PHOBIC DISORDERS AND PANIC IN ADULTS

PHOBIC DISORDERS AND PANIC IN ADULTS:

A Guide to
Assessment
and
Treatment

Martin M. Antony

Richard P. Swinson

American Psychological Association

Washington, DC

Published by
American Psychological Association
750 First Street, NE
Washington, DC 20002

Copies may be ordered from
APA Order Department
P.O. Box 92984
Washington, DC 20090-2984

In the U.K., Europe, Africa, and the
    Middle East, copies may be ordered from
American Psychological Association
3 Henrietta Street
Covent Garden, London
WC2E 8LU England

Typeset in Goudy by World Composition Services, Inc., Sterling, VA

Printer: Port City Press, Baltimore, MD
Cover Designer: Kathy Keler Graphics, Washington, DC
Production Editor: Kristine Enderle

The opinions and statements published are the responsibility of the authors, and such opinions and statements do not necessarily represent the policies of the APA.

Library of Congress Cataloging-in-Publication Data

Antony, Martin M.
    Phobic disorders and panic in adults : a guide to assessment and treatment / Martin M. Antony, Richard P. Swinson.–1st ed.
        p. ; cm.
    Includes bibliographical references and index.
    ISBN 1-55798-696-7 (alk. paper)
    1. Phobias–Treatment. 2. Panic disorders–Treatment. 3. Agoraphobia. I. Swinson, Richard P. II. Title.
    [DNLM: 1. Phobic Disorders. 2. Agoraphobia. 3. Panic Disorder. WM 178 A635p 2000]
    RC535 .P4875 2000
    616.85′22506–dc21

                                                                          00-038094

British Library Cataloguing-in-Publication Data
A CIP record is available from the British Library.

Printed in the United States of America
First Edition

To My Grandmother Mary
M. M. A.

To Rob, Ian, and Emma
R. P. S.

CONTENTS

FOREWORD

Professor S. Rachman

During the past decade we have seen a shift from idiosyncratic psychotherapy, in which the personal preferences of the therapist overrode the particular needs of the patient, to standardized treatments that have been empirically proven to be most effective for patients' particular problems. Recognition of the superiority of these empirically supported treatments has created a need for practical guides for therapists that teach the rationale for the treatment and explain specific procedures for its conduct. This book meets the need for a guide to the assessment and treatment of three major anxiety disorders—panic disorder (with or without agoraphobia), social phobia, and specific phobia.

What should we look for in such a guide? First, one needs assurance that the authors are experienced and authoritative. Second, the empirical support for the treatment and its rationale in particular cases must be convincingly laid out. Third, the interventions described must be comprehensive and up-to-date. This book succeeds admirably on all three counts.

Although these are the essentials, unless the guide is clearly written, it is not worth a bag of beans. Clinicians and clinicians-in-training have neither the time nor the patience to spend their days deciphering thick prose and unnecessary jargon. They need material that is well organized and well written and that is easy to use. This book fulfills all of these requirements: It is clearly written, logically organized, and easy to use. And used it will be.

In addition to meeting these requirements, this guide has one feature that sets it above other, comparable volumes. Although the bulk of the book is devoted to cognitive–behavioral psychotherapy, it also contains a valuable chapter on pharmacological treatment and describes how psychological and pharmacological treatments may be most usefully combined. Given that most patients with anxiety disorders receive drug treatment, the absence of information and advice about pharmacology is a regrettable omission in most other guides.

I expect that this fine guide will be used widely and successfully by beginning and seasoned practitioners alike.

PREFACE

Our motivation for writing this book was to develop a manual that would be different from previous assessment and treatment guides which, in our opinion, have tended to be either too broadly or too narrowly focused. We wanted to write a book that could be used to train our students and to assist our colleagues in assessing and treating people with a full range of phobic disorders—including panic disorder (with or without agoraphobia), social phobia, and specific phobias. We saw the need for a book that would cover these disorders from a psychological as well as a biological perspective and give full coverage to issues related to both assessment and treatment. Finally, we wanted a book that would contain almost everything a reader would need to have on hand to assess and treat people with phobic disorders, such as monitoring forms and diaries, handouts, information on where to obtain assessment materials, lists of self-help books for patients, and suggestions for where to obtain stimuli for exposure treatments.

Our initial ideas for the book were influenced, in part, by a series of workshops that we had presented through the second half of the 1990s at meetings of the American Psychological Association, American Psychiatric Association, Association for Advancement of Behavior Therapy, and various other professional groups. As we developed the volume, two things became clear. First, although the book was intended to be a practical manual for those treating people with phobic disorders, we found it very difficult to discuss the treatment of agoraphobia without also considering the role of panic attacks and panic disorder. Second, we felt that a manual for providing empirically supported assessment and treatment would be incomplete unless it also included a review of the empirical literature on which the relevant strategies were based. In the end, we decided to broaden the focus of the book to include panic disorder (with or without agoraphobia), as well as several chapters that provide detailed literature reviews on the nature and treatment of panic disorder, social phobia, and specific phobia.

The content of this book was influenced by too many people to list individually, as is evidenced by the fact that we have cited almost 1,000 sources. Nevertheless, there are a number of clinicians and researchers who deserve recognition for helping to shape this book by sharing with us important ideas through their teachings and writings. These include David H. Barlow, Aaron Beck, Tim Brown, Michelle Craske, David M. Clark, Rick Heimberg, Donald Klein, Michael Liebowitz, Isaac Marks, Rich McNally, Lars-Göran Öst, Jack Rachman, and Ron Rapee. There are many others as well.

We also thank the following people for reading various chapters and making detailed comments and suggestions: Peter Bieling, Andy Cheok, Linda Cox, Cynthia Crawford, Jane Fogolin, Michelle Jedrzkiewicz, Rich McNally, Elizabeth Meadows, Robert Miranda, Jr., Pauline Nelson, Christine Purdon, Laura Rocca, Deborah Roth, Karen Rowa, Steve Taylor, and Susan Williams. We are grateful to Margaret Schlegel and to the staff at APA Books for their invitation to write this book, as well as for their guidance, support, and patience throughout the process of bringing the project to completion. Finally, we sincerely thank our families for being who they are, for tolerating our busy schedules (once again), and for not taking away our computers.

PHOBIC DISORDERS AND PANIC IN ADULTS

INTRODUCTION

In the *Diagnostic and Statistical Manual of Mental Disorders*, *4th edition* (American Psychiatric Association, 1994), phobic disorders include three main syndromes: agoraphobia, social phobia, and specific phobia. *Agoraphobia* is a fear of situations from which escape might be difficult or embarrassing if one were to experience a panic attack or some uncomfortable physical symptom. Typical situations avoided by people with agoraphobia include crowds, driving, flying, and being far from home. Agoraphobic avoidance is usually associated with panic disorder, and it occurs in up to 5% of the population (Kessler et al., 1994).

Social phobia is an extreme fear of situations in which one might be the subject of evaluation by others (e.g., being at a party, engaging in conversation, public speaking, or eating in front of others). Although estimates of the prevalence of social phobia vary greatly, recent findings from the National Comorbidity Study suggest that more than one in eight Americans suffers from this disorder (Kessler et al., 1994).

A *specific phobia* is an excessive fear of a particular object or situation that causes significant distress and impairment and is not better accounted for by another disorder. Specific phobias include fears of animals, heights, enclosed places, injections, flying, and other discrete situations. Specific phobias are among the most common of psychological disorders, affecting about 11% of the population according to several epidemiological studies (Eaton, Dryman, & Weissman, 1991; Kessler et al., 1994).

In recent years, enormous advances have been made in the understanding and treatment of phobic disorders. With respect to psychological approaches, these advances include the introduction of new interventions as well as the refinement of existing cognitive and behavioral treatment strategies. We now have an improved understanding of the variables that affect treatment outcome and are beginning to understand how different components of treatment can be combined to maximize the benefits achieved. In addition to psychological approaches, advances in the use of pharmacological treatments for phobic disorders have been made, and more is known about the effects of combining biological and psychological treatments.

Despite recent advances in the treatment of anxiety disorders, the vast majority of individuals suffering from phobic disorders do not receive empirically supported treatments. In most cases, individuals suffering from these problems do not even seek treatment. For example, a recent epidemiological survey of adolescents and young adults suffering from social phobia showed that fewer than 10% had ever sought treatment from a mental health professional for their condition (Wittchen, Stein, & Kessler, 1999).

Furthermore, our own data and those of others suggest that, even when people do seek treatment for phobic disorders, they often receive interventions that have little or no empirical support for treating these problems. For example, people with panic disorder and social phobia are more likely to report having received traditional treatments such as psychodynamic psychotherapy and supportive counseling that evidence-based treatments such as cognitive or behavioral therapies (Goisman, Warshaw, & Keller, 1999; Rowa, Antony, Brar, Summerfeldt, & Swinson, in press). These findings support the need to educate clinicians about treatments that have been shown to work for phobic disorders. This is one of the main motivations underlying our decision to write this book.

This text is unique in a number of ways. First, it is the one of the few books to focus exclusively on the three main types of phobic disorders, rather than on the entire range of anxiety disorders. In addition, unlike most other manuals for clinicians, this book integrates research findings and practical recommendations from both psychological *and* pharmacological approaches. It provides detailed, up-to-date reviews of the research on the nature and treatment of phobic disorders, as well as step-by-step instructions for how to assess and treat people with these conditions. The appendixes contain additional resources for clinicians and their patients. Finally, numerous examples of forms and handouts are reprinted throughout the book. These can be freely photocopied and distributed to patients by purchasers of this volume.

OVERVIEW OF THE BOOK

The book is divided into three main sections. The first section includes chapters reviewing the current state of the literature on the nature and treatment of phobic disorders. Each of the first three chapters includes one or more case vignettes, as well as information on the diagnostic criteria, epidemiology, descriptive psychopathology, etiology, biological and psychological correlates, and current controversies pertaining to panic disorder and agoraphobia, social phobia, and specific phobia, respectively. In addition, these initial chapters review the literature pertaining to biological treatments, psychological treatments, and combination treatments for these disorders.

The second section includes chapters on the assessment and treatment of phobic disorders. For example, chapter 4 covers issues related to assessment and diagnosis. The most commonly used diagnostic interview methods are described, and specific recommendations are provided. A detailed discussion of issues related to differential diagnosis is included as well. In this chapter we also discuss other variables that should be assessed during the clinical interview, including the development and course of the problem, the impact on functioning, the pattern of physical symptoms, cognitive features of the disorder, patterns of overt and subtle avoidance, family factors, treatment history, skills deficits, and medical history. Chapter 4 includes comprehensive sections on behavioral assessment, symptom diaries, and self-report questionnaires. Each of the most commonly used measures is described for panic disorder, agoraphobia, social phobia, specific phobia, and related problems that often occur in the context of these conditions.

Chapter 5 provides information on how to integrate the strategies discussed in chapters 6–8 to help clinicians develop and implement a comprehensive treatment plan. In this chapter, we discuss methods of choosing among psychological treatment strategies; choosing between group and individual treatments; when to use psychological, pharmacological, or combined treatments; and issues related to the sequencing of treatment components. Next, we discuss exactly how to present an integrated treatment rationale to patients. This section is followed by information about self-help treatments. We conclude by presenting examples of session-by-session treatment protocols for panic disorder with agoraphobia, panic disorder without agoraphobia, social phobia, and specific phobia.

In chapter 6 we discuss the practical aspects of delivering exposure-based treatments and social skills training, beginning with a discussion of the main types of exposure-based treatment, including in vivo exposure, interoceptive exposure, and imaginal exposure. Detailed instructions on how to prevent the exposure rationale to patients are also provided. Next we provide comprehensive guidelines for maximizing the effectiveness of exposure. Some of the topics that are addressed include the benefits of gradual versus rapid exposure; the role of predictability and control; the importance of structuring practices in advance; the recommended duration, intensity, and frequency of exposure practices; the importance of context during exposure; how to choose exposure stimuli; the effects of distraction and subtle avoidance on exposure; the benefits of therapist-assisted versus self-directed exposure; using technology to aid with exposure practices; and integrating exposure with other therapeutic techniques. This chapter also includes detailed instructions for conducting exposure to feared physical sensations (i.e., interoceptive exposure), as well as a discussion of other issues that are relevant to exposure-based treatments (e.g., assigning homework, dealing with noncompliance, and finding materials that are necessary for exposure). The chapter concludes with a discussion of social skills training as a component of the treatment of social phobia. Throughout this chapter, practical suggestions are supported by relevant research findings.

The focus of chapter 7 is on cognitive interventions for phobic disorders. This chapter begins with a discussion of the underlying principles of cognitive therapy, a review of cognitive distortions and information-processing biases, and a discussion of strategies for identifying anxious automatic thoughts, cognitive schemas, and core beliefs. Next we focus attention on methods for changing phobic thinking, including psychoeducation, examining the evidence regarding phobic thoughts, challenging catastrophic thinking, using rational self-statements, perspective-taking, cost-benefit analysis, and behavioral experiments. Chapter 7 concludes with sections describing ways of avoiding the most common mistakes made by cognitive therapists and a guide for trouble shooting.

Chapter 8 focuses on the practical aspects of treating phobic disorders with medication and other physical approaches (e.g., applied tension for blood-injection-injury phobias and breathing retraining for panic disorder). We start with an overview of the most commonly used medications, how to choose among medications, side effects, interactions among medications, issues related to dosage, recommended duration of treatment, and strategies for discontinuing medications. This section also includes a discussion of newer herbal preparations that are sometimes used to treat anxiety. The chapter continues with sections on using applied tension to overcome blood and injection phobias and using breathing retraining as a component of treating panic disorder. Finally, the chapter ends with a discussion of diet, exercise, sleep, and other health-related issues.

Part 3 of this book includes four appendixes that contain additional information and resources. Appendix A includes information on where to obtain each of the most commonly used assessment tools described in chapter 4. Appendixes B and C include lists of recommended readings for clinicians and patients, respectively. Appendix D includes a wide range of other resources, including information on national and international organizations for people who either suffer from or treat phobic disorders; internet resources that relate to phobias; statistics that may be useful when educating patients with certain specific phobias (e.g., statistics regarding fatalities from automobile crashes, plane crashes, thunderstorms, and drowning); information on commercial programs for overcoming flying phobias; and a list of movies, videos, and television shows that can be used to expose patients to certain phobic stimuli (e.g., animals, blood, injections, surgery, and heights).

There are two additional minor points to keep in mind as you read this book. First, generic names of medications are used throughout the text. In addition, however, chapter 8 contains tables that include both generic and brand names for the major drugs used to treat phobic disorders. Second, the book contains a number of case descriptions and clinical vignettes. Although some aspects of these descriptions are based on actual cases, they are mostly based on composites of many different patients. Furthermore, in all instances, details of cases have been altered to protect patient confidentiality.

CONCLUSION

In summary, this book provides an overview of practically everything that a clinician might need to know when treating a patient with panic disorder (with or without agoraphobia), social phobia, or a specific phobia. Chapters include discussions on the nature and treatment of phobic disorders, practical suggestions for how to assess people with phobias, and in-depth descriptions of each of the major strategies that are used to treat people with phobic disorders. The organization of this book makes it particularly practical and accessible for the busy clinician because it includes numerous headings and subheadings, clinical vignettes, tables, handouts, and samples of diaries and forms, as well as a comprehensive index.

It is our hope that this book will be used by new clinicians, seasoned practitioners, and researchers who have an interest in phobic disorders and their treatment. It should be an invaluable resource for students of psychology, medicine, social work, nursing, and occupational therapy, and for those in other professions who work with people who suffer from these conditions.

I

PHOBIC DISORDERS: AN EMPIRICAL OVERVIEW

1

PANIC DISORDER
AND AGORAPHOBIA

Panic disorder (PD) is an anxiety disorder in which the main feature is unexpected panic attacks and a tendency to be overly concerned about having the attacks. These rushes of fear, which seem to occur out of the blue, are associated with a number of intense physical symptoms as well as a feeling of impending doom. People with PD often develop agoraphobia. That is, they fear a characteristic cluster of situations in which escape might be difficult or in which help might be unavailable in case of a panic attack.

In this chapter we provide an overview of the empirical research on the nature and treatment of PD and agoraphobia. We begin with a discussion of diagnostic issues and definitions of relevant terms and syndromes, such as panic attacks, PD, agoraphobia, and agoraphobia without history of panic disorder. In addition, we discuss in detail special types of panic attacks (e.g., nocturnal panic, nonfearful panic, relaxation-induced panic, and nonclinical panic), as well as the pertinent epidemiological literature. Next, we provide a comprehensive outline of major psychological and biological approaches to understanding the causes of panic and agoraphobia and cite the empirical literature pertaining to these theoretical models. The chapter concludes with a review of the efficacy of psychological, biological, and combination treatments.

DIAGNOSTIC CRITERIA AND
DESCRIPTIVE PSYCHOPATHOLOGY

Panic Attacks

A panic attack is a rush of fear or discomfort that reaches a peak in less than 10 minutes and includes at least 4 of the following 13 symptoms: racing or pounding heart; sweating; shaking or trembling; shortness of breath; choking feelings; chest discomfort; nausea or abdominal discomfort; feeling dizzy, faint, or lightheaded; feelings of unreality or depersonalization; fear of "going crazy" or losing control; fear of dying; numbness or tingling sensations; or chills or hot flushes (American Psychiatric Association, 1994).

Panic attacks can occur across a range of different psychological disorders, including anxiety disorders (e.g., when a person with a snake phobia encounters a snake), eating disorders (e.g., when a person eats a food that is high in fat), and depression. In addition, panic attacks often occur in the absence of any specific psychopathology. For example, it is not unusual for people to experience a panic attack before some stressful event such as a difficult exam or getting married. The fourth edition of the *Diagnostic and Statistical Manual of Mental Disorders* (*DSM-IV*; American Psychiatric Association, 1994) defines three types of panic attacks: unexpected (or uncued), situationally bound, and situationally predisposed.

Unexpected or uncued attacks are those that occur out of the blue without any warning or obvious external trigger. This type of panic attack is most often associated with PD. Situationally bound attacks are those that occur invariably in a particular situation. For example, as is reviewed in chapter 3, people with specific phobias (e.g., animal phobias) almost always experience a rush of fear when confronting the phobic object or situation. Panic attacks that occur in people with specific phobias are usually situationally bound attacks. Situationally predisposed attacks fall somewhere in between those that are unexpected and those that are situationally bound, in that they are more likely to occur in certain situations but do not necessarily occur each time the situation is encountered. People with agoraphobia often report situationally predisposed attacks that are more likely to occur in certain situations (e.g., in crowds) than in others (e.g., at home).

Panic Disorder

According to the *DSM-IV*, the hallmark of PD is the experience of recurrent unexpected panic attacks. In other words, to meet criteria for PD, an individual must have a history of multiple panic attacks, occurring unexpectedly or without any obvious trigger. In addition, the person must experience a period lasting a month or more during which at least one of the following criteria are met: (a) the individual is concerned about having more panic attacks, (b) the individual is concerned about the possible consequences of his or her panic attacks (e.g., that the attack may lead to a heart attack or stroke, loss of control, loss of consciousness, loss of bowel control, etc.), or (c) there is a significant change in behavior related to the attacks (e.g., the person avoids certain activities or places, insists on being accompanied by his or her spouse, insists on carrying some safe object such as a medication bottle, etc.). Additional requirements for a *DSM-IV* diagnosis of PD include provisions that the symptoms are not the direct effects of a substance (e.g., cocaine, caffeine, etc.) or a general medical condition (e.g., hyperthyroidism). In addition, the symptoms are not better accounted for by another psychological disorder. Issues related to differential diagnosis are discussed in chapter 4.

Panic Disorder With Agoraphobia

Panic disorder can be diagnosed as panic disorder with agoraphobia (PDA) or without agoraphobia, although the majority of people with PD have at least some degree of agoraphobic avoidance. In the *DSM-IV*, agoraphobia is defined as a fear of being in situations from which escape might be difficult or embarrassing, or in which help might not be available in the event that one experiences a panic attack or panic-like symptoms. Examples of situations that are often avoided by people with agoraphobia include being home alone, crowds, shopping malls, supermarkets, driving (particularly on highways or in bad traffic), enclosed places (e.g., elevators), movie theaters (especially away from the exit, in the middle of a row), restaurants, airplanes, traveling, and public transportation. For some people with agoraphobia, their pattern of avoidance is limited to certain types of situations (e.g., flying, malls, etc.). Other individuals may define a "safe radius" around their home, outside of which they cannot travel. For example, they may be able to travel anywhere within 2 miles of their home, but not any distance outside of that radius. In severe cases, people with agoraphobia completely avoid leaving their homes, particularly when they are alone.

In addition to avoiding certain places, people with agoraphobia often avoid activities that they perceive as being likely to trigger a panic attack. These may include drinking coffee, becoming sexually aroused, taking certain medications, exercising, getting angry, or being in hot, stuffy rooms. They often feel more comfortable when they are accompanied by a close friend or family member and may also carry with them certain objects (e.g., money to make a phone call, anxiolytic medications, or a bottle of water in case of dry mouth) in case of a panic attack.

Case Vignette: Panic Disorder With Agoraphobia

Sita first presented to the emergency room at age 28, convinced she was having a heart attack. She had been lying in bed the night after finishing her qualifying exams in graduate school when she suddenly began to experience heart palpitations, chest tightness, and difficulty breathing. She soon began to sweat, and her whole body was trembling. She woke her husband, who quickly drove her to a nearby emergency room. By the time she arrived at the hospital, she was feeling quite a bit better. After a brief examination, she was told that nothing was wrong with her and was discharged. The following day, she had a more thorough physical exam by her family physician, who also found no physical abnormality that could account for her symptoms. Although she was initially concerned about the episode (she had never experienced anything like it in the past), she forgot about it after a few days.

About a week later, she experienced a similar episode, this time while driving to school. She pulled over in her car, waited until her symptoms subsided, and then returned home for the rest of the day. The attacks continued to occur about twice per month for a few months. Despite two or three additional visits to the emergency room and several more visits to her family doctor, it was not until 6 months later that Sita was told by an emergency room physician that she was probably having panic attacks.

Although Sita was frequently reassured that she was physically healthy, she was still very frightened of having more attacks and constantly monitored her physical state for any signs that a panic attack might occur. She continued to fear the possibility of having a heart attack, but also feared that she might lose control and embarrass herself during a panic attack. The frequency of her panic attacks gradually increased to a point where they were occurring several times per week. She began to avoid driving anywhere farther than about a mile from her home, in case she had an attack and was unable to find help. Unless she was with her husband or a close friend, she would not go into crowded or enclosed places such as malls, supermarkets, restaurants, airplanes, elevators, or theaters. She also needed to know that help would be available if necessary. Her husband drove her to school and began to carry a pager so that she could reach him at all times.

When she was about 34 years old (6 years after the problem began), Sita responded to an advertisement seeking individuals to participate in a study of cognitive–behavioral treatment for PD. At the time of her assessment for this study, criteria were met for PDA and an additional diagnosis of major depressive disorder (apparently a reaction to having a restricted lifestyle as a result of her panic attacks). She began a 12-session group treatment for PDA. Treatment consisted of in vivo exposure to feared situations, as well as cognitive restructuring and exposure to feared sensations. By the end of treatment, Sita was no longer experiencing panic attacks and was able to comfortably enter all of the situations that she previously feared, except flying in an airplane, which she did not have an opportunity to try during treatment.

Agoraphobia Without History of Panic Disorder

Although most people with agoraphobia also have PD, a small percentage of agoraphobic individuals seen in clinical settings have never met criteria for PD. For these individuals, the *DSM-IV* includes the diagnostic category called agoraphobia without history of panic disorder (AWOPD). Usually, criteria for PD have not been met because typical episodes of fear include fewer than four symptoms, because panic-like episodes do not reach a peak within 10 minutes, or because the individual has not had recurrent panic attacks (e.g., an individual who experiences one unexpected panic attack and subsequently becomes agoraphobic without ever experiencing another attack). In fact, recent findings (Goisman, Warshaw, et al., 1995) suggest that 65% of patients with AWOPD have situational panic attacks, and 57% have what appear to be limited symptom attacks (i.e., panic-like episodes with fewer than the four symptoms needed to meet criteria for a panic attack). Furthermore, these panic-like episodes tend to begin either before or at the same time as the agoraphobic avoidance.

For people with AWOPD, the pattern of agoraphobic avoidance is often similar to that in PDA. In fact, investigators who study this disorder have argued that AWOPD probably belongs on a continuum with PD and PDA, rather than being classified as a separate disorder (Goisman, Warshaw, et al., 1995). As is the case for PD, agoraphobic avoidance in AWOPD must be related to a fear of developing one or more uncomfortable panic-like sensations, such as palpitations, dizziness, nausea, or diarrhea. People suffering from AWOPD often avoid agoraphobic situations for fear of experiencing some physical catastrophe such as a heart attack, fainting, vomiting, or having diarrhea in a public place.

Relationship Between Panic and Agoraphobia

In the *DSM-III* (American Psychiatric Association, 1980), PD and agoraphobia were listed as separate entities. Individuals could be diagnosed as having agoraphobia with panic attacks, agoraphobia without panic attacks, or PD. By the time that the *DSM-III-R* (American Psychiatric Association, 1987) was being produced, a large body of evidence, mostly based on clinical samples, had emerged to suggest that PD and agoraphobia were related and that agoraphobia was probably secondary to a fear of having panic attacks for most individuals (Craske & Barlow, 1988; Turner, Williams, Beidel, &

Mezzich, 1986). With the publication of the *DSM-III-R*, agoraphobia was seen as a feature of PD, rather than the other way around.

Nevertheless, the relationship between panic and agoraphobic avoidance appears to be complex (for a review, see Craske & Barlow, 1988). One common finding in studies of clinical samples is that agoraphobia tends to begin after the first panic attack (Katerndahl & Realini, 1997b; Swinson, 1986; Thyer & Himle, 1985), although in some European studies (e.g., Fava, Grandi, & Canestrari, 1988) the opposite pattern was found. Furthermore, the location of the first panic attack may affect the subsequent development of agoraphobia. Faravelli, Paterniti, Biondi, and Scarpato (1992) found that PD patients with agoraphobia were significantly more likely (i.e., 75.8% of patients) to have their first panic attack in a situation often associated with agoraphobia, compared with only 20% of PD patients without agoraphobia.

In addition, the expectation of having a panic attack during exposure to a particular situation appears to be predictive of subsequent avoidance (Craske, Rapee, & Barlow, 1988; Kenardy & Taylor, 1999; Telch, Brouillard, Telch, Agras, & Taylor, 1989). Social factors such as occupational status (de Jong & Bouman, 1995) and embarrassment about the first panic attack (Amering et al., 1997) also seem to predict the development of agoraphobic avoidance. Finally, although research is limited, it has been suggested that the potential for reinforcement (e.g., secondary gain) may contribute to the development of agoraphobia (Craske & Barlow, 1988).

The expectation of panicking seems to be more strongly related to avoidance than is the actual occurrence of panic (Cox & Swinson, 1994). In fact, with some exceptions (e.g., Turner et al., 1986), current panic frequency, past panic frequency, and panic duration have generally been found to be unrelated to the severity of agoraphobic avoidance (Cox, Endler, & Swinson, 1995; Craske, Sanderson, & Barlow, 1987; Telch et al., 1989). In addition, Cox et al. (1995) found that factors such as fear of anxiety symptoms (i.e., anxiety sensitivity) and the presence of catastrophic panic cognitions (e.g., fear of dying) did not distinguish among people with different levels of agoraphobic avoidance. In contrast, Norton, Pidlubny, and Norton (1999) found a positive relationship between anxiety sensitivity and agoraphobic avoidance.

Although agoraphobia is now generally thought to be secondary to the experience of unexpected panic attacks or panic-like episodes, it should be noted that some investigators (e.g., Fava et al., 1988; Maier et al., 1991; Marks, 1987a) have argued against this view, in favor of the diagnostic approach taken in the *DSM-III*. The largest body of evidence against the view that agoraphobia almost always develops in response to panic attacks comes from epidemiological research. For example, in the Epidemiological Catchment Area (ECA) study (a survey of more than 18,000 Americans, based on *DSM-III* criteria), the majority of individuals with agoraphobia did not report panic attacks (Eaton, Dryman, & Weissman, 1991). More recently, large epidemiological surveys based on *DSM-III-R* criteria (Kessler et al., 1994) and *DSM-IV* criteria (Wittchen, Reed, & Kessler, 1998) also showed that AWOPD was more prevalent than PD with or without agoraphobia.

However, methodological problems inherent in epidemiological surveys such as the ECA study limit the extent to which these data can be considered accurate for PD and agoraphobia (see McNally, 1994, for a review) as well as for other disorders (e.g., Antony, Downie, & Swinson, 1998; Regier et al., 1998). For example, epidemiological studies tend to rely on fully structured interviews (which limit the extent to which the interviewer can ask follow-up questions for clarification) that are conducted by trained lay interviewers rather than experienced clinicians. In addition, the interviews used in these studies have failed to accurately distinguish between agoraphobia and other conditions, most notably specific phobias (McNally, 1994; Wittchen et al., 1998).

For example, Horwath, Lish, Johnson, Hornig, and Weissman (1993) reinterviewed 22 patients who were diagnosed as having agoraphobia without panic attacks in the original ECA study. Using *DSM-III-R* criteria, 86% of these patients no longer met criteria for agoraphobia but rather were diagnosed with specific phobias and fears. In a prevalence study based on *DSM-IV* criteria, Wittchen et al. (1998) found that the prevalence of agoraphobia decreased by more than half when patients were reinterviewed by experienced clinicians. Many of the individuals originally classified as having agoraphobia actually had specific phobias. However, even after controlling for the original diagnostic errors, the prevalence of AWOPD was considerably higher than the prevalence of PD with or without agoraphobia. Interestingly, people with agoraphobia in the absence of panic reported rarely seeking treatment, which might help to explain the fact that these patients are not often seen in clinical practice (Wittchen et al., 1998).

Because people who suffer from AWOPD rarely present for treatment, there has been relatively little research on this condition. The question of what motivates these individuals to exhibit agoraphobic avoidance remains to be answered. As defined in the *DSM-IV*, the avoidance is probably motivated by anxiety over experiencing panic-like sensations, even though full panic attacks may not be experienced.

Special Types of Panic Attacks

Nocturnal panic

Nocturnal panic is the phenomenon of waking from sleep in a state of panic. Up to two thirds of patients with PD report having had at least one nocturnal panic attack at some time in their lives, and about a third of patients report recurrent nocturnal panic attacks (Mellman & Uhde, 1989b). Nocturnal panic attacks tend to occur during late Stage II and early Stage III sleep (Mellman & Uhde, 1989a), rather than during Stage IV (when night terrors are most likely to occur) or rapid eye movement sleep (when dreaming takes place). A detailed review regarding the phenomenon of nocturnal panic was recently published by Craske and Rowe (1997).

In most studies, the types of symptoms reported during daytime and nighttime panic attacks are similar (e.g., Krystal, Woods, Hill, & Charney, 1991; Uhde, 1994), although some researchers have found minor differences in symptom profile (e.g., Craske & Barlow, 1989; Norton, Norton, Walker, Cox, & Stein, 1999). Furthermore, whereas Craske and Barlow (1989) found that individuals with nocturnal panic attacks reported more frequent daytime panic attacks compared with PD patients without nocturnal panic, Norton, Norton, et al. (1999) found no differences in the frequency of daytime panic attacks among those with and without nocturnal panic.

Very little research exists on the effect of treatment on nocturnal panic. However, a preliminary study of 25 PD patients with nocturnal panic attacks (Hsu et al., 1997) suggests that an augmented form of cognitive–behavioral therapy (CBT) for panic may be effective. The investigators modified a standard 11-session cognitive–behavioral program for panic by adding elements specific to nocturnal panic, including education about nocturnal panic, breathing retraining (BRT) prior to sleep, sleep hygiene, cognitive restructuring of sleep-related fears, and exposure to relaxation states. By the end of treatment, 76% of the sample reported no nocturnal panic attacks, 56% reported no daytime panic attacks, and 60% no longer met diagnostic criteria for PD. These findings are promising, although controlled studies are still needed to establish the effectiveness of psychological and biological treatments for nocturnal panic attacks.

Nonfearful panic

In a series of studies and a review, Beitman and colleagues (Beitman et al., 1987; Beitman, Kushner, Lamberti, & Mukerji, 1990; Kushner & Beitman, 1990) described a phenomenon called *nonfearful PD* that occurs in certain medical populations. They found that about one third of cardiology patients with chest pain and current *DSM-III-R* diagnoses of PD reported no fear during their last intense panic attack (Beitman et al., 1987, 1990). Furthermore, although people with nonfearful PD were less depressed and reported fewer cognitive panic symptoms (e.g., fear of dying) than did individuals with fearful panic attacks, there were surprisingly few differences between these groups on measures of panic frequency, physical panic symptoms endorsed, and scores on a number of questionnaires (Beitman et al.,

1987). Supporting the view that nonfearful panic patients are similar to others with PD, Russell, Kushner, Beitman, and Bartels (1991) found that individuals with nonfearful PD were more likely than were control participants to respond to infusion with sodium lactate, which, as is reviewed later in this chapter, has been shown to induce panic attacks in people who suffer from PD.

In one of the few independent attempts to study the phenomenon of nonfearful panic, Wilson, Sandler, and Asmundson (1993) found that nonfearful panic attacks were common among 83 university students who reported a history of unexpected panic. In fact, 27% of this sample reported no fear during their attacks, 36% reported only mild fear, and 37% of the sample reported high fear. Individuals who were highly fearful during their panic attacks were most likely to have elevated scores on measures of psychopathology and were more likely to engage in phobic avoidance than were those in the other groups. However, the groups did not differ with respect to panic frequency.

The idea of a nonfearful PD may seem to go against the very definition of panic. Indeed, some investigators (Antony & Barlow, 1996; Barlow, 1988; Craske, 1991) have argued that panic and fear are identical experiences. Barlow, Brown, and Craske (1994) cautioned against assuming that the nonfearful rushes seen in some cardiac patients are in fact panic attacks. They pointed out that other emotional states (e.g., anger or excitement) are also associated with rushes of physical arousal.

Nevertheless, it is technically possible (according to the *DSM-III-R* and *DSM-IV* definitions of a panic attack) for panic to be a rush of discomfort rather than a rush of fear per se. Furthermore, because the *DSM-III-R* definition of PD did not require worry about panic or a change in behavior caused by the attacks (the presence of four panic attacks in a 4-week period was sufficient), it was possible with *DSM-III-R* criteria for individuals with nonfearful panic attacks to meet criteria for PD. However, with the publication of the *DSM-IV*, it may be less likely that individuals with nonfearful panic attacks would still meet criteria for PD, because they would be less likely to report worry about having panic attacks, worry about the consequences of panic, and perhaps behavioral changes in response to their nonfearful panic. Regardless of whether the phenomenon of nonfearful panic is best considered a true form of panic, it raises interesting questions about the nature of panic and the role of cognitive factors in causing panic attacks.

Relaxation-induced panic

In 1984, Heide and Borkovec reviewed the evidence for a phenomenon that they called "relaxation-induced anxiety." At the time, the evidence that relaxation training could trigger anxiety for some individuals was primarily anecdotal, with the exception of a single study based on chronically anxious patients published a year earlier (Heide & Borkovec, 1983). In the first study to document the psychophysiological correlates of relaxation-induced panic attacks, Cohen, Barlow, and Blanchard (1985) published data on two patients who had experienced full-blown panic attacks while relaxing during a psychophysiological assessment. Essentially, both patients showed dramatic increases in heart rate (almost double for one of the patients) and other psychophysiological measures over a period of 1 to 2 minutes.

Adler, Craske, and Barlow (1987) argued that relaxation-induced panic may share features with nocturnal panic and that the process of interoceptive conditioning (i.e., learning to fear panic-related physical symptoms) may play a role in both phenomena. Although relaxation-induced panic is often discussed in the PD literature, there are still few experimental studies on the topic. An exception is a recent study by Knott, Bakish, Lusk, and Barkely (1997) in which patients with PD did not show the characteristic EEG changes in theta and beta activity that are evidenced by nonanxious individuals who are undergoing relaxation training.

Nonclinical panic

Panic attacks appear to be common in nonclinical populations. Early studies (e.g., Norton, Dorward, & Cox, 1986; Norton, Harrison, Hauch, & Rhodes, 1985) showed that just over a third of university students had experienced a panic attack in the past year, with almost a quarter reporting one or more panic attacks in the 3 weeks prior to the assessment. Based on findings from the Panic Attack Questionnaire (PAQ; Norton et al., 1986), 27.6% of participants reported unexpected/uncued panic attacks, 13.8% reported nocturnal panic attacks, and 8.6% reported panic attacks during relaxation. Findings based on other screening questionnaires have also shown unexpected panic attacks to be common, although not as common as originally found with the PAQ. For example, using a measure called the Anxiety Questionnaire, Telch, Lucas, and Nelson (1989) found that only 12% of college students had experienced at least one unexpected/uncued panic attack.

Other investigators have criticized these findings on the grounds that the self-report measure typically used to measure panic (especially the PAQ) may lead participants to confuse panic with generalized anxiety or other anxiety-related experiences. Wilson, Sandler, Asmundson, Larsen, and Ediger (1991) found that a history of nonclinical panic attacks (as measured by the PAQ) was much less frequently reported among participants who were provided with a written vignette describing a typical panic attack (33.4%) than among participants not provided with a description of panic (51.3%), although the rates were high in both groups. In a related study,

Brown and Cash (1989) used a modified version of the PAQ, specifying for participants the differences between panic and general anxiety. In this study, the investigators found that only 26.6% of participants reported a panic attack in the past year and 14.4% reported an unexpected panic attack. In a follow-up study, using a structured interview assessment of nonclinical panic, Brown and Deagle (1992) confirmed these results, finding a past-year panic prevalence of 29.2%. However, only 2.3% of participants reported an uncued panic attack during this 12-month period. Although panic attacks were common overall, the frequency of uncued panic was low and not much greater than the prevalence of PD in this population (1.2%). Brown and Deagle (1992) found that compared with nonpanickers, individuals with a history of nonclinical panic had higher levels of anxiety sensitivity, trait anxiety, depression, and self-focused attention. Despite difficulties in the assessment of nonclinical panic attacks, the phenomenon of nonclinical panic has provided a convenient analog for studying issues related to panic attacks and PD (for a review, see Norton, Cox, & Malan, 1992). In addition, researchers have begun to include people who panic infrequently to identify risk factors for developing PD.

Epidemiology

Development and course

In a study of 261 agoraphobic individuals, Kenardy, Oei, and Evans (1990) found a mean onset age of 30 ($SD = 10.76$) years and a median of 28 years. Age of onset ranged from 10 to 69 years. These findings are consistent with those from 12 earlier studies reviewed by Öst (1987a) in which the mean age of onset for agoraphobia ranged from 19.7 to 32.0 years (with most studies reporting means in the mid to late 20s). Findings based on an epidemiological sample (from the ECA survey) were in a similar range, with a mean onset age of 24 years for PD (Burke, Burke, Regier, & Rae, 1990). Although PD is most likely to begin in young adults, onsets later in life are also relatively common (Raj, Corvea, & Dagon, 1993), although more research is needed on PD in older adults.

The onset of PD often follows a period of stress—either real or perceived. A number of studies (e.g., Faravelli & Pallanti, 1989; Pollard, Pollard, & Corn, 1989) have shown that people with PD report more stressful life events (e.g., graduation, unemployment, divorce, deaths in the family, etc.) in the year before the onset of their disorder than do nonanxious people during a comparable period. Although Rapee, Litwin, and Barlow (1990) failed to find differences in the number of life events during the 6 months prior to onset as reported by individuals with PD, other anxiety disorders, or no anxiety disorder, participants in the two anxiety-disorder groups did report a more negative impact of such events relative to nonanxious individuals.

Other risk factors for the onset of PD include being female (Keyl & Eaton, 1990), having a history of either substance abuse or dependence (Keyl & Eaton, 1990), and having a history of childhood separation anxiety (e.g., Silove et al., 1995; Silove, Manicavasagar, Curtis, & Blaszczynski, 1996). Among individuals who develop PD later in life, common precipitants also include stress as well as medical illnesses (Raj et al., 1993). Heightened anxiety sensitivity has also been found to be a predictor of the development of spontaneous panic attacks, even after controlling for a history of panic attacks and trait anxiety (Schmidt, Lerew, & Jackson, 1999).

The course of PD appears to be chronic for most individuals. Ehlers (1995) followed patients with current PD and remitted PD for a period of 1 year. In addition, groups of nonclinical panickers and nonanxious individuals were followed. At the end of 1 year, 92% of patients who had current PD continued to experience panic attacks and 41% of the initially remitted patients had relapsed. Also, nonclinical panickers (15%) were more likely to develop PD than were control participants (2%). Predictors of PD maintenance and relapse included anxiety sensitivity (i.e., fear of panic symptoms), good heart beat perception, and phobic avoidance. These findings are consistent with those from a 5-year, naturalistic follow-up study from Italy (Faravelli, Paterniti, & Scarpato, 1995), which also showed that untreated PD generally has a chronic course.

Prevalence

Earlier prevalence estimates, based on the ECA study (e.g., Bourdon et al., 1988; Eaton et al., 1991; Myers et al., 1984; Robins et al., 1984), are limited by the fact that they are based on *DSM-III* criteria (i.e., before the diagnosis of PDA existed in its current form). Therefore, we will limit our discussion to more recent findings, based on the *DSM-III-R* and *DSM-IV*. Initial findings from the National Comorbidity Survey (NCS) of more than 8,000 Americans showed that respondents reported lifetime and 12-month prevalence rates for PD of 3.5% and 2.3%, respectively (Kessler et al., 1994). The corresponding rates for AWOPD were 5.3% and 2.8%, respectively. Two separate follow-up reports provided more detailed findings on PD and agoraphobia, respectively. First, Eaton, Kessler, Wittchen, and Magee (1994) reported that 15% of individuals in the NCS sample reported the occurrence of a panic attack in their lifetime and that 3% reported having a panic attack in the previous month. One percent met criteria for PD in the past month. Of those who met criteria for PD, only 50% also reported symptoms of agoraphobia.

In the second report from the same study (Magee, Eaton, Wittchen, McGonagle, & Kessler, 1996), the lifetime and 30-day prevalence estimates for agoraphobia (regardless of whether panic was also present) were 6.7% and 2.3%, respectively. Contrary to findings from clinical studies reviewed earlier in this chapter, the majority (64.2%) of people with agoraphobia reported neither panic attacks nor PD. PD was present in only 21.6% of individuals with agoraphobia. Taken together, findings from the NCS study suggest that although PD and agoraphobia often co-occur, they frequently occur separately as well. This finding is surprising given that AWOPD is rare in clinical settings (e.g., Pollard, Bronson, & Kenney, 1989).

In a more recent study based on 14- to 24-year-olds living in Germany, Wittchen et al. (1998) also found that the lifetime prevalence of agoraphobia was much higher (8.5%) than that for PD either with (0.8%) or without (0.8%) agoraphobia. Even after correcting for the fact that many people who were identified as having agoraphobia actually had misdiagnosed specific phobias, the lifetime prevalence of agoraphobia was 3.5%, and most agoraphobic individuals reported no prior history of panic.

A number of factors appear to be related to the prevalence of PD and agoraphobia. In the NCS study, both PD and agoraphobia were more than twice as common in women as in men (Kessler et al., 1994; Magee et al., 1996). Furthermore, there is evidence from the ECA study that PD and agoraphobia are more common among people who live in urban areas than among those who live in rural areas (George, Hughes, & Blazer, 1986). Although little is known about the prevalence of PD and PDA across cultures and ethnic groups, prevalence rates appear to be similar in White Americans and African Americans (Horwath, Johnson, & Hornig, 1993) and in Mexican Americans (Karno et al., 1989).

Finally, the prevalence of PD and agoraphobia may be increasing. Magee et al. (1996) found that the lifetime prevalence of agoraphobia was higher in younger cohorts than in older cohorts and that this effect was not as pronounced in either social phobia or specific phobia. Consistent with this finding, Gerdes, Yates, and Clancy (1995) found that the rate at which physicians identified panic attacks and referred patients for treatment of PD increased dramatically from 1980 to 1990. Of course, this finding may be related to improved familiarity among health professionals regarding the diagnostic criteria for PD.

Taken together, these findings suggest that agoraphobia is quite common in the general population. In addition, AWOPD is more common in epidemiological samples than in clinical samples, where agoraphobia is typically associated with panic attacks and PD. Findings from epidemiological studies should be interpreted cautiously, however, because of their limitations with respect to how agoraphobic avoidance was defined and their failure to carefully distinguish between agoraphobia and related conditions such as specific phobias.

Sex differences

As was noted earlier, the prevalence of PD and agoraphobia is higher among women than among men (for a review of this literature and possible reasons for sex differences, see Bekker, 1996). In addition, women with PD are more likely than men with PD to develop agoraphobic avoidance and more likely to experience a recurrence of panic symptoms after a period of remission (Yonkers et al., 1998). Women with agoraphobia also are more likely than men with agoraphobia to require a companion when going outside (Starcevic, Djordjevic, Latas, & Bogojevic, 1998).

A recent study of 96 women and 58 men with PDA (Turgeon, Marchand, & Dupuis, 1998) showed that women with PDA reported more severe symptomatology than men with PDA, as was reflected by more severe agoraphobic avoidance, more catastrophic thoughts, more bodily sensations, and more frequent comorbid diagnoses of either social phobia or posttraumatic stress disorder. For men, lower agoraphobic avoidance was associated with more alcohol use (i.e., men who drank more reported less avoidance). Despite these differences, men and women did not differ on measures of depression, trait anxiety, self-esteem, illegal drug use, stressful life events, and marital adjustment. According to findings from Starcevic et al. (1998), men and women also did not differ with respect to other characteristics, including age of onset, demographic variables, duration of the disorder, and symptom profile during panic attacks.

Functional impairment and economic impact

People with PD report impairment across a broad range of life domains, including work, recreation, and social functioning (Antony, Roth, Swinson, Huta, & Devins, 1998; Ettigi, Meyerhoff, Chirban, Jacobs, & Wilson, 1997; Hoffart, 1997; Hollifield et al., 1997; Katerndahl & Realini, 1997a). In fact, individuals with PD report greater subjective functional impairment than do people with chronic medical conditions such as end-stage renal disease and multiple sclerosis (Antony, Roth, et al., 1998). Although impairment is significant in PD and PDA, it is not significantly higher than that reported by people with other chronic anxiety disorders such as obsessive–compulsive disorder (OCD) and social phobia (Antony, Roth, et al., 1998).

PD and PDA are also costly to the health care system and to society in general. Salvador-Carulla, Segui, Fernandez-Cano, and Canet (1995) estimated the direct health care costs (e.g., therapeutic visits, hospitalization, treatment, medications, etc.) and indirect costs (i.e., lost work productivity) of having PD during the year prior to diagnosis and the year following diagnosis, during which patients were treated for PD. From the period preceding diagnosis to the period following diagnosis, the frequency of visits to nonpsychiatric physicians decreased from a mean of 5.13 per person to 0.25 per person. Visits to hospital emergency rooms decreased from 1.23 per person to 0.11 per person. Similarly, medical tests administered decreased significantly following diagnosis. However, because most patients were offered psychiatric treatment following diagnosis, the overall direct health care costs increased following diagnosis from a mean (in U.S. dollars) per patient of $478 before diagnosis to $758 after diagnosis. The mean indirect costs of decreased work productivity were $1,076 per person in the year preceding diagnosis and $228 in the year following diagnosis. Unfortunately, this study did not report health care utilization and lost productivity costs after treatment was completed.

Siegel, Jones, and Wilson (1990) reported that, compared with the general population, individuals with PD visited physicians seven times more often and missed twice as many work days. Similarly, Leon, Portera, and Weissman (1995) found that nearly 30% of those in the ECA study diagnosed with PD had used the general medical system for issues concerning their emotional well-being. Furthermore, the extent to which people with PD utilize health care services may be greater than that for other anxiety disorders such as social phobia (Rees, Richards, & Smith, 1998). Although people with PD often seek services from health professionals, they rarely receive empirically supported treatments (Swinson, Cox, & Woszczyna, 1992; Taylor et al., 1989). It is possible that these statistics will change as clinicians become more familiar with the nature and treatment of PD.

Comorbidity

In a sample of 86 individuals with a principal diagnosis of PD or PDA (Antony & Swinson, 2000a), the frequency of various current additional diagnoses were as follows: OCD, 5.3%; social phobia, 23.4%; specific phobia, 31.9%; generalized anxiety disorder, 18.1%; posttraumatic stress disorder, 3.2%; major depressive disorder, 11.7%; dysthymic disorder, 6.4%; and somatoform disorders, 6.2%. All diagnoses were based on the Structured Clinical Interview for *DSM-IV* (First, Spitzer, Gibbon, & Williams, 1996).

These findings are consistent with other reports that PD is usually associated with other psychological disorders, including other anxiety disorders (Goisman, Goldenberg, Vasile, & Keller, 1995; Lewinsohn, Zinbarg, Seeley, Lewinsohn, & Sack, 1997; Sanderson, Di Nardo, Rapee, & Barlow, 1990), mood disorders (Chen & Dilsaver, 1995; Lesser et al., 1988; Sanderson et al., 1990), personality disorders (particularly those from the anxious cluster) (Chambless, Renneberg, Goldstein, & Gracely, 1992; Diaferia et al., 1993; Renneberg, Chambless, & Gracely, 1992), and substance use disorders (Cox, Norton, Swinson, & Endler, 1990). For people suffering from multiple psychological disorders, the nonpanic conditions typically precede the onset of PD (Katerndahl & Realini, 1997a; Starcevic, Uhlenhuth, Kellner, & Pathak, 1993).

Initial findings from epidemiological samples showed that people with PD may also be at more risk for contemplating or attempting suicide than nonanxious individuals and people with other psychological disorders (Johnson, Weissman, & Klerman, 1990; Weissman, Klerman, Markowitz, & Ouellette, 1989). However, a reanalysis of these data by Hornig and McNally (1995) failed to confirm the connection between suicide and panic when more appropriate statistical controls for comorbidity were used. Furthermore, studies based on clinical samples of patients suffering from PD have shown that suicide attempts among patients with PD usually occur in the context of depression, substance abuse, and borderline personality disorder (Cox, Direnfeld, Swinson, & Norton, 1994; Friedman, Jones, Chernen, & Barlow, 1992; Warshaw, Massion, Peterson, Pratt, & Keller, 1995). In fact, for most people with PD who have attempted suicide, the attempt usually preceded the onset of PD by several years (Mannuzza, Aronowitz, Chapman, Klein, & Fyer, 1992). Finally, a diagnosis of PD is rare among suicide completers (Henriksson et al., 1996).

PSYCHOLOGICAL ASPECTS OF PANIC DISORDER AND AGORAPHOBIA

We begin this section with a discription of two influential psychological models of panic. Next, we provide an overview of the empirical literature pertaining to psychological mechanisms that are thought to be related to the occurrence of panic attacks and PD. This discussion includes findings on information-processing biases (e.g., body vigilance, attentional factors, and memory biases), as well as findings regarding faulty appraisals and interpretive biases that have been found among people who suffer from PD.

Psychological Models of Panic and Agoraphobia

Since the diagnosis of PD was introduced in the *DSM-III* (American Psychiatric Association, 1980), a variety of psychological theories accounting for panic have been published. These models come from a broad range of theoretical perspectives, including those advocating the importance of hyperventilation (e.g., Ley, 1987), classical conditioning (e.g., Goldstein & Chambless, 1978; Wolpe & Rowan, 1988), psychodynamic factors (e.g., Shear, Cooper, Klerman, Busch, & Shapiro, 1993), evolutionary factors (e.g., Marks, 1987b, Nesse, 1987), cognitive factors (e.g., Beck, Emery, &

Greenberg, 1985; Clark, 1986, 1988; Rapee, 1996), and variations on these approaches (e.g., Barlow, 1988; Ehlers & Margraf, 1989). Although a full review of these approaches is beyond the scope of this chapter, we will highlight two models that have been particularly influential with respect to recent developments in research and treatment.

Clark's cognitive model of panic

According to Clark (1986, 1988), panic results from the catastrophic misinterpretation of benign bodily sensations. The phrase "catastrophic misinterpretation" refers to a belief that these sensations are much more dangerous than they really are and that the danger is imminent. For example, heart palpitations might be catastrophically misinterpreted as an impending heart attack.

The model may be summarized as follows. First there is a trigger. This trigger usually involves noticing a change in physical sensations. The trigger is followed by the perception of threat, which, in turn, causes apprehension. Feelings of apprehension elicit an increase in physical sensations that are then misinterpreted catastrophically. The degree of perceived threat increases, and the cycle continues until the anxiety spirals very quickly into a panic attack. The usual sensations that trigger panic are those that occur during panic or anxiety (e.g., palpitations, breathlessness, dizziness, etc.), although other sensations might trigger panic as well. For example, floaters in the visual field might trigger thoughts of going blind, which in turn might trigger anxiety and the accompanying symptoms such as blurred vision. Consistent with Clark's model, 70% of patients with PD reported that their panic attacks were precipitated by a physical sensation (Breitholtz, Westling, & Öst, 1998).

Clark (1986) described two types of panic attacks. The first type, panic attacks preceded by heightened anticipatory anxiety (i.e., situational attacks), are hypothesized to occur as follows. The person might anticipate an attack in a supermarket or mall and begin to focus on his or her body. Upon focusing on the body, sensations may be noticed and interpreted as an impending panic attack. As anxiety increases, the intensity of sensations increases, and the cycle of panic is begun. The second type, "uncued" attacks, are presumed to begin with the noticing and misinterpreting of sensations caused by triggers such as caffeine, exercise, hyperventilation, or an emotional reaction to some unrelated event (e.g., anger, excitement, sexual arousal). Again, anxiety increases very quickly and peaks in a panic attack.

In addition, Clark (1986) noted the influence of biological factors in panic. Biology is assumed to have several possible roles. As was discussed earlier, physiological factors may produce the triggers of panic. They also may influence the specific symptoms, intensity, or duration of the physical response to a psychological threat. For example, the effects of hyperventilation depend on resting levels of carbon dioxide (CO_2), which vary at different times of the menstrual cycle. Many women report more panic attacks premenstrually. Finally, biological factors may influence the extent to which sudden autonomic surges occur. These sudden surges may then be interpreted as indicating some immediate danger.

Clark (1988) added to the cognitive theory of panic by emphasizing that cognitions need not be conscious to affect behavior. Especially before treatment, the process of misinterpreting sensations may be so quick and automatic that patients are unaware of these thoughts, and the attacks appear to be spontaneous. It should be noted that this idea of unconscious catastrophic interpretations has been criticized as threatening the testability of this model (McNally, 1994).

Barlow's integrated model of panic

Barlow's (1988) model of PD has its roots in emotion theory, expanding upon the work of Izard (1977), Lang (1985, 1988), and others who have tended to distinguish between the states of panic and anxiety. According to Barlow, panic (which in this theory is indistinguishable from the basic emotion of fear) is an alarm reaction in which there is an intense push to escape from potential danger and in which the organism is mobilized, physically and cognitively, for action. Anxiety, in contrast, is a more loosely organized emotional state that is future-oriented and characterized by high negative affect and a sense that upcoming events are uncontrollable and unpredictable. In other words, during panic, an individual reacts to a perception of imminent danger, whereas anxiety is associated with anticipation and worry over some danger that may occur in the future.

Barlow (1988) viewed PD as stemming from a complex interaction among a variety of biological and psychological factors. The model may be summarized as follows. The initial panic attack (also called a *false alarm*) occurs during or following a period of stress in people who have a biological vulnerability (perhaps genetically based) to experience panic attacks in response to stress (i.e., just as other people may be vulnerable to developing headaches, hypertension, ulcers, or colds following stressful periods). Although most people attribute the false alarm to some benign cause (e.g., stress, diet, etc.), some people have a psychological vulnerability to develop anxiety and apprehension over the possibility of experiencing more panic attacks in the future. Essentially, this psychological vulnerability is believed to be related to a poor sense of control and predictability over events in general and emotions in particular.

For people who develop anxious apprehension about having additional panic attacks, physical symptoms become associated (through classical conditioning) with the original false alarm, and the result is what Barlow called *learned alarms*. These learned alarms continue to be triggered by changes in bodily sensations as well as various cognitive cues, leading to the development of PD. Depending on cultural, social, and environmental factors, as well as the presence of safety signals and the extent to which panic attacks are associated with specific situations, agoraphobic avoidance may then develop.

This model differs from the cognitive model in a number of ways. First, panic and anxiety are seen as qualitatively distinct by Barlow (1988) but not by Clark (1986). Second, unlike Clark's view, Barlow's model does not depend on cognitive appraisal to account for panic attacks. Finally, Barlow's model accounts more fully for phenomena such as nonclinical panic. Specifically, the model would view these as examples of false alarms in people who are vulnerable to experiencing panic from time to time (in response to stress) but do not develop anxious apprehension over the attacks and therefore do not develop PD. Antony and Barlow (1996) and Rapee (1996) have recently discussed the evidence for and against each of these views.

Information-Processing Biases

A large number of studies have demonstrated that people with PD and PDA show biases in the way they process threat-related information. These biases include tendencies to show hypervigilance and excessive awareness of panic-related symptoms, heightened attention toward threat-related cues, and biases in memory that are consistent with their fear.

Interoceptive detection and body vigilance

Patients with PD tend to report heightened awareness of physical arousal symptoms on self-report measures, compared with people with other anxiety disorders and nonanxious individuals (Pilkington, Antony, & Swinson, 1998). However, findings have been inconsistent across studies investigating whether people with PD are actually better able to detect particular physical sensations, such as heart rate, compared with individuals in other groups. Although some researchers have shown heightened cardiac acuity among people with PD (e.g., Ehlers & Breuer, 1992), others have shown heightened cardiac acuity only under certain conditions, such as heightened arousal (Richards, Edgar, & Gibbon, 1996; van der Does, van Dyck, & Spinhoven, 1997), and others have failed to find differences among groups under a variety of different conditions (Antony et al., 1995; Asmundson, Sandler, Wilson, & Norton, 1993; Barsky, Cleary, Sarnie, & Ruskin, 1994). Preliminary studies also suggest that patients with PD are no more likely than nonanxious individuals to detect changes in physiological symptoms during panic induction challenges such as CO_2 inhalation (Rapee, 1994a) and hyperventilation (Kroeze & van den Hout, 1998).

Inconsistencies across studies are probably related to methodological differences in how accuracy is measured and how data are analyzed (Ehlers, Breuer, Dohn, & Fiegenbaum, 1995; van der Does, Antony, Barsky, & Ehlers, 2000). In a recent reanalysis of findings from several earlier studies, van der Does et al. (2000) found that a greater percentage of people with PD were able to accurately perceive their heartbeats, relative to several other groups. However, several other anxiety disorders were also associated with heightened cardiac perception. Across a number of studies, the ability to detect heart rate did not seem to change significantly as a result of cognitive–behavioral treatment for PD (Antony, Meadows, Brown, & Barlow, 1994; Ehlers et al., 1995; van der Does et al., 2000).

Attentional biases

Over the past decade or more, investigators have studied the extent to which people with PD allocate attentional resources toward threat-related cues. Many of these studies have been based on a modification of the Stroop (1935) procedure. The modified Stroop task (Mathews & MacLeod, 1985) involves showing participants threat-related words (e.g., *heart, palpitation*) and neutral words (e.g., *book, table*), printed in different colors (e.g., red, green). The participant is instructed to name the *color* of each word as the word is presented, and the time taken to name each color is measured. Differences in the time taken to name the colors of threat-related and neutral words are generally assumed to reflect differences in the amount of attention that the participant is devoting to the word itself, although some authors have cautioned against relying on interpretations based solely on attention (Cloitre, Heimberg, Holt, & Liebowitz, 1992).

Based on response times on the Stroop task, individuals with PD tend to show an attentional bias for panic-related threat words (Ehlers, Margraf, Davies, & Roth, 1988; Maidenberg, Chen, Craske, Bohn, & Bystritsky, 1996; McNally et al., 1994; McNally, Riemann, & Kim, 1990). Furthermore, some studies have shown that this bias is not for panic-related words only, but also exists for words related to other types of threat, such as social threat words and general threat words (Maidenberg et al., 1996; McNally et al., 1994).

Research employing cognitive paradigms other than the Stroop task has confirmed that PD patients have an attentional bias for threat-related words (Asmundson, Sandler, Wilson, & Walker, 1992), although some researchers have failed to replicate this finding (Asmundson & Stein, 1994/1995). Finally, in one of the few studies to examine attentional biases for *actual sensations* rather than just threat-related *words*, Ehlers and Breuer (1995) found evidence that PD patients are quicker than nonanxious individuals to shift their attention toward uncomfortable physical sensations (e.g., mild electrical shocks).

Memory biases

A number of investigators have found that patients with PD and PDA show biases to recall threat-related information. Nunn, Stevenson, and Whalan (1984) found that agoraphobic patients were able to recall more content from a phobia-related passage than from a neutral passage, whereas the reverse was true for nonanxious participants. This finding was replicated by McNally, Foa, and Donnell (1989), who had patients with PD and nonanxious control participants recall lists of threat-related and neutral words that they had been shown previously. More recent studies have provided additional confirmation that individuals with PD have a bias for selectively encoding and recalling threat-related words (Becker, Rinck, & Margraf, 1994; McNally, Hornig, Otto, & Pollack, 1997).

Recently, investigators have begun to study implicit (i.e., nonconscious or automatic) and explicit (i.e., conscious) memory processes separately. In a number of studies using several different paradigms, patients with PD have shown biases for threat-related words (e.g., *stroke, crazy*) in implicit memory (Amir, McNally, Riemann, & Clements, 1996; Cloitre, Shear, Cancienne, & Zeitlin, 1994) and explicit memory (Cloitre et al., 1994; Lundh, Czyzykow, & Öst, 1997). However, other studies have failed to show differences between PD patients and nonanxious control participants on measures of implicit memory (e.g., Lundh et al., 1997; Rapee, 1994b) and explicit memory (Rapee, 1994b).

Finally, in one of the only studies to examine memory biases for stimuli other than words, Lundh, Thulin, Czyzykow, and Öst (1998) found that patients with PDA (but not patients in the control group) showed a bias to recognize photographs of faces that they had previously rated as safe (i.e., a person who seems like he or she could be "counted on" if needed), compared with those that were previously rated as unsafe. Furthermore, this recognition bias was correlated with the severity of agoraphobic avoidance as measured by the Mobility Inventory (Chambless, Caputo, Jasin, Gracely, & Williams, 1985).

Attributions, Appraisals, and Interpretive Biases in Panic Disorder

Individuals with PD and PDA tend to be fearful of physical sensations that are associated with physiological arousal, anxiety, and panic attacks.

In fact, it is this fear of arousal symptoms and the tendency to misinterpret the meaning of normal physical sensations that is central to a number of psychological models of panic and PD (e.g., Clark, 1986, 1988). Two of the most influential measures used to assess the extent to which individuals fear physical arousal sensations are the Anxiety Sensitivity Index (Peterson & Reiss, 1993) and the Body Sensations Questionnaire (Chambless, Caputo, Bright, & Gallagher, 1984), which measure the related constructs known as *anxiety sensitivity* and *fear of fear*, respectively.

Essentially, anxiety sensitivity and fear of fear reflect the extent to which an individual is fearful of experiencing physical sensations that are associated with fear and arousal. For example, individuals who are high on these dimensions are often fearful of experiencing dizziness, palpitations, breathlessness, and related symptoms. Although fear of fear and anxiety sensitivity are elevated across a range of anxiety disorders, they tend to be most elevated in people suffering from PD and PDA (Chambless & Gracely, 1989; Taylor, Koch, & McNally, 1992).

In addition, there is evidence that people with PD are more likely than nonanxious individuals and people with other anxiety disorders to (a) interpret ambiguous physical symptoms as a sign of some immediately impending physical (e.g., heart attack or fainting) or mental (e.g., going crazy or losing control) disaster and (b) to believe these interpretations more strongly (Clark et al., 1997; Harvey, Richards, Dziadosz, & Swindell, 1993). Furthermore, specific types of cognitions appear to be linked to particular physical sensations (Marks, Başoğlu, Al-Kubaisy, Sengün, & Marks, 1991; Westling & Öst, 1993). For example, Marks et al. (1991) found that symptoms such as cardiac sensations, shortness of breath, and numbness/tingling sensations were most closely related to thoughts about physical illness, whereas depersonalization was most closely associated with catastrophic thoughts about the psychosocial consequences of panic.

In a prospective naturalistic study, the expectation that one will experience a panic attack was related to the actual occurrence of panic (Kenardy & Taylor, 1999). However, a number of experimental studies have shown that people with PD tend to overestimate the extent to which they are likely to feel frightened during exposure to agoraphobic situations (Rachman, Lopatka, & Levitt, 1988; Schmidt, Jacquin, & Telch, 1994). Furthermore, findings regarding the effect of repeated exposure on subsequent predictions of fear and panic have been inconsistent. Whereas Schmidt et al. (1994) found that the bias to overpredict fear does not decrease with practice, Rachman et al. (1988) found that exposure trials during which patients correctly predicted panic attacks or had their panic predictions disconfirmed led to subsequent declines in panic predictions.

BIOLOGICAL ASPECTS OF PANIC DISORDER
AND AGORAPHOBIA

This section begins with an overview of biological theories of panic, with an emphasis on the influential work of Donald Klein. Following this theoretical discussion, there is a review of empirical findings related to the biological underpinnings of panic attacks and PD. This review includes neurotransmitter findings, research from family and genetics studies, and brain imaging studies.

Biological Models of Panic Disorder

Most biological models of PD are directly linked to findings from neurotransmitter studies such as those reviewed earlier (for reviews, see Coupland & Nutt, 1995; Nutt & Lawson, 1992). Perhaps the most influential biological model for PD is that developed by Klein (Klein, 1981; Klein & Gorman, 1987). Klein's theory of panic was inspired by studies done by Klein and his colleagues in the early 1960s (Klein, 1964; Klein & Fink, 1962), demonstrating the effectiveness of imipramine for blocking panic attacks but not the anticipatory anxiety accompanying panic. This was the first time that panic attacks had been proposed to be qualitatively different from generalized anxiety. The effectiveness of imipramine and other noradrenergic reuptake blockers led Klein and others to suggest that panic patients had an abnormality in their noradrenergic functioning.

Since this model was first proposed, several theorists have attempted to describe more specifically the nature of the hypothesized biological dysfunction. For example, Gorman, Liebowitz, Fyer, and Stein (1989) reviewed the literature on biological correlates of panic and anxiety and developed a theory that specifies particular brain systems that might be involved in panic attacks, anticipatory anxiety, and agoraphobic avoidance. Their model borrowed heavily from the initial work of Klein, and they expanded on it to suggest specific areas of the brain that may be involved in the proposed dysfunction. First, acute panic attacks were hypothesized to stem from activity in the brainstem area known as the locus ceruleus (which has a high concentration of norepinephrine). Anticipatory anxiety was hypothesized to involve areas of the limbic system, particularly the hippocampus. Finally, phobic avoidance was attributed to activity in the prefrontal cortex.

Klein's suffocation alarm model

Recently, to reflect changes in the current panic literature, Klein expanded and updated his model of panic. Klein's most recent writings describe panic as a pathological misfiring of the "suffocation alarm system" (Klein, 1993, 1994). According to Klein, evolutionary processes have provided humans with two types of alarm reactions and, correspondingly, two types of panic attacks. The first of these systems is mediated peripherally by the hypothalamic-pituitary-adrenal axis. This system controls the emergency alarm reaction that occurs in the presence of some real, immediate danger. It is also activated in cued or situationally triggered panic attacks such as those occurring in specific phobia and agoraphobia.

The second alarm system, according to Klein, is the suffocation alarm system, mediated centrally, presumably by activity in the locus ceruleus. This alarm is triggered by increases in carbon dioxide levels in the blood (pCO_2). From Klein's perspective, it makes sense that the body might develop an alarm reaction in response to increases in pCO_2, because the only time when such increases should occur in the natural world is when a person is forced to breathe his or her own exhaled air.

Klein hypothesized that PD patients have a pathologically lowered threshold for the suffocation alarm response. One factor contributing to the lowered threshold is CO_2 hypersensitivity; however, other factors are presumed to be important as well. According to Klein, it is a physiological misinterpretation of relevant data that precipitates spontaneous panic attacks. During panic, the brain mistakenly concludes that there is not enough air to breathe. This state elicits the suffocation alarm response, which consists of respiratory distress, hyperventilation, and an urge to flee from the situation. In this model, hyperventilation is viewed as a result of panic, not a cause of panic, as is hypothesized in some other models (e.g., Ley, 1987).

In this model, stimuli that predict suffocation should provoke panic in all people. Likewise, panic should be rare unless a person is in a situation where suffocation is likely. In PD, however, the mechanisms that determine the probability of suffocation are defective. As a result, there is a pathological misfiring of an otherwise adaptive response.

It should be noted that these alarm systems are not cognitively mediated, according to Klein (1993). The alarm reaction is developed to protect an organism from an immediate danger. Cognitive processing requires time, and such a reaction must occur before a conscious appraisal can be completed. In other words, there is no time to think in the face of immediate danger. This alarm system is also presumed to exist in phylogenetically primitive organisms without human capabilities for cognitive appraisal.

Finally, Klein described the role of anticipatory anxiety in panic. Anticipatory anxiety and agoraphobic avoidance are primarily determined by learning and cognitive factors. However, in some individuals, frequent limited symptom attacks and chronic breathlessness may themselves maintain or at least intensify chronic levels of anxiety. Furthermore, Klein specified two types of anxiety that are relevant in PD: anticipatory anxiety focused on some danger and anxiety produced by sensitization following repeated trauma. Also, a history of childhood separation anxiety is presumed to contribute to the lowered suffocation alarm threshold; however, the mechanisms by which this occurs are not specified in the model. Overall, findings and opinions regarding the validity of Klein's (1993) model have been mixed (for a thorough review, see Asmundson & Stein, 1994b; Griez & Schruers, 1998; Horwath, Adams, Wickramaratne, Pine, & Weissman, 1997; Ley, 1994; McNally, Hornig, & Donnell, 1995; Schmidt, Telch, & Jaimez, 1996; Taylor, Woody, Koch, McLean, & Anderson, 1996).

Neurotransmitter Findings in Panic Disorder

The neurotransmitters that have been most frequently implicated in PD and agoraphobia include norepinephrine (NE), serotonin (5-HT), and cholecystokinin tetrapeptide (CCK-4), although there is also limited evidence for the involvement of dopamine (e.g., Pitchot, Ansseau, Moreno, Hansenne, & von Frenckell, 1992) and -aminobutyric acid (e.g., Roy-Byrne, Cowley, Greenblatt, Shader, & Hommer, 1990). Findings that suggest that NE, 5-HT, and CCK play a role in the pathogenesis of PD have come primarily from studies of altered receptor functioning, changes in neurotransmitter correlates, patients' responses to panic induction challenges (i.e., inducing panic attacks using substances that are known to affect specific neurotransmitter systems), and changes in PD symptomatology following pharmacological treatments that are known to affect these neurotransmitter systems. A brief summary of some of these findings follows.

Norepinephrine

Among neurotransmitters, NE is the one that is most often implicated in PD and PDA (for a recent review, see Sullivan, Coplan, Kent, & Gorman, 1999). Noradrenergic challenges such as sodium lactate infusion (Liebowitz et al., 1984, 1985), carbon dioxide inhalation (Papp et al., 1993; Rapee, Brown, Antony, & Barlow, 1992), and yohimbine infusions (Charney, Heninger, & Breier, 1984) are effective methods of inducing panic attacks in people with PD, relative to people with other anxiety disorders and nonanxious individuals. However, Beck, Ohtake, and Shipherd (1999) recently found that heightened anxiety occurs equally in response to 5% CO_2 inhalation (a hypercapnic challenge) and 12% O_2 (a hypoxic challenge), suggesting that the anxiety response may have more to do with a hypersensitivity to breathing changes than to CO_2 changes specifically.

In addition, it should be noted that patients' responses to noradrenergic challenges are very much affected by psychological factors such as perceived control over the challenge procedure (Sanderson, Rapee, & Barlow, 1989; Zvolensky, Eifert, Lejuez, & McNeil, 1999; Zvolensky, Lejuez, & Eifert, 1998), the presence of a safe person such as a spouse (Carter, Hollon, Carson, & Shelton, 1995), expectations regarding anxiety during the challenge (van der Molen, van den Hout, Vroemen, Lousberg, & Griez, 1986), and repeated exposure to the challenge procedure (van den Hout, van der Molen, Griez, Lousberg, & Nansen, 1987). In addition, patients with PD are significantly less likely to respond to challenges such as carbon dioxide inhalation (Schmidt, Trakowski, & Staab, 1997) and sodium lactate infusion (Shear et al., 1991) following cognitive–behavioral treatment for PD.

In addition to findings from challenge studies, levels of NE metabolites such as urinary 3-methoxy-4-hydroxyphenylglycol have been shown to predict panic frequency and the severity of panic-related symptoms among people with PD (e.g., Garvey, Noyes, & Cook, 1990). In addition, there is evidence of altered alpha$_2$-adrenoceptor sensitivity in the brains of people with PD (Nutt, 1989). Finally, medications that block reuptake of NE (e.g., imipramine) are effective for preventing panic attacks (Cross-National Collaborative Panic Study, 1992; Mavissakalian & Perel, 1989).

Serotonin

Several recent reviews of the literature on 5-HT and PD have concluded that 5-HT probably plays a role in the pathophysiology of this disorder (e.g., Bell & Nutt, 1998; den Boer & Westenberg, 1991). The strongest evidence for the role of 5-HT comes from studies showing that the selective serotonin reuptake inhibitors (SSRIs) are effective treatments for PD (for a review, see Goddard & Charney, 1998). Additional studies (e.g., 5-HT challenge studies, tryptophan depletion studies) also provide evidence (although inconsistently) of 5-HT involvement in PD, possibly through its interaction with other neurotransmitters (see Bell & Nutt, 1998, for a review).

Cholecystokinin

Studies have consistently demonstrated that infusions of CCK-4 trigger panic attacks in people suffering from PD as well as in healthy volunteers (for a review, see Bradwejn, 1995). Furthermore, treatment with antipanic agents such as imipramine appears to block the effects of CCK on panic (Bradwejn & Koszycki, 1994). However, despite the panicogenic effects of CCK-4, treatment using CCK antagonists does not appear to cause significant improvement in PD symptoms (Kramer et al., 1995; Pande, Greiner, Adams, Lydiard, & Pierce, 1999; Sramek, Kramer, Reines, & Cutler, 1994/1995).

Family and Genetics Research

Family studies

Panic disorder appears to run in families (Cavallini, Perna, Caldirola, & Bellodi, 1999; Fyer, Mannuzza, Chapman, Lipsitz, Martin, & Klein, 1996; Goldstein et al., 1994; Mannuzza, Chapman, Klein, & Fyer, 1994/1995). For example, in one study (Mannuzza et al., 1994/1995), PD was diagnosed in relatives of patients with uncomplicated PD (9%) significantly more often than in relatives of control participants (3%). Furthermore, although a diagnosis of PD increases the chances of an individual's first-degree relatives also having PD, it does not increase their chances of developing other forms of psychopathology, such as other anxiety disorders (except perhaps social phobia), major depression, bipolar disorder, substance use disorders, psychotic disorders, and antisocial personality disorder (Goldstein et al., 1994). The familial pattern of transmission for social phobia and PD appears to be complex. In one study (Fyer et al., 1996), family members of people with comorbid social phobia and PD had an increased risk of having PD but not social phobia, compared with family members of control participants. This was the same pattern as shown by family members of people with PD alone. In contrast, family members of people who had social phobia alone had an increased rate of social phobia but not PD.

Twin and genetic studies

Twin studies have confirmed the importance of genetic factors in the development of PD and PDA, with heritability estimates in the range of 30% to 40% (e.g., Kendler, Karkowski, & Prescott, 1999; Kendler, Neale, Kessler, Heath, & Eaves, 1992, 1993). In a recent study of 120 twins from the general population (Perna, Caldirola, Arancio, & Bellodi, 1997), PD concordance rates were significantly greater for monozygotic twins (73%) than for dyzygotic twins (0%). However, concordance rates (57% vs. 43%) did not differ significantly in this study, with respect to the experience of occasional panic attacks, not meeting criteria for PD.

Overall, genetic linkage studies have not successfully identified a disease gene for PD (Crowe, Noyes, Samuelson, Wesner, & Wilson, 1990; Schmidt, Zoëga, & Crowe, 1993). However, a recent genome-wide screening study in 23 families with a high density of PD (Knowles et al., 1998) revealed some preliminary evidence for involvement in chromosome 20p. More research is needed to better understand the mechanisms by which PD is transmitted across generations.

Brain Imaging Studies

A number of studies suggest that the temporal regions of the brain (especially the right parahippocampal region) are involved in the experience of fear, anxiety, and panic attacks (George & Ballenger, 1992). In a positron emission tomography (PET) study, Reiman, Fusselman, Fox, and Raichle (1989) found increased regional cerebral blood flow (rCBF) in the bilateral temporal poles of healthy volunteers who were anxiously anticipating receiving a painful electrical shock. This finding is consistent with the results of another study from the same group (Reiman, Raichle, et al., 1989), based on drug-free PD patients undergoing a sodium lactate infusion challenge. Compared with those in the nonanxious control group, PD patients experiencing lactate-induced panic attacks had increased rCBF bilaterally in the temporal poles; bilaterally in the insular cortex, claustrum, or lateral putamen; bilaterally in or near the superior colliculus; and in or near the left anterior cerebellar vermis (Reiman, Raichle, et al., 1989).

In more recent PET studies, blood flow differences in the hippocampal regions have also been reported among people with PD, compared with nonanxious individuals. In a study of women in a resting state, Bisaga et al. (1998) found that compared with those in a nonanxious control group, patients with PD had increased glucose metabolism in the left hippocampus and parahippocampal area and decreased metabolism in the right inferior parietal and right superior temporal regions. Other studies have also shown differences in the hippocampal area, although they have differed somewhat with respect to the direction of the differences (i.e., increased vs. decreased rCBF) and whether the differences occurred bilaterally (de Cristofaro, Sessarego, Pupi, Biondi, & Faravelli, 1993; Nordahl et al., 1998).

TREATMENT OF PANIC DISORDER AND AGORAPHOBIA

The American Psychiatric Association (1998) recently published practice guidelines for the treatment of individuals suffering from PD. These guidelines highlighted important issues in the assessment and treatment of PD and PDA and also reviewed the major empirically supported psychological and pharmacological approaches to treating this condition. We now turn our attention to the relevant literature on this topic.

Psychological Treatments

Evidence-based psychological treatments for PD and PDA have primarily included four types of cognitive and behavioral strategies: in vivo exposure to feared situations (e.g., driving on busy highways), interoceptive exposure (IE) exercises (e.g., repeatedly spinning in a chair to overcome a fear of becoming dizzy), cognitive strategies (e.g., examining the evidence that supports and contradicts anxious beliefs), and relaxation-based strategies (e.g., learning to breath more slowly and in a more relaxing way). An exhaustive discussion of all studies is beyond the scope of this chapter, but several recent reviews can be found elsewhere (e.g., Acierno, Hersen, & van Hasselt, 1993; Antony & Swinson, 1996; Barlow & Brown, 1996; Beck & Zebb, 1994; McNally, 1994). In this section we will instead provide an overview of some of the most important findings related to psychological treatments for PD and PDA.

Early studies on the psychological treatment of agoraphobia tended to focus primarily on in vivo exposure to feared situations (e.g., Hand, LaMontagne, & Marks, 1974). Although in vivo exposure is still considered to be an important component of the psychological treatment of agoraphobia, there has been a shift in recent years to include a variety of other strategies designed to directly target panic attacks as well as the fear of experiencing panic. These methods, which include such strategies as cognitive therapy, IE, and BRT, are now thought to be particularly important for the treatment of individuals with PD who have only limited agoraphobic avoidance. Telch et al. (1993) compared cognitive–behavorial therapy (CBT) with a delayed treatment control condition for individuals suffering from PD or PDA. Treatment included education and corrective information, cognitive therapy, BRT, and IE. The percentages of patients in the CBT and control groups who were panic-free at the end of 8 weeks were 85% and 30%, respectively. Numerous additional studies have confirmed that CBT is an effective treatment for PD and that gains tend to be maintained over the long term (Barlow & Brown, 1996).

Differences among CBT strategies and combinations of strategies

A number of researchers have examined the effect of adding panic management strategies (e.g., cognitive therapy, IE, BRT) to in vivo exposure-based treatments for agoraphobia. Although some studies have shown increased efficacy when panic management techniques are used in combination with exposure (e.g., Marchione, Michelson, Greenwald, & Dancu, 1987; Michelson, Marchione, Greenwald, Testa, & Marchione, 1996), others have failed to show any increased benefit for combining situational exposure with these other strategies (e.g., de Ruiter, Rijkin, Garssen, & Kraaimaat, 1989;

Ito, Noshirvani, Başoğlu, & Marks, 1996; Rijken, Kraaimaat, de Ruiter, & Garssen, 1992; van den Hout, Arntz, & Hoekstra, 1994). In a meta-analysis of existing studies, van Balkom, Nauta, and Bakker (1995) concluded that, overall, adding panic management strategies does not add to the efficacy of in vivo exposure for PDA.

Studies in which various CBT strategies for PD and PDA have been compared (e.g., exposure vs. cognitive therapy, cognitive therapy vs. applied relaxation, etc.) have also yielded inconsistent findings, with some showing few differences among strategies (e.g., Bouchard et al., 1996; Hoffart, 1995, 1998; Michelson, Mavissakalian, & Marchione, 1988; Öst & Westling, 1995; Öst, Westling, & Hellström, 1993) and others finding significant differences in the efficacy of particular strategies.

For example, Barlow, Craske, Cerny, and Klosko (1989) found that relaxation training was not as powerful a treatment for PD as was the combination of IE (including a large number of different exercises) and cognitive therapy—a finding that was maintained 2 years after treatment (Craske, Brown, & Barlow, 1991). Confirming this finding, several other investigators have also found that cognitive therapy is more effective than relaxation training, particularly for reducing panic frequency (Arntz & van den Hout, 1996) and agoraphobic fear (Beck, Stanley, Baldwin, Deagle, & Averill, 1994). Finally, Schmidt et al. (in press) found that adding BRT to a standard cognitive–behavioral protocol for PD (i.e., education, cognitive restructuring, IE, and in vivo exposure) did not increase the efficacy of treatment and actually led to a poorer outcome on some measures, although differences were not statistically significant.

Couples treatments for agoraphobia

For some individuals who are treated for agoraphobia, relationship difficulties may develop as the individual becomes more independent and less reliant on his or her partner (Hafner, 1984). Furthermore, relationship difficulties have been shown to be predictive of relapse in people who receive behavioral treatment for agoraphobia (Bland & Hallam, 1981). In light of these findings, several investigators have studied the impact of including partners in the cognitive–behavioral treatment of agoraphobia (for a review of this topic, see Daiuto, Baucom, Epstein, & Dutton, 1998). Including partners in treatment makes intuitive sense for a number of reasons. First, partners can potentially coach patients during early in vivo exposure practices. In addition, being involved in treatment can help partners to gain a better understanding regarding the nature of PDA and learn how not to subtly reinforce agoraphobic behaviors. Finally, partners who are more involved in the treatment process might be expected to feel less threatened as the patient becomes more autonomous. Whereas some studies have shown significantly more improvement in

PDA patients who were treated with their partners, compared with those treated without partners (e.g., Barlow, O'Brien, & Last, 1984; Cerny, Barlow, Craske, & Himadi, 1987), other studies have failed to show differences across groups (e.g., Emmelkamp et al., 1992).

Treatment with minimal therapist contact

Many patients with PD are able to make significant gains with minimal therapist contact. For example, behavioral treatment conducted by telephone is an effective alternative for agoraphobic patients who live far from specialty treatment centers (Swinson, Fergus, Cox, & Wickwire, 1995). In addition, Clark et al. (1999) found that an abbreviated five-session course of CBT (requiring only 6.5 hours of therapy) was as effective as a standard 12-session treatment and superior to a wait-list control condition on all measures. Gains were maintained at a 12-month follow-up. The short-term (10 weeks) and long-term (12 months) effectiveness of a five-session treatment for PD was recently replicated by another group of investigators (Botella & García-Palacios, 1999).

In addition, there is evidence that with early intervention, panic-related symptoms can be treated in as little as one session. Swinson, Soulios, Cox, and Kuch (1992) compared a single session of exposure with a single session of reassurance for individuals presenting to hospital emergency rooms with panic attacks. Forty percent of patients met criteria for PD, and most patients had only recently begun to experience panic attacks. Whereas people who received exposure instructions improved over the next 6 months on measures of panic frequency, phobic avoidance, and depression, those in the reassurance condition showed no improvement on any measure and actually worsened with respect to agoraphobic avoidance.

Finally, several studies have demonstrated that treatment with a self-help manual can be as effective as therapist-administered treatment for many patients suffering from PD or PDA (Gould & Clum, 1995; Gould, Clum, & Shapiro, 1993; Hecker, Losee, Fritzler, & Fink, 1996; Lidren et al., 1994). However, recent findings from Febbraro, Clum, Roodman, and Wright (1999) suggest that self-help treatments may be less effective when they are used on their own, without occasional professional contact to monitor the patient's progress and treatment compliance. In other words, for self-help treatments to be most effective, they should be combined with brief clinical visits.

Predictors of outcome following CBT

A number of factors appear to predict outcome following CBT for PD and PDA. Variables that have been shown to interfere with treatment outcome include chronic life stress (Wade, Monroe, & Michelson, 1993); severity of catastrophic cognitions (Keijers, Hoogduin, & Schaap, 1994);

agoraphobia severity (Keijers et al., 1994); compliance with exposure home-work (Edelman & Chambless, 1993); expressed emotion among family mem-bers, such as emotional overinvolvement or hostility (Chambless & Steketee, 1999); certain characteristics of therapists (Williams & Chambless, 1990); and comorbid personality psychopathology (Keijers et al., 1994). Factors that do not seem to be associated with outcome include perceptions of early parental upbringing (de Beurs, van Dyck, Lange, & van Balkom, 1995), the quality of the therapeutic relationship (de Beurs, van Dyck, et al., 1995), and comorbidity with other anxiety and mood disorders (Brown, Antony, & Barlow, 1995; Laberge, Gauthier, Côté, Plamondon, & Cormier, 1993; McLean, Woody, Taylor, & Koch, 1998). Findings regarding the impact of relationship dissatisfaction (Bland & Hallam, 1981; Keijsers et al., 1994) have been mixed.

Psychotherapy for PD and PDA

In a small number of controlled studies, researchers have examined the use of other psychotherapies for PD and PDA. Hoffart and Martinsen (1990) found that brief psychodynamic treatment was an effective short-term treatment for agoraphobic inpatients. However, relative to an exposure-based treatment, psychodynamic psychotherapy was associated with a sig-nificantly higher rate of relapse 1 year after treatment. Although some studies have shown nondirective therapies (e.g., emotion-focused therapy or client-centered therapy) to be helpful for patients with PD (Shear, Pilkonis, Cloitre, & Leon, 1994; Shear & Weiner, 1997; Teusch, Böhme, & Gastpar, 1997), others have shown nondirective therapies to be relatively ineffective (e.g., Craske, Maidenberg, & Bystritsky, 1995).

Pharmacological Treatments

Controlled clinical trials with a variety of pharmacological agents have led to a large number of medications from which to choose when treating PD or PDA, including SSRIs, tricyclic antidepressants (TCAs), other antide-pressants, and high-potency benzodiazepines. (For additional reviews, see Antony & Swinson, 1996; Cowley, Ha, & Roy-Byrne, 1997; Goddard & Charney, 1998; Jefferson, 1997; Mavissakalian, 1996a; Stein, 1998; Swinson & Cox, 1996; Wilkinson, Balestrieri, Ruggeri, & Bellantuono, 1991.) Note that all drug names in the review are generic; trade names for medications are provided in chapter 8.

Antidepressant trials

Tricyclic antidepressants such as imipramine were among the first medications used to effectively treat PD and PDA (Klein, 1964; Klein &

Fink, 1962). Since these early studies, a number of additional studies have confirmed that imipramine is an effective acute and long-term treatment for this condition (Mavissakalian, 1996b; Mavissakalian & Perel, 1989, 1992, 1995, 1999). In fact, imipramine is the most studied of the medications used for PD. Investigators have also found clomipramine to be effective for blocking panic attacks (e.g., Johnston, Troyer, & Whitsett, 1988). Despite their effectiveness, these medications are now prescribed as first-line treatments less frequently than before, given the difficulty that many patients have tolerating these drugs (e.g., Papp et al., 1997). Although other TCAs have been studied in patients with PD, relatively few controlled trials exist to date.

More recently, controlled trials have established the efficacy of SSRIs for treating PD. Fluoxetine (Michelson, Lydiard, et al., 1998), fluvoxamine (Bakish et al., 1996; Black, Wesner, Bowers, & Gabel, 1993; van Vliet, den Boer, Westenberg & Slaap, 1996), sertraline (Londborg et al., 1998; Pohl, Wolkow, & Clary, 1998; Pollack, Otto, Worthington, Manfro, & Wolkow, 1998; Rapaport, Wolkow, & Clary, 1998), paroxetine (Ballenger, Wheadon, Steiner, Bushnell, & Gergel, 1998; Oehrberg et al., 1995), and citalopram (Wade, Lepola, Koponen, Pedersen, & Pedersen, 1997) have each been shown to be more effective than placebo for the treatment of individuals suffering from PD. Studies comparing SSRIs with TCAs have yielded mixed results. Whereas Bakish et al. (1996) found fluvoxamine and imipramine to be equally effective, Nair et al. (1996) found a strong effect for imipramine but not for fluvoxamine. In contrast, Boyer (1994) concluded in a meta-analytic study that SSRIs are superior to imipramine for alleviating panic attacks.

A number of other antidepressants also appear to be effective for treating PD. A double-blind controlled trial with venlafaxine (Pollack et al., 1996) and two open-label trials with nefazodone (Bystritsky, Rosen, Suri, & Vapnik, 1999; DeMartinis, Schweizer, & Rickels, 1996) suggest that these newer antidepressants are also useful for patients suffering from PD. Although monoamine oxidase inhibitors such as phenelzine (Buigues & Vallejo, 1987) also appear to be effective for blocking panic attacks, they are rarely prescribed because of necessary dietary restrictions for people taking these medications and difficulty tolerating the side effects. Findings regarding reversible inhibitors of monoamine oxidase-A (RIMAs) for treating PD have been mixed. A recent controlled trial with the RIMA brofaromine (van Vliet et al., 1996) showed the drug to be as effective as fluvoxamine and more effective than placebo for alleviating the symptoms of PD. However, another study showed that the RIMA moclobemide was no more effective than placebo in a recent comparative trial (Loerch et al., 1999).

Anxiolytic trials

In 1990, alprazolam became the first pharmacological agent to be approved in the United States for the treatment of PD (Spiegel, 1998). It is now well established that alprazolam is effective for blocking panic attacks and reducing agoraphobic avoidance (Ballenger et al., 1988; Pecknold, Luthe, Munjack, & Alexander, 1994; Schweizer, Patterson, Rickels, & Rosenthal, 1993). However, although side effects of alprazolam are generally well tolerated by patients (O'Sullivan et al., 1994), increased anxiety during discontinuation can be difficult for some individuals, particularly if the drug is tapered quickly (O'Sullivan et al., 1996; Pecknold, Swinson, Kuch, & Lewis, 1988).

Placebo-controlled trials also support the use of clonazepam as a treatment for PD (Beauclair, Fontaine, Annable, Holobow, & Chouinard, 1994; Moroz & Rosenbaum, 1999; Rosenbaum, Moroz, & Bowden, 1997). Furthermore, with a gradual taper, there is evidence (Moroz & Rosenbaum, 1999; Rosenbaum et al., 1997) that clonazepam discontinuation may be easier compared with discontinuation from other benzodiazepines (e.g., alprazolam), based on findings from earlier studies. Other anxiolytics that have appeared to be helpful for PD (based on controlled trials) include lorazepam (Schweizer et al., 1990), diazepam (Dunner, Ishiki, Avery, Wilson, & Hyde, 1986), and adinazolam (Carter, Fawcett, et al., 1995; Davidson et al., 1994). However, controlled trials with the nonbenzodiazepine anxiolytic buspirone showed no significant differences between buspirone and placebo (Sheehan, Raj, Sheehan, & Soto, 1990; Sheehan, Raj, Harnett-Sheehan, Soto, & Knapp, 1993).

Imipramine versus anxiolytics

Comparisons of imipramine and benzodiazepines such as alprazolam (Cross-National Collaborative Panic Study, 1992; Schweizer, Rickels, Weiss, & Zavodnick, 1993) and clonazepam (Svebak, Cameron, & Levander, 1990) have generally shown few differences in the efficacy of these medications after 8 weeks of treatment, although alprazolam appears to work more quickly than imipramine (Cross-National Collaborative Panic Study, 1992). Findings from a preliminary study on the relative efficacy of imipramine, alprazolam, and placebo in older adults (e.g., Sheikh & Swales, 1999) have also shown that these medications have comparable effects and are more effective than placebo. Dosages in this study were about half of those typically used in studies of younger populations. Meta-analytic comparisons of antidepressants and anxiolytics have yielded mixed results. Some researchers have shown few differences between these treatments (e.g., van Balkom et al., 1997; Wilkinson et al., 1991), whereas Cox, Endler, Lee, and Swinson (1992) found alprazolam to be more effective than imipramine on measures of panic and anxiety.

Relative Efficacy of Psychological, Pharmacological, and Combined Approaches

Findings on the efficacy of medications compared with CBT have been mixed. For example, whereas Black et al. (1993) found fluvoxamine to be somewhat more effective than cognitive therapy following acute treatment, Loerch et al. (1999) found 8-week treatment with CBT to be significantly more effective than treatment with moclobemide, which was no better than placebo. Clark et al. (1994) found cognitive therapy to be more effective than imipramine shortly after treatment ended and again at a 15-month follow-up and that relapse rates were considerably higher in the imipramine group (40%) than in the cognitive therapy group (5%).

Studies with a combined treatment condition have also yielded inconsistent findings. A number of researchers have found few differences in the acute effects of CBT, medications (e.g., imipramine, SSRIs, and benzodiazepines), and their combination (e.g., Barlow, Gorman, Shear, & Woods, in press; Marks et al., 1993; Sharp et al., 1996; Wardle et al., 1994), although some researchers have demonstrated added short-term benefit in the combined treatment condition compared with each individual treatment alone (e.g., Cottraux et al., 1995; de Beurs, van Balkom, Lange, Koele, & van Dyck, 1995; Telch, Agras, Taylor, Roth, & Gallen, 1985). Several studies also suggest that CBT can be used to help patients to discontinue their treatment with anxiolytics (e.g., Bruce, Spiegel, Gregg, & Nuzzarello, 1994; Otto et al., 1993; Spiegel, Bruce, Gregg, & Nuzzarello, 1994).

In several recent meta-analytic studies (e.g., Cox et al., 1992; van Balkom et al., 1995; van Balkom et al., 1997), researchers have compared pharmacological, psychological, and combined treatments for PD and PDA. In the largest of these, based on more than 100 studies, van Balkom et al. (1997) found that antidepressants, panic management strategies (e.g., cognitive therapy and IE), high-potency benzodiazepines, and the combination of in vivo exposure and antidepressants were all more effective than control conditions (e.g., placebo) for reducing panic attacks. In this study, in vivo exposure alone was found to be ineffective for reducing panic attacks. The combination of antidepressants and in vivo exposure was superior to other conditions for reducing agoraphobic avoidance. In general, these finding were confirmed in a meta-analysis of long-term effects of these treatments, based largely on naturalistic follow-up data (Bakker, van Balkom, Spinhoven, Blaauw, & van Dyck, 1998).

Despite findings that combined treatments are either as effective or more effective than CBT and pharmacotherapy alone, there is recent evidence that medications may actually interfere with the effects of CBT in the long term. Barlow et al. (in press) recently reported on a large study comparing the relative and combined effects of imipramine and CBT for 303 patients with PD with no more than mild agoraphobic avoidance. This study included two methodological advances that are worth noting. First, in addition to including a CBT *plus imipramine condition*, the study also included a CBT *plus placebo pill condition*, to control for the effects of taking a pill in the CBT plus imipramine group. A second strength of this study was the fact that it was conducted at four sites—two with a primarily pharmacological orientation and two with a primarily psychological orientation. The decision to include sites that are known for having competing therapeutic allegiances was a unique way of controlling for the effects of investigator bias in favor of one treatment or another.

Confirming earlier findings, Barlow et al. (in press) found few differences among active treatment conditions (CBT plus imipramine, CBT plus placebo, CBT alone, and imipramine alone) immediately following treatment, and all four active treatments were more effective than placebo alone. However, 6 months following the end of treatment, individuals who had received imipramine (either alone or in combination with CBT) were more likely to have deteriorated compared with those who had received CBT alone. In addition, the percentage of people considered to be responders at follow-up was higher in the CBT plus placebo condition than the CBT plus imipramine condition.

These findings confirm those from an earlier study by Marks et al. (1993), who compared alprazolam plus exposure, placebo plus exposure, alprazolam plus relaxation, and placebo plus relaxation for 154 patients with PDA. Although alprazolam and exposure were equally effective after 8 weeks of treatment, the gains achieved by alprazolam were lost during follow-up. In fact, following discontinuation, exposure plus alprazolam was slightly less effective than exposure plus placebo. It was found that the extent to which patients believed that their gains were due to the medication rather than the exposure (regardless of whether they were on alprazolam or placebo) was positively correlated with their tendency to experience withdrawal symptoms and worsening during the 6-month follow-up phase (Başoğlu, Marks, Kiliç, Brewin, & Swinson, 1994).

Finally, Sharp et al. (1996) found that individuals who received CBT (either alone, with placebo, or with fluvoxamine) maintained their gains during follow-up to a greater extent than did individuals taking fluvoxamine alone. Taken together, these findings suggest that medications, CBT, and their combination are all effective treatments in the short term for people with PD or PDA. However, given the results of long-term studies, the first-line treatment for PD and PDA should be CBT. For patients who require additional treatment, medication can then be added.

Although CBT and medications seem to be equally effective treatments for PD across groups, they may not be equally efficacious across individuals.

Pollack, Otto, Kaspi, Hammerness, and Rosenbaum (1994) found that among 15 patients who had previously not responded to adequate trials of pharmacotherapy, subsequent CBT led to significant improvements in global functioning and panic frequency. These findings were confirmed in a another case series demonstrating that patients with PD who had previously failed to respond to pharmacotherapy received significant benefit from group CBT (Otto, Pollack, Penava, & Zucker, 1999). In a related study, Hoffart et al. (1993) found that 18 patients with PDA who had previously not responded to treatment with behavior therapy subsequently made moderate gains with clomipramine. Taken together, these studies suggest that for any individual patient, there may be advantages of choosing either pharmacotherapy or CBT. More research is needed to help identify predictors of response to specific treatments such as CBT and various medications.

CONCLUSION

Compared with other anxiety disorders, PD and agoraphobia are undoubtedly the most thoroughly researched. We now have a fairly good understanding of several factors that contribute to the development of this problem and also have treatments that appear to be effective for the majority of people who experience frequent panic attacks. Still, research on PD and agoraphobia remains very active, and new questions are continually being answered.

In the next chapter, we review empirical findings on the nature and treatment of social phobia. Chapter 3 covers similar topics as they relate to specific phobias. The reader will probably find that despite the differences between these conditions, there are also many similarities. As a result, the skills needed to treat any one of these problems overlap greatly with those that are used for treating the other two disorders.

2

SOCIAL PHOBIA

Almost everyone knows what it feels like to be anxious or uncomfortable in a social situation. From surveys of many individuals from across the United States and elsewhere, Zimbardo and his colleagues (Carducci & Zimbardo, 1995; Henderson & Zimbardo, 1998; Zimbardo, Pilkonis, & Norwood, 1975) found that 40% of individuals considered themselves to be chronically shy, to the point of it being a problem. Another 40% reported that they had previously considered themselves to be shy. Fifteen percent more considered themselves to be shy in some situations, and only 5% reported that they were never shy.

Social phobia (also called *social anxiety disorder*) is diagnosed when shyness or performance anxiety becomes so intense and so pervasive that it leads to clinically significant distress and impairment. As is reviewed later in this chapter, social phobia is one of the most prevalent psychological disorders. In this chapter we review the empirical literature pertaining to social phobia and social anxiety. The structure of the chapter is similar to that in chapter 1: We begin with a discussion of diagnostic issues and studies on descriptive psychopathology and epidemiology. Next, we review current theories and empirical evidence pertaining to both psychological and biological approaches to social anxiety. The chapter concludes with an up-to-date review of psychological and biological treatments for social anxiety.

DIAGNOSTIC CRITERIA AND DESCRIPTION

Social phobia is defined in the fourth edition of the *Diagnostic and Statistical Manual of Mental Disorders* (*DSM-IV*; American Psychiatric Association, 1994) as "a marked and persistent fear of one or more social or performance situations in which the person is exposed to unfamiliar people or to possible scrutiny by others. The individual fears that he or she will act in a way (or show anxiety symptoms) that will be humiliating or embarrassing (p. 416)." In addition to anxiety and fear related to social and performance situations, the individual must also (a) experience anxiety or fear almost every time he or she confronts the feared social situations, (b) recognize that the fear is excessive or unreasonable, (c) avoid the feared situations or endure them with intense anxiety or discomfort, (d) have had the problem for at least 6 months (only a requirement if the individual is under 18 years of age), and (e) experience significant distress and/or functional impairment resulting from the problem. Furthermore, the anxiety cannot be better accounted for by another mental disorder or be due to the direct effect of a substance or a general medical condition. Finally, if a general medical condition or mental disorder is present, the fear must be unrelated to it. Issues related to differential diagnosis and diagnostic assessment are discussed in chapter 4.

Not all individuals with social phobia fear the same situations. In fact, the range of feared situations can vary from as few as one (e.g., a fear of public speaking) to as many as almost all situations in which other people are present. Exhibit 2.1 lists situations that may be feared by people suffering from social phobia.

Subtypes of Social Phobia

A number of subtyping strategies were considered when the *DSM-IV* was being developed. In their report to the *DSM-IV* subgroup on social phobia, Heimberg and Holt (1989) proposed three subtypes for the disorder: (a) circumscribed type (for people who fear only one or two situations), (b) generalized type (for people who fear most social situations), and (c) nongeneralized type (for people who have clinically significant anxiety in social interaction situations but have at least one broad domain of social functioning that is not associated with significant anxiety). Another proposal from the Task Force on the *DSM-IV* (American Psychiatric Association, 1991) also involved three subtypes for social phobia: (a) performance type (phobic stimulus includes some activity that is being performed in front of others—e.g., public speaking, eating, drinking, urinating, writing), (b) limited interactional type (phobic stimulus is restricted to one or two interaction situations, such as dating or speaking to strangers), and (c) generalized

Exhibit 2.1
Situations Often Feared by People with Social Phobia

Situations Involving Being Observed or Performing in Front of Others
- Speaking in meetings or in classes
- Arriving late for a class or meeting
- Participating in sports and athletics
  (e.g., aerobics class, working out in a public gym)
- Performing music
- Formal public speaking
- Using public restrooms with other people nearby
- Eating in front of others
- Drinking in front of others
- Speaking in front of others
- Writing in front of others
- Making mistakes in front of other people
- Being in public (e.g., a crowded bus, a shopping mall)

Situations Involving Social Interaction
- Initiating conversations
- Maintaining conversations
- Making "small talk"
- Disclosing personal information to others
- Intimate or sexual situations
- Meeting new people
- Dating
- Talking to strangers
- Expressing disagreement or disapproval
- Conflict situations
- Talking on the telephone
- Talking to people in authority
- Returning items to a store
- Being assertive (e.g., refusing an unreasonable request)
- Going to a party
- Inviting friends over for dinner

type (phobic stimuli include most social situations). More recently, Holt, Heimberg, Hope, and Liebowitz (1992) recommended that individuals with social phobia be classified according to the four situational domains that are feared or avoided: (a) formal speaking/interaction, (b) informal speaking/interaction, (c) observation by others, and (d) assertion.

Despite these different proposals for social phobia subtypes, only the generalized subtype remains in the *DSM-IV*, whereby clinicians are required to specify whether the social phobia is generalized, which is defined to include most social situations. Although the generalized subtype appears to be a reliable and valid way of distinguishing among different types of individuals with social phobia (Mannuzza et al., 1995), the other subtyping strategies described earlier may still be helpful for understanding the nature of social phobia and are often used by researchers who study this disorder. For the interested reader, there are a number of sources for more detailed consideration of issues related to subtypes in social phobia (Hazen & Stein, 1995; Heimberg, Holt, Schneier, Spitzer, & Liebowitz, 1993; Kessler, Stein, & Berglund, 1998).

Case Vignette: Social Phobia

Michael was 34 years old when he presented for an assessment in our anxiety disorders program. The referral letter from his physician explained that Michael was suffering from panic disorder with agoraphobia (PDA) and an essential tremor in both hands. He had been taking propanolol for his tremor and also was taking imipramine, a tricyclic antidepressant (TCA), for his panic attacks. Neither of these medications was particularly helpful. Michael reported fear and anxiety in a range of situations including being in crowds, walking outside (particularly when alone), eating and drinking in front of other people, writing in front of other people, attending parties, speaking in groups, and being assertive. He had outstanding interpersonal skills and appeared to be quite relaxed during the evaluation.

Despite his calm appearance, Michael reported extremely high levels of anxiety during the assessment. While waiting for his appointment, he was unable to complete the patient registration form because other people might notice the tremor in his hands. While being interviewed, he reported feeling very panicky with an increased heart rate, breathlessness, and shaking, although these symptoms were not especially noticeable to the interviewer.

Although he had originally been diagnosed with panic disorder (PD), Michael reported never having had an uncued or unexpected panic attack. In fact, all of his anxiety and fear appeared to be related to the possibility of having his anxiety or some other aspect of his behavior noticed by other people. He feared being out in public because of the possibility of drawing attention to himself. He was especially uncomfortable when alone in public because he believed that other people would notice his anxiety and view him negatively. He felt more comfortable when he was with a friend or with his partner because he assumed that strangers might be distracted from paying attention exclusively to him. Over the course of the evaluation, it became clearer that his diagnosis of PD was probably inappropriate. Given that his anxiety and panic attacks occurred exclusively in the context of what he perceived to be social situations, and because his fear was based exclusively on the possibility of being perceived in a negative light by others, he received a diagnosis of social phobia. In addition, because Michael's tremor occurred only when he was anxious about being observed (e.g., when holding a glass or trying to write in front of other people), his shaking hands were viewed to be tied to social anxiety.

Michael engaged in a variety of behaviors to protect himself from having his anxiety symptoms noticed by other people. Usually, he just avoided situations that made him uncomfortable. When forced to be in a feared situation, he often sat on his trembling hands in order to hide them from people's view. Also, he tended to hold a glass with both hands when drinking in front of others. To feel more comfortable, Michael often drank alcohol in social situations. He reported almost getting into car accidents on two occasions while driving impaired.

Throughout his childhood, Michael's parents had very high expectations regarding his performance in all areas of his life. He was expected to do well in school, excel at sports, and never to do anything that might embarrass his parents. Although he felt a lot of pressure growing up, his social anxiety did not become a problem until he was in his teens. Michael began to take the normal social pressures in high school very seriously. He became very concerned about looking stupid in class and gradually became worried that other people might notice that he was anxious. He ended up quitting high school after 11th grade, despite being very bright and successful in all of his academic subjects.

EPIDEMIOLOGY

Prevalence of Social Phobia

Perhaps more than with any other anxiety disorder, the prevalence of social phobia has been a source of controversy in the literature. In the Epidemiological Catchment Area (ECA) study (Eaton et al., 1991), the lifetime prevalence estimate for social phobia (based on *DSM-III* criteria; American Psychiatric Association, 1980) was 2.73%. This figure is based on structured interviews with more than 13,000 people in five American cities. In contrast, the more recent National Comorbidity Survey (NCS), which was based on structured interviews with just over 8,000 Americans, showed a lifetime prevalence rate of 13.3% for social phobia (Kessler et al., 1994). There are a number of factors that might account for this rather large difference in the estimated prevalence of social phobia.

First, different diagnostic criteria were used in the two studies. Whereas the ECA study used interviews based on *DSM-III* criteria, the NCS interview relied on more recent *DSM-III-R* criteria (American Psychiatric Association, 1987). Second, the sample studied in the NCS study was more representative of the American people at large than the ECA study, which included only people from five specific cities. Most important, however, the interview used in the ECA study (i.e., the Diagnostic Interview Schedule, Version IV

[DIS-IV]; Robins, Cottler, Bucholz, & Compton, 1995) used a very narrow definition of social phobia. Participants were asked only about their fear in three different social situations (i.e., eating in front of others, public speaking, and meeting new people). In addition, the definition of social phobia required only that the fear cause significant impairment in functioning. The presence of significant distress was not considered sufficient to meet the criteria for social phobia, even though the *DSM-III*, *DSM-III-R*, and *DSM-IV* (American Psychiatric Association, 1980, 1987, 1994) permit the diagnosis to be given as long as the person experiences significant distress or impairment.

Interestingly, other studies that have relied on the DIS-IV have also yielded similarly low prevalence rates for social phobia. For example, Bland, Orn, and Newman (1988) found that 1.7% of more than 3,000 individuals in Edmonton, Alberta, Canada, met criteria for social phobia. Recently, however, the overly narrow definition of social phobia used by the DIS-IV has prompted some experts to argue that the prevalence estimates in the ECA and Edmonton studies seriously underestimate the true prevalence of social phobia in the general population (Walker & Stein, 1995).

So, it is likely that social phobia is much more common than is suggested by the ECA findings. Nevertheless, it is still possible that the estimate of 13.3% from the NCS study is an overestimate. Stein, Walker, and Forde (1994) demonstrated in a Canadian sample that the prevalence of social phobia is strongly influenced by the threshold set for distress/ impairment as well as the number of feared situations needed to meet criteria for social phobia. Depending on the threshold used, lifetime prevalence estimates varied from as low as 1.9% to as high as 18.7%. When the threshold was adjusted to conform most closely with the *DSM-III-R* definition of social phobia, the prevalence was 7.1% (Stein et al., 1994).

A recent prevalence study in adolescents and young adults (ages 14–24) confirmed that social phobia continues to be a prevalent problem when the most recent *DSM-IV* definition is used. Wittchen, Stein, and Kessler (1999) found the lifetime prevalence of *DSM-IV* social phobia to be 9.5% in female and 4.9% in male adolescents and young adults. In this study, about a third of participants with social phobia met criteria for the generalized subtype.

Age of Onset, Gender, Ethnicity, and Culture

Age of onset

The mean age of onset for social phobia has been typically found to be in the mid- to late teens (Marks & Gelder, 1966; Öst, 1987a; Schneier, Johnson, Hornig, Liebowitz, & Weissman, 1992; Thyer, Parish, Curtis,

Nesse, & Cameron, 1985). However, there are a number of reasons to interpret these figures cautiously. First, many studies are unclear with respect to what is meant by the term *onset*. Onset may refer to the time at which the fear first appears or to the time at which the fear begins to cause significant impairment or distress. Second, the criteria used to define social phobia differ considerably across studies. In some of the early studies (e.g., Marks & Gelder, 1966), the definition is not based on *DSM* criteria. In other studies (e.g., Schneier et al., 1992), the findings are based on individuals in the ECA study, where social phobia was defined according to *DSM-III* criteria using questions on the DIS-IV. As was discussed earlier, there are serious problems with the way in which social phobia was assessed in the ECA study. In fact, in a recent study using a semistructured interview based on *DSM-IV* criteria, a mean onset age of only 12.8 years was found (Chartier, Hazen, & Stein, 1998).

Third, as was pointed out by Rapee (1995), most estimates of onset age are based on retrospective interviews and are therefore subject to bias. In addition, the means presented in most studies do not adequately capture the fact that the pattern of onset tends to be considerably skewed. For example, Schneier et al. (1992) found that 15% of individuals with social phobia reported having had the problem their whole lives, and it is unclear how such individuals have been counted in most studies of age of onset. An additional 36% of participants in the Schneier et al. (1992) study reported an onset between ages 0 and 10. In only 10% of cases was the onset after age 26. Despite a mean age of onset in the mid- to late teens, social phobia appears to be a somewhat common problem among children and is diagnosed in a considerable percentage of children who are referred to specialty anxiety-disorders clinics (Albano, DiBartolo, Heimberg, & Barlow, 1995).

Gender and social phobia

Most large epidemiological studies (including the ECA and NCS studies) have shown relatively small differences in the prevalence of social phobia among men and women (Eaton et al., 1991; Kessler et al., 1994). Although social phobia tends to be slightly more common among women than men, the differences are relatively small compared with those for other anxiety disorders such as PD, specific phobias, and generalized anxiety disorder (GAD). An exception is the study by Wittchen et al. (1999), in which the lifetime prevalence of *DSM-IV* social phobia was found to be almost twice as high for female (9.5%) as for male (4.9%) adolescents and young adults. Relatively small differences in the prevalence of social phobia in men and women have generally been confirmed in studies based on clinical samples.

Recently, investigators have begun to examine sex differences in the presentation of social phobia. Turk et al. (1998) studied sex differences in a large sample of patients with social phobia who presented for treatment. Compared with men, women reported experiencing more fear when talking to people in authority, talking or performing in front of an audience, working while being observed, entering a room where others are already seated, being the center of attention, speaking at meetings, expressing disagreement, giving a report to a group, and throwing a party. Men were more fearful than women about urinating in public bathrooms and returning goods to a store. Differences between men and women were not significant with respect to patterns of comorbidity, social phobia subtypes, and duration of illness. In a related study, Eskin, Orsillo, Heimberg, Holt, and Liebowitz (1991) reported that women with social phobia tended to score higher on a variety of social anxiety self-report measures than did men with social phobia.

Ethnicity and culture

Weissman et al. (1996) reported on the prevalence of social phobia across samples in the United States, Canada, Puerto Rico, and Korea. All samples were diagnosed using the DIS-IV. Although social phobia was present in all four countries, the prevalence varied somewhat, with the highest prevalence in the United States (2.7%) and the lowest prevalence in Korea (.5%). These findings should be interpreted with caution, however, because of the limitations of the DIS-IV as a diagnostic tool for identifying social phobia.

A broad range of studies have identified people with social phobia and related conditions in additional countries around the world, including Australia and Sweden (Heimberg, Makris, Juster, Öst, & Rapee, 1997), Saudi Arabia (Chaleby, 1987), Japan (Kleinknecht, Dinnel, Kleinknecht, Hiruma, & Harada, 1997), and other East Asian countries (Chang, 1997). There appear to be differences across cultures with respect to the features of social anxiety, the types of situations that produce anxiety, and scores on standard measures of social anxiety (Heimberg et al., 1997; Kleinknecht, Dinnel, et al., 1997). In addition, patients' perceptions regarding the influence of early parenting on subsequent social anxiety appear to be different among American and Chinese American samples, with American samples being more likely to attribute social anxiety to early parenting (Leung, Heimberg, Holt, & Bruch, 1994). Finally, there is evidence that clinicians from different countries may have different diagnostic biases when identifying individuals who are socially anxious. For example, Tseng, Asai, Kitanishi, McLaughlin, and Kyomen (1992) found that diagnoses of social phobia made by Japanese psychiatrists were more likely to be influenced by the ethnic background of the patient than were diagnoses made by American psychiatrists living in Hawaii.

Functional Impairment and Economic and Social Impact

Antony, Roth, et al. (1998) examined the extent to which different anxiety disorders impair functioning across 13 different life domains (e.g., work, recreation, financial situation, social relationships, sexual functioning, etc.). Overall, the levels of impairment reported by individuals with social phobia were similar to those reported by individuals with other severe anxiety disorders (i.e., PD or obsessive–compulsive disorder [OCD]). However, compared with people with PD and OCD, people with social phobia reported more impairment in their social relationships and in their ability to express themselves and engage in self-improvement. In addition, it is interesting to note that impairment was rated significantly higher by all three anxiety disorders groups in the Antony, Roth, et al. study (including social phobia) than by groups of patients with chronic medical illnesses such as end-stage renal disease, insomnia, and multiple sclerosis, as has been reported in previous studies that used the same measure of impairment (Antony, Roth, et al., 1998).

A variety of other studies have confirmed that social phobia is associated with significant impairment. Compared with nonanxious control participants, people with social phobia have reported impairment in the areas of education, employment, family relationships, and other domains of functioning (Schneier et al., 1994). Quality of life also appears to be more impaired in people with social phobia than in those with other anxiety and mood disorders (Bech & Angst, 1996), as well as in nonanxious control participants (Wittchen & Beloch, 1996). Finally, Norton et al. (1996) found that people with social phobia were more likely to be single, living alone, unemployed, and abusing alcohol than were people with PD. Despite the extreme impairment that is associated with this disorder, people with social phobia seem less likely to seek professional help than people with other anxiety disorders (Pollard, Henderson, Frank, & Margolis, 1989). In addition, social phobia tends to go unrecognized in general health care settings (Weiller, Bisserbe, Boyer, Lepine, & Lecrubier, 1996).

Comorbidity

Table 2.1 lists the percentages of individuals from an anxiety disorders clinic who had principal diagnoses of social phobia and various additional diagnoses (Antony & Swinson, 1999). All diagnoses were based on *DSM-IV* criteria and were established using the Structured Clinical Interview for *DSM-IV* (First et al., 1996). The most common additional diagnoses included dysthymic disorder, GAD, specific phobia, and major depressive disorder. Among patients in the program who had other principal diagnoses, social phobia was a common additional diagnosis. For example, of 94 patients with principal diagnoses of PD (with or without agoraphobia), 23% had additional diagnoses of social phobia. Among people with OCD (n = 100), social phobia was the most commonly assigned additional diagnosis, affecting 39% of individuals in this group. Nineteen percent of 21 patients with specific phobia had an additional diagnosis of social phobia.

Data from various other centers around the world confirm that social phobia often co-occurs with other psychological disorders (Goisman, Goldenberg, et al., 1995; Kessler, Stang, Wittchen, Stein, & Walters, 1999; Moras, Di Nardo, Brown, & Barlow, 1994; Sanderson et al., 1990; van Ameringen, Mancini, Styan, & Donison, 1991). In fact, in several of these studies (Sanderson et al., 1990; van Ameringen et al., 1991) it was estimated that 60% to 70% of people with social phobia have one or more additional disorders. The most commonly assigned additional diagnoses among people with social phobia were similar to those identified in the Antony and Swinson (2000a) sample (see Table 2.1), although the rates of comorbidity were even higher in several of these studies.

As an additional diagnosis (i.e., one of lower severity than the principal diagnosis), social phobia often occurs in people with other principal diagnoses, including eating disorders (Schwalberg, Barlow, Alger, & Howard, 1992), a range of anxiety and mood disorders (Goisman, Goldenberg, et al., 1995; Moras et al., 1994), and alcohol abuse or dependence (Kushner, Sher, & Beitman, 1990). Interestingly, for individuals with elevated social anxiety, the amount of alcohol they consume appears to be related to the

Table 2.1
Percentage of Anxiety Disorders Clinic Patients With a Principal Diagnosis of Social Phobia (n = 103) Who Currently Met Criteria for Additional Disorders

Disorder	Percentage of Patients
panic disorder without agoraphobia	4.9%
panic disorder with agoraphobia	9.7%
obsessive–compulsive disorder	5.8%
specific phobia	9.7%
generalized anxiety disorder	10.7%
posttraumatic stress disorder	0%
major depressive episode	9.7%
dysthymic disorder	12.6%
substance use disorder	4.9%
bipolar disorder	0%
psychotic disorder	0%

Note. Unpublished data are from Antony and Swinson (2000a). All patients were diagnosed using the Structured Clinical Interview for DSM-IV Axis I Disorders: Patient Edition (SCID-IP; First et al., 1996). For all patients, social phobia was the principal diagnosis (the disorder currently causing the most distress and/ or functional impairment).

expectation that alcohol will lead to a decrease in anxiety (Tran, Haaga, & Chambless, 1997). Although studies have consistently shown high rates of comorbidity in people with social phobia, these findings should be interpreted cautiously. Most of these studies have been conducted in tertiary treatment settings, and there is evidence that the presence of comorbidity increases the chances that an individual will seek treatment (Galbaud du Fort, Newman, & Bland, 1993).

PSYCHOLOGICAL ASPECTS OF SOCIAL PHOBIA

In recent years, there has been considerable interest in the psychological mechanisms that contribute to social phobia. For example, as with other anxiety disorders, many new studies have focused on the role of cognitive biases in social phobia (for a review, see Rowa, Antony, & Swinson, 1999). This section begins with an overview of recent psychological models of social phobia. This theoretical overview is followed by summaries of research on the relationship between social anxiety and aspects of psychological functioning, including attention, memory, cognitive appraisal, imagery, and social skills.

Psychological Models of Social Phobia

A number of researchers have published comprehensive psychological models to account for social anxiety and social phobia. These include an ethological approach published by Trower and Gilbert (1989), a self-presentation approach described by Leary and colleagues (Leary & Kowalski, 1995; Schlenker & Leary, 1982), and more recent cognitive models that highlight the ways in which people with social phobia perceive and process information (Clark & Wells, 1995; Rapee & Heimberg, 1997; Wells & Clark, 1997). Although each of these approaches share features, they also are different in important ways. A full review of these and other models is beyond the scope of this chapter. Instead, we have chosen to highlight some of the key concepts from recent *cognitive* models, because these have been most thoroughly studied by researchers and are most closely related to varieties of cognitive–behavioral therapy (CBT) that are being increasingly recommended for treating social phobia.

According to Schlenker and Leary (1982), social anxiety occurs when an individual is (a) motivated to make a particular impression on other people and (b) believes that he or she will be unsuccessful in making the desired impression. According to this self-presentation theory, if either of these features is not present, social anxiety should not occur. More recent cognitive models (e.g., Clark & Wells, 1995; Rapee & Heimberg, 1997) are similar in that they view social anxiety as stemming from an individual's beliefs about the impressions he or she makes on others. Clark and Wells (1995) expanded on the Schlenker and Leary (1982) model by suggesting that social anxiety stems from a desire to make a favorable impression on others combined with beliefs that when one encounters a social situation there are risks of (a) behaving in an incompetent and inappropriate way and (b) suffering disastrous consequences (e.g., rejection, loss of worth, etc.) as a result of this behavior. Rapee and Heimberg (1997) have expanded further on the cognitive model by emphasizing the importance of the individual's beliefs regarding the standards of evaluation held by the audience. For example, people with social phobia may assume that their audience (e.g., other people) has high standards for the individual's behavior. This point is consistent with our own research showing that people with social phobia report more perceived pressure from others to behave "perfectly," compared with people with other anxiety disorders and nonanxious individuals (Antony, Purdon, Huta, & Swinson, 1998).

Although these models describe the *process* of social phobia, they do not discuss the *etiology* of social phobia. In other words, they ignore the issue of how social phobia begins. In contrast, Rachman's (1977) model of fear development can be used to explain the onset of social phobia for some individuals. Rachman proposed that fears can develop by three methods: direct conditioning, vicarious acquisition, and information/instruction. Direct conditioning involves learning to fear a particular object or situation through a direct classical conditioning experience involving some traumatic event. In the case of social phobia, this might include being severely teased in social situations or experiencing an unexpected panic attack in a social situation (Barlow, 1988). In each of these examples, the presence of other people has been paired with an aversive stimulus (i.e., teasing or a panic attack), leading to classically conditioned fear.

Vicarious conditioning involves learning by observation or modeling. For example, a person might learn to be anxious in social situations by observing another person who is anxious (e.g., growing up with socially anxious parents) or by seeing another person be teased or hurt in a social situation. Informational and instructional transmission of fear involves learning to fear a situation after being told that the situation is dangerous. This might include being told that one comes across badly, that one should be careful because others are very critical, or that it is always important to make a good impression. Preliminary studies (Hofmann, Ehlers, & Roth, 1995; Öst, 1985; Stemberger, Turner, Beidel, & Calhoun, 1995) suggest that direct conditioning experiences are common in people suffering from social phobia, although onsets following observational or instructional learning appear to be less common. In addition, for public speaking anxiety, direct conditioning experiences often occur only long after the fear has begun, suggesting that they may not be involved in the original onset of the fear (Hofmann et al., 1995).

Rachman's model cannot fully explain how social phobia develops. First, a significant number of people with social phobia do not report onsets related to these three pathways. Second, many people are teased in social situations, grow up with socially anxious individuals, or are exposed to anxiety-provoking information, and yet they do not develop social phobia. A question that remains to be answered is why some people develop social phobia following these types of events whereas others do not. There is evidence that a number of other factors may put people at risk for developing social phobia, including genetic and biological factors (as is reviewed in the next section), parental upbringing (Bruch & Heimberg, 1994; Rapee & Melville, 1997), personality factors such as behavioral inhibition (i.e., a tendency to withdraw from unfamiliar people and situations; Rosenbaum, Biederman, Hirshfeld, Bolduc, & Chaloff, 1991; Turner, Beidel, & Wolff, 1996), and neuroticism (i.e., a tendency to experience negative emotions such as anxiety and depression more frequently and more intensely than others; Stemberger et al., 1995). Perhaps these and other factors mediate whether an individual develops social phobia following conditioning events, observational learning, and instruction.

Attention and Memory Biases in Social Phobia

Attention

Compared with people who are not socially anxious, individuals with social phobia tend to devote more attentional resources to stimuli that represent social threat, relative to neutral stimuli. One of the most popular paradigms for measuring biases in information processing is the modified Stroop color naming task (Mathews & MacLeod, 1985), which is described in chapter 1. In the case of social phobia, a number of studies (e.g., Holle, Neely, & Heimberg, 1997; Hope, Rapee, Heimberg, & Dombeck, 1990; Maidenberg et al., 1996; Mattia, Heimberg, & Hope, 1993; McNeil et al., 1995) have now shown that people with social phobia take longer to name the colors of social-threat-related words, compared with neutral words. Non-anxious individuals tend not to show this bias. These findings suggest that socially anxious individuals have a bias to attend to words that represent social threat.

Furthermore, although other anxiety disorders are also associated with information-processing biases, the attentional bias for *socially related* threat information appears to be most pronounced in social phobia (Hope et al., 1990). Other studies, however, have shown that PD is also associated with longer response times for social-threat words (Maidenberg et al., 1996).

Furthermore, differences in color naming latencies have been found across social phobia subtypes. People with generalized social phobia show increased latencies for a range of different types of threat words, whereas those with circumscribed phobias of making speeches show biased processing only for words related to public speaking (McNeil, Ries, Taylor, et al., 1995). Interestingly, a number of interventions appear to have the effect of suppressing or reducing the attentional bias. These include the induction of heightened anxiety (e.g., by telling patients that they are about to give a speech; Amir, McNally, Riemann, Burns, et al., 1996) and successful treatment of the social phobia (Mattia et al., 1993).

Findings regarding attentional biases in social phobia have been confirmed using paradigms other than the Stroop task. For example, Asmundson and Stein (1994a) used a dot-probe task to demonstrate selective processing of social threat in people with social phobia but not in control-group participants. In addition, a recent study by Mansell, Clark, Ehlers, and Chen (1999) showed that patients with social phobia (but not control participants) tend to direct their attention away from faces presented on a computer screen, compared with neutral household objects presented on the screen. This finding occurred regardless of whether the facial expression was positive, neutral, or negative.

Memory

Studies on memory biases in social phobia have yielded inconsistent results, possibly related to differences in methodology. Cloitre, Cancienne, Heimberg, Holt, and Liebowitz (1995) found that individuals with social phobia and nonanxious participants all showed greater recall and recognition for threat-related and positive words than for neutral words, and there were no significant differences across groups. Rapee, McCallum, Melville, Ravenscroft, and Rodney (1994) also failed to find memory differences between individuals with social phobia and nonclinical control-group participants in a series of studies examining recall, recognition, explicit memory, and implicit memory for threat-related, positive, and neutral words.

Lundh and Öst (1997) found no differences overall between patients with social phobia and nonclinical control participants on measures of implicit and explicit memory, although a subset of patients (those with nongeneralized social phobia) showed an implicit memory bias for social-threat-related words. Amir, Coles, Rutigliano, and Foa (1997) found an implicit memory bias in generalized social phobia patients, compared with nonanxious participants, although there were no differences on measures of explicit memory (recognition). Coles, Amir, Kozak, and Foa (1997) found that people with social phobia had an enhanced ability to forget threat-related information in a directed forgetting experiment. Finally, several recent studies have demonstrated that compared with nonanxious control participants, people with social phobia are better at recognizing faces, particularly when the face has a critical or negative expression (Gilboa-Schechtman, Freshman, Amir, & Foa, 1997; Lundh & Öst, 1996).

Attributions and Appraisals in Social Phobia

A prominent feature of social phobia is a belief that one's symptoms of anxiety (e.g., blushing, sweating, or shaking) will be noticed by other people and that others will interpret the symptoms in a negative light. Interestingly, Mulkens, de Jong, Dobbelaar, and Bögels (1999) recently found that although individuals who were fearful of blushing actually blushed no more than nonfearful individuals during socially stressful challenges, the fearful participants were significantly more likely than nonfearful participants to report significant blushing during the challenge. This study suggests that people's symptoms may actually be less noticeable than they imagine.

In two additional studies, researchers examined ways in which (a) people actually interpret visible anxiety symptoms in others and (b) impressions are formed of people who appear visibly anxious. One study (Roth, Antony, & Swinson, in press) focused on ways in which individuals with social phobia and nonanxious control participants interpreted visible symptoms (e.g., blushing, shaky hands, sweating, etc.) in others, as well as their assumptions regarding the ways in which other people interpreted these symptoms when they themselves exhibited them. Individuals with social phobia did not differ from control participants with respect to how they interpreted symptoms in others. Both groups endorsed a wide range of causal attributions to explain these symptoms in other people, including anxiety, other emotions, medical conditions, and physical states such as being cold or hungry. However, individuals with social phobia and control participants did differ with respect to their assumptions regarding what others thought about them when they showed signs of arousal or anxiety. People with social phobia were more likely than control participants to assume that other people interpreted their anxiety symptoms as a sign of intense anxiety or a psychiatric condition and were less likely than control participants to assume that others attributed their symptoms to some benign physical state such as hunger, fatigue, or cold.

In a related study based on a nonclinical sample, Purdon, Antony, Monteiro, and Swinson (in press) examined whether impressions of various personal characteristics (e.g., intelligence, attractiveness, etc.) are influenced by visible anxiety in a target individual. The relationship between participants' own social anxiety and their impressions of other people who appear anxious was examined in this study. Surprisingly, individuals who reported elevated social anxiety were more likely than nonanxious participants to judge others who appeared anxious to have less "strength of character" and to be less physically attractive than were individuals who did not appear anxious. In other words, socially anxious individuals were actually more judgmental toward others who appeared anxious.

Differences in appraisals among individuals with social phobia and people who are not socially anxious have been investigated in a number of additional studies. Compared with nonphobic individuals, people with social phobia tended to be more critical of their own performance (during a public speaking task), and the differences between their own ratings and those of other people who observed the performance tended to be greater (Rapee & Lim, 1992). Social phobia was also associated with a tendency to view one's performance negatively following a social interaction (Alden & Wallace, 1995; Stopa & Clark, 1993) and to view one's conversation partner's behavior more positively (Alden & Wallace, 1995). In general, socially anxious individuals were more likely than nonanxious control participants to identify ambiguous facial expressions as being negative (Winton, Clark, & Edelmann, 1995) and were less likely to assign positive interpretations to ambiguous interpersonal events (Constans, Penn, Ihen, & Hope, 1999).

Foa, Franklin, Perry, and Herbert (1996) reported that socially phobic individuals were more likely than control participants to rate negative social events as being more probable and more costly, a bias that decreased following treatment. However, it was the potential consequences of the threat, as well as the degree of perceived control over the situation, that appeared to be most relevant to whether an individual experienced fear in social situations (Rapee, 1997). Several other factors appear to affect whether people with social phobia are likely to be anxious in a social situation. These include a tendency to focus on oneself before entering the feared situation (Woody, 1996) and a tendency to focus on the positive attributes of the other person during social interactions (Mahone, Bruch, & Heimberg, 1993).

Social Phobia and Imagery

Recently, investigators have begun to study the types of images held by people who are socially phobic. Hackmann, Surawy, and Clark (1998) found that individuals with social phobia were more likely than nonanxious participants to report experiencing negative imagery when exposed to feared social situations. In addition, several recent studies (Wells, Clark, & Ahmad, 1998; Wells & Papageorgiou, 1999) have shown that people with social phobia are more likely than nonphobic individuals and individuals with specific phobias to take an observer's point of view (i.e., seeing themselves from an external perspective) when imagining social situations but not other types of situations (e.g., nonsocial situations). Interestingly, people with agoraphobia have also reported an observer perspective when recalling anxiety-provoking social situations (Wells & Papageorgiou, 1999). This is not surprising given that social anxiety (e.g., concern about having others notice one's symptoms of panic) is often a feature of PD and agoraphobia.

Social Phobia and Perfectionism

A number of recent studies have indicated that social phobia is associated with heightened levels of perfectionism (e.g., Antony, Purdon, et al., 1998; Juster et al., 1996; Saboonchi, Lundh, & Öst, 1999). Individuals with social phobia consistently report having elevated concerns regarding making mistakes and doubts about whether they have done things correctly. In addition, social phobia is associated with a tendency to report having parents who are overly critical, providing clues about the origins of perfectionism in people with social phobia. Although several other anxiety disorders are also associated with perfectionism (Antony, Purdon, et al., 1998; Antony & Swinson, 1998), concern about making mistakes and having critical parents appear to be highest among people with social phobia, as compared with people with PD, OCD, or specific phobia.

Social Skills Deficits

Given that the treatment of social phobia sometimes includes social skills training (e.g., Turner, Beidel, Cooley, & Woody, 1994; Wlazlo, Schroeder-Hartwig, Hand, Kaiser, & Münchau, 1990), it is surprising that very few researchers have examined the extent to which people with social phobia actually have deficits in social skills. As was reviewed earlier, individuals with social phobia tend to be more critical of their social skills and performance than do independent observers (e.g., Alden & Wallace, 1995). However, a small number of studies suggest that social anxiety may be associated with actual deficits in social and communication skills for some individuals.

For example, Smari, Bjarnadottir, and Bragadottir (1998) found that social anxiety and self-reported social skills were negatively correlated in a sample of undergraduate students. In a study of children with social phobia, Spence, Donovan, and Brechman-Toussaint (1999) found that social phobia was associated with skills deficits on a number of different assessment indices, including self-report, parent-report, an assertiveness questionnaire, and direct behavioral observation. Furthermore, children with social phobia were found to receive fewer positive outcomes during behavioral observations of social interactions with peers.

In a validation study of the Social Performance Rating Scale (a behavioral social skills rating system based on videotaped role plays), Fydrich,

Chambless, Perry, Buergener, and Beazley (1998) found a negative correlation between measures of social anxiety and observed social skills (e.g., eye contact, vocal quality, duration of speech, visible signs of discomfort, and conversation flow). In addition, individuals with social phobia received poorer social skills ratings than did individuals in either an anxious comparison group or a nonanxious comparison group.

A comparison of individuals with a *DSM-III* diagnosis of either social phobia or avoidant personality disorder (Turner, Beidel, Dancu, & Keys, 1986) showed significantly more social skills deficits among people with avoidant personality disorder than among people with social phobia, suggesting that skills deficits are particularly a problem in a subset of socially anxious individuals—those who also have avoidant personality disorder. However, another study (Boone et al., 1999) of the differences in social skills across individuals with a circumscribed speech phobia, generalized social phobia with avoidant personality disorder, or generalized social phobia without avoidant personality disorder showed few differences in observer ratings of participants' gaze, voice volume, intonation, and total skill. The only group difference to emerge was the finding that individuals with social phobia and avoidant personality disorder spoke more quietly than did those in the other groups.

Much more research is needed to establish whether social phobia is in fact associated with skills deficits and, if so, what areas are most affected (e.g., eye contact, conversation skills, assertiveness, public speaking skills, etc.). The small number of existing studies (e.g., Fydrich et al., 1998) have tended to treat skills deficits as a group rather than differentiate among specific types of social skills. Furthermore, this area is probably complicated by the fact that the definition of appropriate social skills is somewhat arbitrary and may differ depending on culture, gender, and other dimensions (e.g., Turner, Beidel, Hersen, & Bellack, 1984).

BIOLOGICAL ASPECTS OF SOCIAL PHOBIA

Neurobiological Findings

Compared with studies of other anxiety disorders, studies of biological correlates have often failed to show significant findings in patients with social phobia (for a review, see Bebchuk & Tancer, 1999). Studies of neuroendocrine functioning in social phobia have failed to show differences between socially phobic patients and nonanxious control participants on measures related to the hypothalamic–pituitary–adrenal axis and hypothalamic–pituitary–thyroid axis (e.g., Martel et al., 1999; Potts, Davidson, Krishnan, Doraiswamy, & Ritchie, 1991; Stein, Huzel, & Delaney, 1993; Tancer, Stein, Gelernter, & Uhde, 1990; Uhde, Tancer, Gelernter, & Vittone,

1994). In addition, studies of abnormal mitral valve functioning (Chaleby & Ziady, 1988) and sleep architecture (Brown, Black, & Uhde, 1994) in social phobia have yielded negative results. In contrast to the negative results often obtained in biological research on social anxiety, a recent study by Schmidt (1999) showed unique patterns of frontal brain electrical activity associated with the personality traits of shyness and sociability. Specifically, shyness was associated with greater relative frontal EEG activity, whereas sociability was associated with greater relative left frontal EEG activity.

Neurotransmitter challenge studies have yielded mixed results. Tancer (1993) failed to find differences between socially phobic patients and non-clinical control participants on an indirect measure of dopamine functioning (eye blink rates and prolactin levels following administration of L-dopa). The same group also failed to show a response to dopaminergic (levodopa) challenges in patients with social phobia (Tancer et al., 1994/1995). Nevertheless, there are studies suggesting that dopamine may play a role in social anxiety. For example, King, Mefford, and Wang (1986) reported that dopamine metabolite levels correlated with measures of extroversion (a personality dimension that is associated with social anxiety). Furthermore, mice bred to be timid have shown deficiencies in brain dopamine concentrations (Lewis, Gariepy, & Devaud, 1989). The differential response of social phobia to monoamine oxidase inhibitors (MAOIs; Liebowitz et al., 1992) but not TCAs (Simpson, Schneier, Campeas, et al., 1998) also supports the view that dopamine plays a role in social phobia. Whereas TCAs act primarily on noradrenergic and serotonergic systems, MAOIs act on noradrenergic, serotonergic, and dopaminergic systems.

With respect to serotonin, studies have yielded mixed results. Tancer et al. (1994/1995) found augmented cortisol response to fenfluramine in patients with social phobia, lending support to the view that social phobia is associated with selective supersensitivity in the serotonergic system. In addition, selective serotonin reuptake inhibitors (SSRIs) have consistently been shown to be effective for treating social phobia (reviewed later in this chapter). However, Stein, Delaney, Chartier, Kroft, and Hazen (1995) found that [^{3}H] paroxetine binding (which reflects serotonergic functioning) was no different in social phobia patients than in nonanxious participants.

Studies of noradrenergic functioning have generally failed to find anything consistent to suggest that norepinephrine plays a significant role in social phobia. Tancer et al. (1994/1995) found no significant differences between patients with social phobia and nonanxious individuals to a noradrenergic challenge in which norepinephrine and growth hormone responses to clonidine administration were measured. Furthermore, as was reviewed earlier, people with social phobia tend not to respond to medications such as imipramine, which are helpful for treating PD and act largely on noradrenergic systems (Simpson, Schneier, Campeas, et al., 1998).

Family and Genetics Studies

Social phobia appears to run in families. In a recent study by Stein, Chartier, et al. (1998), first-degree relatives of patients with generalized social phobia and nonanxious participants were assessed for the presence of avoidant personality disorder, as well as generalized, nongeneralized, and circumscribed forms of social phobia. Relative risks for generalized social phobia and avoidant personality disorder were approximately tenfold for the first-degree relatives of probands with social phobia, compared with relatives of probands in the comparison group. Interestingly, there were no differences across the groups in the prevalence of nongeneralized social phobias. This study confirms findings from previous studies showing that social phobia runs in families (Fyer, Mannuzza, Chapman, Liebowitz, & Klein, 1993).

Of course, the existence of social phobia in multiple family members does not necessarily imply genetic transmission. As was reviewed earlier, there is evidence that fear can be transmitted by observation and modeling. In other words, being around others who are socially phobic may put a person at risk for learning to feel anxious in social situations. Furthermore, it is likely that the risk of developing social anxiety through learning processes is greatest for individuals who have a genetic vulnerability to develop problems with social anxiety. A model that takes into account both genetic and environmental factors may be the most appropriate way to explain the transmission of social anxiety across generations.

To tease out genetic influences from the effects of environment, twin studies, adoption studies, genetic linkage studies, and association studies are often helpful. Of these, only twin studies are available in the social phobia literature, and results have been inconsistent. Kendler et al. (1992) found that a moderate disorder-specific genetic influence, combined with specific and nonspecific environmental influences, best accounted for the transmission of social phobia across family members. A follow-up study (Kendler et al., 1999) showed that the contribution of genetics to the transmission of phobic disorders (including social phobia) was even greater than previously thought, when the effects of unreliable diagnostic interviews were controlled for. Furthermore, the environmental factors that had the strongest impact on the development of phobic disorders were those that were specific to the individual's experience (e.g., experiences outside of the family) rather than those that were shared by other family members.

Studies from other centers have yielded inconsistent findings. Whereas one twin study by Andrews, Stewart, Allen, and Henderson (1990) confirmed the role of genetics in social phobia, other studies (e.g., Skre, Torgersen, Lygren, & Kringlen, 1993) have shown environment to play a larger role. Interestingly, two personality traits that are closely related to social phobia (neuroticism and extroversion) appear to be highly heritable, with average heritability estimates for these traits being close to 50% across a wide range of genetics studies (Plomin, 1989).

TREATMENT OF SOCIAL PHOBIA

Psychological Treatments

Evidence-based psychological treatments for social phobia have primarily included four types of strategies: (a) exposure-based treatments (e.g., graduated in vivo exposure to feared situations, behavioral role play exercises), (b) cognitive treatments (e.g., examining the evidence that supports and contradicts anxious beliefs), (c) applied relaxation (e.g., combining progressive muscle relaxation strategies with gradual exposure to feared situations), and (d) social skills training (e.g., communication training, assertiveness training). In addition, preliminary data support the use of interpersonal psychotherapy (IPT) for treating social phobia. An exhaustive discussion of these studies is beyond the scope of this chapter, but several recent reviews can be found elsewhere (e.g., Antony, 1997; Antony & Barlow, 1997; Antony & Swinson, 1996; Heimberg & Juster, 1995; Turk, Fresco, & Heimberg, 1999; Turner, Cooley-Quill, & Beidel, 1996). We will instead provide an overview of some of the most important findings related to empirically supported treatments for social phobia.

Cognitive–behavioral group therapy versus supportive group psychotherapy

Heimberg, Dodge, Hope, Kennedy, and Zollo (1990) compared cognitive–behavioral group therapy (CBGT), consisting of cognitive restructuring and exposure-based strategies, to an "attention placebo" group psychotherapy consisting of discussion and group support. Both groups were significantly improved following treatment and at 3- and 6-month follow-ups. However, those receiving CBGT were significantly more improved than were those receiving supportive therapy. A portion of the participants in this study were interviewed again a mean of 5 years following treatment. For those who participated in the long-term follow-up assessment, CBGT continued to be superior to supportive group therapy (Heimberg, Salzman, Holt, & Blendell, 1993).

Cognitive therapy versus exposure

Numerous researchers have investigated the relative and combined effects of cognitive strategies and exposure-based strategies for social phobia. In general, cognitive, exposure-based, and combined treatments were each found to be effective. Whereas several studies have shown no differences in the efficacy of these approaches (e.g., Mersch, 1995; Salaberria & Echeburua, 1998; Scholing & Emmelkamp, 1993a; Taylor et al., 1997), other studies have shown differences to varying degrees and in different directions. For example, Hope, Heimberg, and Bruch (1995) found that a pure exposure-based treatment was superior to CBGT (which included exposure and cognitive strategies) on a small number of measures. Emmelkamp, Mersch, Vissia, and van der Helm (1985) found few differences among exposure and two different cognitive treatments, except that exposure-based treatments led to a greater decrease in pulse rate during a behavioral test, compared with the other treatments. In contrast to these findings, Butler, Cullington, Munby, Amies, and Gelder (1984) found that a comprehensive treatment that included exposure and anxiety management (which includes rational self-talk, relaxation, and distraction) was superior to exposure alone. Mattick and Peters (1988) found that adding cognitive restructuring to in vivo exposure increased the effectiveness of treatment, and in a related study, Mattick, Peters, and Clarke (1989) found that the combination of exposure and cognitive restructuring led to improvement on a broader range of measures than either cognitive restructuring alone or exposure alone.

Finally, Scholing and Emmelkamp (1993b) found that the sequencing of treatments affected outcome. The effects of group treatment for social phobia were greatest when cognitive therapy preceded exposure and smallest when cognitive therapy and exposure were both delivered from the start of treatment. At an 18-month follow-up, patients who received 8 weeks of exposure had a superior outcome compared with patients who received a combination of cognitive therapy and exposure, either simultaneously or sequentially (Scholing & Emmelkamp, 1996).

Whether cognitive therapy, exposure, or the combination is most effective remains to be answered. Even meta-analytic studies addressing this issue have yielded conflicting results. In a meta-analysis of 21 studies, Feske and Chambless (1995) found that CBTs (including both cognitive therapy and exposure) and pure exposure-based treatments were equally effective. In contrast, Taylor (1996) found that treatments combining cognitive therapy and exposure were the only treatments to have significantly larger effect sizes than placebo. Treatments involving exposure alone, cognitive therapy alone, and social skills training had effect sizes that were not significantly larger than placebo treatments. Regardless of whether adding cognitive therapy improves the efficacy of exposure, it appears that exposure alone can lead to changes in the cognitive features of social phobia (Newman, Hofmann, Trabert, Roth, & Taylor, 1994).

Social skills training

Social skills training appears to be a helpful treatment for social phobia. It appears to be as effective as in vivo exposure alone and to lead to improvement in both social skills and social anxiety (Wlazlo et al., 1990). Adding social skills training does not appear to have added benefit over and above the effects of exposure alone (Mersch, 1995).

Interpersonal psychotherapy

A large number of studies have shown that interpersonal psychotherapy (IPT) is an efficacious treatment for depression as well as for a number of other forms of psychopathology (Klerman & Weissman, 1993; Markowitz, 1998). To date, the use of IPT in an anxiety disorder has been examined in only one published study. Lipsitz, Markowitz, Cherry, and Fyer (1999) treated nine individuals with social phobia in a 14-week open trial. Following treatment, 78% of participants were independently rated as much or very much improved. These preliminary findings suggest that IPT may be a useful treatment for social phobia, although controlled studies with larger numbers of participants are needed.

Individual response patterns and outcome with therapy

A number of researchers have attempted to discover whether individuals who have particular types of symptoms (e.g., cognitive reactors, physiological reactors, or behavioral reactors) respond differently to specific types of treatment (e.g., cognitive therapy, applied relaxation, or exposure). In general, studies have failed to demonstrate that matching treatments to patients' response styles improves outcome (Jerremalm, Jansson, & Öst, 1986a; Mersch, Emmelkamp, Bögels, & van der Sleen, 1989; Mersch, Emmelkamp, & Lips, 1991). An exception is a study by Öst, Jerremalm, and Johansson (1981), who found that on a number of measures, behavioral reactors responded more to social skills training than to applied relaxation and that physiological reactors responded more to applied relaxation than to social skills training.

Predictors of outcome following therapy

Van Velzen, Emmelkamp, and Scholing (1997) found that comorbidity (e.g., the presence of additional personality, mood, or anxiety disorders) did not affect outcome during exposure-based treatment of social phobia. Similarly, the presence of avoidant personality disorder did not affect outcome during CBT in a study by Brown, Heimberg, and Juster (1995). However, other studies (e.g., Chambless, Tran, & Glass, 1997; Scholing & Emmelkamp, 1999) have shown that the presence of depression and more avoidant personality traits were each associated with poorer outcome on one or more measures.

Another variable that appears to be associated with poorer outcome is more negative expectations regarding the effectiveness of treatment

(Chambless et al., 1997; Safren, Heimberg, & Juster, 1996). In addition, homework compliance appears to affect long-term outcome more than short-term outcome (Edelman & Chambless, 1995). There is also evidence that homework compliance in the early and later sessions of treatment is more closely related to a positive treatment outcome than is compliance in the middle sessions, which may actually be related to a poorer outcome (Leung & Heimberg, 1996). This paradoxical finding remains to be replicated.

Pharmacological Treatments

Based on controlled clinical trials, a variety of effective pharmacological treatments for social phobia have emerged in recent years. These include traditional MAOIs (e.g., phenelzine), reversible inhibitors of monoamine oxidase A (e.g., moclobemide and brofaromine), SSRIs (e.g., sertraline and paroxetine), and benzodiazepines (e.g., clonazepam and alprazolam). Findings from a variety of uncontrolled and controlled trials suggest that several additional medications may also be helpful. Throughout this review, generic names have been used for all medications. Chapter 8 includes generic and trade names for the most commonly used drugs.

Monoamine oxidase inhibitors

In one of the first large controlled studies of MAOIs for social phobia, Liebowitz and colleagues (Liebowitz et al., 1988, 1992), compared phenelzine with atenolol (a beta-adrenergic blocker) and placebo in a randomized, double-blind trial. After 8 weeks, response rates were 64% for phenelzine, 30% for atenolol, and 23% for placebo. Phenelzine was significantly more effective than atenolol and placebo, which were in turn equally effective. After 16 weeks, the difference between phenelzine and placebo was maintained, but atenolol did not differ in effectiveness from either of the other conditions. Participants with generalized social phobia tended to respond more to phenelzine than did patients with circumscribed forms of social phobia (e.g., public speaking phobias). This trial confirmed findings from earlier open trials (e.g., Liebowitz, Fyer, Gorman, Campeas, & Levin, 1986) suggesting that phenelzine is an effective treatment for social phobia.

Despite the efficacy of MAOIs such as phenelzine, they are often not prescribed because of the potential for intense side effects as well as certain dietary restrictions that must be observed by patients taking MAOIs. Foods containing tyramine (e.g., certain cheeses and cured meats) can cause a hypertensive crisis in patients taking MAOIs. Selegiline (L-Deprenyl) is a selective MAOI-B inhibitor. Unlike nonselective MAOIs such as phenelzine, the side effects of selegiline tend to be more manageable, and dietary restrictions tend to be less of a concern (Simpson, Schneier, Marshall, et al., 1998). A recent, 6-week, open trial with selegiline (Simpson, Schneier, Marshall, et al., 1998) suggests that this medication may be helpful for people suffering from social phobia. However, only 9 out of 16 patients completed the trial. Additional placebo-controlled trials with larger samples are clearly needed to replicate this finding.

Recently, investigators have begun to study the reversible inhibitors of monoamine oxidase A (RIMAs) in social phobia. Unlike traditional MAOIs, RIMAs do not require a restricted diet and the side effects tend to be less severe. To date, controlled trials have been conducted with moclobemide and brofaromine. In an initial study comparing moclobemide with phenelzine and placebo, moclobemide appeared to have promise for the treatment of social phobia (Versiani et al., 1992). Side effects for patients taking moclobemide were fewer than those for patients taking phenelzine. After 8 weeks, phenelzine and moclobemide were both more effective than placebo, although improvement with phenelzine was somewhat greater than with moclobemide. By Week 16, 82% of those taking moclobemide and 91% of those taking phenelzine were considerably improved. However, relapse rates were high upon discontinuation for both medications.

Since this initial study, there have been several additional trials with moclobemide, with less promising findings. In a large fixed-dosage, 12-week study, the International Multicenter Clinical Trial Group on Moclobemide in Social Phobia (1997) found that moclobemide was statistically superior to placebo at 600 mg per day but only somewhat superior at 300 mg per day. Another 12-week, fixed-dosage study (Noyes et al., 1997) failed to show significant benefits of moclobemide (compared with placebo) at any of five dosages ranging from 75 mg to 900 mg daily.

This lack of significant findings was confirmed in a recent 8-week study by Schneier et al. (1998), who found relatively low response rates for moclobemide (17.5%) and placebo (13.5%). Oosterbaan, van Balkom, Spinhoven, van Oppen, and van Dyck (1998) found no differences between moclobemide and placebo after 15 weeks of treatment. (This study is discussed in more detail later in this chapter.) Finally, in an uncontrolled long-term trial, moclobemide was found to be helpful in patients treated with the drug for 2 years (Versiani et al., 1996). However, attrition rates were high (39.6%), and 88% of patients relapsed upon discontinuation of the drug.

Two controlled trials with the RIMA brofaromine have each yielded promising results. In a fixed-dosage (150 mg per day) study, patients taking brofaromine for 12 weeks were significantly more improved than were patients taking placebo (Fahlén, Nilsson, Borg, Humble, & Pauli, 1995). This finding was replicated in a variable-dosage study by Lott et al. (1997). Attrition rates were similar across the drug and placebo groups in this study.

Selective serotonin reuptake inhibitors

A recent placebo-controlled study of paroxetine revealed that 12 weeks of treatment led to a response rate of 55% in paroxetine-treated patients and in 23.9% of placebo-treated patients (Stein, Liebowitz, et al., 1998). A recent controlled study by Allgulander (1999) confirmed that paroxetine is an effective treatment for decreasing the symptoms of social phobia. Other placebo-controlled trials with fluvoxamine (Stein, Fyer, Davidson, Pollack, & Wiita, 1999; van Vliet, den Boer, & Westenberg, 1994) and sertraline (Katzelnick et al., 1995) yielded similar findings, suggesting that across a range of these medications, SSRIs are effective for treating social phobia. Uncontrolled open trials with citalopram (Bouwer & Stein, 1998) and fluoxetine (Perugi et al., 1994/1995; van Ameringen, Mancini, & Streiner, 1993) suggest that these SSRIs may also be helpful for people suffering from social phobia.

Other antidepressants

Open trials have been reported with several other antidepressants, including imipramine, nefazodone, and venlafaxine. Although an initial case study suggested that imipramine may be helpful for people suffering from social phobia (Benca, Matuzas, & Al-Sadir, 1986), a more recent uncontrolled open trial with 15 patients did not support the efficacy of imipramine for social phobia (Simpson, Schneier, Campeas, et al., 1998). In contrast, an uncontrolled open trial with the new nonselective antidepressant nefazodone showed the drug to be effective in 66.7% of patients (van Ameringen, Mancini, Oakman, & Collins, 1997).

The use of venlafaxine (a new serotonin and norepinephrine reuptake inhibitor) for treating social phobia in patients who had previously failed to respond to SSRIs has been examined in two preliminary studies. In the first study ($n = 9$), the symptoms of social phobia were significantly reduced for most patients (Kelsey, 1995). However, the social anxiety measure used in this study was limited to a five-item social phobia subscale of a brief questionnaire. In a subsequent study ($n = 12$), using a larger number of measures, venlafaxine was again shown to reduce symptoms of social phobia (as well as depression) in patients who had previously not responded to treatment with SSRIs (Altamura, Pioli, Vitto, & Mannu, 1999). Currently, placebo-controlled trials of venlafaxine for social phobia are underway.

Anxiolytics

Studies of anxiolytics for social phobia have been limited primarily to the high-potency benzodiazepines, clonazepam, and alprazolam, as well as the nonbenzodiazepine, buspirone. In a placebo-controlled study by Davidson et al. (1993), clonazepam was significantly superior to placebo, with 78% of patients taking clonazepam and 20% of patients taking placebo responding to treatment. This study confirmed earlier findings from open trials (e.g., Reiter, Pollack, Rosenbaum, & Cohen, 1990) suggesting that clonazepam is an effective treatment for social phobia. Open trials with alprazolam (e.g., Reich & Yates, 1988) also have yielded positive results with social phobia. However, in a controlled study, Gelernter et al. (1991) found few differences on most measures in a trial comparing phenelzine, alprazolam, CBT, and placebo. However, as is discussed later in this chapter, this study is limited by the fact that all three pharmacotherapy groups received instructions for self-directed exposure (see the section on comparative studies of psychological and pharmacological treatments). Finally, placebo-controlled studies with buspirone have failed to show differences between buspirone and placebo with both circumscribed (Clark & Agras, 1991) and mixed (van Vliet, den Boer, Westenberg, & Ho Pian, 1997) social phobias. Previous uncontrolled trials (e.g., Munjack et al., 1991; Schneier et al., 1993), however, had suggested some benefit to using this medication.

Beta-blockers

A number of early studies in nonpatient groups suggested that beta-blockers may be effective for treating performance anxiety in musicians (James, Burgoyne, & Savage, 1983), people taking exams (Brewer, 1972), and people giving speeches (Hartley, Ungapen, Dovie, & Spencer, 1983). Additionally, in an open trial with social-phobic patients, atenolol was found to be effective for the majority of patients (Gorman, Liebowitz, Fyer, Campeas, & Klein, 1985). Despite these findings, there are no controlled clinical trials in which beta-blockers have been shown to be helpful for individuals with social phobia. In fact, Liebowitz et al. (1992) and Turner, Beidel, and Jacob (1994) found atenolol to be no more effective than placebo. Although beta-blockers are now thought to be ineffective for generalized social phobia, they are still prescribed frequently for circumscribed forms of the disorder (e.g., performance anxiety while public speaking). Nevertheless, there remains a lack of evidence from controlled trials to demonstrate the efficacy of beta-blockers even in circumscribed social phobias.

Gabapentin

Gabapentin is a medication that is traditionally used as an adjunctive therapy in the treatment of partial seizures. A recently published, placebo-controlled trial suggests that gabapentin may be an effective treatment for social phobia as well (Pande, Davidson, et al., 1999). In this 14-week trial, patients taking gabapentin experienced a 28-point decrease in scores on the Liebowitz Social Anxiety Scale, compared with a 12-point decrease in the placebo group. Common side effects of the medication included dizziness, dry mouth, somnolence, nausea, flatulence, and decreased libido. This finding remains to be replicated, and more research is needed to determine whether a dose–response relationship exists.

Relative Efficacy of Psychological, Pharmacological, and Combined Approaches

Several investigators have begun to conduct trials to compare psychological and pharmacological treatments for social phobia. Furthermore, trials are now underway at several centers to study the efficacy of combining psychological and pharmacological treatments. Although findings from combined-treatment studies are not yet available, results from several comparative treatment studies are now published or in press.

Cognitive–behavioral group therapy versus phenelzine

In a 12-week study comparing CBGT, phenelzine, pill placebo, and supportive group psychotherapy (a psychotherapy "attention placebo"), Heimberg et al. (1998) found that both CBGT and phenelzine were more effective than either control condition. Phenelzine worked more quickly than CBGT, and at 12 weeks, phenelzine was superior to CBGT on some measures. However, analyses of long-term outcome showed that during the follow-up period (after treatment had been discontinued) about a third of patients taking phenelzine relapsed, compared with none of the patients who had responded to CBGT (Liebowitz et al., 1999). Group differences during the follow-up phase approached significance. Unfortunately, the long-term results are limited by the relatively small number of participants who participated in the follow-up study. This group, led by Heimberg and Liebowitz, is now conducting a study to compare the combination of CBGT and phenelzine to each treatment individually. However, data from this study are not yet available.

Behavior therapy versus atenolol

In a study by Turner, Beidel, and Jacob (1994), patients with social phobia were randomly assigned to treatment with behavior therapy (flooding), atenolol, and placebo. Behavior therapy was superior to placebo, which did not differ from atenolol. On behavioral measures and composite indices, behavior therapy was also superior to atenolol. At a 6-month follow-up, responders to behavior therapy and atenolol maintained their gains.

Cognitive therapy versus moclobemide

Oosterbaan et al. (1998) compared 15 weeks of cognitive therapy (including cognitive restructuring and behavioral experiments) to treatment with moclobemide or placebo. After the acute treatment phase, cognitive therapy was superior to moclobemide on a composite measure but not different from placebo. At a 2-month follow-up assessment, cognitive therapy was superior to moclobemide and placebo. At no time was moclobemide significantly different from placebo.

Cognitive–behavioral therapy versus alprazolam versus phenelzine

As was reviewed earlier, Gelernter et al. (1991) found that phenelzine, alprazolam, CBT, and placebo were equally effective on most measures. However, on one measure of social and work disability, phenelzine was more effective than the other three groups, which did not differ from one another. Unfortunately, the interpretation of these results is limited by the fact that the definition for "treatment responder" may have been overly stringent, as well as the fact that patients in all four groups were given instructions to expose themselves to feared situations, which probably blurred the differences between groups.

A meta-analytic study

Gould, Buckminster, Pollack, Otto, and Yap (1997) recently conducted a meta-analysis of 24 studies of CBT and pharmacological treatments for social phobia. Overall, the study confirms that both CBT and medications were more effective than were control conditions. Among medications, SSRIs and benzodiazepines have tended to yield the largest effect sizes. Among cognitive–behavioral interventions, treatments involving exposure (alone or with cognitive restructuring) yielded the strongest effect sizes. Forms of CBGT were projected to be the most cost-effective interventions, compared with individual CBT and a variety of different pharmacological approaches.

CONCLUSION

Social phobia is a commonly diagnosed condition that has received increased attention from both researchers and practitioners in recent years. Although researchers have identified unique patterns of thinking that may contribute to the maintenance of social phobia, less is known about the biological underpinnings of this disorder. With respect to treatment, CBT, certain antidepressants, and some anxiolytics have been shown to be useful. However, there are still no published studies investigating the combination of psychological and biological treatments. Several studies of combined treatments are currently underway, and results should be available soon.

3

SPECIFIC PHOBIA

Much of what is known about the nature and treatment of fear has come from research on specific phobias, including fears of animals, heights, blood, injections, enclosed places, flying, and other specific objects and situations. In this chapter we summarize the empirical literature on the nature and treatment of specific phobias. We begin with a discussion of diagnostic considerations, descriptive psychopathology, and epidemiology. This is followed by an overview of psychological and biological correlates of specific phobias. The chapter ends with a review of effective treatments for this condition. Note that additional literature on the treatment of specific phobias is reviewed in the other chapters of this book, particularly the chapter on exposure (chapter 6).

DIAGNOSTIC CRITERIA AND DESCRIPTION

In the fourth edition of the *Diagnostic and Statistical Manual for Mental Disorders* (*DSM-IV*; American Psychiatric Association, 1994), a specific phobia is defined as a "marked and persistent fear that is excessive or unreasonable, cued by the presence (or anticipation) of a specific object or situation." In addition, to meet full criteria for specific phobia, the individual must (a) experience the fear nearly every time he or she encounters the feared object or situation, (b) recognize that the fear is excessive or unreasonable, (c) avoid the feared object or situation or endure exposure with intense anxiety, (d) experience significant distress and/or functional impairment resulting from the fear or avoidance, and (e) have had the problem for at least 6 months (a requirement only if the individual is under 18 years of age). Furthermore, the anxiety should not be better accounted for by another mental disorder.

The criterion of insight into the excessiveness and unreasonableness of the fear was introduced to help clinicians distinguish between phobias and delusional fears, for which there is no insight. Nevertheless, recent findings suggest that some people with specific phobias may have relatively little insight into the inappropriateness of their own fear and distress (Jones, Whitmont, & Menzies, 1996; Menzies & Clarke, 1995a), even though their beliefs may not be of a delusional intensity. Therefore, it is possible that this criterion may inappropriately exclude some individuals from receiving a diagnosis of specific phobia.

Subtypes of Specific Phobia

The *DSM-IV* defines four main subtypes of specific phobia, which are listed here with examples:

1. Animal type: spiders, insects, dogs, cats, rodents, snakes, birds, fish
2. Natural environment type: heights, water, storms
3. Blood–injection–injury type: seeing blood, getting an injection or blood test, watching surgery
4. Situational type: enclosed places, driving, flying, elevators, bridges

In addition, there is a fifth, "other type," to describe phobias that are not easily categorized into one of the four main types, for example, phobias of choking and phobias of clowns or of people wearing masks (common in childhood).

The four main types were created following a series of studies and reports in which it was argued that specific phobias differ on dimensions such as age of onset, sex ratio, comorbidity with other phobias, focus of apprehension, and type of physiological response during exposure to feared situations (Craske & Sipsas, 1992; Curtis, Hill, & Lewis, 1990; Curtis, Himle, Lewis, & Lee, 1989; Himle, McPhee, Cameron, & Curtis, 1989; Hugdahl & Öst, 1985). In addition, some investigators (e.g., Curtis et al.,

1989) have suggested that situational specific phobias are more similar to panic disorder (PD) and agoraphobia on several of these dimensions than are other specific phobia types. Ways in which specific phobia types differ on these dimensions are reviewed later in the chapter.

We have argued elsewhere (Antony, Brown, & Barlow, 1997a) that the usefulness of the specific phobia types is questionable. First, some phobias are not easily classified. This is particularly a problem for the situational and natural environment phobias. For example, on the surface it is not clear whether a fear of the dark belongs in the natural environment type or the situational type. Furthermore, recent factor analytic studies suggest that natural environment and situational fears load on the same factor (Fredrikson, Annas, Fischer, & Wik, 1996; Muris, Schmidt, & Merckelbach, 1999) and that three specific phobia subtypes might be more appropriate than the four that are currently listed in the *DSM-IV*. Finally, it may be argued that specifying specific phobia types is less informative than simply naming the phobia (e.g., assigning the diagnosis "specific phobia, driving" rather than "specific phobia, situational type"). Naming the specific phobia would be briefer, more informative, and more helpful in treatment planning than is the present system of specifying general phobia types.

Case Vignette: Height Phobia

Kalinda first became aware of her fear of heights while in her teens. The fear was fairly mild at first, and it affected her only when she drove over very high bridges while learning to drive. Over the next 10 years or so, her fear began to generalize to other high places. When driving on elevated roads and highways, she preferred to be in the inside lane. She also preferred not to be on balconies or to peer out of windows in tall buildings. Although she was aware of feeling frightened in these situations, she rarely encountered them in her day-to-day life, and she experienced only minimal distress and impairment as a result of the fear.

After marrying at age 25, her fear began to get in the way. Her new partner was an avid skier, and they often went on ski trips together. However, Kalinda was unable to ski because she could not use the chair lift. Also, she had recently started a new job that required her to travel over a large bridge. When she presented for treatment, she was traveling more than an hour out of her way each day to avoid the bridge.

Kalinda reported several anxious beliefs associated with high places. First, she feared that she might lose control if she became too anxious and might possibly jump from the high place. While driving, she was fearful of losing control of the car and driving off a bridge or elevated highway. She tended to avoid these high places at all cost.

Kalinda was treated using a graduated exposure protocol. Her partner attended the treatment sessions and assisted with homework practices, especially early in treatment. To start, a hierarchy of feared situations was generated. Kalinda identified a number of places in town where her fear was problematic, including four different bridges, specific elevated areas on the highway, two different chair lifts at nearby ski resorts, and a balcony at a friend's home. These items were recorded on a hierarchy form, in order of difficulty, and exposure practices were begun. For a number of the situations, exposure began with the therapist or Kalinda's partner present. As the situation became easier, Kalinda practiced being in the situation on her own. Between treatment sessions, Kalinda engaged in exposure homework practices about four times per week. After five weekly sessions, each lasting 2 hours, Kalinda was able to enter all of the situations on her hierarchy with only minimal fear. In addition, she was no longer fearful of losing control in high places. Her gains were maintained when she was seen again a year later.

Physiological Response in Specific Phobias

Findings from a number of studies suggest that phobia types differ with respect to the type of physiological response experienced upon exposure to phobic situations. Although all phobia types are associated with a tendency to experience panic attacks in the phobic situation, only blood-injection-injury phobias are associated with a history of fainting in the feared situation (Antony et al., 1997a; Page, 1994). Individuals with blood-injection-injury phobia experience a diphasic physiological response that includes an initial increase in arousal followed by a sharp decrease in blood pressure and heart rate, which can often lead to fainting. In fact, about 70% of people with blood phobias and 56% of people with injection phobias have reported a history of fainting in the phobic situation (Öst, 1992).

Specific Phobias and Disgust

People with specific phobias of certain animals (e.g., spiders, snakes, and rodents) and of stimuli related to blood and injection injury often report a feeling of disgust (in addition to fear) when they encounter these stimuli. A number of researchers have used scales such as the Disgust Scale (Haidt, McCauley, & Rozin, 1994) and the Disgust Emotion Scale (Kleinknecht, Tolin, Lohr, & Kleinknecht, 1996) to measure disgust sensitivity in people with blood-injection-injury and animal fears. In general, studies on disgust in blood-injection-injury phobia have been based on analog samples (e.g., students reporting higher than normal fears on questionnaire measures), whereas studies on disgust in animal phobias have more often included individuals with clinically relevant phobias.

With respect to blood and injury phobias, findings on the relation between disgust sensitivity and blood-injection-injury-related fears have been inconsistent. Some researchers have found higher levels of disgust sensitivity among students who fear blood and injury than among non-phobic control participants (Sawchuk, Lee, Tolin, & Lohr, 1997; Tolin, Lohr, Sawchuk, & Lee, 1997). In fact, Tolin et al. (1997) found that the reaction of people with blood-injection-injury phobias to medical stimuli was primarily one of disgust rather than of fear. In a related study, Sawchuk, Tolin, Lee, Lohr, and Kleinknecht (1998) showed that disgust among individuals fearful of blood–injection–injury was associated with a fear of contamination.

However, in contrast to Tolin et al. (1997), Merckelbach, Muris, de Jong, and de Jongh (1999) found only modest correlations between disgust and blood-injection-injury-related fear in a group of undergraduate students. In addition, Kleinknecht, Kleinknecht, and Thorndike (1997) found that only blood-injection-injury fear was positively correlated with fainting in blood-injection-injury fearful individuals. In this study, disgust sensitivity was either negatively related or not at all related to fainting, depending on the measure of disgust sensitivity.

Ware, Jain, Burgess, and Davey (1994) examined the relation between disgust sensitivity and animal fears in an analog sample. Although fears of certain animals (e.g., snake, bat, rat, mouse, or spider) were associated with elevated disgust sensitivity, fears of other animals (e.g., "predatory animals" such as tiger, alligator, lion, or bear) were not. Furthermore, for animal fears that were associated with disgust, fear ratings were related to contamination fears.

Although some investigators have failed to find heightened levels of global disgust in people with spider phobias (e.g., Thorpe & Salkovskis, 1998b), several additional studies have shown a relationship between disgust sensitivity and fear of spiders (Merckelbach, de Jong, Arntz, & Schouten, 1993; Mulkens, de Jong, & Merckelbach, 1996; Tolin et al., 1997). Spider-phobic individuals who reported high levels of disgust sensitivity tended to have a greater number of negative conditioning experiences with spiders (Merckelbach, de Jong, et al., 1993) compared with those with lower levels of disgust. In addition, disgust sensitivity in parents tended to be predictive of fear of certain animals (e.g., cockroaches) in offspring. Interestingly, disgust sensitivity has not been shown to be predictive of treatment outcome for spider phobia (Merckelbach, de Jong, et al., 1993), and disgust ratings have tended to decrease along with fear ratings during exposure treatment for spider phobia (de Jong, Andrea, & Muris, 1997).

Prevalence of Specific Phobias

Epidemiological studies such as the Epidemiological Catchment Area (ECA) Study (Eaton et al., 1991) and the more recent National Comorbidity Survey (NCS; Kessler et al., 1994) have consistently shown the lifetime prevalence of specific phobias to be in the neighborhood of 11%, making them among the most common of psychiatric disorders. On the basis of findings from the ECA study, Bourdon et al. (1988) reported the prevalence of particular *DSM-III* simple phobias (renamed "specific phobias" in the *DSM-IV*). These data are summarized in Table 3.1. Because the ECA study did not distinguish well between specific phobias and fears associated with agoraphobia, prevalence rates for phobias of public transportation and enclosed places (which may occur in specific phobias or as part of agoraphobia) should be interpreted with caution.

Curtis, Magee, Eaton, Wittchen, and Kessler (1998) reported the lifetime prevalence rates for particular *DSM-III-R* simple phobias in the NCS study. In a sample of more than 8,000 individuals, the lifetime prevalence rates were 5.3% for height phobias, 3.5% for flying phobias, 4.2% for phobias of enclosed places, 2.9% for storm phobias, 5.7% for animal phobias, 4.5% for blood phobias, and 3.4% for water phobias. Lifetime prevalence rates for "fears" (not necessarily meeting the threshold for a phobia) were two to four times higher than were the rates for clinical phobias. In the only study to examine the prevalence of particular phobias based on *DSM-IV* criteria, Fredrikson et al. (1996) reported on the point prevalence of various specific phobias in 1,000 individuals who completed a mailed questionnaire assessing the *DSM-IV* criteria for various specific phobias. Results are re-

Table 3.1
Lifetime Prevalence of DSM-III Simple (Specific) Phobias in Women and Men, Based on the Epidemiological Catchment Area Survey

Phobia Type	Prevalence (%) women	men	Percent women
Spiders, bugs, mice, snakes	6.63	2.44	73
Heights	4.57	3.36	58
Public transportation (e.g., bus, plane, elevator)	3.80	1.33	74
Being in water (swimming pool, lake)	3.58	1.28	74
Storms	2.95	0.83	78
Being in a closed place	2.67	1.36	67
Other harmless animals	1.42	0.33	81

From "Gender Differences in Phobias: Results of the ECA Community Survey" (pp. 227–241), by K. H. Bourdon, 1988, *Journal of Anxiety Disorders, Volume 2*. Copyright 1988 by Elsevier Science Ltd, Kidlington, England. Adapted with permission.

Table 3.2
Point Prevalence of Particular Specific Phobias in Women and Men,
Based on a Questionnaire Survey of 1,000 Individuals

| Phobia Type | Prevalence (%) | | Total | χ^2 |
	Men	Women		
Snakes	2.4	8.3	5.5	11.6**
Spiders	1.2	5.6	3.5	10.0**
Lightning	0.3	3.7	2.1	10.0**
Closed spaces	2.4	5.4	4.0	4.0*
Darkness	0.0	4.3	2.3	14.6***
Heights	6.3	8.6	7.5	1.3
Flying	1.8	3.2	2.6	1.4
Injections	1.2	1.9	1.6	<1
Dentists	2.1	2.1	2.1	<1
Injuries	2.4	4.0	3.3	1.4

From "Gender and Age Differences in the Prevalence of Specific Fears and Phobias" (pp. 33–39) by M. Fredrikson, P. Annas, H. Fischer, and G. Wik, 1996. Copyright 1996 by Elsevier Science Ltd, Kidlington, England. Adapted with permission.
*p<.05; **p<.01; ***p<.001

ported in Table 3.2. Although prevalence rates are similar to those from other studies, these findings should be interpreted cautiously, because the reliability and validity of the assessment questionnaire are not known.

Sex and Gender Differences

Numerous researchers have reported on the sex ratios among patients with specific phobias presenting for treatment and phobic participants responding to advertisements. However, the relevance of these findings to sex differences in the prevalence of phobias is limited because they are confounded by sex differences in treatment-seeking patterns. For example, although Western studies of people with phobias presenting for treatment include primarily female participants, in a study on phobias in India it was found that only 20% of 83 patients presenting for treatment were women (Raguram & Bhide, 1985). The authors attributed the discrepancy to differences in health-seeking behavior in Indian versus Western cultures. In particular, Indian women are traditionally expected to stay home unless granted permission by the husband to leave and, therefore, may be less likely to seek clinical services.

Nevertheless, although sex differences in therapy-seeking probably affect data on sex composition in clinical samples, these data may be still relevant for examining differences in sex composition across groups, assuming that the relation between sex and therapy-seeking is similar in different phobia types. Curtis et al. (1989) reviewed the literature on sex ratio and phobias and concluded that the percentage of women among people with animal phobias (95%) was higher than that among people with situational phobias (75%–80%), and much higher than that among people with height phobias (54%). These calculations were based on averages across studies, weighted for the number of participants in each. The vast majority of studies reviewed by Curtis et al. (1989) were based on participants presenting for treatment or answering advertisements.

It should be noted that findings based on individuals presenting for treatment are somewhat different from those based on some epidemiological surveys. In a reanalysis of the data from the ECA survey (Robins & Regier, 1991), Curtis et al. (1990) found much more overlap in sex ratios across specific phobia types. In contrast, as is shown in Table 3.2, Fredrikson et al. (1996) did find large differences between men and women in the prevalence of certain specific phobias. Women were significantly more likely to report specific phobias of snakes, spiders, lightning, enclosed places, and darkness. Men and women did not differ with respect to the prevalence of height phobias, flying phobias, and blood-injection-injury-related phobias. Tables 3.1 and 3.2 include prevalence estimates for particular specific phobias in men and women.

Recently, investigators have begun to study reasons for sex differences among individuals with specific phobias. Arrindell, Kolk, Pickersgill, and Hageman (1993) found that biological sex predicted the fear ratings for animal phobias and situational phobias, even after controlling for other confounding variables such as masculine and feminine gender roles. Interestingly, after adjusting for "lie scale" scores, sex differences emerged for blood-injection-injury fears as well, suggesting that men may underreport their fear of these situations.

Findings from Pierce and Kirkpatrick (1992) support this hypothesis. In this study, undergraduate participants estimated their fear of several situations (e.g., rats, mice, roller coasters, etc.) on two occasions—once under normal conditions and once after being told that their fear of these situations was about to be measured objectively (e.g., by heart rate) during a behavior test. Men's fear ratings were significantly higher when they believed that their truthfulness would be subject to evaluation (i.e., during the second test administration), whereas women's fear ratings did not change. The authors concluded that one factor contributing to the sex differences in specific phobias may be the tendency of men to underreport their fears.

Age of Onset

In general, both clinical studies and large epidemiological studies have consistently shown that animal phobias and blood-injection-injury phobias begin in early childhood (e.g., Antony et al., 1997a; Bourdon et al., 1988; Curtis et al., 1990; Himle et al., 1989; Marks & Gelder, 1966; Öst, 1987a).

In contrast, situational phobias such as driving phobia and claustrophobia have typically been shown to begin in the late teens and 20s, closer to the age of onset for agoraphobia (Antony et al., 1997a; Curtis et al., 1990; Himle et al., 1989; Öst, 1987a). Findings regarding the age of onset for natural environment phobias have been inconsistent. Whereas some studies have shown storm phobias (Liddell & Lyons, 1978) and height phobias (Curtis et al., 1990) to begin in the mid-teens, other studies (e.g., Antony et al., 1997a) have shown height phobias to begin in the mid-20s.

Several methodological problems limit the conclusions that can be made from previous research regarding age of onset for specific phobias. First, almost all previous studies are retrospective in nature and, therefore, are subject to biases in retrospective recall. Second, most previous studies (especially those published before the 1990s) failed to include structured clinical interviews to confirm diagnoses or did not adequately distinguish between agoraphobia and specific phobias that are similar in content (e.g., fears of flying, enclosed places, driving, etc.). Finally, investigators have tended to ignore the importance of certain methodological issues such as how to code data from individuals who have had the phobia for as long as they can recall. Therefore, it is often not clear how the issues have been dealt with in these studies. Investigators have also tended to ignore the fact that age of onset for a particular fear may be different from that for the phobia (i.e., the age at which a given fear begins to cause distress or functional impairment). As was illustrated by Antony et al. (1997a), there is an average of 9 years separating the age of onset for the fear and the age at which the fear becomes a phobia.

Comorbidity

Comorbidity among specific phobia types

In a number of factor analytic studies, it has been found that phobias tend to cluster together within types (Arrindell, 1980; Landy & Gaupp, 1971; Liddell, Locker, & Burman, 1991; Wilson & Priest, 1968). In other words, having a phobia from one type (e.g., animal type) makes it more likely that an individual will have an additional phobia within the same type than one from a different type. Several clinical studies have confirmed the findings from factor analytic studies suggesting grouping within specific phobia types. For example, about 70% of individuals with blood phobias tended to have injection phobias as well (Öst, 1992).

However, it should be noted that although there is some consistency across factor analytic studies with respect to the major fear groupings (Arrindell, Pickersgill, Merckelbach, Ardon, & Cornet, 1991), there are also differences across some studies with respect to these dimensions. In addition, the factors on which particular fears load vary somewhat from study to study. One finding that is somewhat consistent across earlier factor analytic studies is the tendency for height phobias to cluster with situational phobias rather than natural environment phobias, even though height phobias are listed in the *DSM-IV* as an example from the natural environment type. Furthermore, as was reviewed earlier, recent factor analytic studies suggest that situational and natural environment phobias load on the same factor (Fredrikson et al., 1996; Muris et al., 1999). This finding raises the question of whether three specific phobia types (i.e., animal phobia, blood-injection-injury phobia, and environment–situational phobia) would be more appropriate than the four-factor structure currently underlying the *DSM-IV* system.

Comorbidity with other psychological disorders

Specific phobias frequently occur with other *DSM-IV* disorders. However, when specific phobias occur in the context of another disorder, they tend to be of a lesser severity compared with the other disorder. In other words, specific phobias tend to occur either alone or as an additional diagnosis, with another more impairing condition. Moras et al. (1994) found that specific phobias were present in 27% of people with PD and agoraphobia, 16% of people with generalized anxiety disorder, and 3% to 9% of people with other anxiety disorders. In another study, Sanderson et al. (1990) found that specific phobias were the most frequently assigned additional diagnoses in patients with anxiety disorders. On average, 32% of patients with anxiety disorders reported additional specific phobias. Overall, the findings from these studies are consistent with other recent findings showing that a significant proportion of individuals who have panic disorder with agoraphobia (20%), social phobia (21%), and generalized anxiety disorder (19%) have additional specific phobias (Goisman, Goldenberg, et al., 1995). Subclinical fears (i.e., fears that do not meet a clinical threshold for distress or functional impairment) of specific objects and situations are also common, affecting about 28% of individuals with a clinical anxiety disorder diagnosis (Antony, Moras, Meadows, Di Nardo, & Barlow, 1994).

PSYCHOLOGICAL ASPECTS OF SPECIFIC PHOBIA

Psychological Approaches to Phobia Acquisition

Fear has a protective function in that it helps us to avoid potentially threatening situations and thereby increase our chances of surviving in the face of danger. From an ethological perspective, it makes sense that organisms would develop an efficient mechanism for acquiring fear when exposed to potentially dangerous objects and situations. In recent years, a number of different investigators have proposed models to explain how specific phobias develop. These include conditioning models (Davey, 1997a; Merckelbach, de Jong, Muris, & van den Hout, 1996), evolutionary models (Menzies & Clarke, 1995c; Merckelbach & de Jong, 1997), and cognitive approaches (Cameron, 1997; Merckelbach, de Jong, et al., 1996).

Perhaps the most influential approaches to understanding specific phobias have been those related to learning theory and conditioning models. In 1939, Mowrer proposed one of the first comprehensive conditioning models to explain the development and maintenance of phobias. According to Mowrer's (1939) two-stage model, phobias begin through classical conditioning, the process by which a neutral stimulus is paired with an aversive stimulus and subsequently becomes a trigger for fear. As an example of classical conditioning, a fear of driving might first develop after a person experiences an accident while driving. The second stage in Mowrer's model concerns the maintenance of fear through operant conditioning. According to Mowrer, avoidance of feared situations maintains the fear through negative reinforcement. By avoiding feared situations, individuals do not experience any discomfort or fear, which in turn maintains their desire to avoid the object or situation. Although Mowrer's model is useful for understanding how some people's phobias originate, the theory has fallen out of favor over the years. One of the most often cited criticisms of the model is the observation that individuals with specific phobias often cannot recall a specific conditioning experience that triggered their fear. In fact, some people report fearing objects and situations that they have never even encountered (e.g., a person who fears flying even though he or she has never been in an airplane).

In response to this and other concerns with Mowrer's theory, Rachman (1976, 1977) proposed three different pathways to developing fear: direct conditioning, vicarious acquisition, and information and instruction. Direct conditioning involves developing a fear through classical conditioning, much as described in Mowrer's (1939) model. Individuals who develop a fear through this pathway typically report having experienced a traumatic event involving the feared object or situation. This usually involves being hurt or frightened in the situation, and it may include events such as falling from a high place, being bitten by a dog, experiencing intense turbulence while flying, or being stuck in an elevator.

Rachman's (1976, 1977) second pathway to fear acquisition is vicarious acquisition. This process involves developing a fear or phobia by seeing someone else behave fearfully in the presence of the feared object or situation or by witnessing some traumatic event experienced by another individual. An example is developing a fear of driving after years of being a passenger with parents who themselves were fearful of driving. Mineka, Davidson, Cook, and Keir (1984) demonstrated the process of vicarious conditioning in a study of snake fear in rhesus monkeys. In this study, after observing their parents behaving fearfully in the presence of real and toy snakes, five out of six young rhesus monkeys quickly developed an intense and persistent fear of snakes.

Information and instruction are the basis of Rachman's (1976, 1977) third pathway to fear development. According to Rachman, reading or hearing that an object or situation is dangerous can cause someone to develop a fear of that object or situation. For example, continually reading about airline crashes in the newspaper may contribute to a fear of flying for some people. Similarly, being warned by one's parents about the dangers of driving may contribute to one's fear of driving.

Rachman's model is an improvement over Mowrer's theory in that it accounts for a greater range of methods by which phobias develop. As was reviewed elsewhere (Antony & Barlow, 1997), a large number of studies have provided support for the model, showing that direct and indirect forms of phobia acquisition occur to varying degrees (e.g., McNally & Steketee, 1985; Menzies & Clarke, 1993b; Merckelbach, Arntz, & de Jong, 1991; Merckelbach, Arntz, Arrindell, & de Jong, 1992; Öst, 1985). However, the percentages of individuals reporting an onset by each of these three pathways differs considerably from study to study, for a number of reasons. First, studies have tended to differ with respect to which events are counted as relevant to the phobia onset. Some studies have included multiple events, whereas others have forced participants to choose a single primary cause. Some studies have counted events without paying attention to the functional relationship between the event and the phobia onset. For example, a car accident that is followed immediately by the onset of a fear of driving is sometimes afforded the same degree of importance as an accident that occurs 10 years before or even 10 years after a phobia begins.

Another problem with many of the early studies is that they tended to overlook important diagnostic issues. For example, some included mixed groups of phobic people (e.g., people who fear driving because of agoraphobia along with those who have a specific phobia of driving). Additionally, previous studies have included very different types of participants, including college students with elevated fear scores, clinical patients with specific phobias, and individuals responding to study advertisements. Finally, a recent study of the stability of driving-fear-acquisition pathways over a 1-year period has brought into question the reliability of retrospective self-reports on the acquisition of phobias (Taylor, Deane, & Podd, 1999). The extent to which participants' reports are unreliable would probably contribute to inconsistent findings across studies.

There have been a number of trends in recent studies that have improved the quality of the research on modes of acquisition for specific phobias. First, researchers have begun to study phobia acquisition in children, using interviews with both children and parents. Because many phobias begin in childhood, this method may provide some protection against the effects of retrospective recall biases that may be present in adults who have had a phobia for many years. In addition, more studies have recently relied on interviews with individuals suffering from carefully diagnosed clinical phobias, rather than just individuals from analog samples. Methods of measuring the origins of phobias have also improved in recent years. Finally, investigators have recently begun to include comparison groups of nonphobic individuals.

Although there is evidence of fear-relevant learning experiences (i.e., conditioning events, vicarious acquisition events, and negative information experiences) in people with specific phobias, these events are also common among people without phobias. In fact, there are now several studies showing that phobic and nonphobic groups do not differ with respect to the number of learning events across studies of people with dog phobias (Di Nardo et al., 1988), water phobias (Graham & Gaffan, 1997), and height phobias (Menzies & Clarke, 1995b). Recent prospective studies on water phobia (Poulton, Menzies, Craske, Langley, & Silva, 1999) and height phobia (Poulton, Davies, Menzies, Langley, & Silva, 1998) also failed to show the expected relationship between fear-related trauma before age 9 and phobia at age 18. In fact, in the Poulton et al. (1998) study, falls resulting in injury between ages 5 and 9 were more frequent for those without a fear of heights at age 18 than for those with a fear of heights.

In contrast, however, there are also studies showing a history of more conditioning experiences (but not more vicarious or information experiences) among spider-phobic individuals than among nonphobic individuals (Merckelbach & Muris, 1997; Muris, Merckelbach, & Collaris, 1997). In addition, Muris, Steerneman, Merckelbach, and Meesters (1996) found that fearfulness in children was associated with fearfulness in mothers (but not fathers) and that the relationship was mediated by the degree to which mothers expressed their fears in front of the children. This study supports a role of vicarious acquisition in the transmission of fear.

The role of conditioning, vicarious acquisition, and informational learning in the development of phobias is still a source of controversy in the literature. There is little doubt that these three pathways are important in the pathogenesis of some phobias. However, there is also consistent evidence that these pathways do not account for all phobias. For example, individuals may report having had a phobia for as long as they can remember and may not report any specific precipitating events. This may be particularly true of phobias that begin in childhood, such as animal phobias (McNally & Steketee, 1985). In addition, Rachman's model does not explain why many people have experiences that are consistent with one or more modes of fear acquisition but still do not develop phobias.

An important issue that remains to be resolved is the question of who develops a phobia following a conditioning event, vicarious experience, or exposure to negative information and who does not become fearful. Antony and Barlow (1997) suggested a number of possibilities. The context of the event (e.g., stress at the time of the event, availability of social support, and the individual's perception of control over the event) may affect people's risk for developing phobias following a traumatic event. In addition, individual difference variables (e.g., trait anxiety or genetic predisposition) may influence whether an individual develops a phobia, given particular experiences.

Also, previous exposure to the object or situation may protect an individual from developing a phobia, perhaps through latent inhibition (which occurs following repeated presentation of a conditioned stimulus alone, before it is actually paired with the unconditioned stimulus). For example, Davey (1989) found that individuals who had a painful experience at the dentist were less likely to report developing a fear of dentists if the experience was preceded by a history of relatively pleasant experiences at the dentist. In addition to previous experience with the feared situation, subsequent exposure may make a difference. For example, getting behind the wheel quickly following a car accident may protect a person from developing a phobia.

Although some investigators (Merckelbach & Muris, 1997; Merckelbach, Muris, & Schouten, 1996) continue to emphasize the role of associative learning in the onset of phobias, others have argued in favor of nonassociative models (e.g., Menzies & Clarke, 1995c), particularly for phobias with an underlying evolutionary function. Menzies and Clarke (1995c) have argued that objects and situations that were historically dangerous (e.g., certain animals, heights, or water) are often feared in the absence of conditioning experiences. In contrast, they proposed that phobias of evolutionarily neutral situations, such as visiting the dentists or flying in an airplane, are more likely to begin through associative learning. Two preliminary studies (Harris & Menzies, 1996; Menzies & Harris, 1997) support this model, showing that more evolutionary-neutral phobias than evolutionary-relevant phobias begin in the context of negative conditioning events.

Attention and Memory Biases in Specific Phobia

Numerous researchers have examined the role of cognitive factors in specific phobias. In general, those using standard information-processing paradigms (e.g., the Stroop color-naming task—see chapter 1 for a description) have found that individuals with specific phobias tend to direct more attentional resources to phobic stimuli (e.g., fear-relevant words) than do nonphobic individuals and that exposure to the feared stimulus tends to decrease this attentional bias (Lavy, van den Hout, & Arntz, 1993b; van den Hout, Tenney, Huygens, & de Jong, 1997; Watts, McKenna, Sharrock, & Trezise, 1986). Furthermore, some investigators have argued that the function of attentional bias in specific phobias is to facilitate escape from danger (Lavy, van den Hout, & Arntz, 1993a). Although Kindt and Brosschot (1997) found that the attentional bias is equally as strong for threat-related words as for threat-related pictures, Merckelbach, Kenemans, Dijkstra, and Schouten (1993) failed to show an attentional bias with pictorial stimuli. However, it should be noted that the Merckelbach, Kenemans, et al. (1993) study had a fairly small sample size (13 participants per group), which may account for the negative findings.

In recent years, a number of additional findings have emerged. In addition to selectively attending to threat cues, there is evidence that individuals with phobias also attend selectively to safety cues (e.g., the door of a room containing a large spider; Thorpe & Salkovksis, 1998a). In addition, studies have recently begun to address the question of whether the attentional bias seen in people with specific phobias is limited to strategic processing (i.e., conscious information processing) or whether there is also a bias for preconscious processing. Whereas some investigators (e.g., van den Hout et al., 1997) have found that attentional bias occurs for both masked and unmasked presentations of threat-related words (indicating both preconscious and strategic information processing, respectively), other investigators (e.g., Thorpe & Salkovskis, 1997) have shown group differences only in the unmasked condition, providing evidence against preconscious processing.

Some studies of memory for threat-related stimuli have shown that people with specific phobias have poorer recognition of fear-related objects, compared with nonphobic control participants. For example, Watts, Trezise, and Sharrock (1986) found that individuals with spider phobias were less able to recognize pictures of spiders (particularly pictures of larger spiders) than were control participants. In this study, focused exposure to spiders increased performance on subsequent recognition tasks, suggesting that the initial poor recall for spider-related details may have been related to distraction or subtle avoidance behaviors. In contrast, Tolin, Lohr, Lee, and Sawchuk (1999) suggested that poor recognition may be related to visual avoidance of phobia-related stimuli, even when individuals are instructed to study the stimuli carefully (i.e., during focused exposure).

However, not all researchers have found poor memory for threat-related information among people with specific phobias. Wessel and Merckelbach (1997, 1998) conducted two studies of the attentional narrowing theory of emotional memory using individuals with spider phobias. In short, the *attentional narrowing theory* suggests that fearful individuals narrow their attention toward the object of their fear (i.e., central details) and decrease their attention to other information (i.e., peripheral details). According to the model, recall for details that are central to the feared objects (e.g., the color of a spider) should be recalled better than are details that are peripheral (e.g., the color of a table in the room).

Consistent with the model, Wessel and Merckelbach (1998) found that, compared with nonphobic participants, individuals with spider phobias had better memory for threat-related stimuli (e.g., photos of spiders) than for non-threat-related stimuli (e.g., photos of babies and pens). In a related study involving exposure to a live spider, spider-phobic individuals had poorer memory for peripheral objects in a room (e.g., a clock) than did nonfearful participants. However, there were no group differences in memory for central details (e.g., characteristics of the spider). This study therefore provided only partial support for the attentional narrowing hypothesis of emotional memory.

Attributions and Appraisals in Specific Phobia

People with specific phobias have more fearful beliefs about the situations they fear than do people without phobias. For example, compared with nonphobic individuals, people with spider phobias are more likely to imagine that spiders are angry and that they are likely to single them out and walk toward them versus walking toward another person in the room (Riskind, Moore, & Bowley, 1995). They are also more likely to provide higher estimates for the probability of being bitten by a spider and for the likelihood that injuries will result from being bitten (Jones et al., 1996). Similarly, people with height phobias are more likely than nonphobic individuals to exhibit catastrophic thoughts about high places, and this tendency to experience catastrophic thinking is a strong predictor of avoidance behavior (Marshall, Bristol, & Barbaree, 1992). Height phobias are also associated with a tendency to give higher estimates for the likelihood of falling from a high place as well as the likelihood of being injured from such a fall (Menzies & Clarke, 1995c).

There is also evidence that people with specific phobias experience perceptual distortions and engage in biased logic when thinking about the objects they fear. People with spider and snake phobias tend to overestimate the amount of activity engaged in by spiders and snakes, respectively (Rachman & Cuk, 1992). Interestingly, these perceptual distortions decline after reduction of the fear. Furthermore, people who fear spiders tend to engage in deductive reasoning that confirms their fearful beliefs rather than in reasoning that disconfirms their beliefs, which may be a factor in maintaining their fear (de Jong, Mayer, & van den Hout, 1997; de Jong, Weertman, Horselenberg, & van den Hout, 1997).

Focus of Apprehension in Specific Phobia

Although anxiety over physical sensations is a feature that is typically associated with PD, there is evidence that individuals with specific phobias are also concerned about experiencing uncomfortable sensations, although not to the extent that is seen in PD. For example, Reiss, Peterson, Gursky, and McNally (1986) reported that people with specific phobias scored a full standard deviation above the norms for nonanxious individuals on the Anxiety Sensitivity Index (ASI; Peterson & Heilbronner, 1987; Peterson & Reiss, 1993), a measure of the extent to which individuals are anxious about experiencing fear-related sensations such as racing heart and breathlessness. Other studies, however, have failed to show significant differences in ASI scores between those with specific phobias and nonanxious individuals (Taylor et al., 1992). Furthermore, in addition to fearing aspects of the situation itself (e.g., being in a plane crash or being bitten by a dog), people with specific phobias also report anxiety over their reactions to the phobic situation (e.g., fears of losing control of the car while driving, having a panic attack, etc.; Arntz, Lavy, van den Berg, & van Rijsoort, 1993; Ehlers, Hofmann, Herda, & Roth, 1994; McNally & Steketee, 1985).

Consistent with the hypothesis that situational specific phobias share features with PD and agoraphobia, there is evidence that people with certain situational phobias are especially anxious about experiencing uncomfortable symptoms. Craske and Sipsas (1992) found that college students with claustrophobia reported greater apprehension over sensations (as was reflected by scores on the ASI) than did nonphobic individuals, whereas individuals with fears of spiders or snakes did not differ from nonphobic people on this measure. However, there is evidence that other specific phobias are also associated with a tendency to focus on internal sensations. Antony et al. (1997a) asked participants with phobias of driving, blood/injections, animals, or heights to estimate the percentage of their fear that was associated with the feared situation versus their reaction to the situation (e.g., fainting, having a panic attack, etc.). People with phobias of heights and blood/injection reported elevated concern about their reactions to the phobic situation, relative to people with animal phobias. In addition, people with driving phobias were in between on this measure and did not differ from those in the other groups.

Compared with people with other anxiety disorders, people with PD tend to react with more fear to biological challenges (e.g., carbon dioxide [CO_2] inhalation) that induce uncomfortable sensations (Rapee et al., 1992). Furthermore, reaction to such challenges appears to be related to the individual's reported fear of uncomfortable sensations (i.e., anxiety sensitivity). To examine differences among specific phobia types in their response to panic-inducing biological challenges, several investigators have compared groups of people with phobias on their responses to CO_2 inhalation. Verburg, Griez, and Meijer (1994) showed that although people with animal phobias did not differ from normal control participants in their response to CO_2 inhalation, a combined group of people with natural environment and situational phobias had a significantly stronger reaction to CO_2 than did control participants. In a related study, Antony, Brown, and Barlow (1997b) found few significant differences between people with animal phobias, height phobias, blood-injection-injury phobias, and driving phobias in their response to CO_2 inhalation. However, for the few measures in which groups differed, there was a tendency for individuals with height and driving phobias to respond more strongly to the CO_2 challenge compared with those with animal and blood-injection-injury phobias.

In summary, there is some evidence that specific phobia types differ with respect to how much fear is associated with the tendency to experience uncomfortable sensations. Several researchers have found heightened fear of sensations among people with situational specific phobias, compared with those with animal phobias. In addition, there is preliminary evidence that people with blood and injection phobias, as well as those with height phobias, report fear regarding how they feel when exposed to the phobic situation. Overall, however, findings have been somewhat inconsistent, with some findings showing relatively few differences among specific phobia types.

BIOLOGICAL ASPECTS OF SPECIFIC PHOBIA

Family and Genetics Studies

Specific phobias tend to run in families. Fyer et al. (1990) conducted a study of 49 first-degree relatives of people with specific phobias and 119 first-degree relatives of people without a history of mental illness. Several interesting findings emerged. First, specific phobias were more commonly diagnosed in family members of people with specific phobias (31%) than in family members of people without a history of psychiatric disorder (11%). In addition, the risk of having disorders other than specific phobia was no higher for family members of people with specific phobia than for family members of people without specific phobias. Although the particular phobia that was transmitted in first-degree relatives was often different from the phobia present in the proband, it was often from the same type (e.g., situational, animal, etc.).

The fact that phobias run in families does not necessarily imply genetic transmission. As was discussed earlier, people can learn phobias by observing other individuals who have a similar fear. To establish genetic transmission, twin, adoption, genetic linkage, and association studies are generally more helpful. Of these methods, only twin studies have been reported in the case of specific phobias, and these have yielded conflicting results.

In an early study, Torgersen (1979) found significantly higher concordance rates for monozygotic twins than for dizygotic twins for a number of different phobia types, including animal phobias, mutilation phobias (including primarily fears from the blood-injection-injury specific phobia type), and nature phobias (including primarily fears from the natural environment and situational specific phobia types). In another twin study, Skre et al. (1993) found that although several of the anxiety disorders had a strong genetic component, environmental influences were most important for specific phobias. Finally, in what may be the most sophisticated twin study on anxiety disorders, Kendler et al. (1992) found that in the case of specific phobias, there was a modest nonspecific genetic vulnerability (e.g., a general predisposition to be anxious) combined with disorder-specific environmental influences (e.g., traumatic conditioning experiences involving the phobic object or situation). The role of genetics in the transmission of phobias appears to be even greater when the effects of unreliable interviews are controlled for (Kendler et al., 1999).

The role of genetics in the transmission of blood-injection-injury phobias has been of particular interest to investigators in recent years. In part, this interest has grown from anecdotal observations that these phobias run in families, as does the tendency to faint in response to blood-injection-injury stimuli. For example, Öst (1992) found that 61% of people with blood phobia and 29% of people with injection phobia reported having a relative with the same fear. Findings from twin studies suggest that both environmental factors (e.g., traumatic events and social learning) and genetic factors (especially related to fainting) contribute to the familial transmission of blood-injection-injury-related fears and phobias (Neale et al., 1994; Page & Martin, 1998).

Neuroanatomical Features of Specific Phobias

In several studies positron emission tomography (PET) has been used to investigate the brain regions that are most active during exposure to phobic stimuli. In an early study (Mountz et al., 1989), no differences in global or regional cerebral blood flow (CBF) were found either at rest or during exposure to fear-relevant stimuli between 7 people with small-animal phobias and 8 control participants. Although there were differences in CBF between the fear-relevant and resting scans, these differences appeared to be accounted for by anxiety-induced hyperventilation.

Subsequent studies have identified specific changes in CBF that occur during exposure to phobic stimuli, although the findings have not been consistent. Fredrikson et al. (1993) found increased regional CBF (rCBF) in the visual associative cortex upon exposure to fear-relevant stimuli in a group of people with snake phobias, but not upon exposure to other aversive stimuli or neutral stimuli. In addition, cortical rCBF and thalamic rCBF were correlated during exposure to phobic stimuli but not during exposure to other aversive or neutral stimuli. In contrast, Rauch et al. (1995) found that provocation with phobic stimuli (e.g., a feared animal in a clear container) led to increased CBF in the anterior cingulate cortex, insular cortex, anterior temporal cortex, somatosensory cortex, posterior medial orbito-frontal cortex, and thalamus, compared with exposure to neutral stimuli (e.g., an empty container). It is difficult to know why these and other studies have failed to show consistent effects of exposure to phobic stimuli on brain function. Likely explanations include differences in the populations studied as well as differences in the methodology and imaging paradigms employed.

Other Physiological Correlates

Exposure to phobic stimuli leads to a wide range of physiological changes in people with specific phobias, including increased heart rate, skin conductance, blood pressure, plasma norepinephrine, epinephrine, insulin, cortisol, and growth hormone (Abelson & Curtis, 1989; Nesse et al., 1985; Prigatano & Johnson, 1974; Teghtsoonian & Frost, 1982). However, there also appears to be desynchrony in the endocrine and cardiovascular responses. That is, there is considerable variability with respect to the timing, consistency, and covariation of these responses (Abelson & Curtis, 1989; Nesse et al., 1985).

There is also evidence that endorphins may stimulate approach behavior in people with specific phobias. In a study of people with spider phobias, Arntz (1993) found that the opiate antagonist naltrexone, but not placebo, negatively influenced approach to spiders, although the drug had no effect on subjective fear. Some investigators (e.g., Carr, 1996) have proposed that it is the release of beta endorphin (and its interaction with adrenocorticotrophic hormone) during exposure to feared stimuli that is in part responsible for the reduction in fear and avoidance seen during exposure-based treatments for phobic avoidance.

TREATMENT OF SPECIFIC PHOBIA

Unlike for other anxiety disorders, it is generally accepted that biological treatments such as medications are not appropriate treatments for specific phobias. Rather, psychological treatments (especially those involving exposure to feared objects and situations) are typically viewed as the treatments of choice (Antony & Barlow, 1998). In addition to this book, detailed treatment manuals for patients (Antony, Craske, & Barlow, 1995) and clinicians (Craske, Antony, & Barlow, 1997) are available for in-depth, step-by-step descriptions of empirically supported treatment procedures for people suffering from specific phobias.

Exposure-Based Treatments

In general, exposure to the feared object or situation is considered to be an essential component of effective treatment for specific phobias. Furthermore, for most phobia types, exposure alone is sufficient for helping patients overcome their specific phobias. Numerous studies have shown that exposure-based treatments are effective for treating phobias of snakes (Gauthier & Marshall, 1977), rats (Foa, Blau, Prout, & Latimer, 1977), spiders (Hellström & Öst, 1995; Öst, 1996a; Öst, Ferebee, & Furmark, 1997; Öst, Salkovskis, & Hellström, 1991), enclosed places (Öst, Johansson, & Jerremalm, 1982; Craske, Mohlman, Yi, Glover, & Valeri, 1995), water (Menzies & Clarke, 1993a), dental treatment (Gitin, Herbert, & Schmidt, 1996; Moore & Brødsgaard, 1994), heights (Baker, Cohen, & Saunders, 1973; Bourque & Ladouceur, 1980), flying (Howard, Murphy, & Clarke, 1983; Öst, Brandberg, & Alm, 1997), and blood (Öst, Fellenius, & Sterner, 1991). Furthermore, for a variety of phobias (e.g., animals, injections, and dental treatment), a single session of in vivo exposure lasting two to three hours has been shown to result in clinically significant improvement in up to 90% of patients (Gitin et al., 1996; Öst, 1989; Öst, Brandberg, & Alm, 1997; Öst, Salkovskis, & Hellström, 1991).

Despite several attempts to identify pretreatment predictors of outcome following exposure-based treatment of specific phobias, few stable predictors have been identified. For example, Hellström and Öst (1996) investigated the relation between a broad range of variables (e.g., age, age of onset, etiology, frequency of the phobia in family members, treatment credibility, treatment expectations, various psychophysiological measures, etc.) and scores on measures of anxiety, fear, and depression. But no consistent predictors of outcome emerged in this study, although diastolic blood pressure at pretest and treatment credibility each predicted outcome for a subset of patients (quite possibly a statistical artifact, given the number of predictors examined in the study). In another study Muris, Mayer, and Merckelbach (1998) showed that trait anxiety, as measured by the State–Trait Anxiety Inventory (Spielberger, Gorsuch, Lushene, Vagg, & Jacobs, 1983), was predictive of outcome for exposure-based treatment of spider phobias. A likely reason for the difficulty in finding consistent predictors of outcome in the treatment of specific phobias is the fact that almost all individuals respond very well to treatment. Further relevant findings regarding particular exposure-based approaches for specific phobias are reviewed in subsequent chapters in this book (e.g., chapter 6). For additional reviews, see Öst (1996b, 1997).

Eye Movement Desensitization and Reprocessing

Eye movement desensitization and reprocessing (EMDR) was originally introduced by Shapiro (1989) as a treatment for posttraumatic stress disorder. Since then, the treatment has been tried for a number of other anxiety disorders, including specific phobia. The introduction and promotion of EMDR has probably generated more controversy and debate among clinical scientists than has any other recent development in the treatment of anxiety disorders (for recent reviews, see Cahill, Carrigan, & Frueh, 1999; de Jongh, Broeke, & Renssen, 1999; Lohr, Lilienfeld, Tolin, & Herbert, 1999; Lohr, Tolin, & Lilienfeld, 1998; Shapiro, 1999). Essentially, EMDR involves having patients expose themselves in imagination to a feared image or memory while simultaneously engaging in horizontal eye movements induced by the therapist's hand moving back and forth. Recently, other forms of bilateral sensory stimulation have been tried as an alternative to eye tracking, including listening to tones and tapping the hands. However, most research has focused on the more commonly used eye movement methods.

Although some case studies have yielded promising results for EMDR in the treatment of specific phobias (Kleinknecht, 1993; Lohr, Tolin, & Kleinknecht, 1995, 1996), the positive findings have often been limited to subjective measures of fear rather than psychophysiological indices or measures of phobic avoidance (e.g., Lohr et al., 1995, 1996; Muris & Merckelbach, 1995). Furthermore, larger group studies with specific phobia patients have either failed to show any differences between EMDR and traditional exposure-based treatments (e.g., Sanderson & Carpenter, 1992) or have shown greater effects with traditional exposure therapies compared with EMDR (Muris, Merckelbach, Holdrinet, & Sijsenaar, 1998; Muris, Merckelbach, van Haaften, & Mayer, 1997). In fact, one study showed no differences in fear reduction between EMDR and a no-treatment comparison group (Bates, McGlynn, Montgomery, & Mattke, 1996).

Overall, it seems that EMDR is an effective treatment for some individuals. However, because imaginal exposure is a component of EMDR, it is possible that the effectiveness of EMDR is due primarily to the effects of exposure. In other words, "what is effective in EMDR is not new, and what is new is not effective" (McNally, in press). In a comprehensive review of the literature, Lohr et al. (1998) made several conclusions about the current state of the literature on EMDR. First, the effects of EMDR appear to be limited to subjective verbal reports. Second, eye movements appear to be unnecessary for clinical improvement. Finally, the conceptual basis of EMDR is not supported by scientific findings regarding the role of eye movements in this treatment.

Cognitive Therapy and Specific Phobia

In a study of individuals with fears of enclosed places, spiders, or snakes, Craske, Mohlman, et al. (1995) investigated the effect of combining in vivo exposure with either relaxation training or correcting misappraisals regarding bodily sensations during two treatment sessions. Overall, there were no differences in the effectiveness of the two treatment conditions for people with spider or snake fears. In contrast, for people who feared enclosed places, there was short-term benefit of adding cognitive restructuring to change beliefs about uncomfortable sensations. However, these differences were no longer present 4 weeks after treatment ended.

Booth and Rachman (1992) compared in vivo exposure, exposure to feared sensations (interoceptive exposure), and cognitive restructuring for the treatment of claustrophobia. Although in vivo exposure was the most effective of the treatments on most measures, people receiving cognitive therapy also made significant gains compared with a control group. Interoceptive exposure led to only modest gains on most measures. Regardless of the specific treatment received, changes in anxious cognitions regarding being trapped, suffocating, or losing control was predictive of fear reduction during treatment (Shafran, Booth, & Rachman, 1993).

A number of researchers have also examined the efficacy of cognitive treatments for dental phobias. Jerremalm, Jansson, and Öst (1986b) compared self-instructional training (teaching patients to replace negative thoughts with more realistic ways of thinking) with applied relaxation (relaxation training combined with gradual exposure) for dental phobias. Both treatments were conducted over nine 90-minute group sessions. During the last three sessions, the patients in each treatment were encouraged to use the strategies during exposure to dental procedures. Both treatment conditions led to significant improvement and were equally effective on most measures. Individual response patterns (i.e., whether patients were classified as cognitive vs. physiological reactors) did not predict outcome across conditions. Additional recent studies (de Jongh, Muris, et al., 1995; Getka & Glass, 1992) have confirmed that cognitive strategies are useful for individuals with dental phobias, particularly over the short term. In summary, cognitive strategies may be useful, particularly when combined with exposure for some phobias (e.g., phobias of enclosed spaces or dentists). More research is needed to evaluate the benefits of cognitive therapy for other specific phobias.

Applied Tension for Blood Phobia

As was discussed earlier, blood and injection phobias are the only fears that are often associated with fainting upon exposure to the phobic situation. Fainting in blood-injection-injury phobia occurs when an individual experiences vasovagal syncope accompanied by a sudden drop in systolic and diastolic blood pressure, reduced heart rate, and a reduction in muscle tone. In 1981, Kozak and Montgomery published the first case report describing the use of applied muscle tension to help prevent fainting in people with blood-injection-injury phobias. Essentially, the method involved teaching patients to tense all the muscles of their body, thereby increasing their blood pressure and preventing fainting. Cognitive strategies and exposure to feared stimuli were gradually introduced until the patient no longer experienced the fainting feelings and no longer feared the previously phobic situation.

Several years after Kozak and Montgomery's (1981) report, Öst and Sterner (1987) developed further the applied tension treatment into a five-session protocol for blood phobia treatment. This updated version included only the muscle tension and exposure components of the original treatment. Preliminary findings with 10 patients were very promising, and gains were maintained at a 6-month follow-up (Öst & Sterner, 1987). A number of larger controlled studies have lent additional support for the use of applied tension. Hellström, Fellenius, and Öst (1996) found that a single session of therapist-directed applied tension was equally effective as the standard five-session treatment, provided that the single session was followed by a maintenance program of self-directed exposure. In fact, 70% of individuals who received a single session of applied tension were clinically improved at follow-up.

Öst, Fellenius, and Sterner (1991) compared applied tension, tension only (without exposure to blood-injection-injury stimuli), and in vivo exposure for the treatment of blood phobia. After five sessions of treatment, all three groups were significantly improved, although applied tension was significantly more effective than exposure alone. The percentages of patients who were clinically improved were 90%, 80%, and 40% for the three groups, respectively. One year later, the corresponding percentages were 100%, 90%, and 50%.

Medications and Specific Phobia

Although medications are sometimes prescribed for certain specific phobias, there have been very few studies of the use of medications for specific phobias. In one of the few published studies, Whitehead, Robinson, Blackwell, and Stutz (1978) examined the effects of combining diazepam versus placebo with exposure therapy for the treatment of small-animal phobias. The addition of diazepam had no effect on the length of time taken to treat the phobia. A similar study showed no effects of adding alprazolam to exposure for the treatment of people with spider phobias (Zoellner, Craske, Hussain, Lewis, & Echeveri, 1996).

In contrast, Wilhelm and Roth (1996) found that alprazolam decreased fear, compared with placebo, during a flight taken by women who were fearful of flying. However, during a second flight taken a week later without medication, individuals who had taken alprazolam during their first flight reported more fear and more panic attacks than did individuals who had taken placebo during their first flight. In other words, although it was effective in the short term, alprazolam appeared to interfere with the effects of in vivo exposure for flying phobia in the long term. This finding is consistent with previous findings on the effect of combining exposure and alprazolam for agoraphobia (Marks et al., 1993).

Although studies are lacking, it is possible that the effects of medication may be different with different types of specific phobia. As was reviewed earlier, some investigators have argued that situational specific phobias share more features with agoraphobia than do other specific phobia types. It is possible that medications that work for PD and agoraphobia may also be more effective for situational specific phobias (e.g., fears of flying, driving, or enclosed places) than for other phobia types. The findings from the few studies reviewed in this section are consistent with that possibility. However, it is likely that even if some medications are effective for situational specific phobias in the short term, they are unlikely to be the treatment of choice in the long term for most patients, because of problems with relapse and possible interference with the effects of exposure-based treatments.

Relapse and Return of Fear

Several factors appear to predict whether a patient's fear is likely to return following exposure-based treatment. In general, it seems that patients for whom fear decreases more quickly during exposure are less likely to experience a return of fear compared with patients for whom fear decreases more slowly (Rachman & Whittal, 1989a). In addition, the extent to which anxious cognitions are changed as a result of treatment appears to be a significant predictor of whether fear returns in the future (de Jong, van den Hout, & Merckelbach, 1995; Shafran et al., 1993). Finally, the presence of an elevated heart rate at the start of treatment is a strong predictor of whether fear returns (Craske & Rachman, 1987; see Rachman, 1989, for a review). Factors such as experiencing a fear-related aversive event (Rachman & Whittal, 1989a) and experiencing only partial fear reduction during treatment (Rachman & Lopatka, 1988; Rachman, Robinson, & Lopatka, 1987) have generally not been found to predict return of fear, at least not among individuals with fear of spiders or snakes.

CONCLUSION

Specific phobias are common in the general population. Although people with specific phobias are less likely to seek treatment than are those with other anxiety disorders, this condition is one of the most easily treated of all psychological problems. Unlike with other anxiety disorders, the role of biological factors in the etiology and maintenance of specific phobias is not well established. In addition, there are almost no studies supporting the use of medications for the treatment of people with specific phobias.

II

ASSESSMENT AND TREATMENT OF PHOBIC DISORDERS

4

ASSESSING PHOBIC DISORDERS

A thorough assessment is essential before treatment begins. The assessment process has several functions:

- to establish a diagnosis and rule out alternative diagnoses
- to measure the severity of the presenting problem and associated problems
- to help in the selection of appropriate treatment strategies
- to measure the individual's response to treatment

In the assessment of phobic disorders in particular, a multimodal approach should be used, which may include structured and unstructured interviews, self-report questionnaires, behavioral assessments, diaries, psychophysiological assessment, and medical examination.

In this chapter we present an overview of the assessment process and a discussion of diagnostic assessment for phobic disorders, providing information on the most commonly used structured and semistructured interviews for establishing a diagnosis, guidelines for differential diagnosis, and an overview of the relationship between diagnosis and treatment. Next, there are comprehensive sections on conducting clinical interviews, behavioral assessment strategies, and the value of a complete physical examination by a physician. The chapter ends with a detailed review of the major self-

and clinician-administered instruments that are often used for assessing the symptoms of phobic disorders.

AN OVERVIEW OF THE ASSESSMENT PROCESS

There are many different ways of arranging the assessment strategies discussed in this chapter to form a comprehensive clinical evaluation. Usually, the first 2 or 3 weeks of clinical contact is spent on assessment. Sessions usually occur weekly and should last 1 to 2 hours each, depending on the amount of material that needs to be covered and practical considerations such as the availability of the therapist and patient. At the very least, the initial evaluation should include a clinical interview lasting from one to two sessions and completion of self-report measures. Later in the chapter we recommend specific content areas that should be covered during the clinical interview, and we recommend specific self-report questionnaires to use for particular problems. In managed care settings, the clinician may be under pressure to obtain information in a relatively brief period. Although not ideal, one way of handling this situation is to rely more heavily on self-report instruments than on interview-based evaluation.

If a semistructured diagnostic interview (as is described later in the chapter) is to be administered, it will probably take up an entire session (about 2 hours), and remaining parts of the clinical interview will probably need to be administered in a separate meeting with the patient. During the initial period of assessment, the patient may also be asked to complete various monitoring forms and diaries. For example, if a person is experiencing panic attacks, he or she should complete a Panic Attack Diary (see Exhibit 4.10) for several weeks before treatment begins, as well as during the course of treatment. The diaries that are completed before treatment are used to establish the baseline frequency of attacks.

In addition to symptom diaries, we describe other forms of behavioral assessment, including the behavioral approach test (BAT) and the fear and avoidance hierarchy. If a BAT is to be used, it will probably be administered before treatment begins. Typically, the BAT takes only 5 to 30 minutes and is easy to combine with part of the clinical interview or at the start of the first treatment session. As is discussed later in this chapter, we recommend that the BAT be repeated periodically throughout treatment. Usually, exposure-based treatments begin by the therapist and patient developing a fear and avoidance hierarchy. This can be done during the initial assessment or after treatment has begun, immediately before starting exposure. In the rest of this chapter, we provide detailed descriptions of each major assessment strategy that is typically used in the evaluation of people suffering from phobic disorders. We start this discussion with an overview of the diagnostic assessment process.

DIAGNOSTIC ASSESSMENT

The purpose of diagnostic assessment is to establish an appropriate diagnosis and rule out diagnoses that do not apply to a particular individual. Although diagnostic assessment is often conducted during the course of an unstructured clinical interview, we recommend the use of a structured or (preferably) a semistructured clinical interview. Previous studies have shown that about a third of diagnostic disagreements are related to inconsistencies on the part of the diagnostician, as opposed to inadequacies of the diagnostic criteria (for a review, see Blanchard & Brown, 1998). Structured and semistructured interviews limit the extent to which diagnostic assessment methods vary across clinicians, thereby improving diagnostic reliability. In fact, in a recent National Institute of Mental Health consensus development conference on the treatment of panic disorder (PD), it was recommended that all research on the treatment of PD include a structured or semistructured interview (Shear & Maser, 1994).

Structured and Semistructured Diagnostic Interviews

Structured and semistructured diagnostic interviews include detailed questions that help the diagnostician assess the relevant criteria for a variety of psychological disorders. Compared with unstructured interviews, they ensure that the clinician remembers to ask about a more complete range of psychological problems and also protect against the possibility of forgetting to ask about important diagnostic criteria for a particular disorder. For each psychological problem assessed by the interview, questioning begins with a general screening probe. For example, for social phobia, the screening questions might address whether the individual experiences excessive fear in certain social situations such as public speaking, meeting new people, or eating in front of others. For patients who answer affirmatively to the screening question, the clinician continues to ask specific questions to assess the other diagnostic criteria for the disorder. For patients who respond negatively to the screening question, the clinician may skip to the next section in the interview. Although fully structured and semistructured interviews are both often referred to as structured interviews, there are important differences between these approaches, and we prefer to distinguish between them.

Structured interviews have been developed generally for use in large epidemiological studies. They are designed to be administered by trained lay interviewers and have often been adapted for administration by computers. Questions regarding diagnostic criteria are asked exactly as written, and additional questions to follow up on patients' responses are not permitted (except for limited number of specific follow-up questions that are specified in the interview). An important difference between a fully structured and semistructured interview is the degree to which the clinician is permitted to ask follow-up questions to clarify responses given by the patient.

Semistructured interviews have been developed primarily for use in clinical research settings. Like structured interviews, semistructured diagnostic interviews require that the clinician initially ask the required questions exactly as written. However, semistructured questions may be followed up with unstructured questions to clarify information provided by the patient and to assist patients who may have misunderstood a question from the interview. Semistructured interviews are designed to be administered by experienced clinicians and are typically thought to be inappropriate for administration by lay interviewers.

Choosing among diagnostic interviews can be a complex task. As was reviewed by Blanchard and Brown (1998), interviews differ on many different dimensions including the following:

- the diagnostic system on which they are based
- the availability of up-to-date versions
- the availability of computerized versions
- the time needed for administration
- coverage of relevant disorders
- comprehensiveness of coverage for each disorder (e.g., Is each diagnostic criterion assessed? Are other associated features assessed?)
- how signs and symptoms are rated (e.g., dichotomous ratings of presence and absence vs. continuous ratings of severity)
- the degree to which lifetime diagnoses are assessed
- the population for which the instrument is designed
- the amount of training and experience needed to administer the interview
- the availability of manuals and training opportunities
- psychometric properties (e.g., reliability and validity)

Examples of commonly used diagnostic interviews are provided in Table 4.1.

In general, we recommend the use of semistructured interviews such as the Structured Clinical Interview for DSM-IV Axis I Disorders (SCID-IV; First et al., 1996) and the Anxiety Disorders Interview Schedule for DSM-IV (ADIS-IV; Di Nardo, Brown, & Barlow, 1994; see also Brown, Di Nardo, & Barlow, 1994) instead of structured interviews such as the Composite International Diagnostic Interview (CIDI; Robins et al., 1988; World

Table 4.1
Commonly Used Structured and Semistructured Interviews for
Diagnosing Phobic Disorders

Acronym	Title and sources
ADIS-IV	Anxiety Disorders Interview Schedule for DSM-IV
	Brown, Di Nardo, & Barlow, 1994 (lifetime version); Di Nardo, Brown, & Barlow, 1994
CIDI	Composite International Diagnostic Interview
	Robins et al., 1988; World Health Organization, 1990
DIS-IV	Diagnostic Interview Schedule, Version IV
	Robins, Cottler, Bucholz, & Compton, 1995
MINI	Mini-International Neuropsychiatric Interview
	Sheehan et al., 1998
PRIME-MD	Primary Care Evaluation of Mental Disorders
	Recently revised into a self-report version, Patient Health Questionnaire (PHQ)
	Spitzer et al., 1994
SADS-LA	Schedule for Affective Disorders and Schizophrenia—Lifetime Anxiety Version
	Fyer et al., 1989; Mannuzza et al., 1989
SCID-IV	Structured Clinical Interview for DSM-IV Axis I Disorders
	First, Gibbon, Spitzer, & Williams, 1996

Health Organization, 1990) and Version IV of the Diagnostic Interview Schedule (DIS-IV; Robins, Cottler, Bucholz, & Compton, 1995). Diagnoses assigned by a fully structured interview tend to have poor diagnostic agreement with semistructured interviews and have recently been shown to overdiagnose a number of disorders, compared with semistructured interviews conducted by expert clinicians (Antony, Downie, & Swinson, 1998; Ross, Swinson, Larkin, & Doumani, 1994). The ADIS-IV and SCID-IV have additional advantages over the other measures listed in Table 4.1. First, unlike several other instruments, they have been updated for the *DSM-IV*. Second, they are much more comprehensive than briefer measures such as the PRIME-MD and MINI[1], which do not provide as detailed an assessment of the *DSM* criteria for each anxiety disorder. Finally, the SCID-IV and ADIS-IV are the most commonly used and best studied measures among clinical researchers and other experts in the area of anxiety disorders for diagnosing anxiety-related problems.

Despite their advantages, the ADIS-IV and SCID-IV may not be appropriate for all settings. Compared with other measures, they are time consuming. In some primary care and managed care settings, briefer instru-

---

[1]Note that there is a more comprehensive version of the MINI called the MINI Plus. This version screens for more disorders and has more detailed questions for each disorder, compared to the standard version of the MINI.

ments may be more practical to administer. In addition, the ADIS-IV or SCID-IV can be administered in parts, focusing only on the modules that are of interest. Although the ADIS-IV and SCID-IV are both considered to be excellent for the purpose of diagnosing anxiety disorders, each has advantages over the other. The features of these measures are compared in Table 4.2.

Although we recommend that a semistructured clinical interview such as the ADIS-IV or SCID-IV be used to establish a *DSM-IV* diagnosis, we recognize that administering such an interview in its entirety is not always practical. If time does not allow for the use of a semistructured interview, the criteria for particular disorders can still be assessed in a systematic way during an unstructured clinical interview. We recommend that the clinician use questions similar to those in standardized interviews and bring notes to the assessment interview that can serve as reminders to ask all the relevant questions.

Differential Diagnosis

Panic disorder with agoraphobia (PDA), social phobia, and specific phobia are sometimes difficult to distinguish from one another and from other related problems. Although ambiguity in the *DSM-IV* may make it difficult to make a differential diagnosis at times, asking the right questions during the diagnostic interview can often help a clinician to tease apart the features of two or more problems to make an appropriate diagnosis. We provide guidelines here for distinguishing phobic disorders from one another and from other conditions. For a small number of individuals, making the distinction may be almost impossible, even for the experienced diagnostician. For others, differential diagnosis is fairly straightforward. Finally, in some cases multiple diagnoses may be appropriate. For example, an individual with PD who avoids flying in part because of his or her fear of having an unexpected panic attack and in part because he or she fears that the plane will crash may receive diagnoses of PDA and specific phobia, assuming that all the relevant criteria are met for both problems.

Panic disorder with agoraphobia

One of the most important questions in trying to determine whether an individual has PDA versus some other disorder is whether the individual has unexpected or uncued panic attacks. In anxiety disorders other than PDA, panic attacks tend to be cued by some situation or thought. In social phobia, panic attacks are associated exclusively with exposure to social situations. In specific phobia, panic attacks are associated exclusively with exposure to the feared object (e.g., a snake) or situation (e.g., flying in an airplane).

Table 4.2

Comparing the ADIS-IV and SCID-IV for the Diagnosis of Anxiety Disorders

ADIS-IV	SCID-IV
Versions available	
1. Standard version (current Axis I diagnoses only)	1. Axis I research version (includes current diagnoses for most disorders as well as lifetime diagnoses for a few disorders; comes in patient and nonpatient versions)
2. Lifetime version (includes current and lifetime Axis I diagnoses)	2. Axis I clinician version (shortened for clinical practice–less comprehensive coverage of diagnostic criteria)
	3. Axis II version (for personality disorders)
Time to administer	
2–4 hours (for lifetime version)	1–3 hours (for research version)
Format of symptom ratings	
Continuous ratings (using a Likert-type scale) for all symptoms	Symptoms are coded as absent, present at a clinical threshold, or present at a subclinical threshold.
Development and use	
Developed by psychologists and has tended to be more popular among psychological researchers (e.g., for cognitive–behavioral therapy trials) than among medical researchers. Suitable for diagnosing anxiety disorders in both psychological and medical settings.	Developed by psychiatrists and has tended to be more popular among medical researchers (e.g., for pharmacotherapy trials) than among psychological researchers. Suitable for diagnosing anxiety disorders in both psychological and medical settings.
Coverage of *DSM-IV* disorders	
Includes detailed diagnostic criteria for all anxiety disorders, mood disorders, somatoform disorders, and substance use disorders. Also includes screening questions for certain other disorders (e.g., psychotic disorders).	Research version includes detailed diagnostic criteria for all anxiety disorders, mood disorders, somatoform disorders, substance use disorders, and psychotic disorders. Also available with a psychotic screening module, which includes screening questions (instead of full diagnostic criteria) for psychotic disorders. SCID-IV includes more detailed questions than ADIS-IV regarding mood disorder specifiers (e.g., atypical depression, melancholic depression, etc.).

(continued)

Table 4.2
(Continued)

ADIS-IV	SCID-IV
Comprehensiveness of anxiety disorders sections	
Much more comprehensive than the SCID-IV. Includes detailed questions about a broader range of specific phobias and agoraphobia and social phobia situations. Also includes detailed questions regarding etiology, age of onset, panic frequency, and other relevant variables.	Research version assesses all diagnostic criteria but very few additional variables. In addition, screening questions for agoraphobia, social phobia, and specific phobia ask about a relatively small number of situations. For example, specific phobias of driving, storms, or water are unlikely to be picked up by the SCID-IV. Also, the social phobia screening question is more likely to identify people with performance-related fears (e.g., public speaking) than with interpersonal fears (e.g., fears of meeting new people, parties, casual conversation).
Manuals and training tapes	
Manual and training tapes are available.	Manual and training tapes are available.
Psychometric properties	
There are no published studies on the current DSM-IV version. However, previous versions for the DSM-III (Di Nardo, O'Brien, Barlow, Waddell, & Blanchard, 1983) and the DSM-III-R (Di Nardo, Moras, Barlow, Rapee, & Brown, 1993) have been shown to be reliable, particularly for phobic disorders.	There are no published studies on the current DSM-IV version. However, previous versions for the DSM-III (Williams, Spitzer, & Gibbon, 1992) and DSM-III-R (Segal, Hersen, & van Hasselt, 1994; Skre, Onstad, Torgersen, & Kringlen, 1991; Spitzer, Williams, Gibbon, & First, 1992; Williams, Gibbon, et al., 1992) have been shown to be reliable, particularly for phobic disorders.

Panic attacks may also be triggered by thoughts. For example, in generalized anxiety disorder (GAD), panic attacks are cued by worries about finances, family, work, or some other topic. In obsessive–compulsive disorder (OCD), panic attacks may be triggered by an obsession or the inability to perform a compulsion. These would not be considered to be uncued panic attacks because they are triggered by thoughts that are associated with another disorder. If you suspect that a patient has GAD, a helpful question to ask is, "Do you ever have panic attacks when you are not worrying about . . . ?"

As is discussed in chapter 1, proponents of the cognitive model of panic disorder argue that most panic attacks that are perceived by patients to be uncued are actually cued by benign physical sensations such as dizziness, palpitations, or shortness of breath. Differential diagnosis can be complicated by the fact that some patients with PDA are aware of the internal triggers for their uncued panic attacks. When assessing for the presence of uncued panic attacks, it can be helpful to ask about the individual's first few attacks, before he or she recognized the connection between the panic attacks and the feared physical sensations that trigger them.

The clinician should be careful to distinguish the panic attacks experienced by people with PD from those experienced by people with hypochondriasis. In both conditions, panic attacks are often triggered by benign physical sensations. Unlike in PD, anxiety in hypochondriasis is focused on the possibility of developing a serious physical illness (e.g., cancer or multiple sclerosis), rather than the possibility of having another panic attack. In addition, people with hypochondriasis often are fearful of symptoms that are not typically associated with panic attacks (e.g., headaches may be interpreted as a sign of a brain tumor). Finally, agoraphobic avoidance is not typically reported by people with hypochondriasis.

Panic attacks are associated with all of the anxiety disorders, as well as a range of other problems (e.g., depression, somatoform disorders, eating disorders, psychotic disorders, etc.). In fact, even uncued panic attacks may occur from time to time in conditions other than PD and in people with no particular *DSM-IV* diagnosis (e.g., individuals with nonclinical panic attacks). An individual who is depressed may have occasional uncued panic attacks that tend to go away as the depression remits. However, unlike people with PD, people with depression alone are unlikely to report worrying about the consequences of the panic attacks, worrying about having more panic attacks, or changing their behavior because of the panic attacks. In case of uncertainty, helpful questions to ask the patient include "Do the rushes of panic frighten you?" and "Do you worry about having more panic attacks?"

Keep in mind that people with PDA and people with certain other disorders may avoid similar situations. In order to choose the most appropriate treatment for a given individual, it is important to differentiate PDA from other phobic disorders, such as social phobia and specific phobias. When delivering cognitive–behavioral therapy (CBT), for example, the specific types of situations and thoughts that are targeted during treatment typically depend on the full range of situations that are feared or avoided by the individual, as well as the reasons for which the person avoids situations.

Many people with PDA avoid social situations because they fear that they may have a panic attack in front of other people. However, unlike people with social phobia, they also have panic attacks that are uncued and often experience attacks that are cued by places other than social situations. Similarly, people with social phobia often avoid situations that are often associated with agoraphobia (e.g., crowded places, malls, or public transportation). However, for them, it is exclusively the social aspects of these situations (e.g., looking unattractive, making a mistake, or having other people evaluate them in a negative way) that are frightening. Furthermore, unlike in PDA, panic attacks tend not to happen when an individual with social phobia is alone. Helpful questions for distinguishing between PDA and social phobia include "What are you afraid will happen if you are exposed to . . . ?" and "Are you fearful of being judged in social situations for reasons other than looking anxious, such as appearing unattractive, incompetent, or boring?"

As is the case with social phobia, people with specific phobias may avoid similar situations (e.g., flying or driving) as do some people with agoraphobia. However, there are two important differences between PDA and specific phobias. First, people with PDA have uncued and unexpected panic attacks outside the phobic situation. Second, people with PDA often report having different reasons for avoiding these situations than do people with specific phobias. For example, a typical specific phobia of flying is usually related to a fear of the plane crashing, whereas a typical agoraphobic fear of flying is associated with a fear of having a panic attack and not being able to escape (McNally & Louro, 1992). Helpful questions to distinguish PDA from specific phobias include "Do you ever have panic attacks in situations other than . . . ?" and "What are you afraid might happen if you are exposed to . . . ?"

It can be particularly difficult to decide between PDA and a specific phobia of enclosed places (claustrophobia). As is the case in PDA, people with claustrophobia tend to be fearful of the sensations they experience (e.g., breathlessness) and of not being able to escape. However, people with claustrophobia tend to report having panic attacks only when exposed to enclosed places, whereas people with PDA report panic attacks in other situations as well.

Another condition that shares features with PDA is agoraphobia without history of panic disorder (AWOPD). People with AWOPD often avoid similar situations as do people with PDA and typically avoid these situations for similar reasons (e.g., a fear of having a panic-like reaction or experiencing uncomfortable physical sensations). However, people with AWOPD do not meet the criteria for PDA, usually because they do not experience unexpected or uncued panic attacks, as defined in the *DSM-IV*. For example, for some patients the panic-like episodes include only three symptoms instead of the minimum of four that is needed to diagnose panic attack. For other individuals, the panic-like episodes may peak over a period longer than the maximum of 10 minutes that is allowed in the definition of a panic attack.

A diagnosis of anxiety disorder, not otherwise specified, may also be appropriate for some patients who have panic-like episodes that do not meet criteria for panic attacks. An example would be a person who is not agoraphobic (therefore not meeting criteria for AWOPD) but is still fearful of having episodes of fear that are associated with dizziness and palpitations but has no other associated symptoms. Undifferentiated somatoform disorder may also be an appropriate diagnosis for such an individual. Finally, one should consider giving a diagnosis of anxiety disorder caused by substance use or by a medical condition for cases in which it seems likely that the symptoms of PD are all accounted for by a psychoactive substance (e.g., caffeine) or a medical condition that directly causes panic-like episodes (e.g., hyperthyroidism).

Social phobia

It is easy to confuse social phobia with other psychological disorders. As was reviewed earlier, social phobia can be mistaken for PDA and vice versa. Social phobia may also be difficult to distinguish from depression, body dysmorphic disorder, certain personality disorders (e.g., avoidant personality disorder or schizoid personality disorder), and other conditions that are associated with social anxiety (e.g., eating disorders or OCD). Social phobia may also be misdiagnosed in people who have subclinical fears of public speaking or other social situations.

An important rule to remember is that social phobia should not be diagnosed in people whose social anxiety is exclusively related to having the symptoms of another psychological or medical condition that is noticed by other people. For example, a man who fears socializing exclusively because other people might notice his stuttering would not receive a diagnosis of social phobia, nor would a woman with an eating disorder who is fearful of eating in front of others because they might notice her peculiar eating habits. People with OCD sometimes avoid socializing for fear of being ridiculed for performing certain compulsions. However, such an individual would not receive a diagnosis of social phobia unless he or she also feared being judged negatively for other reasons (e.g., being boring, unattractive, etc.). Finally, an individual with body dysmorphic disorder would not receive a diagnosis of social phobia if he or she were fearful of social situations only because other people might notice some (imagined) defect in his or her appearance. Helpful questions to ask include "What are you afraid might happen if you are exposed to . . . ?" and "Are you afraid of doing . . . for reasons other than . . . ?"

An important difference between the avoidance of social situations in depression and social phobia is that people who are depressed are often not particularly interested in socializing. Furthermore, their interest in socializing typically returns when the depression remits. In contrast, the typical person with social phobia avoids socializing because of fear rather than a lack of interest per se. Questions that are helpful for making this distinction include "Do you enjoy socializing when you are not feeling depressed?" and "If you were sure that others would enjoy your company and think highly of you, would you be more interested in socializing?"

As with depression, schizoid personality disorder can sometimes be mistaken for social phobia. However, unlike social phobia, schizoid personality disorder is associated with a tendency to be indifferent to praise and criticism from others, as well as a genuine lack of interest in becoming more comfortable around other people. In contrast, people with social phobia are likely to be very sensitive to being criticized and would prefer to be more comfortable around others.

Clinicians often wonder how to distinguish social phobia from avoidant personality disorder. Research on this topic suggests that this particular distinction is neither useful nor practical in many cases. Studies of the relationship between these two conditions have generally shown that they differ primarily in severity and not in quality (e.g., Widiger, 1992). Most people with avoidant personality disorder also tend to have social phobia, and both conditions tend to respond to similar treatments. However, individuals with avoidant personality disorder often display more interpersonal sensitivity and have poorer social skills than do socially phobic patients without avoidant personality disorder (Turner, Beidel, Dancu, & Keys, 1986).

Finally, social phobia should be distinguished from normal states of fear and anxiety. Many individuals report mild shyness in certain social situations or intense fears of public speaking that neither bothers them particularly nor causes significant interference in their day-to-day lives. To meet criteria for social phobia, an individual must report significant distress over having the fear or must report significant interference in his or her work, social life, or leisure activities.

Specific phobia

In an earlier section, we discussed strategies for distinguishing between certain specific phobias (e.g., fears of flying, driving, and enclosed places) and PDA. Certain specific phobias may also be mistaken for OCD, posttraumatic stress disorder (PTSD), eating disorders, or hypochondriasis. Finally, it is important to distinguish between a true specific phobia (one that either bothers an individual or causes clinically significant impairment) and subthreshold fears that can sometimes be quite severe but still not meet criteria for specific phobia (e.g., a person who is terrified of snakes but never encounters them and rarely even thinks about them).

In some individuals, specific phobia may be difficult to distinguish from OCD. For example, we recently treated a patient with contamination obsessions who also was terrified of snakes. Although we initially thought she had a specific phobia of snakes, it turned out that her fear of snakes was better accounted for by her fear of contamination. Snakes were in fact one of many different objects that she believed were contaminated.

Some forms of PTSD can also be confused with specific phobias. For example, although some people develop PTSD following a serious automobile accident, others may develop a specific phobia of driving. Both conditions are typically associated with avoidance of driving. However, whereas PTSD is associated with reexperiencing symptoms (e.g., having nightmares about the crash, flashbacks, or intrusive memories), specific phobias are typically not. Finally, careful questioning should be used to distinguish between medical phobias and hypochondriasis (both conditions may be associated with avoidance of doctors and hospitals, but for different reasons) and between eating disorders and choking phobias (both disorders may be associated with avoidance of certain foods).

The Relationship Between Diagnosis and Treatment

The particular diagnosis assigned to a patient should inform the clinician's decisions and expectations regarding treatment. For example (as is reviewed in chapters 1–3), although tricyclic antidepressants have been shown to be helpful for PD, they are not particularly useful for the treatment of social phobia or specific phobias. In contrast, selective serotonin reuptake inhibitors are often effective for treating either PD or social phobia, but there is little evidence regarding their usefulness for treating specific phobias. Diagnostic factors should also influence the selection of cognitive and behavioral strategies. Whereas the combination of cognitive and exposure-based techniques are often used for the treatment of PD and social phobia, exposure alone is more likely to be used with specific phobias.

In addition to diagnostic factors, treatment decisions should also take into account the specific features of the disorder. For example, applied muscle tension (see chapter 8) is likely to be helpful for individuals with blood or injection phobias who have a history of fainting in the phobic situation but not for those without a history of fainting. Similarly, although interoceptive exposure (see chapter 6) is useful for people who are fearful of the sensations they experience when anxious (regardless of diagnosis), exposure to internal cues is not particularly relevant for phobic patients who are not fearful of experiencing panic attacks or uncomfortable physical sensations. Finally, as is reviewed in chapter 8, choice of medications is often determined by the profile of symptoms reported by a patient. For example, an individual with PD who experiences severe dizziness during panic attacks and wishes to be treated with pharmacotherapy should not be given a medication for which dizziness is likely to be a side effect.

Choosing among problems to be treated

Most people with anxiety disorders typically meet diagnostic criteria for more than one disorder. Therefore, the clinician and patient often must make a decision regarding which problem to work on first. The following are questions that should be answered before making the decision:

- Which problem causes the most impairment (e.g., interference with work, social life, domestic responsibilities, leisure activities, etc.)?
- Which problem is most distressing to the patient?
- Which problem does the patient want most to work on first?
- Which problem is most likely to respond quickly to treatment?
- What is the functional relationship among the problems (e.g., is one problem causing an exacerbation of the other?)?
- Are there treatments that are more likely to lead to improvement in several or all of the conditions simultaneously?
- Is one problem likely to interfere with the treatment of one or more of the other problems?

Depending on the responses to these questions, the clinician may decide to treat one problem first or to target several problems simultaneously. In general, the problems that should be worked on first are those that are most impairing and distressing, those that the patient is most motivated to work on, those that are likely to respond to treatment, and those for which treatment is most likely to have a positive impact on associated problems. For example, there is evidence that for people with a principal diagnosis of PD who also have GAD, treating the PD alone tends to lead to significant improvement in the symptoms of GAD (Brown, Antony, & Barlow, 1995).

In some cases, the decision of which problem to treat first can be quite complex. For example, individuals with social phobia who also abuse alcohol often drink to reduce their anxiety. Treating the alcohol abuse may be ineffective if the treatment ignores the social anxiety that appears to be underlying the drinking. Conversely, attempting to treat the social anxiety alone may be problematic if the patient is unable to complete homework assignments because of his or her drinking or if the patient attends treatment sessions while intoxicated. For such a patient, it might be important to treat the alcohol abuse and social phobia simultaneously.

UNSTRUCTURED CLINICAL INTERVIEWS

Perhaps the most commonly used method of collecting information in clinical practice is the unstructured clinical interview. Although a formal interview often occurs at the start of treatment, the interview process should continue throughout treatment so that the clinician can assess changes in symptoms and other features of the problem. One purpose of the unstructured clinical interview is to establish a differential diagnosis in cases where a semistructured interview cannot be administered. Exhibit 4.1 summarizes the variables that should be assessed during an unstructured interview with patients suffering from a phobic disorder. A more detailed description of these factors follows, with the exception of differential diagnosis, which was discussed earlier in the chapter.

Development and Course of the Problem

Generally, CBTs pay more attention to the factors responsible for maintaining the disorder than to those initially responsible for causing the problem. Nevertheless, it is often helpful for the clinician to obtain information regarding the early developmental factors that may have contributed to the development of the disorder. Understanding the role of

Exhibit 4.1
Variables to Assess During an Unstructured Clinical Interview

---

- Diagnostic criteria for relevant *DSM-IV* disorders (differential diagnosis)
- Development and course of problem
- Impact on functioning
- Pattern of physical symptoms
- Cognitions, beliefs, predictions, and cognitive biases
- Focus of apprehension (e.g., internal vs. external)
- Patterns of overt avoidance
- Subtle avoidance strategies (e.g., distraction, overprotective behaviors, safety signals)
- Parameters of the fear (i.e., variables affecting fear)
- Family factors and social supports (e.g., family history of the problem; family accommodation; potential for family and friends to help with treatment)
- Treatment history
- Skills deficits (e.g., communication skills, driving skills)
- Medical history and physical limitations

---

stressful life events, traumatic experiences, early parenting, and other developmental factors can help the clinician and patient to have a better understanding of how the problem began, thereby setting the stage for changing the thoughts and behaviors that currently maintain the problem. Having information about the development of a problem can also be helpful for making differential diagnoses. For example, if panic attack symptoms began only around the time that a patient began to use cocaine and improved after the cocaine use stopped, a diagnosis of PD may not be appropriate because of the probable role of the cocaine use.

Understanding the course of the problem provides a context in which to interpret changes that occur during treatment. If a patient's symptom course has been steady and constant for many years, changes that occur during treatment can more confidently be attributed to the treatment. It may be more difficult, however, to know whether changes are in fact related to treatment for a patient whose course fluctuates from week to week or from month to month. Single-case experimental methods (e.g., taking baseline measures or withdrawing treatment) can be used to increase confidence that changes occurring during the course of treatment are in fact related to treatment rather than to extraneous variables (for a review, see Hayes, Barlow, & Nelson-Gray, 1999).

Impact on Functioning and Pattern of Physical Symptoms

To understand the day-to-day impact of a particular disorder, questions should be asked about the ways in which a problem interferes with various life domains such as work, relationships, hobbies, leisure activities, socializing, diet, exercise, and other areas of functioning. The patient should also be asked about the types of symptoms experienced during periods of elevated anxiety and fear. For example, people with PD should be asked about the frequency of their panic attacks and the typical symptoms that occur during their attacks. People with social phobia should be asked about the physical symptoms that they experience during exposure to social situations, particularly about those symptoms that are likely to be noticed by others (e.g., shaking, sweating, blushing, shaky voice, losing train of thought, etc.). People with specific phobias should also describe the physical sensations that they experience. Individuals with blood and injection phobias should be asked whether they have ever fainted in the phobic situation and about symptoms associated with fainting (e.g., light-headedness). People with other specific phobias should be asked about the presence of panic attacks in the phobic situation and about particular physical sensations that they find disturbing. For example, people who are claustrophobic often are concerned about feeling breathless in claustrophobic situations.

Cognitions, Beliefs, Predictions, and Cognitive Biases

The interview should include questions to assess a patient's beliefs, expectations, and predictions regarding the phobic situation. Examples of open-ended questions are listed in Exhibit 4.2. Open-ended questions may be followed up with closed-ended questions to assess other common beliefs that are associated with the particular disorder. See chapter 7 for examples of beliefs that are often associated with phobic disorders.

In addition to asking questions about thoughts and beliefs, it is also helpful to assess the extent to which a patient has specific information-processing biases that are likely to lead to problems such as repeatedly confirming anxious beliefs or causing heightened fear. Examples of information-processing biases include the tendency for patients with PD to scan their bodies for uncomfortable sensations, the tendency for socially phobic individuals to interpret ambiguous social cues (e.g., a friend wanting to get off the telephone) as evidence that the other person is judging them in a negative way, and the tendency of people with specific phobias of flying to

---

Exhibit 4.2
Examples of Open-Ended Questions to Assess Fearful Beliefs
and Cognitions

Panic Disorder and Agoraphobia
- What do you think might happen if you have a panic attack?
- What are you afraid will happen if you can't leave the theater?
- What might happen if you feel anxious while driving?
- When you are experiencing panic symptoms, what do you imagine will happen?
- If you were alone and began to feel anxious, what might happen to you?

Social Phobia
- What do you imagine happening when you ask a question in class?
- What might people think of you if you stumble on your words during a presentation?
- If people notice your blushing, why would that be a problem? What might they think?
- What frightens you about meeting new people?
- Do you have any frightening images of what might occur if you ask someone out on a date?

Specific Phobia
- What if you looked down and noticed a spider on your arm? What might happen to you?
- What do you fear might happen to you on an airplane?
- What thought bothers you the most when you imagine getting an injection?
- Imagine getting stuck on an elevator. Why would that be a problem?
- When you are on a high ledge, what do you imagine happening? Falling? Jumping? Being pushed?

---

pay much more attention to information about airplanes that crash (e.g., from media coverage) than to airplanes that arrive at their destination safely (e.g., from statistical information about the number flights that occur each year).

Focus of Apprehension

It is helpful to assess the extent to which a patient's fear is focused on his or her reaction to the situation versus aspects of the situation itself. For people with PDA, anxiety is primarily focused internally, on the possibility of experiencing a panic attack, on uncomfortable physical sensations, or on some physical (e.g., a heart attack) or emotional catastrophe (e.g., losing control or going crazy). Rather than fearing possible threats arising from the situation itself, people with agoraphobia tend to be more fearful of their own reaction to being in the agoraphobic situation.

In social and specific phobias, the focus of fear is likely to include concerns about the situation itself (e.g., being bitten by a dog or being struck by lightening), as well as concerns about one's reaction to the situation (e.g., jumping from a high place). A man with social phobia might fear that others will find him to be boring, unattractive, or incompetent. However, he might also believe that his own anxious reaction to social situations (e.g., blushing or shaking) may increase the likelihood of others to form negative judgments about him. Similarly, a woman with a specific phobia of elevators may be fearful of the elevator getting stuck or falling, but she may also fear losing control and embarrassing herself on the elevator.

The extent to which an individual is fearful of his or her own reactions to the phobic situation will influence the treatment strategies that are recommended. For example, hyperventilation exercises (a method of exposing an individual to feelings of lightheadedness and other uncomfortable feelings) may be helpful to a person who is fearful of fainting in enclosed places. Some questions that may be used to assess patients' focus of apprehension include "Are you fearful of the physical sensations that you experience in the situation?" and "Do you worry that something terrible might happen if your anxiety gets too high?"

Patterns of Overt Avoidance

It is essential that the assessment generate a detailed list of situations that are avoided by a patient so that appropriate exposure practices can assigned. In addition to asking open-ended questions such as "Are there situations that you avoid because of your fear?" we recommend that the clinician ask the patient to rate his or her fear and avoidance of particular

Exhibit 4.3
Situations Avoided by Individuals With Panic Disorder and Agoraphobia

- Shopping (e.g., malls, supermarkets, department stores)
- Driving (e.g., highway driving, city driving, being a passenger)
- Walking or driving over a bridge
- Public transportation (e.g., buses, trains)
- Flying in an airplane
- Crowded places (e.g., sports events, concerts)
- Enclosed places (e.g., elevators, tunnels, small rooms)
- Being far from home
- Eating in restaurants
- Theaters (e.g., movies, live theater)
- Museums and galleries
- Arousing activities (e.g., sex, exercise, amusement park rides)
- Standing in long lines
- Going for walks
- Situations that are difficult to leave (e.g., going to the dentist, getting a haircut)
- Areas that are far from a public washroom, exit, pay telephone, or some other safety cue
- Being at home alone

situations that are likely to be problematic. Exhibit 4.3 lists examples of situations that individuals suffering from PDA might avoid, and Exhibit 4.4 provides a similar list for specific phobias of heights. Similar lists for each of the main specific phobia types are available elsewhere (Antony, Craske, & Barlow, 1995). For ideas regarding situations avoided by people with social phobia, see the section in chapter 6 on exposure practices.

Exhibit 4.4
Situations Avoided by Individuals With a Specific Phobia of Heights

- Balconies and windows in tall buildings
- Sitting in the upper levels of a theater or sports stadium
- Escalators, glass elevators, open stairs (e.g., a fire escape)
- Standing near railings (e.g., on the upper level of a shopping mall)
- Careers involving high places (e.g., construction)
- Standing on chairs or ladders (e.g., to change light bulbs)
- Fixing the roof
- Walking or driving over bridges or elevated roads (e.g., highway ramps)
- Flying in airplanes
- Mountain climbing and hiking in elevated areas (e.g., near cliffs)
- Skiing, parachuting, diving off diving boards, and other sports involving high places
- Amusement park rides (e.g., Ferris wheel)
- Watching people in high places (e.g., in-person or on film)
- Looking up at the sky or at the tops of sky scrapers

Exhibit 4.5
Subtle Avoidance Strategies and Related Behaviors in Individuals
With Phobic Disorders

Panic Disorder and Agoraphobia
• Carrying medication, money, cellular telephone, pager, water, or other safety cues
• Always knowing where one's spouse is
• Insisting on being accompanied when leaving the house
• Sitting near exits when at the movies or at a restaurant
• Checking one's pulse or blood pressure
• Distraction (e.g., reading a book on the subway)
• Avoiding caffeine, alcohol, or other substances

Social Phobia
• Wearing a turtleneck shirt to hide blushing on the neck
• Making an excuse to leave a party early
• Avoiding eye contact
• Overcompensating by memorizing a presentation
• Avoiding certain topics of conversation
• Having several glasses of wine before going to a party
• Dimming the lights when eating with friends
• Spending most of the evening (during a party) preparing food and cleaning up
  rather than socializing with the guests
• Arriving at a store with a check already filled out, to avoid writing in public

Specific Phobias
• Wearing long pants so that spiders will not crawl on legs
• Sitting away from the window during a thunderstorm
• Driving only at certain times, in certain lanes, or on certain roads
• Requesting particular "safe" seats on an airplane
• Riding only on glass elevators to avoid feeling closed in
• Carrying pepper spray in case of being attacked by a dog
• Checking the neighborhood for birds before walking from the house to the car
• Closing eyes during films that have scenes involving surgery

Subtle Avoidance Strategies

For the purpose of designing appropriate exposure practices, it is important to identify the ways in which a patient engages in subtle avoidance,
overprotective behaviors, and overreliance on safety cues. These coping
strategies may be identified by asking the patient questions such as "Are
there things that you do or things that you carry with you to feel more
comfortable when you are on an airplane?" or "When you visit a friend who
has a dog, are there things that you do to protect yourself?" Exhibit 4.5 lists
examples of subtle avoidance strategies.

Parameters of the Fear

Identifying the variables that affect an individual's fear is important
for the purpose of developing an exposure hierarchy and for implementing

exposure-based treatments. As an illustration, Exhibit 4.6 includes a list of variables that can affect fear and anxiety among individuals with social phobia. Comparable lists are available elsewhere for each of the main specific phobia types (Antony, Craske, & Barlow, 1995). Similar lists can be generated for patients with PDA.

Family Factors and Social Supports

It may be helpful to find out if a patient has family members who suffer from the same anxiety disorder or another anxiety-related problem. In addition, family-related variables that are relevant to the etiology and treatment of the presenting problem should be assessed. This is particularly

Exhibit 4.6
Variables Affecting Fear Among Individuals With Social Phobia

Aspects of the Target Person
- Age (e.g., older, younger, same age)
- Gender (e.g., same sex, opposite sex)
- Relationship status (e.g., married, single)
- Relation (e.g., supervisor, coworker, employee)
- Physical attractiveness
- Nationality or ethnicity
- Perceived confidence of the individual
- Perceived aggressiveness or pushiness
- Perceived intelligence
- Perceived social status or income

Relationship With the Target Person
- Level of intimacy between patient and target person
- Familiarity (e.g., stranger vs. family member) of the target person to the patient
- History of hostility between patient and target person

Aspects of the Patient
- Fatigue
- Familiarity with the material being discussed or presented
- General life stress at the time of exposure

Aspects of the Situation
- Lighting
- Formality of the situation (e.g., eating at a wedding reception vs. a casual dinner with friends)
- Number of people involved (presenting to a few coworkers vs. a filled auditorium)
- Activity involved (e.g., eating, speaking, writing, etc.)
- Position (e.g., seated, standing, etc.)
- Ability to use alcohol or drugs
- Duration of exposure
- Other details specific to the situation (e.g., eating messy vs. clean foods when on a date)

important in families where there has been significant accommodation to a patient's anxiety symptoms (e.g., engaging in behaviors that make it easier for a patient to continue to avoid the feared objects or situations). Examples of ways in which family members might have contributed to the etiology or maintenance of phobic disorders include the following:

- Parents were overly critical and had unreasonably high standards—they may have contributed to the patient's social anxiety and concern about being judged negatively by others.
- Parents were overprotective during the patient's childhood—they may have contributed to the patient's fear of exploring new situations.
- Parents continually told the patient to be careful when driving—they may have contributed to the patient's fear of driving as an adult.
- The patient's spouse has taken over most of the family responsibilities outside the home (e.g., shopping, driving, running errands, etc.)—making it easier for the patient to continue to avoid these situations.
- The patient relies on his or her children to check the basement for spiders before going downstairs—an avoidance of the basement helps to maintain the patient's spider phobia.
- The patient insists that his or her spouse carry a pager so that he or she can be reached at any time in the event of a panic attack—thus maintaining the patient's belief that he or she cannot be alone during a panic attack.

Finally, it can be useful to assess the extent to which the patient has family members or other support people who can help with the treatment process (e.g., accompanying agoraphobic patients during exposure practices or gathering spiders for a spider phobic individual to be used during exposure practices).

Treatment History

A careful assessment of the previous treatments tried by a patient, as well as the response to these treatments, can be helpful in deciding which treatments to administer. If a treatment has not worked in the past, an alternative treatment could be tried. Similarly, a treatment that has worked in the past might be attempted again. Clinicians should not assume that because a patient reports having received a treatment previously that the treatment was delivered competently, at an adequate dosage, and for an adequate duration. Patients are often treated with medications at dosages that are too low to be effective or for too brief a period. Similarly, patients will often report having had "behavior therapy" for a phobia, when in fact treatment may have included only biofeedback or relaxation training, neither of which are especially helpful for people suffering from phobic disorders.

Skills Deficits

It is important to establish whether a patient has any significant skills deficits that could be contributing to his or her fear. For example, in the case of social phobia, an individual with interpersonal skills deficits (e.g., lack of assertiveness, poor eye contact, or poor conversation skills) may require social skills training in addition to exposure-based and cognitive treatments. Similarly, an individual with a driving phobia who also has poor driving skills (perhaps because of a lack of experience and practice) may require driving lessons in addition to CBT.

Medical Conditions and Physical Limitations

Certain medical conditions may affect the treatment of patients with phobic disorders. We recommend that a patient's medical history and current physical status be assessed carefully. When the possibility of a relevant medical condition seems likely, a patient should obtain permission from his or her physician before engaging in any treatment procedures that might be dangerous. Illustrations of how medical conditions can affect treatment include the following:

- Blood-phobic patients with a cardiac condition that makes it dangerous for them to experience a significant drop in blood pressure should not be exposed to situations in which they are likely to faint.
- Certain medical conditions (e.g., seizure disorders, heart disease, back and neck injuries) may interfere with a patient's ability to safely engage in symptom-induction exercises to overcome a fear of panic sensations.
- Certain medical conditions (e.g., epilepsy or organic brain disorders) may interfere with a driving-phobic patient's ability to drive safely.
- Certain medical conditions and possible drug interactions may affect the types of medications that a patient can take for his or her anxiety problem.
- Some patients with phobias of blood tests have very small veins that make it difficult and painful for them to have blood taken.
- Vestibular disorders may affect a height-phobic patient's ability to safely conduct exposure practices in high places.

Behavioral and Medical Assessment

Behavioral assessment provides an opportunity for the clinician to obtain additional information over and above what can be obtained from interviews and self-report scales. Because patients often avoid the situations that they fear, they may not be able to recall the specific symptoms, thoughts, and behaviors that they typically experience during exposure to feared objects and situations. Assessing these and other variables during actual exposure to the situation increases the likelihood of obtaining accurate information. Furthermore, it gives the clinician the opportunity to corroborate information previously provided by the patient and to notice behaviors of which the patient may be unaware.

The most commonly used form of behavioral assessment for phobic disorders is the behavioral approach test (BAT). During the BAT, the patient is asked to enter a feared situation or approach a feared situation while his or her reactions are measured. The specific content of the BAT can be selected in a number of ways. For example, the progressive BAT involves having a patient engage in progressively more difficult steps involving exposure to a feared object. Steps may be selected from a standard hierarchy or from a hierarchy developed especially for the patient. For this type of BAT, the variables to be assessed may include how close the patient can get to the feared object, the number of steps that the patient is able to complete, the patient's fear level at each step, the types of thoughts and behaviors that occur at each step of the assessment, and perhaps the patient's psychophysiological reaction (e.g., heart rate). Typically, fear levels are measured using a Likert-type scale called the subjective units of discomfort scale (SUDS). Using this procedure, the patient rates his or her level of discomfort, fear, or anxiety on a scale of 0 (*no discomfort*) to 100 (*as uncomfortable as can be imagined*), where 50 = *moderately uncomfortable*. It is also common to use a scale other than 0–100 (e.g., 0–8, 0–10, etc.). An example of a progressive BAT hierarchy for a patient with a specific phobia of spiders is provided in Exhibit 4.7.

Some problems may lend themselves to a selective BAT, an alternative to the progressive BAT in which the clinician selects particular situations from a list or hierarchy and asks the patient to enter them while his or her reactions are measured. For example, in social phobia the BAT may involve a behavioral exercise in which the individual is asked to role-play one or more specific social interactions (e.g., a presentation, a job interview, a casual conversation, etc.) while paying attention to his or her thoughts, feelings, and behaviors. BATs for agoraphobia may also involve having a patient enter one or more situations from a list of feared situations while measuring his or her reactions. Situations selected for the BAT can involve those from the top of the hierarchy or from several different places on the

Exhibit 4.7
Steps in a Behavioral Approach Test for a Specific Phobia of Spiders

1. Walk toward a spider in the glass jar (placed on a table).	Fear (0–100) _____
2. Closest distance from the spider: _____ cm	Fear (0–100) _____
3. Touch the glass jar (for at least 10 seconds).	Fear (0–100) _____
4. Lift the jar (for at least 10 seconds).	Fear (0–100) _____
5. Remove the cover from the jar.	Fear (0–100) _____
6. Touch the spider with a pencil (for at least 10 seconds).	Fear (0–100) _____
7. Put the spider in a plastic tub.	Fear (0–100) _____
8. Touch the spider with your finger (for at least 10 seconds).	Fear (0–100) _____
9. Let the spider walk on your hand (for at least 10 seconds).	Fear (0–100) _____

hierarchy (e.g., one from near the top, one from near the bottom, and one from the middle). They may also include a specific challenge test such as asking a patient with PD to hyperventilate for 90 seconds or to undergo some other panic-induction procedure (see chapters 1 and 6).

As with the progressive BAT, a number of variables may be measured during the selective BAT, including physical symptoms reported, anxious automatic thoughts, subtle avoidance strategies, escape or refusal to enter a situation, heart rate, and SUDS ratings. We recommend that the BAT be repeated from time to time during treatment (e.g., every five sessions) and again following treatment. Repeating the BAT is helpful for measuring improvements that occur during treatment.

Developing a fear and avoidance hierarchy

In order to identify situations to use as selective BAT items, the clinician and patient should generate a fear and avoidance hierarchy. The hierarchy should include 10 to 20 specific situations that the patient could potentially enter, ranging from mildly fear-provoking to extremely fear-provoking (often so fear-provoking that the patient would refuse to enter the situation). One way to complete this task is to generate a range of possible situations and to record them on index cards. Next, the patient can sort the cards so that the items are in order of difficulty. Finally, the list should be typed up in order, and the patient should rate his or her fear and desire to avoid each situation, using a scale ranging from 0 (*no fear or avoidance*) to 100 (*maximum fear or avoidance*), or some similar scale. An example of a fear and avoidance hierarchy for agoraphobia is provided in Exhibit 4.8. Note that the hierarchy items are quite detailed, including such variables as the day of the week, the duration of exposure, and who else is present in the situation. In addition to providing items for the BAT, fear and avoidance hierarchies are also useful for identifying items that the

Exhibit 4.8
Sample Fear and Avoidance Hierarchy for Agoraphobia

Situation	Fear	Avoidance
1. Ride a subway for 60 minutes alone at rush hour	90	100
2. Shop at Springfield Mall (second floor) alone for 60 minutes	85	100
3. Go to large concert with a friend	80	90
4. Stay overnight with spouse in a hotel	65	65
5. Ride subway for 60 minutes with spouse at rush hour	55	55
6. Drive to Springfield Mall alone on a Saturday	55	45
7. Walk around the block alone at night	40	50
8. Ride in an elevator for 15 minutes	35	35
9. Stay home alone all day	35	35
10. Go to corner store alone	30	30

patient can practice during exposure-based treatments. This issue is discussed in more detail later (see chapter 6). A blank fear and avoidance hierarchy form is included in Exhibit 4.9.

Psychophysiological assessment

Psychophysiological assessment is often used in research studies, but it can also be useful in clinical practice. Although a number of different psychophysiological functions can be measured during the BAT or during treatment (e.g., electrodermal response, respiration rate, blood pressure, etc.), the most commonly used psychophysiological measure is heart rate. Inexpensive heart rate monitors are available from companies that sell exercise equipment. We use a monitor that is worn around the wrist, like a wrist watch. Data are stored in the monitor, which can then be used to transfer the information to a computer. Heart-rate data can be summarized and graphed if desired.

Monitoring diaries

It is helpful to have patients use diaries before, during, and following treatment in order to continually monitor their progress. A number of sample diaries are included throughout this book. For patients with PD, we recommend that they complete a Panic Attack Diary each time they experience a panic attack (e.g., de Beurs, Chambless, & Goldstein, 1997). Exhibit 4.10 is an example of what a panic attack diary may be used to record. Some patients prefer to have smaller diaries, so that they can be carried around in a pocket, wallet, or bag. It is important to teach the patient to use the record appropriately (e.g., to differentiate between panic attacks, anxiety, and other related experiences). In addition, an Exposure Monitoring Form (see chapter 6) should be completed by patients each time they practice exposure to a feared situation or object. Finally, we

Exhibit 4.9
Fear and Avoidance Hierarchy

Instructions: Please list feared situations in order of difficulty, beginning with the most difficult situation. Please rate your fear and avoidance of each situation, using a scale ranging from 0 *(no fear or avoidance)* to 100 *(maximum fear or avoidance)*.

Situation	Fear rating (0–100)	Avoidance rating (0–100)

recommend the use of other specific diaries and monitoring forms for patients who are learning particular cognitive and behavioral techniques (e.g., cognitive restructuring, interoceptive exposure, etc.). Examples of these forms are included in the relevant chapters of this book.

Medical Examination

In addition to providing medical history during the clinical interview, we recommend that individuals who report concerns about physical symptoms (e.g., especially patients with PD) obtain a full medical work-up with their family physician to rule out medical conditions that may mimic the symptoms of panic attacks and PD. Specifically, it is important to rule out conditions such as endocrine disorders (e.g., hyperthyroidism), cardiovascular disease, respiratory disorders (e.g., asthma), temporal lobe epilepsy, and vestibular disorders. In addition, the clinician should rule out substance-

Exhibit 4.10
Panic Attack Diary

Instructions: Please complete this form each time you experience a rush of fear or panic.

Date _____   Time _____

Describe Situation:
Where were you? _____
What were you doing? _____
Who were you with? _____

Check One   Check One
_____ Expected   _____ Cued by Situation or Thought
_____ Unexpected   _____ Uncued or Spontaneous

Intensity of Panic Attack Symptoms (rate 0–100)
_____ Racing or pounding heart   _____ Nausea or abdominal discomfort
_____ Breathlessness or smothering   _____ Feeling unreal or detached
_____ Trembling or shaking   _____ Numbness or tingling sensations
_____ Sweating   _____ Chills or hot flushes
_____ Feeling of choking   _____ Fear of dying
_____ Chest pain or discomfort   _____ Fear of losing control or going
                                           "crazy"
_____ Feeling dizzy, unsteady, or faint _____ Other _____

Anxious Thoughts and Predictions During the Attack:

Countering Anxious Thoughts and Predictions:

Anxious Behaviors During the Attack:

---

related anxiety that may occur with intoxication from drugs such as caffeine, cocaine, or amphetamine, or withdrawal from drugs such as alcohol, barbiturates, or opiates.

STANDARD ASSESSMENT MEASURES

In this section we review self-report and standard interview measures that are commonly used to measure symptoms of PD, PDA, social phobia, and specific phobias. In addition, we discuss more general measures that are often helpful for assessing individuals suffering from phobic disorders. The specific battery of measures that are used will depend on many different factors, and it is difficult to recommend a particular package that will work in all clinical settings and for all patients. For example, clinicians who are actively involved in research may be more likely to use certain scales than are those in settings that exclusively provide service.

In our setting, we administer to all patients the Depression Anxiety Stress Scales (Lovibond & Lovibond, 1995) to measure symptoms of generalized anxiety and depression, the Illness Intrusiveness Rating Scale (Devins et al., 1983) to measure functional impairment, and the Anxiety Sensitivity Index (Peterson & Reiss, 1993) to measure anxiety over experiencing physical sensations. In addition, everyone completes forms that ask questions about life history, demographic information, and medical history. Additional questionnaires are added to the package, depending on the most likely diagnosis. Patients with PD or PDA complete the Anxiety Sensitivity Profile (Taylor & Cox, 1998a), Agoraphobia Cognitions Questionnaire (Chambless et al., 1984), the Mobility Inventory (Chambless et al., 1985), and our own Panic Frequency Questionnaire (Antony & Swinson, 1999). Individuals with social phobia complete the Social Phobia Scale and Social Interaction Anxiety Scale (Mattick & Clarke, 1998), as well as the Social Phobia Inventory (Davidson, 1998). Finally, individuals with specific phobia are provided with additional scales, depending on the particular type of phobia (see Exhibits 4.11 and 4.12 for examples). Details regarding these and other measures are provided throughout this section.

Measures for Panic Disorder With or Without Agoraphobia

Self-report assessment of PD should include instruments that measure (a) panic frequency and symptomatology, (b) fear of anxiety-related sensations, (c) cognitions associated with panic attacks, and (d) degree of agoraphobic avoidance. An exhaustive review of all measures is beyond the scope of this chapter. In addition to the most commonly used instruments that are reviewed in this section, other measures that may be worth considering include the following:

- Agoraphobia Scale (Öst, 1990)
- Agoraphobic Cognitions Scale (Hoffart, Friis, & Martinsen, 1992)
- Agoraphobic Self-Statements Questionnaire (van Hout, Emmelkamp, Koopmans, Bogels, & Bouman (in press)
- Albany Panic and Phobia Questionnaire (Rapee, Craske, & Barlow, 1994/1995)
- Body Sensations Interpretation Questionnaire (Clark et al., 1997)
- Body Vigilance Scale (Schmidt, Lerew, & Trakowski, 1997).
- Catastrophic Cognitions Questionnaire (Khawaja & Oei, 1992)
- NIMH Panic Questionnaire (Scupi, Maser, & Uhde, 1992)

Exhibit 4.11
Popular Self-Report Measures for Spider Phobias and Blood-Injection-Injury Phobias

---

Spider Phobia Measures

Fear of Spiders Questionnaire
- Authors: Szymanski & O'Donohue (1995)
- Measures fear of spiders
- 22 items rated on a Likert-type scale
- Good psychometric properties (Muris & Merckelbach, 1996)

Spider Phobia Beliefs Questionnaire
- Authors: Arntz, Lavy, van den Berg, & van Rijsoort (1993)
- Measures beliefs among people with spider phobias—regarding spiders and regarding their reactions to spiders
- Good psychometric properties and sensitivity to treatment changes

Blood-Injection-Injury Phobia Measures

Mutilation Questionnaire
- Authors: Klorman, Hastings, Weerts, Melamed, & Lang (1974)
- 30 true/false items
- Good psychometric properties (Kleinknecht, 1992; Kleinknecht & Thorndike, 1990)
- Two factors: (a) repulsion/revulsion toward blood, injury, and mutilation and (b) fear of bodily harm (Kleinknecht & Thorndike, 1990)

Medical Fear Survey
- Authors: Kleinknecht, Thorndike, & Walls (1996)
- 70 items rated on a 5-point scale
- Good psychometric properties (Kleinknecht, Kleinknecht, Sawchuk, Lee, & Lohr, 1999; Kleinknecht, Thorndike, & Walls, 1996)

- Panic and Agoraphobia Scale (Bandelow, 1995, 1999; Bandelow, Hajak, Holzrichter, Kunert, & Rüther, 1995; Bandelow et al., 1998)
- Panic Appraisal Inventory (Feske & de Beurs, 1997; Telch, 1987)
- Panic Attack Cognitions Questionnaire (Clum, Broyles, Borden, & Watkins, 1990)
- Panic Attack Questionnaire—Revised (Cox, Norton, & Swinson, 1992; Norton et al., 1986)
- Panic Attack Symptoms Questionnaire (Clum et al., 1990)
- Panic Disorder Self-Report (Newman, Zuelig, & Kachin, 1998)
- Panic Disorder Severity Scale (Shear et al., 1997)
- Texas Safety Maneuver Scale (Kamphuis & Telch, 1998)

Exhibit 4.12
Citations for Other Self-Report Measures for Specific Phobias

Blood-Injection-Injury Phobia Measures
- Blood-Injection Symptom Scale (Page, Bennett, Carter, Smith, & Woodmore, 1997)
- Fear Questionnaire (Marks & Mathews, 1979)

Claustrophobia Measures
- Claustrophobia Questionnaire (Radomsky, Rachman, Thordarson, McIsaac, & Teachman, in press)
- Claustrophobia Situations Questionnaire (Febbraro & Clum, 1995)
- Claustrophobia General Cognitions Questionnaire (Febbraro & Clum, 1995)

Dental Phobia Measures
- Dental Anxiety Inventory (Stouthard, Hoogstraten, & Mellenbergh, 1995)
- Dental Cognitions Questionnaire (de Jongh, Muris, Schoenmakers, & Ter Horst, 1995)
- Dental Fear Survey (McGlynn, McNeil, Gallagher, & Vrana, 1987; Kleinknecht & Bernstein, 1978)

Height Phobia Measures
- Acrophobia Questionnaire (Cohen, 1977)

Snake Phobia Measures
- Snake Questionnaire (Klorman, Hastings, Weerts, Melamed, & Lang, 1974). Also known as the Snake Anxiety Questionnaire (see Klieger, 1987, 1994)

Spider Phobia Measures
- Spider Questionnaire (Klorman, Hastings, Weerts, Melamed, & Lang, 1974)
- Spider Phobia Questionnaire (Watts & Sharrock, 1984)
- Spider Phobia Questionnaire—Extended Version (Barker & Edelmann, 1987)

Anxiety Sensitivity Index

The Anxiety Sensitivity Index (ASI; Peterson & Reiss, 1993) is a 16-item self-report questionnaire designed to measure anxiety sensitivity—or the extent to which an individual is fearful of the sensations associated with anxiety and panic attacks. Items include statements such as "It scares me when I feel faint," each of which are rated on a 5-point scale (ranging from 0 = *very little* to 4 = *very much*) to indicate the degree of agreement. The ASI is scored by adding the responses on each of the 16 items. Although the factor structure of the ASI has been a source of controversy in the literature (Peterson & Reiss, 1993), a recent factor analytic study based on a large sample (Zinbarg, Barlow, & Brown, 1997) showed that the ASI has a single higher-order factor and three lower-order factors representing physical concerns, social concerns, and mental incapacitation concerns. The ASI has been shown to have a satisfactory degree of internal consistency, test–retest reliability, criterion validity, and construct validity (Peterson & Heilbronner, 1987; Peterson & Reiss, 1993; Reiss et al., 1986). Among people with anxiety disorders, ASI scores tend to be most elevated in people with PD, although they are also somewhat elevated in the other anxiety disorders as well (Taylor et al., 1992).

Variations of the Anxiety Sensitivity Index

Apfeldorf, Shear, Leon, and Portera (1994) found that although the ASI distinguished between people with PD and people with other anxiety disorders, an abbreviated version of the ASI distinguished just as well among these groups. This abbreviated version, called the Brief Panic Disorder Screen, consists of only four items from the original ASI—Items 3, 4, 6, and 10, which measure fears of shaking, feeling faint, racing heart, and shortness of breath, respectively.

Taylor and Cox (1998b) recently published data on an expanded version of the ASI. The new measure has 20 additional items, for a total of 36. It was designed to strengthen the measure by adding items to assess each of the lower-order factors identified in previous research (e.g., Zinbarg et al., 1997) and by removing items that were too general to assess these lower-order factors. This measure appears to have four lower-order factors, loading on a single higher-order factor: (a) fear of respiratory symptoms, (b) fear of publicly observable anxiety reactions, (c) fear of cardiovascular symptoms, and (d) fear of cognitive dyscontrol. As with the original ASI, people with PD tend to score higher on the expanded ASI compared with individuals with other anxiety disorders (Taylor & Cox, 1998b). Additional data on the reliability and validity of the expanded ASI are needed.

Taylor and Cox (1998b) recently published a measure called the Anxiety Sensitivity Profile. This 60-item measure is designed to assess the extent to which an individual assumes that a particular physical sensation is a sign that something bad is about to happen. Like the revised ASI, the Anxiety Sensitivity Profile has four lower-order factors, loading on a single higher-order factor: (a) fear of respiratory symptoms, (b) fear of cognitive dyscontrol, (c) fear of gastrointestinal symptoms, and (d) fear of cardiac symptoms. This factor structure is based on a university student sample and remains to be replicated in a clinical sample. In addition, psychometric studies on the reliability and validity of the Anxiety Sensitivity Profile are lacking.

Body Sensations Questionnaire

The Body Sensations Questionnaire (BSQ; Chambless et al., 1984) is an 18-item self-report inventory designed to assess fear of bodily sensations in people with PD and related conditions. The scale consists of a list of 17 physical sensations (e.g., sweating, heart palpitations, etc.) that patients rate on a 5-point scale (rated from 1 to 5) to indicate how frightened they are by each sensation. The questionnaire is scored by taking the mean of all 17 items. In addition, an 18th item allows patients to write in an additional sensation that they find frightening. Like with the ASI, BSQ scores tend to be most elevated in people with PD and agoraphobia, but they are also somewhat elevated in other anxiety disorders, compared with scores in normal control participants (Chambless & Gracely, 1989). The scale has good test–retest reliability, internal consistency, predictive validity, construct validity, and discriminant validity (Arrindell, 1993; Chambless et al., 1984).

Agoraphobic Cognitions Questionnaire

The Agoraphobic Cognitions Questionnaire (ACQ; Chambless et al., 1984) is a 15-item self-report measure designed to assess cognitions that are associated with panic attacks and anxiety in individuals with agoraphobia. The scale consists of a list of 14 thoughts (e.g., "I am going to pass out" and "I am going to go crazy") that patients rate on a 5-point scale (ranging from 1 to 5) to indicate how frequently they experience each thought when anxious. The questionnaire is scored by taking the mean of the 14 items, although it can also be broken into two subscales representing loss of control concerns and physical concerns (see Schutte & Malouff, 1995, pp. 158–162). In addition, an 15th item allows patients to write in an additional thought that occurs when they are anxious. Like scores on the ASI and BSQ, ACQ scores tend to be most elevated in people with PD and agoraphobia, but they are still somewhat elevated in people with other anxiety disorders (Chambless & Gracely, 1989). The scale has good test–retest reliability, internal consistency, predictive validity, construct validity, and discriminant validity (Arrindell, 1993; Chambless et al., 1984)

Mobility Inventory

The Mobility Inventory (MI; Chambless et al., 1985) is a 27-item self-report inventory designed to measure severity of agoraphobic avoidance. The instrument lists 26 situations (e.g., supermarkets and subways) that are often avoided by people with PD and agoraphobia. Each item is rated on a 5-point Likert-type scale indicating the extent to which the situation is avoided because of discomfort or anxiety. Each item is rated twice—once to measure avoidance when alone and a second time to measure avoidance when accompanied. In addition, a 27th item is included for patients to write in and rate an additional situation that they avoid. Finally, there is a space to write in the number of panic attacks experienced in the previous week. The MI has good test–retest reliability, internal consistency, and sensitivity to change following treatment (Chambless et al., 1985). Although some factor analytic studies have identified three factors (Public Places, Enclosed Places, and Open Places) underlying the MI (e.g., Arrindell, Cox, van der Ende, & Kwee, 1995; Cox, Swinson, Kuch, & Reichman, 1993), others have shown that a two-factor solution (Crowded/Social Situations and Enclosed/Riding Situations) fits best (Kwon, Evans, & Oei, 1990).

Swinson, Cox, Shulman, Kuch, and Woszczyna (1992) examined the psychometric properties of an adapted version of the MI. In addition to the "alone" and "accompanied" ratings that are provided on the original version of the MI, Swinson, Cox, Shulman, et al. (1992) added a third column on which patients rated their degree of avoidance "without medication." In addition to confirming the psychometric properties of the original subscale, these researchers found that the new "without medication" subscale was a useful addition. Scores on this subscale were significantly higher than those on the original subscales, underscoring the relationship between medication use and agoraphobic avoidance. The "without medication" subscale had good internal consistency.

Fear Questionnaire

The Fear Questionnaire (FQ; Marks & Mathews, 1979) is a 24-item self-report questionnaire designed to measure agoraphobic fear, social anxiety, and fear of blood-injection-injury stimuli. The first section consists of 17 items, each of which is rated by the patient on a 9-point scale indicating the degree to which the situation is avoided. The first item provides a rating of the "main phobia" that the patient wants treated (described in his or her own words). Next, there are 15 situations listed, of which 5 measure agoraphobic fears (e.g., traveling alone by bus or coach), 5 measure social fears (e.g., speaking or acting to an audience), and 5 measure blood-injection-injury fears (e.g., injections or minor surgery). Item 17 allows patients to write in and rate any additional situations that are avoided.

The first section of the FQ generates subscale scores for agoraphobia, social phobia, and blood-injection-injury phobia, based on Items 2–16. The second section (Items 18–23) has the patient rate on a 9-point scale the extent to which he or she is bothered by various symptoms such as depressed mood, irritability, and tension. Finally, Item 24 asks the patient to rate the extent to which his or her phobic symptoms are disturbing or disabling, based on a 9-point scale.

Despite its brevity, the FQ appears to have good internal consistency and seems to be a reliable and valid measure for discriminating between agoraphobia and social phobia (Cox, Swinson, & Shaw, 1991; Oei, Moylan, & Evans, 1991). A number of researchers have also confirmed the three-factor structure of the FQ (Cox, Parker, & Swinson, 1996; Cox, Swinson, Parker, Kuch, & Reichman, 1993; Oei, Moylan, & Evans, 1991). Finally, the

FQ appears to be sensitive to change in agoraphobic patients (Mavissakalian, 1986). Although the psychometric properties of the main section of the FQ (with items measuring fears of agoraphobic situations, social situations, and blood-injection-injury situations) are well established, little is known about the reliability, validity, and clinical usefulness of the second section, where patients rate the severity of associated symptoms such as anxiety and depression.

Panic Frequency Questionnaire

The Panic Frequency Questionnaire (PFQ; Antony & Swinson, 1999) is an unpublished self-report scale designed to assess PD symptomatology during the previous month. Items are included to measure cued and uncued panic frequency, worry about having more panic attacks, concern over the consequences of having panic attacks, behavioral changes caused by panic attacks, and symptoms experienced during typical panic attacks. Although the psychometric properties of the scale are not yet established, the PFQ may be a helpful way of supplementing and confirming information obtained during the clinical interview. The scale is reproduced in Exhibit 4.13.

Measures for Social Phobia

Self-report and interview assessments for social phobia primarily include instruments that assess the severity of social anxiety. An exhaustive review of social phobia measures is beyond the scope of this chapter. Instead, we provide an overview of the most commonly used measures for social phobia. Other measures that are not covered in this section but may still be of interest include the following:

- Fear of Negative Evaluation Scale (Oei, Kenna, & Evans, 1991; Turner, McCanna, & Beidel, 1987; Watson & Friend, 1969)
- Index of Social Phobia Improvement (Turner, Beidel, & Wolff, 1994)
- Personal Report of Confidence as a Speaker (Paul, 1966; Phillips, Jones, Rieger, & Snell, 1997)
- Social Avoidance and Distress Scale (Oei, Kenna, & Evans, 1991; Turner et al., 1987; Watson & Friend, 1969)
- Social Cognitions Questionnaire (Freshman, Amir, Foa, & Clark, 1997)

Additional comprehensive reviews on assessment instruments that are often used to assess social phobia are available elsewhere (e.g., Cox & Swinson, 1995; Heimberg, 1994; McNeil, Ries, & Turk, 1995).

Exhibit 4.13
Panic Frequency Questionnaire

A panic attack is a period of intense fear or discomfort that begins suddenly and peaks in 10 minutes or less. Panic attacks must be accompanied by at least four of the following symptoms:

1. racing or pounding heart
2. sweating
3. trembling/shaking
4. shortness of breath
5. chest pain/discomfort
6. choking feeling
7. nausea/abdominal discomfort
8. dizzy, unsteady, lightheaded, faintness
9. feeling unreal or detached
10. numbness/tingling sensations
11. chills/hot flashes
12. fear of dying
13. fear of going crazy/losing control

1. In the past month, approximately how many panic attacks (see above definition) have you had out of the blue or when you did not expect to have a panic attack?   _____ attacks

2. In the past month, approximately how many attacks did you have that were triggered by a specific situation or occurred when you expected to have a panic attack?   _____ attacks

   What were these situations or places? _____

   _____

3. During the past month, how worried or concerned were you about having more panic attacks. Estimate your average level of concern by circling a number on the scale below from 0 to 8, where 0 = *no worry or concern about panicking* and 8 = *constantly worried about having a panic attack over the past month.*

   0----------1------------2----------3--------4------------5-------------6------------7----------8
   not at all   mildly   moderately   very   constantly
   worried   worried   worried   worried   worried

4. During the past month, how worried or concerned were you about something bad happening (e.g., dying, going crazy, losing control, being embarrassed, vomiting, fainting, losing bowel control, etc.) during your panic attacks. Estimate your level of concern by circling a number on the scale below from 0 to 8, where 0 = *no worry or concern about something bad happening during panic* and 8 = *constantly worried about something bad happening during panic.*

   0----------1------------2----------3--------4------------5-------------6------------7----------8
   not at all   mildly   moderately   very   constantly
   worried   worried   worried   worried   worried

(continued)

Exhibit 4.13
(*Continued*)

5. During the past month, to what extent have you behaved differently (e.g., avoiding situations, avoiding activities, using drugs or alcohol to reduce anxiety, carrying certain objects with you, etc.) because of your panic attacks. Estimate the degree to which your panic attacks affected your behavior by circling a number on the scale below from 0 to 8, where 0 = *no change in behavior related to panic* and 8 = *very extreme changes in behavior related to panic*.

```
0----------1------------2----------3----------4------------5-------------6------------7----------8
none        mild        moderate            extreme            very extreme
```

6. During a typical panic attack in the past month, how intensely did you feel each of the following symptoms? Write a number to the left of each symptom, using the following scale:

0 = *not at all;* 1 = *mild;* 2 = *moderate;* 3 = *severe;* 4 = *very severe.*

____racing or pounding heart	____dizzy, unsteady, lightheaded, faintness
____sweating	____feeling unreal or detached
____trembling/shaking	____numbness/tingling sensations
____shortness of breath	____chills/hot flashes
____chest pain/discomfort	____fear of dying
____choking feeling	____fear of going crazy/losing control
____nausea/abdominal discomfort	

Brief Social Phobia Scale

The Brief Social Phobia Scale (BSPS; Davidson et al., 1991) is an 11-item clinician-administered scale with two sections. The first section requires that the clinician rate separately the fear and avoidance (using a 5-point Likert-type scale) of seven different social and performance situations (e.g., speaking in public or in front of others and social gatherings). In the second section, the clinician uses a 5-point scale to rate the severity of four different physical symptoms (e.g., blushing or palpitations) experienced by the patient when exposed to or thinking about being in a feared social situation. Initial psychometric studies suggest that the BSPS has good test–retest reliability, interrater reliability, internal consistency, concurrent validity, and sensitivity to change following treatment (Davidson et al., 1991, 1997). Recently, this scale was adapted for administration by a computer by Kobak et al. (1998). (See Heimberg, Mennin, & Jack, 1999, for additional comments on the computerized version.)

Liebowitz Social Anxiety Scale

The Liebowitz Social Anxiety Scale (LSAS; Liebowitz, 1987), previously called the Liebowitz Social Phobia Scale, is a 24-item clinician-administered scale designed to measure the severity of anxiety in social and performance situations. Each item is rated on two dimensions (fear and avoidance), using a 4-point scale. The LSAS generates two separate subscores—one based on 11 social interaction situations (e.g., going to a party) and one based on 13 performance situations (e.g., speaking up at a meeting). Furthermore, Kobak et al. (1998) recently reported findings based on a computer-administered version of the scale (also see Heimberg, Mennin, & Jack, 1999).

The LSAS appears to have good internal consistency, convergent validity, and discriminant validity (Heimberg, Horner, et al., 1999). Although there is preliminary evidence of sensitivity to treatment effects following pharmacotherapy (Heimberg, Horner, et al., 1999), sensitivity to changes following CBT may be weaker compared with other social anxiety measures (Cox, Ross, Swinson, & Direnfeld, 1998). Furthermore, limited evidence regarding the factor structure of the LSAS does not support the two factors (Performance Anxiety and Social Interaction Anxiety) of the scale, which tend to be highly intercorrelated (Slavkin, Holt, Heimberg, Jaccard, & Liebowitz, 1990). More studies on the psychometric properties of this scale are needed.

Fear Questionnaire

The FQ (Marks & Mathews, 1979) is designed to measure the severity with which individuals avoid situations related to agoraphobia, social phobia, and blood-injury-injection phobia. This measure is described in more detail in the earlier section on measures for PD with or without agoraphobia.

Social Phobia Scale and Social Interaction Anxiety Scale

The Social Phobia Scale (SPS; Mattick & Clarke, 1998) is a 20-item self-report scale designed to measure anxiety related to social performance. Items include statements such as "I become anxious if I have to write in front of other people" and "I fear I may blush when I am with others." Each item is rated on a 5-point scale ranging from 0 (*not at all*) to 4 (*extremely*). The Social Interaction Anxiety Scale (SIAS; Mattick & Clarke, 1998) is a 20-item self-report scale designed to measure anxiety related to social interaction. Items include statements such as "I tense up when I meet an acquaintance on the street" and "I am nervous mixing with people I don't know well." Like with the SPS, each item is rated on a 5-point scale ranging from 0 (*not at all*) to 4 (*extremely*).

The SPS and SIAS are designed to be administered together. They are relatively brief and easy to score. They appear to be both reliable and valid (Brown, Turovsky, et al., 1997; Mattick & Clarke, 1998; Osman, Gutierrez, Barrios, Kopper, & Chiros, 1998) and are sensitive to change following treatment (Brown, Turovsky, et al., 1997; Cox et al., 1998). Findings regarding the factor structure of the combined scales (based on pooling the items from both measures) have been mixed. Using a confirmatory factor analysis in undergraduate students, Osman et al. (1998) found support for a two-factor solution, suggesting that the SIAS and SPS tap different dimensions. However, other studies, including a confirmatory factor analysis in patients with social phobia (Safren, Turk, & Heimberg, 1998) and an exploratory factor analysis in university students (Habke, Hewitt, Norton, & Asmundson, 1997), have suggested that a three-factor solution is more appropriate.

Social Phobia and Anxiety Inventory

The Social Phobia and Anxiety Inventory (SPAI; Turner, Beidel, & Dancu, 1996) is a 45-item self-report scale designed to measure social anxiety and agoraphobia severity. It includes a 32-item Social Phobia scale and a 13-item Agoraphobia scale. In practice, the scale is used much more frequently to measure social anxiety than to measure agoraphobic fear. Furthermore, most of the psychometric research has been with socially anxious and non-anxious samples, with relatively little research on the usefulness of the scale in agoraphobic individuals. Compared with other social anxiety measures, the SPAI is more complicated to score and interpret.

The SPAI has been shown to have good test–retest reliability, internal consistency, construct validity, external validity, and concurrent validity (Beidel, Borden, Turner, & Jacob, 1989; Beidel, Turner, Stanley, & Dancu, 1989; Herbert, Bellack, & Hope, 1991; Turner, Beidel, & Dancu, 1996; Turner, Beidel, Dancu, & Stanley, 1989; Turner, Stanley, Beidel, & Bond, 1989). In addition, it appears to be sensitive to changes following treatment (Beidel, Turner, & Cooley, 1993; Cox et al., 1998). The SPAI has recently been adapted for use with children (Beidel, Turner, & Fink, 1996; Beidel, Turner, & Morris, 1995).

Social Phobia Inventory

The Social Phobia Inventory (SPIN; Davidson, 1998) is a 17-item self-report scale designed to measure social anxiety and avoidance of social situations. This relatively new instrument contains 17 statements that reflect social anxiety (e.g., "I am afraid of people in authority"), each of which is rated on a 5-point (0–4) scale. A preliminary psychometric study (Connor, Davidson, et al., 1999; in press) suggests that this instrument is useful for the assessment of social phobia. In addition, despite the lack of extensive research, pharmaceutical companies have recently started to promote this instrument, and it is becoming more popular in pharmacotherapy trials for social phobia. Recently, the Mini-SPIN (a subset of three items from the

SPIN) has been shown to be a relatively sensitive brief screening tool for identifying individuals with social phobia (Connor, Kobak, et al., 1999).

Measures for Specific Phobia

Fear survey schedules

Several different fear survey schedules have been published and researched since the 1950s. Generally, these scales were developed to identify specific objects and situations that people fear. The first of these, developed by Akutagawa (1956), was a survey of 50 items representing commonly occurring fears. Although the scale was never used widely, it was used in at least one published study (Lang & Lazovik, 1963) to measure outcome following behavior therapy. In 1965, Geer published a second Fear Survey Schedule (FSS-II) patterned after the original scale by Akutagawa. This 51-item scale was empirically derived from an original item pool of 111 items. Geer (1965) designed the scale to be used as a research tool for identifying objects and situations that people fear. Wolpe and Lang (1964) published a third Fear Survey Schedule (FSS-III) based on an early version of Geer's scale. Unlike the FSS-II, the 72-item FSS-III was designed to be used in clinical settings.

Although there have been other fear survey schedules developed over the years, the FSS-II and FSS-III remain the most popular versions. However, despite their popularity, investigators have questioned their validity (e.g., Klieger & Franklin, 1993). Furthermore, in addition to including items that are related to common specific phobias (e.g., injections, airplanes), social phobias (e.g., speaking in public), and agoraphobic situations (e.g., crowds), they also tend to include a large number of questions about situations and objects that are not typically associated with fear in people with phobic disorders (e.g., noise of vacuum cleaners, sirens, ugly people, nude men and women, and parting from friends). Therefore, as a general method of assessing fears in people with specific phobias, fear survey schedules may not be ideal. There is a need for the development of an updated fear survey schedule that more closely reflects the types of situations and objects feared by people with specific phobias.

Other specific phobia measures

Numerous instruments for assessing severity of particular specific phobias have appeared in the literature. Although a detailed discussion of these measures is beyond the scope of this chapter, Exhibit 4.11 includes an overview of some of the most commonly used measures for spider phobias and blood-injection-injury phobias, for which there tend to be more available and better studied measures, relative to other phobia types. In addition, citations are listed in Exhibit 4.12 for other instruments that may be of interest. The patient manual, *Mastery of Your Specific Phobia* (Antony, Craske, & Barlow, 1995), includes additional measures to assess the types of situations that a patient fears as well as the beliefs that are associated with each of the main specific phobia types. Although these scales have not been subjected to systematic research, they may be used for providing relevant clinical information.

Self-Report Measures for Other Relevant Dimensions

Generalized anxiety measures

Perhaps the two most popular self-report measures of generalized anxiety are the Beck Anxiety Inventory (BAI; Beck & Steer, 1990) and the State-Trait Anxiety Inventory (STAI; Spielberger, 1983). Both measures are brief and easy to score and interpret. However, despite their popularity, each has limitations. The BAI has been criticized for being more a measure of panic symptomatology than of generalized anxiety per se (Cox, Cohen, Direnfeld, & Swinson, 1996). Most items tend to assess physical symptoms of fear, such as shakiness and faintness, and relatively few items ask about features that are more characteristic of generalized anxiety, such as worry, irritability, and muscle tension. Nevertheless, the BAI is generally thought to have good psychometric properties (Beck & Steer, 1990).

The STAI is available in two versions—one that measures state anxiety and one that measures trait anxiety. Although both are psychometrically sound, based on a number of different criteria (Spielberger, 1983), the trait anxiety version has recently been demonstrated to be a poor measure of generalized anxiety. In fact, in a recent factor analytic study (Bieling, Antony, & Swinson, 1998), more than half of the items were shown to measure depression rather than anxiety.

In light of the problems with the BAI and STAI, we recommend the Depression Anxiety Stress Scale (DASS; Lovibond & Lovibond, 1995) as a measure of generalized anxiety. This 42-item measure (a 21-item version is also available) has three subscales: (a) a Depression subscale to assess depressed mood (e.g., "I felt that life was meaningless"), (b) an Anxiety subscale to assess symptoms of fear and physiological arousal (e.g., "I was able to feel the action of my heart in the absence of physical exertion"), and (c) a Stress subscale to assess symptoms of negative affect such as worry and agitation (e.g., "I found it difficult to relax"). Unlike the STAI, the DASS does an excellent job at separating anxiety and depression. Furthermore, unlike the BAI, the DASS includes items that measure negative affect and not only symptoms of fear and panic. The DASS has excellent psychometric properties for patients with anxiety disorders (Antony, Bieling, Cox, Enns, & Swinson, 1998; Brown, Chorpita, Korotitsch, & Barlow, 1997).

Depression measures

A number of different instruments may be used for measuring depression in phobic patients. Perhaps the most popular of these is the second edition of the Beck Depression Inventory (BDI-II; Beck, Steer, & Brown, 1996). This familiar 21-item scale is brief and easy to score and interpret, and it has excellent psychometric properties. Alternatively, the DASS (described earlier) is also an excellent choice as a measure of depression in phobic individuals.

Perfectionism measures

Perfectionism is often associated with anxiety disorders such as social phobia and PDA (Antony, Purdon, et al., 1998). Two different perfectionism scales (both called the Multidimensional Perfectionism Scale) have been used to measure perfectionism in anxious groups. The first scale (Frost, Marten, Lahart, & Rosenblate, 1990) measures six different dimensions of perfectionism: (a) personal standards, (b) doubts about actions, (c) concern over mistakes, (d) organization, (e) parental expectations, and (f) parental criticism. The second scale (Hewitt & Flett, 1991) measures three different aspects of perfectionism: (a) self-oriented perfectionism, (b) other-oriented perfectionism, and (c) socially prescribed perfectionism. Although both measures have good psychometric properties (Frost et al., 1990; Frost, Heimberg, Holt, Mattia, & Neubauer, 1993; Hewitt, Flett, Turnbull-Donovan, & Mikail, 1991), the Frost et al. (1990) scale tends to show more differences across anxiety disorders groups than does the Hewitt and Flett (1991) scale (Antony, Purdon, et al., 1998). However, a recent factor analytic study raised questions about whether the six-factor solution is the most appropriate way to organize the items from the Frost et al. (1990) questionnaire (Purdon, Antony, & Swinson, 1999).

Functional impairment

The Illness Intrusiveness Rating Scale (IIRS; Devins et al., 1983) is a 13-item scale that measures the extent to which an individual experiences interference in 13 different domains of functioning caused by a particular illness or its treatment. Although the scale has been used primarily in populations with chronic medical conditions, a recent study (Antony, Roth, Swinson, Huta, & Devins, 1998) provides norms for various anxiety-disorder groups. The 13 domains of functioning that are assessed by the IIRS are (a) health, (b) diet, (c) work, (d) active recreation (e.g., sports), (e) passive recreation (e.g., reading), (f) financial situation, (g) relationship with partner, (h) sex life, (i) family relations, (j) other social relations, (k) self-expression/self-improvement, (l) religious expression, and (m) community and civic involvement. For each item, interference is rated on a scale ranging from 1 to 7. The IIRS has been shown in previous research to have good construct validity and high internal consistency for a variety of illnesses (Binik, Chowanec, & Devins, 1990; Devins et al., 1983, 1990, 1992, 1993) and is not contaminated by defensive response styles (Devins et al., 1990).

CONCLUSION

In this chapter we provided an overview of strategies used for the assessment of phobic disorders, including clinical interviewing, behavioral assessment, and questionnaire measures, among others. As highlighted at the beginning of the chapter, an important function of the assessment process is to facilitate the process of selecting appropriate treatments. Another important function is to measure the effects of treatment. In chapter 5 we provide an overview of how to choose among treatment strategies, in part based on the results of the initial assessment findings.

5

DEVELOPING A COMPREHENSIVE TREATMENT PLAN

In chapter 5 we provide an overview of how to develop a detailed treatment plan that is most likely to be effective. We guide the clinician through the best ways of integrating the strategies discussed in chapters 6–8. Generally, treatment should be based on empirically supported strategies and should be symptom focused. In most cases, treatment will also be short-term, consistent with the current climate of managed care in the United States.

The chapter is divided into several sections. It begins with a discussion of how to choose among available treatment options (e.g., choosing between medication and psychological treatment or choosing among psychological strategies). Next, there is a detailed discussion of how to present the rationale for cognitive–behavioral therapy (CBT) to the patient. This is followed by discussions on ending therapy and how to integrate self-help readings into the treatment. The chapter ends with examples of comprehensive, step-by-step CBT protocols for panic disorder (PD), social phobia, and specific phobia.

Choosing Among Pharmacological, Psychological, and Combined Treatments

Panic disorder with and without agoraphobia

As is reviewed in chapter 1, pharmacological treatments (e.g., with antidepressants or high-potency benzodiazepines) and CBT have generally been found to be about equally effective in the short term, assuming that the patient does not drop out of treatment. Furthermore, research on combined treatments suggests that the combination of pharmacotherapy and CBT is about as effective in the short term as is either approach alone, with only a few studies showing greater short-term improvements with combined treatments.

However, findings on the long-term benefits of each approach tell a different story (see chapter 1 for a review). After treatment ends, relapse rates tend to be considerably higher following discontinuation of pharmacotherapy than following discontinuation of CBT. Furthermore, there is preliminary evidence that people who receive combined treatments do not do as well as people who receive CBT alone (Barlow, Gorman, Shear, & Woods, in press; Marks et al., 1993) and that the extent to which people who are treated with both approaches attribute their improvement to the medication is predictive of withdrawal symptoms experienced during discontinuation from medication (Başoğlu et al., 1994).

Considering the long-term effects of pharmacological, psychological, and combined treatments, the first-line treatment for most individuals with PD and panic disorder with agoraphobia (PDA) should be CBT. Medications are an appropriate option (instead of, or in addition to, CBT) for individuals who do not respond following an adequate trial of CBT alone. In addition, medication or combined treatment may be a preferred option for patients who are likely to be noncompliant with the CBT procedures, who have difficulty understanding the CBT procedures, who insist on taking medications, who have significant comorbidity (e.g., severe depression that could interfere with CBT), and who are already being treated successfully with medications. For patients who wish to discontinue their medications, CBT appears to be an effective method of helping people to do so, particularly for those who are taking benzodiazepines (Bruce et al., 1995; Otto et al., 1993; Spiegel et al., 1994). Detailed descriptions of how to use CBT to help patients discontinue their medications may be found in recently published manuals for therapists and patients (Otto, Jones, Craske, & Barlow, 1996; Otto, Pollack, & Barlow, 1996).

Social phobia

As is reviewed in chapter 2, pharmacological and cognitive–behavioral approaches to treating social phobia appear to be equally effective in the short term according to most comparative studies. In a meta-analysis of 24 studies (Gould et al., 1997), selective serotonin reuptake inhibitors (SSRIs) and benzodiazepines tended to yield the largest effect sizes among medications. Among cognitive–behavioral interventions, treatments involving exposure (alone or with cognitive restructuring) yielded the strongest effect sizes. Cognitive–behavioral group treatments were the most cost-effective interventions, compared with individual CBT and most pharmacological approaches. However, as is the case with PD, there is preliminary evidence that relapse rates following treatment may be higher among people treated with antidepressants than among people treated with CBT (Liebowitz et al., 1999). In addition, there are currently no published data on the short-term or long-term effects of combining pharmacotherapy and CBT for social phobia.

In light of these findings, as well as our clinical experience, it appears that CBT, pharmacotherapy, and the combination of these approaches are equally likely to be helpful in the short term. Which of these approaches to choose should depend on factors such as the patient's preference, the relative availability and cost of each approach, and the patient's response to previous treatments. If a patient is treated with medication, it may be helpful to provide several sessions of CBT at the time that medication is discontinued to help ensure that gains are maintained. Note that in light of the relative lack of research on long-term outcome following treatment of social phobia with medication versus CBT, as well as the lack of data on short-term and long-term findings following combined treatments, these recommendations could change in the next few years.

Specific phobia

As is reviewed in chapter 3, there is no empirical evidence supporting the use of pharmacotherapy or combination treatments for specific phobias. Furthermore, in light of the fact that exposure alone is so effective, usually in a small number of sessions, it is hard to justify using pharmacotherapy to treat specific phobias. Despite the lack of empirical support for pharmacotherapy and combined treatments, patients with certain specific phobias (e.g., flying phobias) are sometimes prescribed a benzodiazepine to take while flying. There is also a published anecdotal report of two patients' flying phobia remitting after being treated with fluoxetine for depression (Abene & Hamilton, 1998). If any specific phobias are eventually found to respond to pharmacotherapy, they are likely to be the situational-specific phobias (e.g., claustrophobia), because their symptom profiles, age of onset, and other features overlap most strongly (compared with other specific phobia types) with those of PD and agoraphobia (see chapter 3 for a review). This hypothesis remains to be tested.

Sequencing of combined treatments

For patients who are treated with a combination of CBT and medication, the recommended order in which these treatments are given depends on the reason for which the two treatments are being combined. For example, in cases where medication is being used to make exposure practices more palatable to the patient (e.g., for individuals who initially refuse to enter feared situations without medication), pharmacotherapy should begin before or around the same time as CBT. In cases in which CBT is used to help a patient discontinue pharmacotherapy, then CBT will obviously begin after the medication has already been in use for some time. Finally, CBT or medication may be added as an augmentation treatment if a patient has responded only partially to one or the other. Regardless of whether CBT and pharmacotherapy are introduced together or sequentially, the therapist should consider providing CBT during the time that the patient discontinues the medication, to prevent a return of symptoms during discontinuation.

Choosing Among Psychological Strategies

The empirical literature regarding various psychological treatment strategies (e.g., exposure, cognitive restructuring, etc.) and their combinations is reviewed in chapters 1–3. This section focuses instead on clinical recommendations for choosing particular strategies, based on the research findings that were reviewed previously as well as years of experience using these treatments for patients with phobias.

Panic disorder with mild or no agoraphobia

Our standard protocol for PD with no more than mild agoraphobia typically lasts between 10 and 12 one-hour sessions. Initially, the sessions are weekly (the first few sessions may be even more frequent), and the last two or three sessions are biweekly. The first one to two meetings involve psychoeducation regarding the nature of panic and anxiety and an overview of methods for overcoming the problem (see the treatment protocol outline later in this chapter). These are followed by meetings in which the patient is taught the main panic management skills such as breathing retraining (BRT) (when relevant; see chapter 8), cognitive restructuring (see chapter 7), and interoceptive exposure (IE; see chapter 6). In addition, exposure to agoraphobic situations and elimination of safety signals (e.g., carrying medication or a mobile telephone) are included if they are relevant to the particular patient (chapter 6).

Which of these strategies to include for a given patient depends on a number of factors. We recommend that the therapist consider using the cognitive strategies for almost all patients who suffer from PD with no more than mild agoraphobia. For patients who are unable to use the cognitive strategies effectively (e.g., because of intellectual impairment or difficulty identifying their anxious cognitions), greater emphasis may be placed on other, more behavioral strategies. We also recommend that IE be used with most patients. However, patients for whom the symptom-induction exercises do not trigger fear (even when they are conducted alone or in the context of situational exposure practices) are unlikely to benefit from IE. Similarly, patients who have certain medical conditions (see chapter 6) may be unable to use certain IE exercises safely. Finally, we recommend that all patients be encouraged to practice exposure to feared situations and to eliminate their reliance on safety cues and overprotective behaviors.

Generally, we recommend that BRT not be included in the standard treatment for panic (see chapter 8 for a detailed discussion of this issue), but rather that it be reserved only for patients who specifically request it or who clearly have difficulties related to hyperventilation. If BRT is to be included, it is typically the focus of about one and a half sessions, beginning immediately after the initial psychoeducation sessions and before sessions involving cognitive restructuring. When BRT is not used, cognitive restructuring is typically taught after the initial psychoeducation meetings. Symptom-induction testing, IE, and situational exposure should begin after the first two sessions of cognitive restructuring. Later sessions are generally spent practicing the various treatment strategies, with the last two sessions including discussions about termination and relapse prevention. A sample protocol for the treatment of PD with no more than mild agoraphobia is provided later in this chapter.

Panic disorder with moderate to severe agoraphobia

For patients with significant agoraphobic avoidance, situational exposure is an essential part of treatment. Some patients may be willing to attempt exposure practices on their own, whereas others tend to need the assistance of a therapist or family member, particularly early in treatment. In severe cases, treatment may have to start in the patient's home until the patient is able to come to the therapist's office alone or with a friend or family member. It may also become necessary to schedule telephone contacts early in treatment to facilitate the completion of homework assignments.

Effective treatments for PDA vary considerably from site to site. At some centers, treatment is quite brief and based entirely on intensive exposure (e.g., six 3-hour sessions of therapist-assisted exposure conducted over 8 weeks, combined with exposure homework between sessions). At other centers, treatment consists of 12 to 15 one-hour sessions, consisting of situational-exposure homework assignments, cognitive therapy, and IE. In our experience, either approach (as well as a number of variations on these approaches) is equally likely to be effective. Factors such as the number of sessions, the degree of the therapist's involvement in exposure practices, the intensity of treatment, and whether to include strategies other than situational exposure typically depend on the individual patient's needs and the preferences of the patient and therapist, as well as any practical constraints that may exist (e.g., availability of the therapist and cost of treatment).

In our standard treatment, we tend to begin with a session of psychoeducation (e.g., presenting the treatment rationale), followed by one to two sessions of formal cognitive restructuring (which continues for part of each session throughout the rest of the treatment). Situational (in vivo) exposure begins by the fourth session and includes exposure homework assignments as well as longer sessions that include therapist-assisted exposure, depending on whether the patient is able to practice exposure alone. After three to five sessions of situational exposure, the IE exercises are introduced. The patient is encouraged to practice relevant exercises at home as well as in agoraphobic situations. We are even more reluctant to include BRT with agoraphobic patients than we are with patients who have PD without agoraphobia, primarily because of the increased time needed for situational exposure.

Social phobia

As with PD, treatment of social phobia typically includes a combination of cognitive and behavioral strategies. The initial session or two should include education regarding the nature of social phobia and an overview of the strategies for overcoming the problem. The next two to three sessions focus on cognitive restructuring, after which patients may begin exposure to feared situations and in-session role-play simulations. Delaying exposure until after patients have learned the cognitive strategies is consistent with research findings by Scholing and Emmelkamp (1993b), who found that the effects of group treatment for social phobia were greatest when cognitive therapy preceded exposure and smallest when cognitive therapy and exposure were delivered simultaneously.

We recommend that social skills training be tailored to the individual's needs. For example, whereas some patients may benefit from some assertiveness training, others may instead require strategies for meeting new people or dating. Some patients may need more intensive work in a larger number of areas, and for many patients, social skills training may be unnecessary and irrelevant. We tend to integrate social skills practices, as needed, with the patient's exposure homework and in-session role-plays.

Specific phobia

Treatment of a specific phobia is unlikely to be effective unless it includes in vivo exposure. Furthermore, for certain types of phobias (e.g., animal or blood phobia), patients are especially unlikely to be able to practice exposure without the assistance of a therapist, especially early in treatment. Exposure sessions typically last between 90 minutes and 3 hours. The number of sessions needed varies, depending on the phobia type. A single session of exposure lasting 2 to 3 hours has been shown to lead to clinically significant, lasting change for animal phobias (Öst, Salkovskis, & Hellström. 1991), blood and injection phobias (Öst, 1989), and flying phobias (Öst, Brandberg, & Alm, 1997). Single-session treatments have not been investigated for most other specific phobias, and, in our experience, at least several sessions are usually needed to overcome phobias of heights, driving, and enclosed places.

As is discussed in chapter 6, adding IE exercises during in vivo exposure practices may be helpful for patients who are fearful of the physical sensations that they experience when they are anxious (e.g., a patient with claustrophobia who is fearful of feeling breathless when in an enclosed place). Although it is not necessary to include formal cognitive restructuring (e.g., with monitoring forms, homework, etc.) when treating specific phobias, cognitive strategies may be used informally during therapist-assisted exposure practices (e.g., while standing on a bridge with a height-phobic patient, the therapist might discuss the patient's beliefs regarding the probability of falling or jumping).

Choosing Between Group and Individual Approaches

Research findings

Numerous studies have demonstrated that CBT for PD can be effectively delivered in groups (e.g., Cerny et al., 1987; Penava, Otto, Maki, & Pollack, 1998; Telch et al., 1993), as well as individually (e.g., Barlow et al., 1989; Marks et al., 1993), with up to 85% of patients no longer experiencing panic attacks (e.g., Telch et al., 1993) following treatment. Furthermore, a preliminary comparison of individual and group treatment for PD revealed few differences in efficacy between these two approaches (Neron, Lacroix, & Chaput, 1995). Overall, findings regarding CBT for social phobia are similar to those for panic disorder, with group treatment working as well as individual treatment (Scholing & Emmelkamp, 1993b; Wlazlo et al.,

1990). However, there is some evidence that exposure conducted in groups is more effective for patients with more severe social skills deficits, compared with exposure conducted individually (Wlazlo et al., 1990).

Relatively speaking, there have been few studies of the use of group treatments for specific phobias. In one study of individuals with dental phobias, Moore and Brødsgaard (1994) compared brief desensitization treatments conducted in groups versus two different individual treatments. In all conditions, treatment involved relaxation training (conducted in dental chairs) combined with gradual exposure to dental stimuli. In the group treatment and in one of the individual treatment conditions, exposure was conducted using videotaped dental scenes. In the second individual treatment condition (clinical rehearsal), exposure was conducted using actual simulated exposure to dental instruments and situations. Although the group treatment led to the greatest reduction in fear during treatment, people who received individual treatment using clinical rehearsal were most likely to subsequently seek dental care.

Öst (1996a) compared the effects of treatment in large groups (7 to 8 patients) versus treatment in small groups (3 to 4 patients) for individuals with spider phobia. Treatment involved a single session lasting 3 hours, consisting of exposure and modeling. Both conditions were equally effective on most measures, with 82% and 70% of people meeting criteria for clinically significant improvement in the small and large groups, respectively. At a 1-year follow-up, improvement was even greater, with 95% and 75% being significantly improved in the small and large groups, respectively. Taken together, these studies on treating dental phobias and spider phobias suggest that specific phobias may respond to group treatments.

Recommendations

Group and individual treatments each have advantages. Group treatments provide patients with an opportunity to meet other people with the same problem, which may help the patient to realize that other people also struggle with anxiety and fear. Group treatments also provide patients with an opportunity to learn from other people's mistakes and successes. Helping to apply the cognitive and behavioral strategies to other people's problems may facilitate patients' application of the techniques to their own symptoms. The group setting also provides social support and a degree of peer pressure, which may help to increase homework compliance for some patients. For patients with social phobia, the group provides a natural opportunity to practice exposure as well as any newly acquired social skills. For patients with agoraphobia, group members can accompany one another on exposure practices. Finally, group treatments allow the therapist to use his or her time more effectively and are more cost-effective for patients.

An obvious advantage of individual treatment over group treatment is that it allows the therapist to pay more attention to individual patients. For example, more time can be spent challenging a particular patient's thoughts and conducting relevant therapist-assisted exposure practices. In addition, individual treatment allows the therapy to be better tailored to the patient's needs. For example, the duration of each session, the number of sessions, and the types of strategies used can be chosen to suit a particular patient's symptoms. Another advantage of individual treatment is that there is less of a cost to missing sessions. In a group treatment, a patient who misses one or two sessions because of illness or vacation may fall far behind and may be more likely to drop out of the group. Missed sessions may require the therapist to help the patient catch up with additional individual meetings. In contrast, patients who miss individual treatment sessions can pick up where they left off at the next session. Individual treatment also allows flexibility with respect to scheduling. The more patients involved in the treatment, the harder it is to find a time that suits everyone. In addition, patients may have to wait longer to start treatment if there are not enough individuals to form a group. Finally, individual treatment may be preferable for patients who refuse to participate in a group (e.g., some severely socially phobic patients).

For group treatment, we recommend that the group members be as similar as possible to one another so that the treatment remains fairly focused and so that patients are likely to benefit from one another's experiences and contributions. Rather than running treatments for mixed groups of anxiety disorder patients, we suggest that patients be homogeneous at least with respect to diagnosis and, if possible, with respect to the severity of their symptoms. Group sessions for PD and social phobia typically last 90 minutes to 2 hours. The number of sessions is similar to that for treatments conducted individually. Despite preliminary evidence supporting the use of group treatments for specific phobias, we suggest that this approach be used cautiously. Individuals with certain specific phobias may need more individual attention (e.g., helping them to hold a snake) during exposure practices, compared with those with social phobia and agoraphobia.

Group sizes typically range from 2 or 3 patients, up to 10 patients. In fact, we recently found that people with social phobia can benefit from psychoeducational treatments presented in a large group format with up to 30 patients (Liss, Antony, Purdon, & Swinson, 1999). However, in our experience, smaller groups are often associated with fewer dropouts and better outcomes. Most research studies on group treatments for phobic disorders are based on groups of 4 to 6 patients. Therapists may also consider using a combination of group and individual treatment. For example, early sessions (consisting of psychoeducation) could be delivered in a group format, with later sessions (consisting of exposure practices) being delivered in smaller groups or individually.

THE INITIAL SESSION: PRESENTING THE TREATMENT RATIONALE

The initial presentation of a model for phobic fear and an overview of the treatment procedures is as important as the treatment procedures themselves. Because patients' expectations regarding treatment have such an enormous impact on treatment compliance as well as treatment outcome, it is essential that patients understand and accept the rationale before treatment starts. In this section, we provide an overview of how the rationale may be presented to patients. The suggestions presented here are adapted from recommendations by Craske and Barlow (1993) for the treatment of PD. The discussion begins with an overview of the nature of fear and phobias, followed by education regarding common myths that the patient might hold about the phobic situation or about the fear itself. Next, the patient is taught to think of his or her fear in terms of three components, namely the physical, cognitive, and behavioral aspects, as well as their interactions. Finally, an overview of the treatment procedures is presented, with a special emphasis on the importance of homework between sessions.

Presentation of the rationale typically takes a full session or two for patients with PD and social phobia. In addition to the general rationale presented early in treatment, more detailed instructions are provided for particular treatment procedures (e.g., exposure or cognitive restructuring) that begin after the first few sessions of treatment (see chapters 6 and 7). For specific phobias, the initial overview may be combined with the rationale and instructions for exposure, which tends to the principal focus of the entire treatment (see chapter 6).

The Nature of Anxiety, Fear, and Panic

Presentation of the treatment rationale should begin with a general discussion of the nature of anxiety, fear, panic attacks, and phobias. Several points should be made here. The patient should be told that anxiety and fear are basic emotions, experienced by all people and across animal species. In addition, the therapist should remind the patient that the goal of treatment is not to remove all anxiety and fear, but rather to bring these emotions to a level where they are no longer interfering. The therapist should also emphasize that the reactions associated with anxiety and fear are time-limited and manageable. The body is designed so that panic and fear will not last forever.

The therapist should engage the patient in a brief discussion of the advantages and survival value of fear and anxiety. All of the symptoms experienced during fear and panic are designed to activate the body for quick escape. For example, the heart beats harder and more quickly to get oxygen to the parts of the body that require it, breathing becomes faster to increase the amount of available oxygen, and we perspire so that our bodies are cooled down and we can perform more efficiently. Our bodies have developed the capacity to react very quickly and automatically to potentially dangerous situations. Although phobias are associated with a tendency to react this way in the absence of real danger, the mechanism of the reaction is the same. In other words, panic and fear protect us from danger. They are not dangerous in and of themselves.

For patients with PD, it may be reassuring to hear that their panic reactions are not dangerous. Similarly, people with social phobia may be relieved to hear that other people also experience fear from time to time and that discomfort in social situations is particularly common. For people with social phobia, it is helpful to emphasize the survival function of social anxiety in addition to the more general discussion regarding the survival value of fear and anxiety. Specifically, it can be argued that our concern about negative evaluation from other people motivates us to behave in a socially acceptable way (e.g., to get to work on time, dress appropriately, etc.). Of course, in social phobia, the concern to look good in front of others is out of proportion to the actual threat. Because PD and social phobia are both maintained in part by beliefs that one should not experience panic and fear, just knowing that it is okay to feel anxious can set the stage for overcoming these problems. Ironically, once patients are more willing to experience panic attacks or to have other people notice their anxiety symptoms, they will be less likely to experience panic and excessive fear.

For people with specific phobias, a discussion of how fear is normal may also be helpful. People often feel as though they are different from everyone else because they have an irrational fear. In addition to discussing the survival value of fear, it can be helpful to speculate regarding the survival value of fainting when treating people with blood and injection phobias who have a history of fainting in the phobic situation. Just as panic helps us to survive when faced with certain types of danger (e.g., being chased by a dangerous animal), fainting in the presence of blood may also have a survival function. If one were bleeding, it could be helpful to experience a drop in blood pressure in order to prevent an excessive loss of blood. It is this drop in blood pressure that causes fainting among people with blood phobia. As with panic, fainting upon seeing blood or receiving injections is a natural, normal, and adaptive response that happens to occur too easily and in situations where it is not needed.

Presenting a Model of the Patient's Fear

After the therapist and patient have discussed the fact that anxiety, panic, and fear are normal responses that are designed to facilitate escape from danger, it is helpful to provide patients with a cognitive–behavioral model with which to understand their problem and how it started. For patients with PD, it can be helpful to describe the problem as stemming from a complex interaction of biological and psychological factors (e.g., Antony & Barlow, 1996). Specifically, some people appear to have a genetically transmitted predisposition for experiencing panic attacks during or following periods of life stress (e.g., graduation, a stressful job, unemployment, a new marriage, divorce, financial strain, etc.), just as other people are predisposed to have other physical reactions to stress (e.g., stomach aches, increased blood pressure, more frequent colds, etc.). For many people, after the stress goes away, the panic attacks subside.

However, for some people, the panic symptoms themselves become a source of fear. In short, the person develops a phobia or fear of the physical sensations associated with panic attacks. Because physical sensations often occur out of the blue, people who fear the symptoms start to experience panic attacks, seemingly out of the blue, although actually they occur in response to benign physical sensations. Eventually, the person may start to avoid situations where it would be particularly embarrassing or dangerous to experience the symptoms (e.g., being alone, driving, crowds, etc.). The patient may also start to scan his or her body for sensations, making it more likely that panic attacks will be experienced. This increased vigilance for panic symptoms may even occur when a person is sleeping, resulting in nocturnal panic attacks. Just as new parents are quick to waken upon the sound of their infant crying, people who are concerned about feeling certain feared physical symptoms may be more likely to wake up in a panic upon experiencing these sensations while asleep.

For patients with social phobia and specific phobias, we recommend presenting a model that describes the cognitive and learning processes that contribute to these disorders. In the case of social phobia, it may also be helpful to discuss the role of genetics and biological factors that contribute to shyness, anxiety, and related personality characteristics. A helpful framework for presenting the etiology of social and specific phobias is Rachman's (1976, 1977) model of phobia development (see chapter 3 for a detailed description). In short, Rachman argued that fears develop through three different pathways. The first is direct traumatic conditioning (e.g., developing social phobia after being teased repeatedly in high school or developing a fear of dogs after being bitten by a dog as a child), the second is observational learning (e.g., growing up with a phobic role model, such as a shy parent or a sibling with a fear of heights), and the third includes other forms of information transmission (e.g., developing a fear of flying after repeatedly reading about airline crashes or developing a fear of meeting new people after being taught as a child that it is always important to make a good impression on others).

As is discussed in chapter 3, this model does not apply to all patients. For example, many patients report having had their fear for as long as they can recall and are aware of no relevant events that may have triggered the fear. Nor does the theory explain why some people develop a fear following a traumatic event and other people do not. In chapter 3 we discuss some of the possible reasons why these fear pathways affect different people differently.

Correcting Myths and Misconceptions

It is helpful to educate the patient with respect to specific myths and misconceptions that he or she holds regarding the nature of panic or the nature of the object or situation that he or she fears. Exhibit 5.1 provides a list of common misconceptions and corrective information that can be provided to patients with panic disorder and agoraphobia. People with social phobia or specific phobia may also hold misconceptions that need to be corrected. For example, some people with social phobia may believe that others can notice their anxiety symptoms, even if this is not the case. They may also falsely believe that almost all other people feel confident in social situations and rarely experience symptoms such as blushing, shaking, sweating, or losing their train of thought. In addition, people with phobias of thunderstorms, flying, elevators, or driving may be misinformed regarding the likelihood of mishaps in these situations. People with spider phobias may falsely assume that spiders can sense their fear and that they are more likely to be approached or attacked by the spider as a result. They may also misinterpret specific movements made by the spider.

Three Components of Anxiety, Fear, and Panic

People with phobic disorders often view their panic and fear reactions as an overwhelming force that hits them, sometimes out of the blue. Instead, it can be helpful to teach patients to view their fear and anxiety in terms of three components: the physical, the cognitive, and the behavioral. Definitions and examples of each component should be provided for the patient.

Exhibit 5.1
Common Myths and Misconceptions Regarding Panic Attacks and
Related Symptoms

Myth: I will "go crazy" as a result of my panic attacks.

Corrective Information: Although people often feel as though they are losing touch with reality during their panic attacks, this is something that simply does not occur. Although symptoms such as unreality, depersonalization, visual changes, and dizziness may be uncomfortable and frightening for some people, none of these are dangerous in any way. Psychological problems such as schizophrenia, in which people do sometimes lose touch with reality (i.e., experiencing symptoms such as hallucinations and delusions), are not at all related to problems with panic and agoraphobia. They are caused by different factors, and they respond to different treatments.

Myth: My panic attacks will lead to a heart attack or stroke.

Corrective Information: Although the symptoms of panic may mimic certain symptoms that people associate with heart attack and stroke (e.g., chest tightness or dizziness), there is no evidence that panic can directly cause any physical catastrophe or damage. The changes experienced in the body are similar to those that occur during exercise, sexual excitement, and other forms of physical arousal. Although they may be uncomfortable, they are not dangerous.

Myth: My panic attacks will cause me to faint.

Corrective Information: Although people with panic attacks often experience symptoms that make them feel as though they might faint (e.g., dizziness), fainting is very rare among people who experience panic attacks. In most cases, even when a person with panic attacks has fainted in the past, the fainting is not even during a panic attack. Rather, it may have occurred as a result of a physical illness (e.g., the flu) or while getting a needle or some other medical procedure. In fact, phobias of blood, needles, and surgery are the only types of phobias that tend to be associated with fainting. Furthermore, when people do faint, they are typically unconscious for only a few seconds.

Myth: Even if I do not have a heart attack now, the cumulative effect of having panic attacks will cause me to die young.

Corrective Information: Although there is evidence that frequent stressful events such as poverty, unemployment, divorce, and job stress increase the risk of developing certain physical illnesses, that does not mean that most people who are under stress develop such problems early in life. Stress is just one of many different factors that affect the risk of heart disease, along with family history of illness, being overweight, smoking, alcohol and drug use, diet, sleep habits, and exercise. In addition, despite good evidence regarding the relationship between stress and health, we know very little about the relationship between panic attacks and long-term health. There is little convincing evidence that having panic attacks is directly related to the development of health problems in the future.

Physical component

The physical component of fear and panic includes all the different physical symptoms that are associated with fear, such as a racing heart, breathlessness, dizziness, blurred vision, muscle tightness, nausea, sweating, shaking, chest tightness, and other uncomfortable physical sensations. The physical component may also include fainting, in the case of blood and injection phobias, and blushing, in the case of social phobia. The patient should also be reminded that the physical component is not fear in and of itself, but rather just a component of the fear. This point is especially important when treating people with PD, who tend to overemphasize the physical component of their fear. Patients with PD should be reminded that the physical sensations that occur during panic attacks are the same as those that occur during other intense emotions (e.g., anger or excitement). In fact, some people go out of their way to seek out the same sensations that people with PD try to avoid experiencing. For example, children spin around to feel dizzy, and many people go on amusement park rides specifically to experience the symptoms associated with fear.

As in the case of PD, people with social phobia often tend to focus on the physical sensations (particularly those that might be noticed by other people) that they experience in social situations. Therefore, individuals who are socially anxious can also benefit from understanding that it is possible to experience blushing, sweating, shaking, and other uncomfortable sensations in social situations and not necessarily be frightened by the feelings. In contrast, patients with certain specific phobias (e.g., animal phobias) are typically less concerned about the physical symptoms that are associated with their fear. Therefore, the discussion of the physical components can be relatively brief. For patients with other specific phobias (e.g., claustrophobia), a more detailed discussion of the physical component may be warranted if the patient is fearful of his or her physical reactions to the phobic situation.

Cognitive component

The cognitive component of fear includes the beliefs, assumptions, predictions, and interpretations that contribute to an individual's discomfort. For example, people with PD may assume that a racing heart is a sign of an impending heart attack. People with social phobia may interpret a friend's being unable to get together for dinner as a personal rejection. People with dog phobias may believe that most dogs are aggressive. Many more examples of phobic thinking are provided in chapter 7.

Another aspect of the cognitive component is the tendency to seek out information that confirms one's phobic beliefs and the tendency to differentially attend to information that is consistent with one's beliefs. For example, people with flying phobias are more likely to attend to information about airplanes that have crashed (e.g., in newspaper articles) than to information regarding planes that have landed safely. Similarly, people with PDA selectively attend to their uncomfortable physical sensations. Information-processing biases help to maintain phobic fear by preventing patients from attending to evidence that might otherwise help them to overcome their fearful thoughts.

Behavioral component

The behavioral component of fear includes the various strategies that people use to avoid the feared situation or to avoid their uncomfortable sensations. Typically, this includes overt avoidance or escape (e.g., not going to parties for fear of feeling humiliated, running away from a spider, or not driving on busy highways). However, phobic behavior can also include more subtle forms of avoidance, such as distraction (e.g., reading a book while flying in an airplane), reliance on safety cues (e.g., carrying a cellular phone when entering crowds, in case a panic attack occurs), drinking alcohol (e.g., before entering a feared social situation), or reliance on other overprotective behaviors (e.g., checking for dogs in the neighborhood before leaving the house). Chapter 4 includes examples of subtle avoidance strategies engaged in by people with phobic disorders. As is reviewed in chapter 6, avoidance behaviors help people to feel more comfortable in the short term. However, in the long term, they serve to maintain the phobic symptoms because the person is prevented from ever learning that the phobic object, situation, or sensations are safe and that the fear is unwarranted.

Interactions among the three components

After discussing the nature of each of the three components of anxiety and fear, the therapist should engage the patient in a discussion of how the components interact with one another. The cycle of fear can begin with any one of the three components, depending on the type of anxiety disorder and the specific situation. For example, a patient with PD might experience an uncomfortable sensation (e.g., dizziness) from some benign cause (e.g., standing up quickly). This in turn might trigger the thought that he or she is going to lose control. This fearful interpretation often leads to more sensations, which in turn reinforce the fearful prediction regarding losing control. As the panic becomes more intense, various coping behaviors (e.g., avoidance, escape, etc.) are used to reduce the anxiety.

The cycle can also begin with an anxious thought. For example, a person who is fearful of public speaking might expect to feel nervous and, as a result, blush and shake during a presentation. During the talk, he or she would probably be vigilant for these uncomfortable feelings, making them more likely to be experienced, and thereby intensifying the thoughts. The increased intensity of the fearful thoughts would lead to an increase in the intensity of these symptoms, which are a normal part of fear.

Finally, the cycle can begin with the behavioral component of fear. Avoidance for an extended period can have the effect of increasing fear during the next encounter with the feared situation. Just as it is often hardest to drag oneself to an unpleasant job on Monday (after a weekend away), it is harder to enter a feared situation after a long absence. Avoidance has the effect of maintaining or increasing an individual's fear over time.

Overview of Treatment Strategies

After the therapist has discussed with the patient the nature of fear and anxiety and their components, an overview of the treatment strategies should be provided. The therapist should also emphasize how each of the treatment strategies targets particular components of the phobia and how the problem can be overcome by breaking the fear cycle by targeting either the cognitive, behavioral, or physical components. For example, cognitive therapy targets the fearful thoughts and misconceptions that contribute to the fear. Exposure targets the behavioral component of fear (e.g., avoidance), which in turn helps to change the fearful predictions by demonstrating for the patient that they are unfounded. Finally, strategies such as BRT and medication break the cycle of fear by targeting the physical component of fear.

Homework

From the first session, the patient should understand that homework is an important part of each session and that compliance with homework will be the key to overcoming the fear. The time commitment necessary for the homework should be discussed in advance, and any concerns that the patient has should be addressed. Having the patient monitor the physical, cognitive, and behavioral aspects of his or her fear (using the Three Components of Anxiety and Panic Monitoring Form) is an appropriate homework assignment for the week following the first session. A sample of a completed monitoring form (for a patient with PD) is included in Exhibit 5.2. A blank copy of this form as well as the other forms suggested as homework in the "Sample Protocols for Phobic Disorders" section of this chapter can be found in the following exhibits:

- Exhibit 4.10: Panic Attack Diary
- Exhibit 5.3: Three Components of Anxiety and Panic Monitoring Form

- Exhibit 6.4: Symptom Induction Testing Form
- Exhibit 6.5: Interoceptive Exposure Monitoring Form
- Exhibit 6.7: Exposure Monitoring Form
- Exhibit 7.8: Cognitive Monitoring Form

FINAL SESSIONS: TERMINATION AND STRATEGIES FOR MAINTAINING GAINS

As the end of treatment approaches, the therapist should discuss with the patient his or her feelings about terminating CBT or, if applicable, discontinuing medication. A number of steps may be taken to minimize any negative effects of ending treatment. First, patients should know at the start of treatment the approximate number of treatment sessions, and the patient's progress should be reviewed periodically to assess the extent to which the treatment goals are being met. In other words, termination should be discussed right from the start and periodically throughout the course of therapy. Patients should be prepared in advance for the time when treatment eventually ends.

A number of factors can contribute to the return of fear after treatment has ended. First, patients who have made only partial gains may be at risk for experiencing a return of fear. For example, continuing to hold the belief "It would be a disaster to have another panic attack" may leave an individual with PD at risk for experiencing a return of symptoms if he or she actually has another panic attack. Second, a long period of avoidance may also contribute to a return of fear. For example, a professor who is fearful of teaching in large classes may be more fearful in the early fall, after not having had the opportunity to teach during the summer. Third, a trauma in the feared situation (e.g., being bitten by a dog after having overcome a fear of dogs) may lead to a quick return of fear. Fourth, increased life stress (e.g., relationship problems or financial strain) may lead to an increase in phobic symptoms, even if the content of the phobic fear is unrelated to the stress. Finally, patients may experience an increase in fear if they encounter a situation that is more difficult than those practiced during treatment (e.g., panicking on the Golden Gate Bridge in San Francisco after having overcome a fear of smaller bridges in a different city).

In order to minimize the chances of the fear returning, a number of steps may be taken. First, treatment should be withdrawn gradually. Medications should be discontinued slowly, and CBT should end after a period of gradually spacing out the last few sessions. Also, as is reviewed in chapter 6, there is evidence that gradually expanding the time between exposure practices over the course of treatment may protect an individual from experiencing a return of fear (e.g., Rowe & Craske, 1998a). In addition,

Exhibit 5.2

Three Components of Anxiety and Panic Monitoring Form (Sample for Panic Disorder)

Place/situation/ date/time	Fear rating (0–100)	Sensations	Anxious thoughts	Anxious behaviors
March 3 at a movie	55	felt breathless, started sweating	I will have to leave I will pass out I will suffocate People will think I'm strange	went to the washroom until my panic symptoms went away
March 7 lying in bed	90	heart pounding, feeling unreal, chest pain	I am having a heart attack I am going crazy	left the light on, watched TV until I fell asleep
March 9 driving in the car	70	very dizzy, blurred vision, racing heart	I am going to crash the car I am dying	stayed in the right lane, drove slowly, distracted myself with the radio

Exhibit 5.3
Three Components of Anxiety and Panic Monitoring Form

Place/situation/ date/time	Fear rating (0–100)	Sensations	Anxious thoughts	Anxious behaviors

patients should be reassured that further treatment can be made available if there is a return of symptoms in the future.

Specific treatment strategies can be adapted for relapse prevention as well. For example, cognitive techniques can be used to prepare the patient for hypothetical traumatic scenarios that could occur in the future (e.g., experiencing a very severe panic attack, having a car accident, or being criticized or rejected by another person). Patients should also be encouraged to continue occasional exposure practices even after the fear has subsided. For example, an individual who was previously phobic of heights can be encouraged to spend a few minutes near the edge whenever he or she encounters a high place.

If a patient does experience a return of symptoms, he or she should be encouraged to start using the treatment strategies again. Rereading a good self-help manual may remind the patient of the techniques that were most helpful the first time around. In addition, a small number of "booster" treatment sessions may be enough to bring patients back to where they were before the symptoms returned.

BIBLIOTHERAPY AND SELF-HELP READINGS

We recommend that self-help readings be integrated into the treatment plan in order to reinforce the principles learned during the treatment sessions (see Pantalon & Lubetkin, 1995, for a discussion of this topic). There is evidence, however, that the bibliotherapy works best when it is combined with visits to a professional who can monitor the patient's progress and compliance (Febbraro et al., 1999). In Appendix C, we have listed a number of self-help readings that we often recommend to our patients. These include stand-alone books that summarize empirically supported strategies for overcoming anxiety and fear (e.g., Antony & Swinson, 2000b; Markway, Carmin, Pollard, & Flynn, 1992; Zuercher-White, 1997a), as well as a series of step-by-step manuals that are available in both clinician and client versions (see Appendixes B and C).

For example, the Psychological Corporation publishes therapist and client manuals for PD (Barlow & Craske, 1994; Craske & Barlow, 1994; Craske, Meadows, & Barlow, 1994) and specific phobias (Antony, Craske, & Barlow, 1995; Craske et al., 1997) in their *TherapyWorks* series. New Harbinger Publications has recently begun a similar series of manuals (e.g., Bourne, 1998a, 1998b), referred to as the *Best Practices* series. Other publishers, such as Jason Aronson, have also begun to publish self-help manuals (e.g., Rapee, 1998) for phobic disorders, with accompanying clinician manuals (e.g., Bruce & Sanderson, 1998; Rapee & Sanderson, 1998). Although the quality of these manuals is generally quite good, they differ from one another considerably with respect to price and availability (e.g., the ease with which they can be found in local book stores). Finally, it may be helpful to recommend books (when appropriate) on overcoming other problems that are often associated with phobic disorders, including other anxiety disorders (e.g., Foa & Wilson, 1991), depression (Burns, 1989; Greenberger & Padesky, 1995), anger management (McKay, Rogers, & McKay, 1989), and perfectionism (e.g., Antony & Swinson, 1998).

SAMPLE PROTOCOLS FOR PHOBIC DISORDERS

In other chapters we provide detailed instructions for teaching patients to use exposure, cognitive strategies, and other therapeutic techniques to overcome their fear and phobias. In previous sections of this chapter, we provided overviews of how to present the treatment rationale and how to deal with issues related to termination. The purpose of this section is to integrate the suggestions from other parts of this book in order to provide session-by-session outlines for treating PD, social phobia, and specific phobias. These protocols are based on the assumption that the patient has already had a thorough assessment and that the therapist has a detailed picture regarding variables such as the cognitive features of the patient's fear or phobia, the patient's range of avoidance, specific coping strategies used by the patient, and previous treatment history.

Note that these treatment plans are flexible. For example, although we recommend 11 sessions for PD, there will be some patients (e.g., with very mild or infrequent panic attacks) who will need only 3 or 4 sessions of treatment (primarily psychoeducation). Other patients with more severe symptoms may require more treatment sessions than we recommend in these sample protocols. Patients may also differ with respect to how much time is spent on particular strategies. For example, a patient with PD who does not experience any fear in response to the IE exercises might benefit more from focusing on other treatment strategies.

Panic Disorder With Mild or No Agoraphobia

Session 1

Duration: 1 hour.

Introduction and rationale for treatment: This session focuses on providing an overview of the rationale for treatment, including (a) the nature of panic and anxiety (e.g., fear is normal, time-limited, and has a survival function), (b) myths and misconceptions regarding panic, (c) a model of panic attacks and PD, (d) the three components of panic (i.e., physical, cognitive, and behavioral) and their interactions, (e) an overview of the treatment strategies, and (f) the importance of homework compliance.

Homework: The patient is instructed to monitor his or her panic attacks in the coming week using the Three Components of Anxiety and Panic Monitoring Form and the Panic Attack Diary. In addition, patients may be instructed to begin self-help readings on the nature of panic and agoraphobia (e.g., Barlow & Craske, 1994; Zuercher-White, 1997a).

Session 2

Timing: 1 week after Session 1.
Duration: 1 hour.
Review of the previous week: This session begins with an overview of the previous week's events, lasting about 20 to 30 minutes. The therapist reviews the monitoring forms and provides corrective feedback. In addition, the therapist answers any questions that the patient has about the self-help readings. While discussing anxiety and panic episodes from the previous week, the therapist may begin the process of Socratic questioning to help the patient to identify anxious thoughts and to consider alternative explanations for panic-related symptoms.

Introduction to cognitive biases: After reviewing the previous week's events, the therapist provides an overview of how cognitions influence panic and anxiety. Detailed descriptions of the common information-processing biases (e.g., arbitrary inference, selective abstraction, catastrophic thinking) are provided, and the patient is taught how to identify his or her anxious thoughts.

Homework: The patient is instructed to monitor his or her panic attacks in the coming week using the Panic Attack Diary. In addition, he or she should continue to complete the Three Components of Anxiety and Panic Monitoring Form, paying special attention to the cognitive features of anxiety and panic. Finally, the patient should be instructed to continue the self-help readings, with a focus on chapters pertaining to cognition and panic.

Session 3

Timing: 1 week after Session 2.
Duration: 1 hour.
Review of the previous week: This session begins with a 20- to 30-minute review of the homework and the previous week's events, with an emphasis on challenging episodes of anxious thinking that occurred through the week.
Introduction to cognitive restructuring: After the review, the rationale and instructions for cognitive restructuring are provided. The patient is

taught methods of challenging arbitrary inferences, selective abstractions, catastrophic thinking, and related cognitive biases. In addition, detailed instruction in how to use the cognitive monitoring forms is provided.

Homework: The patient is instructed to monitor his or her panic attacks in the coming week using the Panic Attack Diary. In addition, he or she should now start using the Cognitive Monitoring Form to identify and challenge panic-related cognitions. Finally, the patient should be instructed to continue the self-help readings, with a focus on chapters pertaining to cognition and panic.

Session 4

Timing: 1 week after Session 3.
Duration: 1 hour.
Review of the previous week: This session begins with a 20-minute review of the homework and the previous week's events, with an emphasis on challenging episodes of anxious thinking that occurred through the week.
Rationale for exposure: Following the review, the rationale and general principles of effective exposure are provided (e.g., exposure should be predictable, prolonged, repeated frequently, etc.).
Rationale for interoceptive exposure: Next, the therapist engages the patient in a brief discussion of the rationale for IE.
Symptom-induction testing: The patient is asked to attempt each of the exercises on the Symptom-Induction Testing Form and to report the types of symptoms experienced, the intensity of the symptoms, the level of fear during or immediately following the exercise, and the extent to which the experience was similar to his or her naturally occurring panic attacks.
Homework: The patient is instructed to continue completing the Panic Attack Diary and Cognitive Monitoring Form and to continue the self-help readings, with an emphasis on chapters pertaining to IE.

Session 5

Timing: 1 week after Session 4.
Duration: 1 hour.
Review of the previous week: This session begins with a 20-minute review of the homework and the previous week's events, with an emphasis on challenging episodes of anxious thinking that occurred through the week.
Completion of symptom-induction testing: Following the review, symptom-induction testing is continued if there was not enough time to complete the testing during Session 4.
Interoceptive-exposure practices: Next, an interoceptive exercise that successfully triggered fear is selected for repeated practice. The patient should

attempt the exercise four or five times in a row, with a short break between each trial (a few minutes, or long enough for the symptoms to abate). Over the course of the repeated trials, the therapist and patient monitor the extent to which the fear decreases from trial to trial.

Homework: The patient is instructed to continue completing the Panic Attack Diary and Cognitive Monitoring Form and to continue the self-help readings, with an emphasis on chapters pertaining to IE. In addition, the patient should select one or two IE exercises and practice them at home in sets of four to five trials (twice per day). The Interoceptive Exposure Monitoring Form should be completed at each practice.

Session 6

Timing: 1 week after Session 5.

Duration: 1 hour.

Review of the previous week: This session begins with a 20- to 30-minute review of the homework and the previous week's events, with an emphasis on challenging episodes of anxious thinking that occurred through the week and reviewing the patient's progress with the IE practices.

Interoceptive-exposure practices: The patient and therapist continue to practice IE using exercises that are relevant to the patient.

Introduction to in vivo exposure: The therapist and patient identify situations or activities that the patient tends to avoid or in which the patient engages in subtle avoidance, reliance on safety cues, or reliance on overprotective behaviors.

Homework: The patient is instructed to continue completing the Panic Attack Diary and Cognitive Monitoring Form and to continue the self-help readings, with an emphasis on chapters pertaining to in vivo exposure. In addition, the patient should continue to practice IE exercises and should introduce in vivo exposure practices three to four times per week. During in vivo exposure practices, the patient is encouraged to discontinue subtle avoidance methods such as distraction. The Exposure Monitoring Form and Interoceptive Exposure Monitoring Form should be completed at each practice.

Session 7

Timing: 1 week after Session 6.

Duration: 1 hour.

Review of the previous week: This session begins with a 20- to 30-minute review of the homework and the previous week's events, with an emphasis on challenging episodes of anxious thinking that occurred through the week and reviewing the patient's progress with the interoceptive and in vivo exposure practices.

Introduction to combining interoceptive and in vivo exposure: The therapist and patient identify possible practices in which IE and in vivo exposure can be combined (e.g., breathing through a straw while stuck in traffic).

Homework: The patient continues to complete the Panic Attack Diary, Cognitive Monitoring Form, and Exposure Monitoring Form. Throughout the following week, the patient continues to practice cognitive restructuring, IE, and in vivo exposure on most days. During in vivo exposure practices, the patient is encouraged to induce feared sensations using IE exercises.

Session 8

Timing: 1 week after Session 7.

Duration: 1 hour.

Review of the previous week: This session begins with a 30-minute review of the homework and the previous week's events, with an emphasis on challenging episodes of anxious thinking that occurred through the week and reviewing the patient's progress with the interoceptive and in vivo exposure practices.

Discussion of the worst panic attack: The therapist and patient identify the worst panic attack that the patient has ever experienced and attempt to challenge any unrealistic or anxious beliefs that the patient still holds regarding this experience.

Homework: The patient continues to complete the Panic Attack Diary, Cognitive Monitoring Form, and Exposure Monitoring Form. Throughout the following 2 weeks, the patient continues to practice cognitive restructuring, IE, and in vivo exposure on most days.

Session 9

Timing: 2 weeks after Session 8.

Duration: 1 hour.

Content of session: The purpose of this session is to help the patient to consolidate his or her gains. The session is spent reviewing the homework and the previous 2 weeks' events, with an emphasis on challenging episodes of anxious thinking that occurred since the last session and reviewing the patient's progress with the interoceptive and in vivo exposure practices.

Homework: The patient continues to complete the Panic Attack Diary, Cognitive Monitoring Form, and Exposure Monitoring Form. Throughout the following 2 weeks, the patient continues to practice cognitive restructuring, IE, and in vivo exposure on most days.

Session 10

Timing: 2 weeks after Session 9.
Duration: 1 hour.
Content of session: The purpose of this session is to help the patient to consolidate his or her gains. The session is spent reviewing the homework and the previous 2 weeks' events, with an emphasis on challenging episodes of anxious thinking that occurred since the last session and reviewing the patient's progress with the interoceptive and in vivo exposure practices.
Homework: The patient continues to complete the Panic Attack Diary, Cognitive Monitoring Form, and Exposure Monitoring Form. Throughout the following 2 weeks, the patient continues to practice cognitive restructuring, IE, and in vivo exposure on most days.

Session 11

Timing: 2 weeks after Session 10.
Duration: 1 hour.
Review of the previous 2 weeks: This session begins with a 30-minute review of the homework and the previous 2 weeks' events, with an emphasis on challenging episodes of anxious thinking that occurred since the last session and reviewing the patient's progress with the interoceptive and in vivo exposure practices.
Maintenance strategies and termination: The patient and therapist discuss strategies for maintaining gains and for coping with a possible return of symptoms in the future.
Homework: The patient should continue to use the strategies that were most helpful during the treatment.

Variations on the Treatment Protocol

There are a number of ways in which this protocol may be altered to suit particular patients' needs:

- Include BRT (early in treatment, before introducing the cognitive strategies) for patients who engage in chronic hyperventilation.
- Consider having more frequent sessions (particularly at the beginning) to increase the rate of improvement.
- Consider increasing or decreasing the total number of sessions, depending on the patient's progress.
- Add a follow-up or "booster" session 1 to 3 months after treatment ends in order to check on the patient's progress and review strategies for maintaining gains.

- Spend more or less time on in vivo exposure, depending on the patient's degree of agoraphobic avoidance.
- Consider conducting the protocol using a group format (with meetings lasting between 90 minutes and 2 hours, depending on the size of the group).
- Consider involving the patient's partner, a close friend, or a family member in the treatment sessions and homework practices.
- Consider including a few sessions of therapist-assisted situational exposure for patients who are unable or unwilling to attempt exposure practices unaccompanied between sessions.

Panic Disorder With Agoraphobia

Session 1

Duration: 1 hour.
Introduction and rationale for treatment: The focus of this session is on providing an overview of the treatment rationale, including (a) the nature of panic and anxiety (e.g., fear is normal, time-limited, and has a survival function); (b) myths and misconceptions regarding panic; (c) a model of panic attacks, PD, and agoraphobia; (d) the three components of panic (i.e., physical, cognitive, and behavioral) and their interactions; (e) an overview of the treatment strategies; and (f) the importance of homework compliance.
Homework: The patient is instructed to monitor his or her panic attacks in the coming week using the Three Components of Anxiety and Panic Monitoring Form and the Panic Attack Diary. In addition, patients may be instructed to begin self-help reading on the nature of panic and agoraphobia (e.g., Barlow & Craske, 1994; Zuercher-White, 1997a).

Session 2

Timing: 1 week after Session 1.
Duration: 1 hour.
Review of the previous week: This session begins with an overview of the previous week's events, lasting about 20 to 30 minutes. The therapist reviews the monitoring forms and provides corrective feedback. In addition, the therapist answers any questions that the patient has about the self-help readings. While discussing anxiety and panic episodes from the previous week, the therapist may begin the process of Socratic questioning to help

the patient to identify anxious thoughts and to consider alternative explanations for his or her panic-related symptoms.

Introduction to cognitive biases: After reviewing the previous week's events, the therapist provides an overview of how cognitions influence panic and anxiety. Detailed descriptions of common information-processing biases (e.g., arbitrary inference, selective abstraction, and catastrophic thinking) are provided, and the patient is taught how to identify his or her anxious thoughts.

Homework: The patient is instructed to monitor his or her panic attacks in the coming week using the Panic Attack Diary. In addition, he or she should continue to complete the Three Components of Anxiety and Panic Monitoring Form, paying special attention to the cognitive features of anxiety and panic. Finally, the patient should be instructed to continue the self-help readings, with a focus on chapters pertaining to cognition and panic.

Session 3

Timing: 1 week after Session 2.
Duration: 1 hour.
Review of the previous week: This session begins with a 20- to 30-minute review of the homework and the previous week's events, with an emphasis on challenging episodes of anxious thinking that occurred through the week.
Introduction to cognitive restructuring: After the review, the rationale and instructions for cognitive restructuring are provided. The patient is taught methods of challenging arbitrary inferences, selective abstractions, catastrophic thinking, and related cognitive biases. In addition, detailed instruction in how to use the cognitive monitoring forms is provided.
Homework: The patient is instructed to monitor his or her panic attacks in the coming week using the Panic Attack Diary. In addition, he or she should now start using the Cognitive Monitoring Form to identify and challenge panic-related cognitions. Finally, the patient should be instructed to continue the self-help readings, with a focus on chapters pertaining to cognition and panic.

Session 4

Timing: 1 week after Session 3.
Duration: 1 hour.
Review of the previous week: This session begins with a 20-minute review of the homework and the previous week's events, with an emphasis on challenging episodes of anxious thinking that occurred through the week.

Rationale for exposure: Following the review, the rationale and general principles of effective exposure are provided (e.g., exposure should be predictable, prolonged, repeated frequently, etc.).

Development of exposure hierarchy: The patient and therapist develop a detailed hierarchy of situations that will be used to plan exposure practices conducted for homework and during in-session exposures.

Homework: The patient is instructed to continue completing the Panic Attack Diary, to practice cognitive restructuring using the Cognitive Monitoring Form, and to continue the self-help readings, with an emphasis on chapters pertaining to exposure. In addition, if the patient is able, he or she should attempt repeated (e.g., five times per week) exposure to a situation that is relatively low on his or her hierarchy. An Exposure Monitoring Form should be completed after each practice.

Sessions 5–8

Timing: Weekly.

Duration of each session: 1.5 to 2.5 hours.

Review of the previous week: Each session begins with a 20- to 30-minute review of the homework and the previous week's events, with an emphasis on challenging episodes of anxious thinking that occurred through the week and discussion of the previous week's exposure homework practices.

Exposure practices: The therapist accompanies the patient on exposure practices selected from the exposure hierarchy or from other situations that are feared by the patient. As the patient's fear improves, the exposure practices shift to being conducted alone, and contact with the therapist during the session includes only a brief discussion before and after the practice.

Homework: The patient is instructed to continue completing the Panic Attack Diary and Cognitive Monitoring Form and to continue self-help readings that are relevant to the content of the sessions. In addition, the patient continues to practice in vivo exposure at least 5 days per week, between treatment sessions, each time completing the Exposure Monitoring Form.

Session 9

Timing: 1 week after session 8.

Duration of session: 90 minutes.

Review of the previous week: The session begins with a 20- to 30-minute review of the homework and the previous week's events, with an emphasis on challenging episodes of anxious thinking that occurred through the week and discussion of the previous week's exposure homework practices.

Rationale for interoceptive exposure: The therapist engages the patient in a brief discussion of the rationale for IE.

Symptom-induction testing: The patient is asked to attempt each of the exercises on the Symptom-Induction Testing Form and to report the types of symptoms experienced, the intensity of the symptoms, the level of fear during or immediately following the exercise, and the extent to which the experience was similar to a naturally occurring panic attack.

Homework: The patient is instructed to continue completing the Panic Attack Diary, to practice cognitive restructuring using the Cognitive Monitoring Form, and to continue self-help readings, with an emphasis on chapters related to IE. In addition, the patient continues to practice in vivo exposure at least 5 days per week, each time completing the Exposure Monitoring Form. Finally, the patient should select one or two IE exercises and practice them at home in sets of four to five trials (twice per day). The Interoceptive Exposure Monitoring Form should be completed following each IE practice.

Session 10

Timing: 1 week after Session 9.
Duration: 1 hour.
Review of the previous week: This session begins with a 20- to 30-minute review of the homework and the previous week's events, with an emphasis on challenging episodes of anxious thinking that occurred through the week and reviewing the patient's progress with the interoceptive and in vivo exposure practices.

Introduction to combining interoceptive and in vivo exposure: The therapist and patient identify possible practices in which IE and in vivo exposure can be combined (e.g., breathing through a straw while riding an elevator).

Homework: The patient is instructed to continue completing the Panic Attack Diary and Cognitive Monitoring Form and to practice interoceptive and in vivo exposure exercises at least three to four times per week. During in vivo exposure practices, the patient is encouraged to attempt to induce feared sensations using IE exercises. The Exposure Monitoring Form and Interoceptive Exposure Monitoring Form should be completed.

Session 11

Timing: 2 weeks after Session 10.
Duration: 1 hour.
Content of session: The purpose of this session is to help the patient to consolidate his or her gains. The session is spent reviewing the homework and the previous 2 weeks' events, with an emphasis on challenging episodes

of anxious thinking that occurred since the last session and reviewing the patient's progress with the interoceptive and in vivo exposure practices.

Homework: The patient continues to complete the Panic Attack Diary, Cognitive Monitoring Form, and Exposure Monitoring Form. Throughout the following 2 weeks, the patient continues to practice cognitive restructuring, IE, and in vivo exposure on most days.

Session 12

Timing: 2 weeks after Session 11.

Duration: 1 hour.

Review of the previous 2 weeks: This session begins with a 30-minute review of the homework and the previous 2 weeks' events, with an emphasis on challenging episodes of anxious thinking that occurred since the last session and reviewing the patient's progress with the interoceptive and in vivo exposure practices.

Maintenance strategies and termination: The patient and therapist discuss strategies for maintaining gains and for coping with a possible return of symptoms in the future.

Homework: The patient should continue to use the strategies that were most helpful during the treatment.

Variations on the Treatment Protocol

There are a number of ways in which this protocol may be altered to suit particular patients' needs:

- Consider having more frequent sessions to increase the rate of change during treatment.
- Consider increasing or decreasing the total number of sessions, depending on the patient's progress.
- Add a follow-up or "booster" session 1 to 3 months after treatment ends in order to check on the patient's progress and review strategies for maintaining gains.
- Consider changing the relative amounts of time spent on cognitive restructuring, IE, and in vivo exposure, depending on the patient's response to each particular strategy.
- Consider conducting the protocol using a group format (with the duration of each session depending on the size of the group).
- Consider involving the patient's partner, a close friend, or a family member in the treatment sessions and homework practices

- Consider increasing or decreasing the amount of therapist-assisted exposure, depending on the degree to which the patient is able to practice unaccompanied or with a family member or friend.

Social Phobia

Session 1

Duration: 1 hour.
Introduction and rationale for treatment: This session focuses on providing an overview of the treatment rationale, including discussions regarding (a) the nature of fear and social anxiety (e.g., occasional social anxiety is normal and has a survival function), (b) myths and misconceptions regarding fear and social anxiety, (c) a model of social phobia (d) the three components of fear (i.e., physical, cognitive, and behavioral) and their interactions, (e) an overview of the treatment strategies, and (f) the importance of homework compliance.
Homework: The patient is instructed to monitor his or her anxiety in social situations over the coming week using the Three Components of Anxiety and Panic Monitoring Form. In addition, patients may be encouraged to begin self-help readings on the nature and treatment of social phobia (e.g., Markway et al., 1998).

Session 2

Timing: 1 week after Session 1.
Duration: 1 hour.
Review of the previous week: This session begins with an overview of the previous week's events, lasting about 20- to 30-minutes. The therapist reviews the monitoring forms and provides corrective feedback. In addition, the therapist answers any questions that the patient may have about the self-help readings. While discussing episodes of social anxiety from the previous week, the therapist may begin the process of Socratic questioning to help the patient to identify anxious thoughts and to consider alternative explanations, interpretations, and predictions.
Introduction to cognitive biases: After reviewing the previous week's events, the therapist provides an overview of how cognitions influence social anxiety. Detailed descriptions of common information-processing biases (e.g., arbitrary inference, selective abstraction, and catastrophic thinking) are provided, and the patient is taught how to identify his or her anxious thoughts.

Homework: The patient continues to complete the Three Components of Anxiety and Panic Monitoring Form, paying special attention to the cognitive features of his or her social anxiety. Finally, the patient should be instructed to continue the self-help readings, with a focus on material pertaining to cognition and social anxiety.

Session 3

Timing: 1 week after Session 2.
Duration: 1 hour.
Review of the previous week: This session begins with a 20- to 30-minute review of the homework and the previous week's events, with an emphasis on challenging episodes of anxious thinking that occurred through the week.
Introduction to cognitive restructuring: After the review, the rationale and instructions for cognitive restructuring are provided. The patient is taught methods of challenging arbitrary inferences, selective abstractions, catastrophic thinking, and related cognitive biases. In addition, detailed instruction in how to use the Cognitive Monitoring Form is provided.
Homework: The patient is instructed to start using the Cognitive Monitoring Form to identify and challenge anxious cognitions. In addition, the patient should continue the self-help readings, with a focus on sections pertaining to cognition and social anxiety.

Session 4

Timing: 1 week after Session 3.
Duration: 1 hour.
Review of the previous week: This session begins with a 20-minute review of the homework and the previous week's events, with an emphasis on challenging episodes of anxious thinking that occurred through the week.
Rationale for exposure: Following the review, the rationale and general principles of effective exposure are provided (e.g., exposure should be predictable, prolonged, repeated frequently, etc.).
Development of exposure hierarchy: The patient and therapist develop a detailed hierarchy of situations that will be used to plan exposure practices conducted for homework and during in-session exposures.
Homework: The patient is instructed to continue practicing cognitive restructuring using the Cognitive Monitoring Form and to continue the self-help readings, with an emphasis on chapters pertaining to exposure. In addition, he or she should attempt repeated exposure (e.g., three to five times during the week) to a situation that is relatively low on his or her hierarchy. An Exposure Monitoring Form should be completed after each practice.

Sessions 5–8

Timing: Weekly.

Duration of each session: 1.5 to 2 hours.

Review of the previous week: Each session begins with a 20- to 30-minute review of the homework and the previous week's events, with an emphasis on challenging episodes of anxious thinking that occurred through the week and discussion of the previous week's exposure homework practices.

Exposure practices: The therapist may accompany the patient on exposure practices selected from the exposure hierarchy or from other situations that are feared by the patient. In-session exposures may include role-play simulations (e.g., a simulated job interview) or in vivo exposures accompanied by the therapist (e.g., returning items to a store).

Homework: The patient is instructed to continue practicing cognitive restructuring using the Cognitive Monitoring Form and to continue self-help readings that are relevant to the content of the sessions. In addition, the patient continues to practice in vivo exposure at least 5 days per week, between treatment sessions, each time completing the Exposure Monitoring Form.

Session 9

Timing: 1 week after Session 8.

Duration of session: 1 hour.

Review of the previous week: The session begins with a 20- to 30-minute review of the homework and the previous week's events, with an emphasis on challenging episodes of anxious thinking that occurred through the week and discussion of the previous week's exposure homework practices.

Social skills training: If warranted, the therapist engages the patient in a brief discussion of the rationale for social skills training, after which the therapist and patient identify and begin to change specific behaviors that have been targeted for social skills training.

Homework: The patient is instructed to continue practicing cognitive restructuring using the Cognitive Monitoring Form and to continue self-help readings, with an emphasis on material related to social skills training (e.g., McKay, Davis, & Fanning, 1995). In addition, the patient continues to practice in vivo exposure at least 5 days per week, integrating specific social skills training exercises as necessary. The Exposure Monitoring Form should be completed following each situational exposure practice.

Session 10

Timing: 1 week after Session 9.

Duration: 1 hour.

Content of session: The purpose of this session is to help the patient to continue to consolidate his or her gains. The session is spent reviewing the homework and the previous week's events, with an emphasis on challenging episodes of anxious thinking that occurred since the last session and reviewing the patient's progress with in vivo exposure and social skills training practices.

Homework: The patient continues to complete the Cognitive Monitoring Form and Exposure Monitoring Form. Throughout the following 2 weeks, the patient continues to practice cognitive restructuring, in vivo exposure, and social skills practices on most days.

Session 11

Timing: 2 weeks after Session 10.

Duration: 1 hour.

Content of session: The purpose of this session is to help the patient to consolidate his or her gains. The session is spent reviewing the homework and the previous 2 weeks' events, with an emphasis on challenging episodes of anxious thinking that occurred since the last session and reviewing the patient's progress with in vivo exposure and social skills training practices.

Homework: The patient continues to complete the Cognitive Monitoring Form and Exposure Monitoring Form. Throughout the following 2 weeks, the patient continues to practice cognitive restructuring, in vivo exposure, and social skills practices on most days.

Session 12

Timing: 2 weeks after Session 11.

Duration: 1 hour.

Review of the previous 2 weeks: This session begins with a 30-minute review of the homework and the previous 2 weeks' events, with an emphasis on challenging episodes of anxious thinking that occurred since the last session and reviewing the patient's progress with the in vivo exposure and social skills training practices.

Maintenance strategies and termination: The patient and therapist discuss strategies for maintaining gains and for coping with a possible return of symptoms in the future.

Homework: The patient should continue to use the strategies that were most helpful during the treatment.

Variations on the Treatment Protocol

There are a number of ways in which this protocol may be altered to suit particular patients' needs:

- Consider meeting more frequently to facilitate quicker improvement during treatment.
- Consider increasing or decreasing the total number of sessions, depending on the patient's progress.
- Add a follow-up or "booster" session 1 to 3 months after treatment ends in order to check on the patient's progress and review strategies for maintaining gains.
- Consider changing the relative amounts of time spent on cognitive restructuring and in vivo exposure, depending on the patient's response to each particular strategy.
- Consider eliminating, reducing, or increasing the time spent on social skills, depending on the patient's needs.
- Consider conducting the protocol using a group format (with each session lasting about 2 hours).
- Consider involving the patient's partner, a close friend, or a family member in the treatment sessions and homework practices.
- Consider increasing or decreasing the amount of therapist-assisted exposure, depending on the degree to which the patient is able to practice unaccompanied or with a family member or friend.
- Consider integrating IE with situational exposure exercises for patients who are frightened of experiencing symptoms of physical arousal (e.g., blushing or sweating) when in social situations.

Specific Phobia

Session 1

Duration: 1 to 1.5 hours.

Introduction and rationale for treatment: The initial part of the session focuses on providing a general overview of the treatment rationale, including (a) the nature of fear and phobias (e.g., fear is normal and has a survival function), (b) myths and misconceptions regarding the feared object or situation, (c) a model of the patient's specific phobia (d) the three components of fear (i.e., physical, cognitive, and behavioral) and their interactions, (e) an overview of the treatment strategies that will be used in subsequent sessions, and (f) the importance of homework compliance.

Exposure rationale and instructions: The rationale and general principles of effective exposure are provided (e.g., exposure should be predictable, prolonged, repeated frequently, etc.).

Development of exposure hierarchy: The patient and therapist develop a detailed hierarchy of situations that will be used during exposure homework practices and in-session exposures.

Homework: The patient is encouraged to begin self-help readings on the nature and treatment of his or her specific phobia (e.g., Antony, Craske, & Barlow, 1995; Bourne, 1998a; Brown, 1996).

Subsequent sessions

Timing: Weekly or more frequently.

Duration of each session: 1.5 to 3 hours.

Number of sessions: Ranges from as few as 1 (e.g., for some people with animal phobias) to 10 (e.g., for some people with driving phobias).

Review of the previous week: Each session begins with a brief review of the homework and the previous week's events, with an emphasis on the previous week's exposure practices as well as on challenging anxious thinking related to the phobic object or situation.

Exposure practices: The largest portion of each treatment session consists of therapist-assisted exposure to the feared object or situation.

Cognitive restructuring: Cognitive restructuring is used informally during the therapist-assisted exposure practices.

Maintenance strategies and termination: At the last session, the patient and therapist discuss strategies for maintaining gains and for coping with a possible return of symptoms in the future.

Homework: Each session ends with the patient being encouraged to practice exposure almost daily between sessions and to complete the Exposure Monitoring Form at each practice. In addition, the patient is encouraged to continue self-help readings that are relevant to the phobia.

Variations on the Treatment Protocol

There are a number of ways in which this protocol may be altered to suit particular patients' needs:

- Consider meeting more frequently to facilitate quicker improvement during treatment.
- Consider increasing or decreasing the number of sessions, depending on the patient's progress.
- Add a follow-up or "booster" session 1 to 3 months after treatment ends in order to check on the patient's progress and review strategies for maintaining gains.
- Consider involving the patient's partner, a close friend, or a family member in the treatment sessions and homework practices.

- Consider increasing or decreasing the amount of therapist-assisted exposure, depending on the degree to which the patient is able to practice unaccompanied or with a family member or friend.
- Consider including IE exercises for patients who are frightened of experiencing symptoms of physical arousal when in their feared situation (e.g., as is often the case in claustrophobia).

CONCLUSION

In this chapter we provided an overview of how to present the rationale for treatment to a new patient and how to integrate the various strategies discussed in chapters 6–8. Chapter 6 begins with a detailed description of how to use exposure-based strategies for treating phobic disorders. In the second part of the chapter, we discuss practical suggestions for social skills training, which is sometimes used in combination with situational exposure for social phobia. Chapter 7 teaches the basics of how to use cognitive methods to combat phobic thinking. Finally, chapter 8 covers physical management strategies, including pharmacotherapy, herbal preparations, BRT, and applied tension for blood and injection phobias.

6

EXPOSURE-BASED STRATEGIES AND SOCIAL SKILLS TRAINING

Exposure to feared stimuli, objects, and situations is considered by many experts to be an essential component of effective treatment for phobic disorders (Davey, 1997b). This is especially true in the case of specific phobias, for which little else other than exposure-based treatments has been shown to help. In this chapter we describe the basic principles of exposure-based treatments for phobic disorders. Empirical research supporting these principles is provided throughout the chapter. In many cases, the research on process issues in exposure therapy tends to be based on individuals with specific phobias. Although there is relatively less research on the mechanisms underlying exposure therapy for social phobia and agoraphobia, the findings that are available suggest that the variables that affect outcome following exposure therapy are similar across phobic disorders. As is reviewed in chapter 2, social skills training is sometimes included in the treatment of social phobia (Turner, Beidel, Cooley, & Woody, 1994; Wlazlo et al., 1990). Because social skills training is often incorporated into exposure-based practices (e.g., behavioral role-plays), this topic is included in this chapter.

We begin with an overview of different types of exposure, then we provide detailed instructions regarding how to present the rationale for exposure to patients as well as guidelines for how to use exposure more effectively. In this section we include detailed suggestions as well as support from empirical research regarding factors such as the role of predictability during exposure practices; optimal duration, intensity, and frequency of practices; the effects of distraction and safety signals; the role of context; the relative benefits of therapist-assisted and self-administered exposure; and the use of technology to supplement exposure-based treatments.

Next, there is a comprehensive section on interoceptive exposure (IE) for people suffering from panic disorder (PD) or other conditions in which there is heightened anxiety over experiencing symptoms of arousal. This section includes instructions for presenting the rationale, determining which exercises to use, and combining IE with situational exposure. This part is followed by a consideration of practical issues that arise during exposure-based treatment, including the assignment of homework. Next, there is a section providing solutions for some of the most common problems that arise during exposure therapy. The chapter concludes with a discussion of social skills training for people with social phobia. This section includes information on presenting the rationale for social skills training as well as specific strategies for improving skills such as nonverbal communication, making conversation, and communicating assertively.

TYPES OF EXPOSURE

Imaginal Versus In Vivo Exposure

Exposure can be conducted in imagination or in vivo (i.e., real-life exposure in the actual situation). In general, in vivo exposure appears to be more effective than exposure in imagination. Emmelkamp and Wessels (1975) compared imaginal exposure, in vivo exposure, and a combination of the two approaches for treating people with agoraphobia. In vivo exposure alone was the most effective of the three approaches and was significantly more effective than imaginal exposure. This study confirmed earlier findings by Stern and Marks (1973). So, although early exposure-based treatments such as systematic desensitization (Wolpe, 1958) relied on exposure in imagination, we generally recommend that in vivo exposure be used whenever possible.

Nevertheless, there are some situations in which imaginal exposure may be appropriate. These include (a) exposure to objects or situations in which the patient initially refuses to practice in vivo exposure (imaginal exposure may help a patient reach a point at which he or she is willing to attempt in vivo exposure); (b) exposure to situations that are impossible or impractical to practice frequently, such as thunderstorms or flying in an airplane (for these phobias, imaginal exposure may be a useful adjunct to in vivo exposure, in that it increases the frequency of exposure); and (c) exposure to situations in which in vivo exposure may be dangerous or unethical (e.g., exposure to traumatic memories in posttraumatic stress disorder).

Often there are alternatives to imaginal exposure that can be used when in vivo exposure is impractical or is refused by the patient. Pictures or videotapes of the phobic object are sometimes useful for people who suffer from certain specific phobias (e.g., spiders, snakes, rodents, blood, or injections). In addition, role-play simulations (e.g., a simulated job interview) are routinely used with individuals suffering from social phobia, before having them attempt exposure in the real situation. Finally, as is reviewed later in this chapter, virtual reality may be helpful for individuals suffering from certain phobias (e.g., heights).

For imaginal exposure, one way of presenting the rationale is to describe imaginal exposure as akin to watching the same scary movie over and over in one's head; with each "viewing," it gets less frightening and eventually becomes boring.[1] It is important to assist the patient in achieving an extremely vivid image of the feared situation. The clinician may describe the situation in detail (or provide an audiotaped description) or have the patient describe the situation during the practice. The more detailed the description the better. For example, if the patient is imagining being exposed to a spider, he or she should be encouraged to imagine all aspects of the situation, including the size, color, and shape of the spider; the location of the spider; the nature and speed of the spider's movements; and the imagined environment in which the exposure is being conducted.

Foa and Rothbaum (1998) recommended asking the patient a number of additional questions to enhance the richness of the exposure experience, including the following: What are you feeling? What are you thinking? Are you experiencing any physical reactions? What is your body feeling? What are you seeing/smelling/doing now? Imaginal exposure sessions should last 30 to 60 minutes, during which the difficulty of the exposure is gradually increased as the patient's fear decreases. During the session, the therapist should ask the patient to rate his or her anxiety periodically, using a 0–100 or similar scale.

Graduated Versus Rapid Exposure

The evidence regarding the benefits of conducting exposure gradually versus starting at the top of the hierarchy or moving through the hierarchy steps very quickly has been mixed. Everaerd, Rijken, and Emmelkamp (1973)

---

[1] We thank Rich McNally for providing this analogy.

found that graduated exposure and in vivo flooding (i.e., rapid exposure) were both effective for the treatment of agoraphobia, with few differences overall. In contrast, Fiegenbaum (1988) found ungraded exposure to be more effective for treating people with agoraphobia than was graded exposure.

In our clinical experience, both approaches have been effective, but each has advantages over the other. More gradual exposure is often more palatable to the patient and less likely to cause a refusal to engage in a particular exposure practice. However, when exposure is conducted too gradually, the fear may change too slowly and cause the momentum of the treatment to be compromised. Generally, we recommend that exposure begin with a moderately difficult task and that steps be taken to increase the difficulty of the exposure as quickly as the patient is willing.

Situational Versus Interoceptive Exposure

In addition to exposing patients to objects and situations that they fear (i.e., situational exposure), it is often helpful to expose patients to the physical sensations that they fear, using IE exercises (e.g., spinning to produce dizziness). Interoceptive exposure is most often used to treat people with PD—with or without agoraphobia. However, for some people with social phobia and certain specific phobias, exposure to feared sensations, especially in the context of the feared object or situation (e.g., wearing a sweater during a presentation to increase sweating, or hyperventilating to increase breathlessness during exposure to a claustrophobic situation), may be helpful for decreasing the patient's fear of particular physical sensations.

INTRODUCING EXPOSURE TO PATIENTS

Presentation of the rationale for exposure should include a number of components, including (a) a description of how exposure works, (b) a discussion of why exposure may not have worked in the past, (c) an overview of the guidelines for how exposure should be conducted, and (d) a discussion of the costs and benefits of exposure. This section includes an overview of each of these topics.

Describing How Exposure Works

In describing how exposure works, any of a number of explanations may be used. For example, those who think in terms of learning theory might use an extinction model to explain the effects of exposure. From this perspective, exposure causes a conditioned stimulus (e.g., a car) to be repeatedly paired with the absence of an unconditioned stimulus (e.g., being in an accident) until the fear is eventually extinguished. Instead, we tend to use a cognitive model to explain the effects of exposure. In short, the patient is told that exposure works by disconfirming fearful predictions regarding the feared object or situation. Unlike cognitive restructuring, which relies on changing beliefs through logical analysis, exposure changes beliefs by providing new experiences that are inconsistent with the individual's anxious beliefs. In fact, for some phobias (e.g., specific phobias), exposure appears to be a more powerful method than is cognitive restructuring for changing fearful beliefs. The following case vignette with a dog-phobic individual illustrates how to present the idea of exposure to a patient.

> **Therapist:** Can you think of anything that you once feared that no longer bothers you?
> **Patient:** No, not off hand.
> **Therapist:** What about some childhood fear, like the dark? Or, can you remember ever being nervous when you started a new job but eventually becoming more comfortable over time?
> **Patient:** Actually, yes. When I first started teaching, I was terrified. After a couple months, I got used to it, and it got easier.
> **Therapist:** Why do you think that is?
> **Patient:** I do not really know. I guess I just realized that I could do it. I got used to it over time.
> **Therapist:** Do you notice a difference in your anxiety after the summer, when it is time to return to teaching?
> **Patient:** Yes, even now, after having taught for more than 10 years, I still feel nervous on the first day of classes. I think that's normal, though. I know that a number of other teachers feel the same way.
> **Therapist:** Your experience with teaching illustrates the effect of avoidance on fear as well as the effect of exposure on decreasing a person's fear. Just as a summer away from teaching leads to an increase in your anxiety on the first day back to school, avoiding dogs also serves to maintain or even increase your fear of dogs. In contrast, gradual exposure to dogs will have the effect of decreasing your fear.
> **Patient:** I expect that it will be much harder for me to overcome my fear of dogs than it was to get used to teaching.
> **Therapist:** Overcoming your fear of dogs may be more frightening than was overcoming your anxiety while teaching. Nevertheless, the same principles apply to both situations. Exposure is one of the most powerful ways to reduce almost any fear. Frequent and repeated exposure teaches an individual that his or her negative predictions do not come true, thereby decreasing the fear of the situation or object.

Discussing Why Exposure Has not Worked in the Past

It is important for the therapist to recognize that, in the past, the patient has probably encountered numerous people (e.g., family members and friends) and self-help books suggesting that that patient expose him- or herself to frightening situations in order to overcome the fear. The therapist's job is to present the rationale for exposure in a way that is more convincing and credible than has been the case in the past. After the therapist suggests that exposure will help to decrease the patient's fear, the patient may be skeptical. He or she may be quick to point out, "I am already exposed to . . . (e.g., spiders, being at work, having panic attacks, etc.), and my fear has not gotten any better. In fact, it is worse now than it used to be." It is important to point out the reasons why exposure may not have worked well in the past. In everyday life, the type of exposure that occurs is different from therapeutic exposure in several important ways, as is summarized in Table 6.1. It is likely that the patient's previous exposures have been unpredictable, uncontrollable, infrequent, brief, and characterized by catastrophic thinking and subtle avoidance behaviors.

Table 6.1
Differences Between Naturally Occurring and Therapeutic Exposures for Patients With Phobic Disorders

Typical exposure (naturally occurring)	Therapeutic exposure (during treatment)
Unpredictable and uncontrollable (e.g., the patient is surprised by a spider; the patient experiences an unexpected panic attack)	Predictable and controllable (e.g., the patient makes a decision to be exposed to a spider in a predictable way; the patient purposely hyperventilates during an IE practice, thereby bringing on panic sensations in a predictable and controllable way)
Brief duration (e.g., the patient becomes anxious and leaves the situation, thereby learning "when I am in the situation, I feel frightened; when I escape, I feel better")	Prolonged (e.g., the patient stays in the situation until the fear subsides, thereby learning that he or she can be in the situation and feel calm)
Infrequent (because the patient typically avoids, exposure is infrequent under normal circumstances and each exposure practice is like starting over)	Frequent (exposure is repeated frequently so that benefits of previous exposure are cumulative)
Includes catastrophic thinking (patient typically experiences catastrophic thoughts such as "I am going to die" and "I will crash the car")	Includes cognitive restructuring (the patient uses cognitive restructuring to challenge anxious thoughts)
Subtle avoidance strategies are used (e.g., distraction, alcohol use, overprotective behaviors, etc.)	Subtle avoidance strategies are eliminated (patient is taught to eliminate subtle avoidance strategies, thereby learning that he or she can master the situation without these aids, confirming that the situation is in fact safe)

Presenting the Guidelines, Costs, and Benefits of Exposure

As is suggested in Table 6.1, the way exposure is conducted can affect the outcome. For example, exposure that is frequent, predictable, and prolonged generally leads to more fear reduction than does infrequent, brief, unpredictable exposure. For example, surprising a snake-phobic individual by tossing a snake at him or her obviously would not lead to fear reduction. However, describing the snake to the patient and having him or her gradually approach it would probably lead to a significant decrease in fear over a period of 2 or 3 hours.

When discussing the rationale for exposure-based treatment (guidelines are provided in the next section), the therapist should also discuss the benefits of exposure, as well as the costs and barriers that may arise during treatment. Usually, the patient will acknowledge that the long-term benefits of conducting exposure practices are worth the short-term costs. With respect to benefits, exposure is likely to lead to a reduction in fear, because it teaches the patient that his or her anxious thoughts are not true and helps a person to replace anxious beliefs with more realistic beliefs. However, in addition to this obvious benefit, there are other positive effects of exposure. For example, exposure provides a context in which the patient can practice other anxiety management strategies, such as cognitive restructuring and applied tension for blood phobia. In addition, exposure provides an opportunity to improve one's skills in the situation. For example, following repeated practice, people with driving phobias are likely to become better drivers. Similarly, people with social phobia are likely to learn what works and does not work in social situations, thereby improving their skills at socializing, speaking in public, and other social activities. Finally, exposure often has other positive effects, including meeting new people (e.g., after overcoming social phobia), being able to return to work or school (e.g., after overcoming severe agoraphobia), or enhancing general self-confidence.

The most obvious cost of conducting exposure practices is the discomfort that patients feel during the session. However, there are other potential costs. People often report feeling very tired after exposure practices and may need several hours or even the rest of the day to recuperate from an exposure session. At the beginning of treatment, patients may also report increased feelings of anxiety, tension, irritability, and sleeplessness. They may also report being agitated and frustrated by minor stresses and may experience nightmares. Patients should be informed of possible negative effects when they start exposure and should be reassured that these feelings typically subside as treatment progresses.

Patients may be worried about other possible negative consequences during exposure, most notably that their negative beliefs will be confirmed (e.g., the plane will crash, they will die during a panic attack, others will find them to be boring or unattractive, etc.). They may also provide other reasons for not conducting exposure, including a lack of time, money, or opportunities to practice, as well as skepticism about whether exposure will work and anxiety about being overwhelmed during the exposure practices. The therapist should be prepared to address these and other concerns as they arise.

GUIDELINES FOR EXPOSURE PRACTICES

In this section we provide guidelines for therapists to keep in mind when conducting exposure practices. Exhibit 6.1 is a handout summarizing the most important of these guidelines, which may be distributed to patients to aid them in developing their own practices.

Structuring Exposure Sessions in Advance

To the extent possible, exposure homework practices should be planned and structured in advance. By setting aside specific times to practice exposure, patients will be less likely to forget to practice or to report that they were too busy to practice. In addition, patients should be encouraged to practice regardless of how they feel on a particular day. Individuals with panic disorder with agoraphobia (PD and agoraphobia) often report that it is easier for them to practice exposure on "good days" than on days when they are particularly anxious. By planning exposure practices in advance, patients will be less likely to practice only on good days. Finally, it is important to have a back-up plan so that if a homework practice becomes impractical, there are one or more alternative practices that can be completed.

Predictability and Perceived Control

A sense of predictability and control appear to be important for patients who are undergoing exposure-based treatments for a phobic disorder. In a study of predictability and exposure in snake-fearful individuals, Lopatka (1989) found that unpredictable exposure to a snake led to greater subsequent avoidance compared with predictable exposure to the snake. However, findings regarding the importance of perceived control during exposure have been mixed. Although some researchers (e.g., McGlynn, Rose, & Lazarte, 1994; Rose, McGlynn, & Lazarte, 1995) have found a greater treatment response when participants controlled the intensity of exposure compared with when exposure intensity was not controlled by participants, other researchers have failed to show group differences in people who fear spiders (Craske, Bunt, Rapee, & Barlow, 1991) and snakes (McGlynn, Rose, & Jacobson, 1995).

Exhibit 6.1
Guidelines for Conducting Exposure

1. **Exposure practices should be planned, structured, and predictable.** Decide in advance what you will do in the situation and how long you will stay. Plan in advance when you will complete your practice and put it in your schedule. Have a back-up plan in case the original plan does not work out.
2. **Exposure pace can be gradual.** Do not assume that you must do the most difficult thing you can imagine right away, but be sure to choose practices that are challenging. The more difficult the items that you practice, the quicker you will learn to become more comfortable. Try to choose practices that are challenging but not so difficult that you will not complete them.
3. **Do not use subtle avoidance strategies during exposure practices.** Try to complete the practices without the use of distraction, alcohol, leaving early, avoiding eye contact, and other such strategies.
4. **Rate your fear on a scale from 0 to 100.** When in the feared situation, it can be helpful to pay attention to how you are feeling and to notice the variables that make your anxiety go up and down during the practice.
5. **Try not to fight your fear.** Fighting the anxiety will have the effect of increasing your anxious feelings. Instead, just let it happen. The worst thing that is likely to happen is that you will feel uncomfortable.
6. **Exposure practices should be repeated frequently and spaced close together.** The more closely spaced the practices, the more fear reduction that you are likely to experience. It is a good idea to practice being in the same situation repeatedly until it becomes easier.
7. **Exposure practices should last long enough to experience a significant decrease in anxiety.** Sometimes this can take several hours!
8. **Use the cognitive coping strategies to counter anxious automatic thoughts during exposure practices.**
9. **Expect to feel uncomfortable.** It is perfectly normal to feel awful during initial exposure practices. Also, these practices may leave you feeling tired and anxious afterwards. With repeated practices, these feelings will decrease. Success should not be judged by how you felt in the situation. Rather, success should be judged by whether you were able to stay in the situation despite feeling awful.
10. **If you experience social anxiety, use specific exercises to enhance your anxiety and to draw attention to yourself in the feared situation.** For example, if you fear sweating, wear a heavy sweater. Or, if you fear having others notice your shaky hands, purposely shake your hand while holding a drink. If you are fearful of losing your train of thought, you can purposely allow yourself to have trouble finding the right words during a conversation.

Nevertheless, it is typically recommended that exposure practices be predictable and maximize the patient's perception of control in the situation.

Despite the benefits of predictable and controlled exposure, some situations may be inherently unpredictable. For example, if a patient with social phobia is being instructed to ask another individual to have lunch, the outcome may be unpredictable. In these situations, it can be helpful to have the patient anticipate possible outcomes before the exposure practice begins and to think about how he or she can cope with each of these outcomes. Although the outcome will still be unknown in advance, at least the patient will be better prepared for a range of possible negative outcomes that might occur.

In later exposure sessions, it is helpful to purposely build in unpredictability to better prepare the patient for unpredictable events that may occur in his or her daily life. For example, the treatment of claustrophobia might begin with predictable practices that provide the patient with control over the situation (e.g., standing in an unlocked closet from which escape is easy). Subsequent exposures might involve standing in a locked closet for 5 minutes (here, the patient has given up control of his or her ability to leave the situation but still is able to predict when the exposure will end). Later practices could involve standing in a locked closet for an unknown duration (e.g., anywhere from 5 to 15 minutes), controlled by the clinician.

At such a time when the patient is ready to begin unpredictable exposures, he or she should always be prepared in advance for what is likely to occur. For example, it would be a mistake to tell a claustrophobic patient that the locked closet will be opened in 5 minutes but not to actually open it for 15 minutes. Similarly, when conducting a social phobia role-play with a patient who is fearful of being criticized unexpectedly, the patient should be warned in advance if you intend to be particularly nasty or to criticize the patient as part of the role-play. In other words, the patient should agree to including unpredictable or uncontrollable events in an exposure session before the practice begins.

Duration of Exposure

In an early study with agoraphobic patients, Stern and Marks (1973) demonstrated that a single 2-hour exposure session led to more fear reduction than did four 30-minute practices spread out over the course of an afternoon. Because prolonged exposure is more effective than briefer exposures, it is generally recommended that before moving on to a more difficult step within an exposure session, the therapist and patient should wait until the fear has decreased significantly. Also, an exposure session should not be terminated until there has been a significant reduction in fear. If the patient's fear becomes so overwhelming that he or she must leave the situation, there still may be benefit from the exposure practice if the patient immediately returns to the phobic situation after a short break (de Silva & Rachman, 1984; Rachman, Craske, Tallman, & Solyom, 1984).

The issue of exposure duration gives rise to two questions: (a) How should fear be measured in order to determine the optimal exposure duration? and (b) How much fear reduction should occur before moving on to the next step or before ending the session? Generally, fear can be measured in three ways: self-report (e.g., patient's ratings on a 0–100 point subjective units of discomfort scale [SUDS]—see chapter 4), observer ratings (e.g., a therapist's ratings of how fearful the patient appears), and psychophysiological measures (e.g., heart rate). We recommend that the therapist use a combination of the patient's self-report ratings as well as his or her own impressions of whether the fear has decreased. There is evidence (based on a study with snake-fearful undergraduate students) that treatment outcome is superior when changes in observer ratings are used to estimate the optimal duration for exposure compared with using changes in heart rate to determine when exposure practices should end (Gauthier & Marshall, 1977).

With respect to how much fear reduction should occur before increasing the intensity of the exposure, we usually recommend that fear decrease to a mild to moderate level (e.g., a SUDS level of 30 to 50). In addition, treatment sessions should not end until a patient's fear of a particular situation has decreased to a mild or moderate level. In other words, we suggest ending the session on a high note whenever possible.

Intensity of Exposure

From a study of imaginal exposure in rat-phobic students, there is evidence that intense horror does not lead to increased improvement compared with exposure under more pleasant circumstances (Foa et al., 1977). In fact, in this study, the key was to make sure that exposure was prolonged, regardless of whether horrifying scenes were introduced during the imaginal exposure. Typically we recommend that the intensity of fear experienced during exposure be moderate to high (e.g., generating SUDS ratings of about 70 out of 100). If exposure intensity is too high, patients are less likely to stay in the situation without engaging in subtle avoidance strategies, such as distraction. If the intensity of fear is too low, it is possible that the effects of exposure will not generalize to more difficult situations.

Massed Versus Spaced Exposure

Foa, Jameson, Turner, and Payne (1980) demonstrated that 10 daily exposure sessions were more effective for decreasing agoraphobic fear and avoidance than were 10 weekly sessions. It is generally recommended that patients practice exposure frequently. This may include large practices three to six times per week, as well as brief practices throughout the day. For example, an individual with agoraphobia might be expected to practice driving to and from work each day, as well as driving smaller distances (e.g., to the corner store) as opportunities arise.

In a series of new studies, Craske and her colleagues have investigated the benefits of using an *expanding spaced exposure schedule*. In the first of these studies (Rowe & Craske, 1998a), spider-fearful groups were treated either with massed sessions (four exposure trials in 1 day) or with an expanding spaced schedule (four sessions distributed over 1 week, each time doubling the time between sessions). Essentially, the expanding spaced exposure schedule had elements of both massed exposure (at the beginning of treatment) and spaced exposure (toward the end of treatment). Confirming previous findings on massed versus spaced exposure (e.g., Fiegenbaum, 1988; Foa et al., 1980), massed exposure led to greater fear reduction across sessions than did the expanding spaced exposure schedule. However, return of fear 1 month later was significantly greater in the massed exposure group than in the expanding spaced exposure group. These findings suggest that over the long term, the expanding spaced exposure schedule may be more effective than a massed exposure approach.

Attempts to replicate these findings have yielded mixed results. Lang and Craske (2000) failed to find any significant long-term advantage to treating people with height phobias using an expanded spaced exposure schedule compared with a massed exposure schedule. In contrast, Tsao and Craske (in press) found that an expanding spaced treatment schedule was less likely to lead to a return of fear following treatment than was a massed exposure schedule. In this study, participants were treated for a fear of public speaking. Overall, it is still too early to say whether the long-term outcome following expanding spaced exposure is superior to the outcome following massed exposure. However, initial findings are promising, and it is likely that this issue will be clarified as more research findings become available.

Varied-Stimulus Exposure Versus Same-Stimulus Exposure

To help a patient overcome fear in a specific situation, we recommend that exposure practices be carried out in a variety of different versions of that situation to ensure maximum long-term improvement. For example, rather than working with only one spider, an individual with a spider phobia should practice exposure with a variety of spiders. Similarly, an agoraphobic individual who fears shopping malls should practice exposure in a variety of different shopping malls. Varying the stimulus across exposure practices increases the long-term benefits of exposure and makes the fear less likely to return (Rowe & Craske, 1998b).

The Importance of Context

Findings from animal studies show that exposure conducted in multiple contexts protects against relapse, compared with exposure in only one context (Gunther, Denniston, & Miller, 1998). Furthermore, people who have been treated for spider fears have been found to experience more return of fear when tested in novel contexts compared with when tested in contexts where the exposure treatment originally occurred (Mineka, Mystkowski, Hladek, & Rodriguez, 1999; Rodriguez, Craske, Mineka, & Hladek, 1999). In order for the effects of exposure to generalize to the patient's day-to-day life, it is recommended that exposure practices occur in the contexts in which the patient is likely to encounter the phobic object or situation in his or her everyday life. For example, in addition to practicing exposure to spiders in the therapist's office, the patient should practice exposure to spiders in the bedroom, car, backyard, basement, and other places where he or she normally sees spiders. Similarly, an individual who is nervous about speaking with co-workers should practice speaking to people at work, in addition to practicing making small talk in other situations. On a related note, the situations and objects chosen for exposure should be as similar as possible to those that the patient is likely to encounter in his or her day-to-day life. For example, if a person is fearful of small basement spiders, exposure to tarantulas may not help the individual's fear of house spiders.

Effects of Distraction on Exposure

Distraction has been hypothesized to interfere with the effects of exposure (e.g., Foa & Kozak, 1986), although studies of this issue have yielded mixed findings. In a study of spider- and snake-phobic individuals, focused exposure led to increases in subjective anxiety during a 6-minute period, whereas anxiety did not change over the 6 minutes for individuals who were instructed to distract themselves during exposure (Craske, Street, Jayaraman, & Barlow, 1991). Similarly, Antony, Leeuw, Ing, and Swinson (1998) found no effects of distraction on outcome following a single session of exposure for specific phobias of spiders.

However, in another study (Rodriguez & Craske, 1995), distraction was found to interfere with fear reduction during high-intensity exposures but not low-intensity exposures. In addition, Haw and Dickerson (1998) found that although distraction did not interfere with fear reduction in the short term, individuals who were distracted during an exposure-based treatment for spider fears were more likely than people who were not distracted to show increased anxiety during the follow-up period. This study confirmed the findings from an earlier study on agoraphobic individuals (Craske, Street, & Barlow, 1989), showing that focused exposure led to greater improvement during follow-up than exposure with instructions to distract.

Rodriguez and Craske (1993) speculated on why studies on distraction and exposure have tended to yield conflicting results, concluding that methodological differences across studies (e.g., attentional demand created by the distracter or affective quality of the distracter) may be in part responsible.

In addition, studies have tended to differ with respect to the duration of exposure, the period of measurement (e.g., effects of within-session change vs. between-session change), and the population studied (e.g., people with agoraphobia, specific phobia, etc.). Furthermore, in all studies of the effects of distraction, distracted participants are instructed to distract themselves during the exposure. This process may be different from distraction that occurs during naturally occurring exposure, in which individuals are more likely to distract themselves as a form of escape—which may be interpreted as a loss of control in the situation. In experimental studies, individuals have typically been instructed to distract themselves regardless of how they feel, which may be more likely to foster a sense of perceived control in the situation.

In addition to the equivocal findings regarding the effects of distraction on exposure, there is also some evidence that attempting to suppress intrusive negative thoughts can lead to increased frequency as well as increased distress and discomfort, although these findings, too, have been mixed (Purdon, 1999). These effects have tended to be shown most often in normal populations and in people with obsessive–compulsive disorder (OCD); however, an effect of thought suppression on phobic anxiety remains to be demonstrated (Purdon, 1999).

Generally, we recommend that patients not distract themselves during exposure practices and not attempt to suppress their fear. Rather, we view distraction and suppression of fear as subtle forms of avoidance and suggest that instead of engaging in these behaviors, patients maintain their focus on the situation. In the case of specific phobias, this involves focusing on the feared object or situation (e.g., looking at a spider or looking down from a high place). For people with social phobia, we recommend that the patient focus on aspects of the social situation. In fact, there is preliminary evidence that focusing on the social situation during exposure for social phobia leads to more within-session reduction in fear than does focusing on oneself (Wells & Papageorgiou, 1998). Finally, in PD, for which the feared stimulus is often the occurrence of internal sensations, we recommend that the patient allow him- or herself to be aware of the uncomfortable feelings and not attempt to be distracted from them.

On a related note, we recommend that patients try not to fight their fear. Fighting the fear among people with phobic disorders has effects that are analogous to trying to fall asleep among people with insomnia. Some people with insomnia can be up for hours when they try too hard to fall asleep. It is not until they stop trying so hard that they fall asleep fairly quickly. Similarly, trying to make discomfort go away can have the paradoxical effect of maintaining or increasing the discomfort (Wegner, Broome, & Blumberg, 1997). The more that patients are able to accept the way they feel when they are fearful, the less fearful they will be.

Safety Signals and Overprotective Behaviors

As is reviewed in chapter 4, patients with phobic disorders often rely on safety signals and overprotective behaviors to manage their fear. People with agoraphobia may insist on being accompanied by their spouse or may carry certain objects (e.g., a cellular phone, bottled water, or money) that may be helpful in the event of a panic attack. Similarly, an individual with a storm phobia may compulsively watch the television weather forecast repeatedly before leaving the house. Although these behaviors may lead to short-term reductions in fear, they probably help to maintain fear in the long term.

In two recent studies of socially phobic individuals, those who decreased in-session safety behaviors during exposure benefited more from treatment than did those who continued these behaviors during exposure (Morgan & Raffle, 1999; Wells et al., 1995). In light of these and other findings, we recommend that patients discontinue their use of safety signals and overprotective behaviors during their exposure practices. For patients who are too fearful to give these up at the beginning of treatment, these behaviors may be discontinued gradually as treatment progresses.

Vicarious Exposure (Modeling) and Exposure

Menzies and Clarke (1993c) investigated the effects of vicarious exposure (having the patient observe another person, such as a therapist or family member, being exposed to the feared situation) on childhood water phobias. Although vicarious exposure was not an effective treatment on its own and did not add to the short-term effects of in vivo exposure, there was some evidence of vicarious exposure enhancing the maintenance of gains during in vivo exposure at a 3-month follow-up.

Similar findings were recently found in a study of adults with specific phobias of spiders (Öst, Ferebee, & Furmark, 1997). In this study, direct exposure (in which patients were directly exposed to spiders) was compared with direct observation (in which patients watched another individual be exposed to spiders) and indirect observation (in which patients watched on videotape another individual interacting with spiders). All treatments were conducted in a single 3-hour session, in a group format. Direct exposure was significantly more effective than direct observation and indirect observation, with 75%, 7%, and 31% showing clinically significant improvement in the three groups, respectively. In contrast, findings from an in vivo exposure study with height-phobic individuals failed to show any differences between participants for modeling, exposure, and the combination of modeling and exposure (Bourque & Ladouceur, 1980). Although we do not recommend modeling or vicarious exposure as an exclusive treatment, we do recommend that the therapist model appropriate behaviors for the patient during exposure practices. For example, before asking a height-phobic patient to stand near a high ledge, the therapist should demonstrate how to do the practice.

Therapist-Directed Versus Self-Directed Exposure

In a study of in vivo exposure for snake-fearful individuals, O'Brien and Kelley (1980) investigated the effects of varying the degree of the therapist's involvement. Overall, treatment was effective in the self-directed and therapist-directed conditions. However, individuals who received therapist-directed exposure responded more than individuals who received self-directed exposure. In a more recent study (Öst, Salkovskis, & Hellström, 1991), spider-phobic individuals received a single 3-hour session of therapist-directed exposure or a 2-week self-directed exposure-based treatment using a self-help manual. Significantly more individuals evidenced clinically significant improvement following therapist-directed exposure (71%) than following the self-administered treatment (6%). Results were maintained after a 1-year follow-up.

This finding was replicated in a comparison study of therapist-directed exposure and various manualized treatments for spider phobia (Hellström & Öst, 1995). Although therapist-directed exposure was more effective than manualized treatments overall, self-administered treatments were more effective when they were conducted in a clinic setting (instead of at home) and when the manual was tailored to the specific fear. In this study, the proportion of patients who evidenced clinically significant improvement was 80% for therapist-directed exposure, 63% for the specific manual used in the clinic, 10% for the specific manual used at home, 10% for the general manual used at the clinic, and 9% for the general manual used at home. An early study by Baker et al. (1973) showed that self-directed (using audiotapes) and therapist-directed systematic desensitization (relaxation combined with graduated imaginal exposure) were equally effective at posttreatment. However, those who received self-directed exposure continued to make gains during an 8-month follow-up period, whereas those who received therapist-directed exposure maintained their posttreatment gains.

In our clinical experience, whether to use self-directed or therapist-assisted exposure often depends on the individual patient. Although it is often helpful to begin with therapist-assisted exposure to make sure that the practices are being conducted properly, patients who are willing and able to conduct subsequent practices on their own should be encouraged to do so. For some patients (e.g., those who are too fearful to practice on their own), more intensive therapist-assisted exposure may be necessary.

The goal by the end of treatment should still be to have the patient conduct exposure practices unaccompanied.

There may be differences between diagnostic groups with respect to the patient's willingness to practice exposure unaccompanied. In our experience, people with certain specific phobias (e.g., spider phobias) almost always require a therapist to be present during the initial exposure practices. In contrast, some patients with agoraphobia or social phobia may be more willing to practice exposure on their own.

Although therapist-assisted exposure is often time-consuming, there are a number of strategies that can be used to minimize the face-to-face time spent between the patient and therapist. One is to include other people in the treatment (e.g., family members or friends of the patient, trainees or volunteers who work with the therapist, etc.). When a helper is asked to assist, the person who is going to assume that role should be instructed in the model and rationale for exposure and should first attend an exposure session with the therapist and patient. Another strategy for reducing therapy time, while still ensuring that the patient completes the exposure practice, is to meet with the patient immediately before and after an exposure practice but to allow the actual practice to be conducted alone. For example, before going to a shopping mall for 2 hours, an agoraphobic patient could be scheduled for a 20-minute session to plan the exposure practice and a second 20-minute session immediately after the practice in the mall for debriefing.

Using Technology to Enhance Exposure

Technological advances such as virtual reality, computer simulations, and cellular telephones may be useful methods of enhancing exposure to certain phobic stimuli. Case reports suggest that virtual reality may be an effective treatment for people with fears of heights (Rothbaum et al., 1995b), flying (Rothbaum, Hodges, Watson, Kessler, & Opdyke, 1996), and spiders (Carlin, Hoffman, & Weghorst, 1997). In addition, a group study in which 12 height-fearful students were treated with virtual reality showed significant benefits of the treatment, compared with a wait-list condition in which individuals' fear was unchanged (Rothbaum et al., 1995a). To date, there are no published studies in which virtual reality treatments have been compared with traditional exposure-based treatments for phobic disorders. However, because the effectiveness of exposure is probably related to the extent to which the exposure practice matches the types of situations that the individual normally avoids, it is likely that virtual-reality exposure on its own is less effective than in vivo exposure, although it is perhaps more effective than imaginal exposure. As the technology for virtual reality continues to improve and becomes more accessible, it is possible that this method of treatment may be appropriate for simulating situations for which it is impractical to conduct in vivo exposure, or for which the patient refuses to conduct in vivo exposure, particularly early in treatment. For a review of research on virtual reality for treating people with phobias, see Rothbaum and Hodges (1999).

Several preliminary studies and case reports suggest that exposure-based treatments delivered by a computer can be effective for some people suffering from dental fears (Coldwell et al., 1998) and spider fears (Nelissen, Muris, & Merckelbach, 1995). Palm-held computers have also been used to increase the effectiveness of brief cognitive–behavioral therapy (CBT) for PD (Newman, Kenardy, Herman, & Taylor, 1997). In addition, Denholtz and Mann (1975) found that flight-phobic individuals benefited significantly from an exposure-based treatment (e.g., desensitization, modeling, and positive reinforcement) delivered by nonprofessionals using an automated audio-visual program. Case reports suggest that maintaining radio contact with a patient (Levine & Wolpe, 1980) or communicating with mobile telephones (Flynn, Taylor, & Pollard, 1992) can be useful adjuncts to exposure-based treatments for driving phobias.

Integrating Exposure and Other Strategies

Exposure may be combined with other treatment strategies. For example, applied tension (see chapter 8) involves combining muscle tension with exposure to blood-related stimuli in order to prevent fainting in people with blood phobias. Similarly, cognitive techniques (see chapter 7) can be used to prepare patients for exposure practices or to help patients process the results of practices after they are completed. The use of cognitive strategies as an adjunct to exposure appears to be especially helpful for people suffering from social phobia and PD. Adding cognitive therapy appears to be less important when treating people with specific phobias.

Finally, applied relaxation involves combining progressive muscle relaxation and cue-controlled relaxation with exposure to feared situations. As is reviewed in Part 1 of this book, applied relaxation has been shown to be a useful treatment for PD and agoraphobia (Arntz & van den Hout, 1996; Clark et al., 1994; Jansson, Jerremalm, & Öst, 1986; Öst, 1988a; Öst & Westling, 1995); Öst et al., 1993), social anxiety (Jerremalm, Johansson, & Öst, 1980; Osberg, 1981), and certain specific phobias (Öst et al., 1982; Öst, Lindahl, Sterner, & Jerremalm, 1984). However, because combining relaxation training with standard exposure-based treatments has rarely been shown to add any benefit over and above exposure alone, applied relaxation is not described in detail in this book. For a more thorough discussion of this technique, see Öst (1987b, 1988b).

Measuring the Success of a Particular Practice

Patients and new therapists often measure the success of an exposure practice by how a patient feels during the practice; a successful practice is incorrectly viewed to be one in which a patient feels comfortable. Instead of judging success by what how a patient feels, success should be judged by what a patient does during the practice. The patient should expect to feel uncomfortable. During an ideal practice, the patient will become anxious and uncomfortable during the initial part of the session and will gradually become more comfortable as the session progresses. If a patient does not experience fear during a practice, it may mean that the practice was not difficult enough. We encourage the patient to do things that make him or her uncomfortable. The first feature to change following exposure is often the patient's behavior. Changes in fear and anticipatory anxiety are likely to follow changes in the patient's behavior rather than the other way around.

Determining How Far to Take the Exposure Practice

It is recommended that exposure-based treatments continue until a patient is able to face situations that are more difficult than those that are typically encountered. For example, even though the most difficult situation that a person with a snake phobia is likely to encounter normally is seeing a snake on the ground or in a pet store, we recommend that the patient take the exposure to a point where he or she can comfortably hold a harmless snake. By taking the exposure to increasingly difficult levels, the patient learns even more strongly that the situation is safe. In addition, he or she is somewhat protected from a relapse if some of the fear returns. Although it is helpful to continue to assign increasingly difficult exposure practices, the patient should never be asked to do anything that is likely to be dangerous (e.g., handling a poisonous snake, driving at excessively high speeds, etc.).

INTEROCEPTIVE EXPOSURE

Interoceptive exposure refers to a method of exposing people to uncomfortable physical sensations (e.g., dizziness or a racing heart) using a series of exercises (e.g., hyperventilation or spinning around). It is an appropriate treatment strategy for patients who are particularly fearful of the physical sensations that they experience when feeling anxious or panicky. Although IE has been studied primarily in trials of CBT for PD, it may also be useful for some patients with social phobia and specific phobias. In deciding whether to use IE, it is important to determine whether the patient is fearful of his or her uncomfortable physical sensations. The answer to this question will almost always be "yes" for patients with PD and agoraphobia. In addition, many socially phobic individuals report being fearful of certain sensations—particularly those that might be noticeable to others (e.g., shaking, sweating, blushing, or a shaky voice). If a patient is not fearful of the physical sensations that occur when he or she is anxious, IE is unlikely to be helpful.

Among people with specific phobias, fear of sensations may or may not be a problem. For example, most (but not all) individuals with animal phobias are much more concerned about the animal causing them harm than they are about their anxiety symptoms being dangerous. In contrast, people with claustrophobia are often very afraid of feeling breathless and suffocating in enclosed places. Similarly, people with height and driving phobias may fear becoming dizzy or unsteady (e.g., having "rubbery" legs) in the phobic situation. Individuals with blood and injection phobias are often fearful of feeling faint during an injection or when seeing blood. The extent to which the patient is fearful of these and other sensations should influence the clinician's decision of whether to incorporate IE into the treatment program.

Implementing Interoceptive Exposure

Interoceptive exposure typically involves four main steps: (a) presenting the rationale, (b) symptom induction testing, (c) assigning IE practices, and (d) integrating IE with situational exposure. Note that in planning IE practices, many of the general guidelines described earlier for exposure therapy (e.g., regarding exposure frequency, duration of exposure, context, etc.) are relevant. The following suggestions for conducting IE are based, in part, on recommendations from a number of sources (e.g., Antony, Craske, & Barlow, 1995; Barlow & Craske, 1994; Craske & Barlow, 1993; Zuercher-White, 1997b).

Presenting the rationale

The general guidelines and recommendations for IE are similar to those for situational exposure. Practices should be predictable, prolonged, and frequent, so as to maximize their effectiveness. When presenting the rationale, it should be explained to the patient that IE will probably help to decrease his or her fear of the physical sensations, just as situational exposure will probably decrease an individual's fear of objects, activities, or situations in the environment (e.g., snakes or public speaking).

Before beginning IE, it is important to assess whether the patient has any medical problems that might affect the safety of particular exercises. For example, individuals with chronic asthma should not be asked to hyperventilate. Also, patients with neck or back problems should be excused from exercises that may aggravate their conditions (e.g., shaking their head from side to side or stationary running). Other physical conditions, such as cardio-vascular disease, migraines, vestibular conditions, and seizure disorders may also affect the extent to which IE can be used safely. We recommend that the patient receive permission (in writing, if possible) from his or her physician before beginning IE if there is any possibility of a relevant medical condition being present.

Symptom-induction testing

Before beginning IE practices, it is important to first establish which exercises are likely to be effective for a particular patient. In order to select exercises, the therapist and patient should first attempt a broad range of exercises that are likely to be effective. An appropriate exercise is one that (a) creates uncomfortable physical sensations, (b) triggers anxiety or fear, and (c) creates a reaction that is similar to naturally occurring anxiety, fear, or panic. Initially, symptom-induction testing typically takes an entire session and may extend into part of a second session. Symptom-induction testing is often tiring for both the patient and therapist, and both may leave the session with a headache or other uncomfortable feelings.

Exhibit 6.2 includes a comprehensive list of IE exercises. This list includes the most common sensations experienced during each exercise, based, in part, on preliminary findings from systematically collected data on 14 patients with PD (Roth, Antony, & Swinson, 1999). Exhibit 6.3 is a handout for patients that lists these exercises. This handout can be distrib-uted to patients to facilitate their use of the IE exercises between sessions. In addition to these exercises, panic-provocation procedures that are often used in laboratory studies (e.g., carbon dioxide inhalation) also appear to be useful for inducing panic sensations in the context of providing CBT (for a review, see Hofmann, Bufka, & Barlow, 1999).

Before attempting each exercise, the therapist should first demonstrate the exercise for a few seconds. In addition, we suggest that the therapist conduct each exercise along with the patient. Following each exercise, the therapist should ask the patient to report the symptoms experienced, the intensity of his or her fear, and the similarity between the experience and his or her naturally occurring fear or panic attacks. For each item, a scale of 0–100 may be used to provide an estimate. A Symptom Induction Testing Form, on which to record the patient's responses, is included in Exhibit 6.4.

Note that it is not always necessary to try all of the IE exercises during symptom-induction testing. For some patients, it may be very clear that only certain sensations (e.g., breathlessness) are relevant to their fear. For such an individual, it may be appropriate to focus on exercises that trigger these sensations. Nevertheless, it is often helpful to try a broader range of

Exhibit 6.2
Exercises for Inducing Physical Sensations for Interoceptive Exposure

1. **Shake head from side to side (30 sec.)**
   Primary symptoms: dizziness or lightheadedness
   Additional symptoms: breathlessness or smothering feelings, racing or pounding heart
2. **Spin around in a swivel chair (60 sec.)**
   Primary symptoms: dizziness or lightheadedness
   Additional symptoms: racing or pounding heart, derealization, nausea, trembling or shaking
3. **While sitting, bend over and place head between legs for 30 sec., then sit up quickly**
   Primary symptoms: dizziness or lightheadedness
   Additional symptoms: breathlessness or smothering feelings
4. **Hold breath (30 sec. or as long as possible)**
   Primary symptoms: breathlessness or smothering feelings
   Additional symptoms: racing or pounding heart, dizziness or lightheadedness, chest tightness
5. **Hyperventilate (shallow breathing at a rate of about 100–120 breaths per min.) (60 sec.)**
   Primary symptoms: breathlessness or smothering feelings, dizziness or lightheadedness
   Additional symptoms: racing or pounding heart, derealization, trembling or shaking, numbness or tingling sensations
6. **Breathe through a narrow, small straw (plug nose if necessary) (2 min.)**
   Primary symptoms: breathlessness or smothering feelings, racing or pounding heart
   Additional symptoms: choking feelings, dizziness or lightheadedness, chest tightness, trembling or shaking
7. **Place a tongue depressor on the back of the tongue (a few seconds or until inducing a gag reflex)**
   Primary symptoms: gag reflex, choking feelings
   Additional symptoms: nausea, racing or pounding heart
8. **Wear a tie, a turtleneck shirt, or a scarf (5 min.)**
   Primary symptom: tightness in the throat
   Additional symptoms: breathlessness or smothering feelings
9. **Stare at a light on the ceiling for 60 sec. and then try to read**
   Primary symptom: blurred vision
   Additional symptoms: dizziness or lightheadedness, derealization
10. **Stare at self in a mirror (3 min.)**
    Primary symptom: derealization
11. **Stare at a small dot (about the size of a dime) posted on the wall (3 min.)**
    Primary symptom: derealization
12. **Stare at an optical illusion (e.g., rotating spiral, "psychedelic" computer screen saver) (2 min.)**
    Primary symptom: derealization
    Additional symptoms: dizziness or lightheadedness
13. **Tense all the muscles in the body or hold a push up position (60 sec. or as long as possible)**
    Primary symptoms: trembling or shaking
    Additional symptoms: breathlessness or smothering feelings, racing or pounding heart, dizziness or lightheadedness,
14. **Run on the spot (or run up and down stairs) (60 sec.)**
    Primary symptoms: racing or pounding heart, breathlessness or smothering feelings
    Additional symptoms: chest tightness, sweating, trembling, or shaking

(continued)

Exhibit 6.2
(*Continued*)

---

15. **Sit in a hot, stuffy room (e.g., a sauna, hot car, or small room with a space heater) (5 min.)**
    Primary symptom: sweating
    Additional symptoms: breathlessness or smothering feelings, hot flushes
16. **Sit with head covered by a heavy coat or blanket (5 min.)**
    Primary symptoms: breathlessness or smothering feelings
    Additional symptoms: sweating, hot flushes
17. **Drink a hot drink**
    Primary symptoms: sweating, hot flushes

---

exercises, just in case one or more unexpectedly trigger fear. Several exercises (hyperventilation, spinning, and breathing though a straw) are particularly effective for bringing on feared symptoms and should always be tried, especially for individuals with PD.

Assigning IE practices

After a number of fear-inducing exercises have been identified, the next step is to practice the appropriate exercises repeatedly until the fear has decreased. With repeated practice, the exercises will probably continue

Exhibit 6.3
Exercises for Inducing Physical Symptoms

---

1. Shake head from side to side (30 sec.)
2. Spin around in a swivel chair (60 sec.)
3. While sitting, bend over and place head between legs for 30 sec., then sit up quickly
4. Hold breath (30 sec. or as long as possible)
5. Hyperventilate (shallow breathing at a rate of about 100–120 breaths per min.) (60 sec.)
6. Breathe through a narrow, small straw (plug nose if necessary) (2 min.)
7. Place a tongue depressor on the back of the tongue (a few seconds or until inducing a gag reflex)
8. Wear a tie, a turtleneck shirt, or a scarf (5 min.)
9. Stare at a light on the ceiling for 60 sec. and then try to read
10. Stare at self in a mirror (3 min.)
11. Stare at a small dot (about the size of a dime) posted on the wall (3 min.)
12. Stare at an optical illusion (e.g., rotating spiral, "psychedelic" computer screen saver) (2 min.)
13. Tense all the muscles in the body or hold a push up position (60 sec. or as long as possible)
14. Run on the spot (or run up and down stairs) (60 sec.)
15. Sit in a hot, stuffy room (e.g., a sauna, hot car, or small room with a space heater) (5 min.)
16. Sit with head covered by a heavy coat or blanket (5 min.)
17. Drink a hot drink

Exhibit 6.4
Symptom-Induction Testing Form

Instructions: For each symptom-induction exercise, (1) list the physical SYMPTOMS that were experienced, (2) rate the intensity of FEAR using a scale of 0 (no fear) to 100 (maximum fear), and (3) record the SIMILARITY of the experience to typical episodes of anxiety and fear using a scale from 0 (not at all similar) to 100 (identical).

Exercise	Symptoms	Fear (0–100)	Similarity (0–100)
Shake head from side to side (30 sec.)			
Spin around in a swivel chair (60 sec.)			
While sitting, bend over and place head between legs for 30 sec., then sit up quickly			
Hold breath (30 sec. or as long as possible)			
Hyperventilate (shallow breathing at a rate of about 100–120 breaths per min.) (60 sec.)			
Breathe through a narrow, small straw (plug nose if necessary) (2 min.)			
Place a tongue depressor on the back of the tongue (a few seconds or until inducing a gag reflex)			
Wear a tie, a turtleneck shirt, or a scarf (5 min.)			
Stare at a light on the ceiling for 60 sec. and then try to read			
Stare at self in a mirror (3 min.)			
Stare at a small dot (about the size of a dime) posted on the wall (3 min.)			
Stare at an optical illusion (e.g., rotating spiral, "psychedelic" computer screen saver) (2 min.)			
Tense all the muscles in the body or hold a push up position (60 sec. or as long as possible)			
Run on the spot (or run up and down stairs) (60 sec.)			
Sit in a hot, stuffy room (e.g., a sauna, hot car, or small room with a space heater) (5 min.)			
Sit with head covered by a heavy coat or blanket (5 min.)			
Drink a hot drink			

to cause uncomfortable sensations, but the fear associated with the exercises will gradually decrease. As with situational exposure, it is often helpful to create a hierarchy of exercises and to have the patient work through the exercises until the most difficult exercises can be done with minimal fear (see the later section on creating exposure hierarchies).

For patients with PD, we recommend practicing each exercise in sets of five trials. For example, when practicing hyperventilation, the patient should complete five trials of hyperventilation (each lasting 60 seconds) in a row, with short breaks between each trial to allow the symptoms to subside. These sets of five trials should be repeated two to three times per day until the exercise no longer causes fear. With practice, the patient will probably experience a reduction of fear, both within practices and between practices.

A form for recording responses to IE practices (Interoceptive Exposure Monitoring Form) is included in Exhibit 6.5. This form is designed so that patients can record their responses to IE practices while also using the cognitive strategies described in chapter 7 to challenge anxious thoughts that occur during these practices. On the form, the individual records the specific exercise, date, and time. For each practice trial, the following information is also recorded: symptoms experienced, fear level (on a 0–100-point scale), anxious thoughts and predictions, and countering of anxious thoughts. We recommend that the clinician complete a sample form in session before having the patient use it on his or her own. For patients with social phobia and specific phobias, IE practices are unlikely to create fear outside of the phobic situation. Therefore we recommend combining IE with situational exposure for individuals with social or specific phobias.

Combining interoceptive and situational exposure

IE may be used in the context of situational exposure. In treating PD, this is often the next step after a patient has learned to be comfortable conducting IE practices in a safe location (e.g., at home or in the therapist's office). In the case of social and specific phobias, IE is more likely to be helpful if it is used in the presence of the phobic object or situation right from the start (as opposed to beginning with practicing IE in safe situations). Exhibit 6.6 lists examples of how IE can be combined with situational exposure practices.

PRACTICAL ISSUES IN EXPOSURE-BASED TREATMENT

Teaching Patients to Have Realistic Expectations

During exposure-based treatments, patients often become discouraged, particularly if their progress is slower than what they had hoped for, or if

Exhibit 6.5
Interoceptive Exposure Monitoring Form

Instructions: This form should be completed each time you practice interoceptive exposure. For each interoceptive exposure trial, (1) list the physical SYMPTOMS that were experienced, (2) rate the intensity of FEAR using a scale of 0 *(no fear)* to 100 *(maximum fear)*, (3) list specific anxious predictions regarding the exercise (e.g., what might happen during the exercise?), and (4) list alternative nonanxious predictions and evidence supporting these predictions (i.e., countering).

Describe the Exposure Exercise _____ Date and Time _____

Trial #	Symptoms experienced	Fear (0–100)	Anxious thoughts and predictions	Countering
1				
2				
3				
4				
6				
7				

Exhibit 6.6
Combining Interoceptive and Situational Exposure: Examples

Panic Disorder With Agoraphobia
- Stand on one leg at the mall to induce unsteadiness
- Hyperventilate while sitting in the passenger seat of a car
- Run on the spot while standing alone in a small closet
- Walk around quickly while shopping at the supermarket
- Drink a cup of coffee at a party
- Wear a tight scarf while flying on an airplane

Social Phobia
- Carry around heavy bags before filling out a form at the bank (to trigger shaking hands)
- Wear a warm sweater while giving a presentation
- Eat hot soup to induce flushing and sweating at a dinner party
- Run up and down the stairs before guests arrive for a party
- Hyperventilate just before calling someone on the telephone

Specific Phobia
- Breathe through a straw while sitting in a small, locked closet
- Hold your breath while riding in an elevator
- Increase the heat and close the windows while driving to work
- Turn your head quickly when in a high place
- Hyperventilate in an elevator or other enclosed place
- Walk up a flight of stairs before confronting a feared animal

they experience a worsening of symptoms after having made some progress. From the start, patients should be reminded that changes take time and that setbacks are a natural part of overcoming the problem. It is normal to experience one step back for every two or three steps forward. An inability to practice for a couple of weeks (e.g., due to the flu or a heavy exam schedule at school) can lead to a worsening of symptoms, as can an increase in general stress levels. Patients should be encouraged to learn from their negative experiences during exposure. For example, if an individual with social phobia experiences a rejection in a social situation, he or she should be encouraged to learn how he or she could approach the situation differently next time.

Patients should not treat a particular practice as their last chance to "get it right." Rather, each practice should be thought of as part of a learning process. For example, people with social phobia often avoid taking social risks (e.g., asking another person for a date or applying for a new job). When they finally take such a risk, a rejection may lead them to avoid taking a similar risk again for months or years. Of course, by avoiding these situations, they are successfully prevented from experiencing rejection, but they also are prevented from experiencing successes. For example, a person who avoids interviewing for jobs for fear of being rejected should be reminded that if the probability of being offered a job following an interview is 1 in 10, interviewing for jobs once per year will result in an offer every 10 years. In contrast, interviewing daily will result in an offer once every 10 days. In other words, more frequent social risks will lead to more rejections but also more successes.

Finally, as was discussed earlier, patients should expect to have things go wrong sometimes during exposure practices. Despite the patient's best intentions, he or she may experience a panic attack or feel too frightened to stay in a feared situation. Or, while practicing exposure to a feared social situation, he or she may make some interpersonal error (e.g., telling a joke that nobody laughs at, inadvertently offending someone, etc.). These experiences are normal from time to time and should not lead one to give up on the whole exposure process.

Setting and Duration of Treatment Sessions

Unlike traditional psychotherapies, exposure therapies tend to take place in the situations that are feared by the patient. Therefore, treatment may include activities such as driving over bridges with a patient who fears heights, eating in a restaurant with a patient who has social phobia, or shopping at a mall with a patient who has agoraphobia. The costs incurred by these activities (e.g., tolls to go over bridges) are typically paid for by the patient.

The fact that treatment often occurs outside of the office raises an important issue. It is particularly important that the patient and therapist be aware of boundary issues and that the patient is clear about the purpose of the session. For example, if you are eating in a restaurant with a patient, he or she should understand that your relationship is not a friendship, but rather that eating in a restaurant is part of the treatment. There may be situations in which you might want to invite a co-therapist or a member of the patient's family to be present during the treatment. These include practices that occur in secluded areas (e.g., standing near a cliff to overcome a fear of heights), practices that occur in the patient's home, or practices in which the patient is likely to scream (e.g., seeing cockroaches) or faint (e.g., exposure to blood).

The duration of exposure sessions will vary, depending on the patient, the particular fear, and the rate at which the patient's fear decreases. Exposure sessions should typically last between 1 and 3 hours. At the initial exposure session, we often schedule a 2-hour meeting, and we typically adjust the length of future meetings, depending on the progress of treatment.

Assigning Homework

Studies with agoraphobic individuals (Edelman & Chambless, 1993) and patients with social phobia (Leung & Heimberg, 1996) have consistently shown a relationship between homework compliance and outcome of exposure-based treatments. Exposure practices between sessions are important for helping the patient overcome his or her phobic anxiety and may be even more important than the therapist-assisted exposure that occurs during treatment sessions (Al-Kubaisy et al., 1992). The therapist should ensure that homework is assigned at the end of each session and discussed at the beginning of the following session.

Exposure homework has two main functions. First, it increases the number of hours of practice over and above what occurs during the treatment session. Second, homework allows for generalization of the treatment effects from the office setting to naturally occurring situations in the patient's life. Despite the benefits of homework, however, patients often are noncompliant with homework assignments. Identifying the reasons for noncompliance can often help to take care of the problem before it becomes worse.

Reasons for homework noncompliance

One of the most common reasons why patients do not complete their exposure homework is because they did not understand the task. Often the therapist waits until the very end of each session to assign the homework and may rush through the instructions. Enough time should be left to ensure that the patient understands the homework instructions and is involved in planning the homework. In addition, the homework should be relevant to the patient. For example, an agoraphobic patient who fears riding the bus (among other situations) is unlikely to practice in this situation if riding buses is not important to him or her. Asking the patient to practice doing things that will probably lead to an improved quality of life when the fear decreases should lead to improved compliance.

Patients may also avoid doing exposure homework because the task is too difficult. This problem can be overcome by having the patient involved in the process of generating homework assignments and by having back-up plans in place if an assignment ends up being too difficult. In addition, patients may be more likely to comply with difficult homework tasks when family members are involved in the process or when the therapist arranges for a telephone contact just before the homework is completed, just after the homework is completed, or both. After compliance has improved, telephone contact can often be gradually discontinued.

Another reason for a lack of compliance with homework is the failure of the therapist to ask about homework at the start of each session. Unless the therapist reviews homework each week, the patient will quickly get the message that the homework is not important. Finally, homework compliance may be compromised in patients who have other demands, problems, or stresses in their lives (e.g., several small children, a demanding work schedule, depression, marital difficulties, etc.) or for whom interpersonal factors (e.g., poor therapeutic alliance or personality disorders) are affecting the treatment. In such cases it is important to address these issues with the patient.

Choosing Items for Exposure Practices

In chapter 4 we discuss how to prepare a *hierarchy of feared situations*. To summarize, the therapist and patient should generate a list of 10 to 15 specific situations that are feared by the patient and that are appropriate situations in which to practice exposure. These situations should be rank ordered according to difficulty, and the patient should rate the difficulty level for each item using a 0–100 or similar scale.

Next, items can be selected from the hierarchy for exposure practices. Exposure practices should begin with a moderately difficult item and should continue through the various items on the list until the most difficult items can be completed with relative comfort. At the start of treatment, patients may be skeptical about their ability to practice items near the top of the hierarchy. However, with each step taken, the remaining steps on the hierarchy will become somewhat easier to complete.

As exposure practices continue, the hierarchy may change. Items that were once very difficult may no longer be relevant. In addition, it may be useful to add new items to the hierarchy as treatment progresses. The hierarchy should be viewed as a helpful guide for planning exposure practices. However, it should be used with flexibility. It is okay to skip items, add items, and remove items as the treatment progresses. An example of an exposure hierarchy for social phobia is provided in Table 6.2.

Measuring the Effects of Exposure

Immediately following an exposure practice, the patient should complete an Exposure Monitoring Form (Exhibit 6.7 is a blank copy of this form). This form is used to monitor changes in fear over the course of a situational exposure practice (a separate form is included for monitoring responses during IE). Although the form is somewhat complex, it has the advantage of being combined with elements of a Cognitive Monitoring Form (see chapter 7) and therefore can also be used to challenge anxious beliefs regarding the exposure practice. When this form is being used, there is no need for the patient to also complete cognitive monitoring forms.

Table 6.2
Exposure Hierarchy for Social Phobia

Item	(Fear 0–100)
1. Have a party and invite everyone from work.	99
2. Go to Christmas party for 1 hour without drinking.	90
3. Invite Cindy to have dinner and see a movie.	85
4. Go for a job interview.	80
5. Ask boss for a day off work.	65
6. Ask questions in a meeting at work.	65
7. Eat lunch with coworkers.	60
8. Talk to a stranger on the bus.	50
9. Talk to cousin on the telephone for 10 minutes.	40
10. Ask for directions at the gas station.	35

If the patient finds this form to be too complicated, a simpler form can be developed.

At the top of the Exposure Monitoring Form, the individual describes the practice situation, the date, time, and duration of the practice, and his or her fear level before and after the practice. The middle part of the form is essentially used for testing the validity of fearful predictions about the exposure practice. The first three columns are completed before the practice, and the last column is completed after the practice. In the first column, the individual records his or her emotional response to the upcoming practice. Columns 2 and 3 are used for recording fearful predictions and evidence regarding the validity of the predictions. After the practice is completed, the individual records the outcome of the practice, as well as his or her reappraisal of the validity of his or her original predictions.

In the lower part of the form, there is space to record the patient's fear level periodically during the practice using a scale ranging from 0 (*no fear*) to 100 (*maximum fear*). The frequency with which fear ratings are recorded will depend on the duration of the practice. For example, ratings might be recorded every minute for a practice lasting 10 minutes or every 30 minutes for a practice lasting all day. The last step in completing this form is to plan for the next practice by answering the question, "Based on this experience, what exposure will you do next?"

Safety Issues

Before starting treatment, the clinician should make sure that there are no particular safety issues that are of concern. For example, if working with animals to help a person overcome an animal phobia, the clinician should make sure that he or she is familiar with the animal's behavior and that the animal is unlikely to become aggressive or agitated during the

Exhibit 6.7
Exposure Monitoring Form

Describe the Exposure Situation _____   Date and time _____

Initial fear level (0–100) _____   Fear level at end (0–100) _____   Duration of exposure _____

COMPLETE BEFORE THE EXPOSURE PRACTICE	COMPLETE AFTER THE EXPOSURE PRACTICE
What emotions and feelings (e.g., fear, anger, etc.) do I have about the exposure?	What anxious thoughts, predictions, and assumptions do I have about the exposure? What do I expect will happen during the exposure practice?	What evidence do I have that my fearful thoughts are true?	1. What was the outcome of this practice? What actually happened? 2. What evidence did I gain from this practice? How accurate were my original thoughts and predictions?

1. Outcome:

2. Evidence:

Fear levels (0–100) during the exposure practice (rate every _____ minutes)

1. _____   4. _____   7. _____   10. _____   13. _____   16. _____   19. _____   22. _____   25. _____   28. _____
2. _____   5. _____   8. _____   11. _____   14. _____   17. _____   20. _____   23. _____   26. _____   29. _____
3. _____   6. _____   9. _____   12. _____   15. _____   18. _____   21. _____   24. _____   27. _____   30. _____

Based on this experience, what exposure will I do next?

Reprinted with permission. © 2000 Peter J. Bieling, Ph.D., and Martin M. Antony, Ph.D.

treatment. The clinician should also be aware of any medical conditions that may affect the patient's safety during the treatment. For example, before doing exposure with a blood-phobic individual, it is wise to obtain permission from the patient's physician, indicating that it is safe for the patient to begin practices that could lead to fainting. There may also be issues related to insurance that need to be clarified. Clinicians should ensure that they are covered in the event that a patient is hurt during a session (e.g., being bitten by a dog during an exposure practice, getting into a car accident while practicing driving, etc.). The clinician may want to consider developing a consent form or waiver for patients to sign before starting treatment.

Finding Relevant Materials and Situations

Table 6.3 and Exhibit 6.8 list ideas for exposure practices for people suffering from specific phobias and social phobia, respectively. For additional exposure ideas (particularly for people suffering from PD and agoraphobia), chapter 4 is a good source.

TROUBLESHOOTING FOR EXPOSURE THERAPY

Fear Does Not Decrease With Exposure

There are a number of reasons why a patient's fear may not decrease during a particular practice or between practices. As a first step, clinicians should examine the patient's cognitions during the practice. For example, if a person with social phobia is interpreting his or her behavior very critically following a practice (e.g., "I made a fool of myself"), this may undermine the effects of the exposure. Similarly, if a person who fears flying attributes his or her success during a particular practice to luck, the fear may not decrease between practices. In these cases, it may be helpful to combine exposure with some of the cognitive strategies described in chapter 7.

It is also important to assess whether the patient is engaging in subtle avoidance strategies, relying on safety cues, using overprotective behaviors, or using substances during practices. All of these can undermine the benefits of exposure. In addition, increasing the duration or frequency of the exposure may improve the outcome. Finally, if all else fails, the patient can decrease the difficulty of the exposure practice or switch to a completely different practice.

A Medical Condition Interferes With Treatment

Occasionally, a medical condition may affect exposure therapy. For example, an inner ear disorder, mitral valve prolapse, or asthma may

Table 6.3
Finding Materials and Situations for Exposure in
Specific-Phobia Treatment

Phobia	Ideas for finding materials and situations
Bugs, spiders, rodents	Researchers in university psychology (rodents) and zoology (bugs, spiders) departments
	Biological supply companies (that supply schools and researchers)
	Gardens, homes, basements, wooded areas (bugs and spiders)
	Pet stores (rodents, crickets)
	Ask friends or colleagues to bring in pet mice and rats
	Ask friends or colleagues to look for bugs and rodents
	Use books, nature videos, or movies that depict bugs, spiders, or rodents
	Bee keepers (for bee phobias)
Dogs, cats, birds, snakes	Use your own pets
	Ask friends or colleagues to bring in their pets
	Ask a pet store owner if you can conduct exposure at the store (possibly after hours)
	Ask a pet store owner if you can borrow or rent an animal
	Go to places where these animals can be found (e.g., parks, zoos, homes of pet owners, Humane Society)
	Use books, nature videos, or movies that depict the feared animal (most likely to be effective for fears of snakes or birds)
Heights	Look over the railing at a mall, fire escape, balcony, etc.
	Stand near ledges, on ladders, on chairs
	Look out the window of a tall building
	Walk or drive slowly over a bridge
	Stand on a flat rooftop
	Ride on a chair lift while skiing or a Ferris wheel
Storms	Arrange to have a telephone session with a patient on the day of a storm to plan in vivo exposure practices
	Conduct imaginal exposure, using thunderstorm cassettes to simulate thunder and a camera flash to simulate lightning
	Watch simulated thunderstorm videos on a large screen television
	During a storm, sit near the window (perhaps with the window or door open
	Stop planning activities around the possibility of bad weather
Blood, injection, injury	Arrange to watch live surgery at a hospital
	Use books, educational videos, or movies that show blood, surgery, or injections (check a medical school library)
	Observe people giving blood at a lab or blood donor clinic
	Use finger prick blood test kit (from pharmacy) to draw blood from the patient or therapist's finger
	Obtain a blood test at a lab or a physician's office
	Give blood at a blood donor clinic
Enclosed places	Reverse the lock on a small room or closet so that individual can be locked inside
	Sit in the back seat of a small two-door car
	Ride on old, small, slow elevators
	Arrange to have an elevator put on "service" so that it will remain stationary until the button is pushed and held
	Sit in a small doctor's office
	Sit in a cramped attic, crawl space, or closet

(continued)

Table 6.3
(*Continued*)

Phobia	Ideas for finding materials and situations
Flying	Practice taking several short, inexpensive flights in the same week
	Hire a private pilot with a small airplane who charges by the hour for rides
	Choose travel with multiple connections instead of direct flights
	Enroll in airline course for fearful flyers
	Ask airline staff for permission to sit in a grounded airplane
	Visit an airport and watch airplanes take off and land
Driving	Practice driving when the road is empty (e.g., weekend mornings)
	Practice making left hand turns over and over again
	Drive on city streets or the highway during rush hour
	Practice merging with traffic on highways
	Practice switching lanes on the highway
	Drive in an empty parking lot

contribute to a person's symptoms of panic. Having small veins may exacerbate a fear of blood tests, as the result of an increased likelihood of experiencing pain or bruising. Poor night vision can exacerbate a fear of driving.

As is discussed in chapter 4, we recommend that clinicians ask patients about medical conditions that may contribute to their fear. In many cases, treatment can work around these or take these into account. For example, if the patient has poor night vision, perhaps he or she should not be driving at night. Instead, treatment can focus on overcoming the fear of driving during the day. If a patient's veins are so small that it is very difficult and painful to have blood taken from the arm, recommend that the patient only have blood taken by experienced laboratory technicians and have the patient request that the blood be taken from another location in the body, where he or she has had success in the past. In consultation with the patient's physician, clinicians should sort out how much of the fear is realistic and how much is exaggerated or excessive. In addition, they should find out whether there are certain behavioral exercises that could be dangerous for the patient.

Fear Is Too High for the Patient to Benefit From Exposure

If a patient's fear is too high during a particular exercise, there are generally two options for the therapist: taking a short break and then trying the same exercise again and switching to a less difficult practice.

The Feared Situation Is Difficult to Create

If the conditions needed for a particular exercise cannot be created, patients can practice in other situations for which the benefits of exposure

Exhibit 6.8
Ideas for Exposure Practices for People Suffering From Social Phobia

---

Practices Involving Public Speaking
- Speak in meetings at work
- Go to a public lecture and ask questions
- Enroll in or audit a university or college course (ask questions)
- Make an impromptu speech or toast
- Take a public speaking course (e.g., Toastmasters)
- Take a drama class
- Give a lecture at a local high school or college about your work

Practices Involving Informal Socializing (Making Small Talk)
- Have friends over for a get together
- Speak to strangers on elevators, in lines, etc.
- Ask for directions or for the time
- Go to a social event (e.g., party, gallery opening)
- Talk to coworkers or classmates
- Talk to neighbors (or invite them over for a drink)
- Talk to dog owners who are walking their dogs
- Talk to cashiers in stores
- Give or receive compliments
- Express a controversial opinion
- Join an ongoing conversation
- Talk to parents of other children (e.g., at parents' night, swimming lessons, etc.)
- Meet two or three friends at a café
- Join a club or organization (e.g., bowling league, volleyball league, bingo, etc.)

Practices Involving Conflict Situations
- Ask someone to change his/her behavior (e.g., stop talking in a movie theatre)
- Stay stopped in your car when the light turns green (with traffic backed up behind you)
- Say no when you do not want to do something
- Return an item at a store
- Send food back in a restaurant
- Ask a stranger not to smoke

Practices Involving Being the Center of Attention
- Take an aerobics class
- Say something incorrect
- Spill your drink
- Talk about yourself
- Ask for help in a store
- Wear a shirt or dress inside out
- Knock over a display in a store or supermarket

Practices Involving Eating or Drinking in Front of Others
- Invite people over for a meal
- Have a meal at other people's homes
- Meet a friend at a restaurant for dinner
- Have lunch with co-workers
- Eat a snack at your desk
- Eat alone in a food court or another public place

Practices Involving Writing in Front of Others
- Fill out or sign checks at a store
- Fill out forms or applications (e.g., at a bank)

(*continued*)

Exhibit 6.8
(*Continued*)

Practices Involving Job Interviews
- Apply for many jobs (even jobs you do not want)
- Practice interviews with family members or friends

Practices Involving Being Around Strangers
- Go to a mall or supermarket
- Walk down a busy street
- Go to a concert or sporting event
- Read in a library
- Make eye contact while riding a bus or subway
- Join the YMCA or a health club

Practices Involving Talking to Authority Figures
- Have a meeting with your boss or teacher
- Ask a pharmacist questions about a medication
- Ask your doctor to explain a particular medical condition

may generalize to the hard-to-create situation. For example, an individual who fears flying as part of agoraphobia may experience a decrease in fear of flying by practicing in other agoraphobic situations (e.g., driving or crowds). Imaginal exposure or simulated exposures (behavioral role-plays for the treatment of social phobia) are other options.

The Situation Is by Definition Very Brief in Duration

There are some situations, such as asking a stranger for directions, taking an elevator, turning left in a car, or crossing a bridge, that are inherently brief. Because prolonged exposure works best, we recommend that creative ways be found to lengthen the duration of these practices. Usually, this will mean repeating the practice over and over, until the fear has decreased. For example, patients can be instructed to ride an elevator up and down for an hour, drive over a bridge repeatedly until the fear subsides, or ask for directions many times over the course of an afternoon.

The Patient Refuses to Do a Practice

If a patient refuses to do a suggested practice, the clinician has several options. Usually, the best option is to choose an easier practice. For example, if a patient is able to drive accompanied but refuses to drive alone, he or she may practice driving with the therapist crouched down in the back seat. Next, the patient may drive with the therapist following in the car behind. Similarly, if a spider-fearful patient refuses to touch a spider, he or should could be asked to touch close to the spider.

Another option for dealing with a patient's refusal to try a particular practice is to examine his or her anxious predictions and to challenge them using cognitive restructuring strategies (chapter 7). In addition, it may be helpful to explore the costs and benefits of conducting the practice, before giving up on it completely. In most cases, the only cost to conducting exposure is temporary discomfort.

An Unexpected Negative Event Occurs During a Practice

Although rare, it is possible that an unexpected negative event will occur during an exposure practice. For example, a patient may be bitten by an animal, may almost crash a car, may have a very bad panic attack, or may be laughed at during a presentation. If this occurs, it is reasonable to expect some return of fear, and it may be necessary to resume exposure with an easier item on the hierarchy. Additionally, it may be helpful to use cognitive restructuring techniques to help the patient re-process the negative event.

Fear Returns Between Sessions

This is normal to some extent. With continued practice, the fear will decrease more quickly during practices and will not return as intensely between practices. One way of preventing return of fear between practices is to increase the frequency of the exposures, particularly early in treatment.

The Exposure Situation Is Difficult to Control

Although exposures work best when they are predictable, structured, and controlled, some types of situations are inherently difficult to control. For example, birds may fly away during exposure practices for bird phobias. Traffic may be unpredictable during exposures to driving. To minimize unpredictable events when working with animals, use cages, leashes, aquariums, boxes, and other restraints to control the animal. Also, try to use animals that are easier to control (e.g., a dog that does not bark much). When working with other phobias, encourage the patient to practice at times when the situation is easier to control (e.g., driving when the roads are empty, practicing exposure to social situations using role-play simulations). Once the individual has mastered practicing under more controlled circumstances, he or she should be encouraged to practice in situations that are less predictable and controlled.

The Patient Still Has Fear Despite Exposure

Occasionally, a person will report having intense fear despite confronting feared situations. An example is a person who flies frequently despite having white knuckles from being so frightened. Generally, there are two strategies that can be used to manage these patients. The first is to assess whether the patient is engaging in subtle avoidance strategies, reliance on safety cues, overprotective behaviors, substance use, or other strategies that may be undermining the effects of the exposure. If so, the person should be encouraged to discontinue these behaviors. The second is to examine the patient's cognitions during exposure. Cognitive restructuring (chapter 7) may be helpful for changing fearful thoughts and predictions that are maintaining the fear despite frequent exposures.

The Patient Lacks Certain Necessary Skills

For some patients, a skills deficit may be contributing to fear. For example, some patients who fear driving are poor drivers. Similarly, some socially phobic people behave awkwardly in social situations and may actually be at a greater risk for being negatively evaluated. In these cases, we recommend arranging for the patient to develop the needed skills through driving lessons, assertiveness training, or another form of skills training.

A Particular Interoceptive Exposure Does Not Trigger Fear

There are four reasons why a particular IE exercise may not cause fear: (a) the exercise does not trigger sensations that are normally feared by the patient, (b) the patient is not fearful of the exercises because he or she knows what is causing the uncomfortable sensations, (c) the context in which the exercises are being practiced (e.g., therapist's office) increases the patient's perceived safety, and (d) in the absence of the feared object or situation, the sensations created by the exercise are not frightening. If an exercise does not trigger fear in the therapist's office, it may still be worth having the patient try the exercise at home or in the presence of the feared situation or object. It may also be helpful to practice the IE exercises during naturally occurring episodes of fear or panic (as an alternative to avoidance strategies).

SOCIAL SKILLS TRAINING FOR SOCIAL PHOBIA

Many patients with social phobia have outstanding social and interpersonal skills, despite their anxiety and fear in social situations. However, because social phobia is associated with avoidance of certain types of social contact, some patients may not have had the opportunity to develop particular social or interpersonal skills that other people take for granted. Furthermore, for some people, social skills deficits can contribute to rejection from other people, confirming the patient's assumption that other people will judge him or her negatively. Exercises for improving social skills can be integrated into exposure practices for patients who stand to benefit from refining their social and communication skills.

Social skills training involves teaching the patient to change specific behaviors while performing or interacting with others, with the goal of increasing the likelihood of a positive response from the other people. Methods that can be used to facilitate social skills training include the following:

- Psychoeducation (e.g., teaching the patient about the differences between assertive communication, passive communication, and aggressive communication).
- Monitoring and changing specific social behaviors during exposure practices throughout the week (e.g., asking the patient to increase his or her eye contact during casual conversations).
- In-session role-plays with feedback from the therapist (and from other patients if treatment is being conducted in a group—e.g., giving the patient feedback on his or her performance during a simulated job interview).
- Videotaped in-session role-plays with feedback and discussion centering around the tape (e.g., videotaping a simulated presentation by the patient and watching it together so that specific suggestions can be made by the patient and therapist for improving the performance next time).

Examples of behaviors that may be the target of social skills training are listed in Exhibit 6.9.

Presenting the Rationale for Social Skills Training

Presenting to a patient the notion that he or she could benefit from improved social skills is sometimes a delicate matter. Social phobia is often associated with an intense fear of rejection, and telling patients that they have poor social skills could be interpreted as evidence supporting the patient's negative self-image and the belief that he or she is likely to be judged negatively by others. In addition, people with social phobia are often already too aware of how they are coming across and may already focus on behaviors that they perceive as evidence of incompetence or social ineptness (e.g., saying the wrong thing, looking anxious, etc.). The therapist should be careful to ensure that attempts at social skills training do not serve to increase or maintain a patients' self-focused attention.

There are several measures that can be taken, when presenting the rationale, to increase the likelihood that patients will benefit from the social

Exhibit 6.9
Behaviors That Can Be Targeted in Social Skills Training

- Eye contact (e.g., making appropriate eye contact when talking to other people)
- Body language (e.g., learning to have an "open" posture and to stand at an appropriately close distance to other people during conversations)
- Tone and volume of speech (e.g., avoiding talking too quietly)
- Conversation skills (e.g., learning to stop apologizing unnecessarily and to stop putting oneself down in front of others, learning to disclose information about oneself, learning to use open-ended questions instead of closed-ended questions)
- Public speaking skills (e.g., learning to talk to an audience during a presentation instead of reading from a paper; using slides, overheads, and audiovisual aids; answering audience questions and criticisms clearly and without alienating the audience)
- Interview skills (e.g., preparing for an interview—what to wear, what questions to ask, what questions to expect from the interviewer)
- Dating skills (e.g., asking another individual to lunch or dinner)
- Assertiveness skills (e.g., learning how to ask for things assertively, without being either too passive or too aggressive)
- Conflict skills (e.g., learning how to deal with other people who are angry or hostile)
- Listening skills (e.g., listening to other people when they are talking instead of comparing oneself to the other person, ruminating about what to say next, etc.)
- Other interpersonal skills (e.g., learning the difference between imposing on others' time and privacy and making reasonable requests for help or social contact)

skills training. First, it is often helpful to begin by having the patient identify particular social behaviors that he or she would like to work on improving, rather than pointing out social skills deficits that the patient may not even be aware of. Social skills deficits should be described as habits that most people engage in from time to time and to varying degrees, rather than serious problems that are unique to the patient. Patients should also be taught to recognize that there is no such thing as perfect social skills. A person whose social skills work well in one situation may not be particularly effective in other situations.

In addition, social skills training should progress in steps, so that patients are unlikely to be overwhelmed with trying to change too many behaviors at once. Finally, at the same time that patients are encouraged to change certain behaviors, they should also give themselves permission to make mistakes. Integrating cognitive strategies during social skills training sessions may help the patient to be more accepting of his or her social behaviors. The following vignette illustrates how to initially present the topic of social skills training to a patient.

> **Therapist:** Sometimes when people are nervous about how other people
> will react to them, they engage in certain behaviors that actually increase
> the likelihood of being judged negatively by others. For example, at a

party, a person who is nervous about seeming boring or unattractive is more likely to talk very quietly and avoid making eye contact and say too much. As a result, others may be less inclined to talk to the person, choosing instead to talk to other people who either seem easier to talk to or more interested in talking. In short, the person who is nervous about being rejected may end up contributing to the outcome of which he or she is most afraid.

Patient: I know that I avoid eye contact when I am nervous.

Therapist: That's quite a normal response for people to have when they feel anxious in a social situation. In fact, there are lots of ways in which people's behavior in social situations is different when they feel anxious compared with when they're not anxious. Are there are times when you notice that it is easier to make eye contact?

Patient: When I am with my close friends or family, it's not a problem at all.

Therapist: Because people who are socially anxious tend to avoid the situations that make them nervous, they may never have the opportunity to develop certain social skills. Just like learning to drive or to play the piano requires repeated rehearsal, learning to give presentations or to ask someone out on a date takes practice. To achieve these skills, a person has to be willing to take a risk, knowing that he or she will probably make mistakes.

Patient: That makes sense.

Therapist: Can you think of areas in which you could benefit from improving certain social skills or changing certain social behaviors?

Patient: I'm pretty bad at small talk. I never seem to have anything to say.

Therapist: Is small talk always difficult for you?

Patient: Actually, I'm fine over the phone. I'm also fine with people I know well. It's hardest with people I do not know, like at a party.

Therapist: You mentioned some difficulty making eye contact. Do you think there are other ways that your body language says "stay away?"

Patient: It's possible. I have been told that some people at work think I'm snobby or aloof. If I am doing anything to give off that message, I have no idea what it is.

Therapist: How about situations demanding assertiveness? Can you say "no" to an unreasonable request? If a person's behavior is bothering you, do you often keep it to yourself rather than saying something?

Patient: That's definitely me.

Therapist: Most people have difficulty being assertive from time to time. Do you think being assertive is harder for you than for most people?

Patient: I think it is harder for me. I cannot even return something to a store if it does not work properly.

Therapist: How about public speaking? Is it important for you to improve your public speaking skills?

Patient: I am terrified of public speaking, but it never really comes up. I do not see that as a problem.

Therapist: Are there other types of behaviors or skills that you would like to develop or improve in order to help you feel more comfortable in social situations?

Patient: None that I can think of.

Therapist: So let's summarize the items that you mentioned. You said that you would like to improve your conversation skills, particularly when making small talk with people you do not know well. You mentioned difficulty making eye contact and that you may give off other nonverbal signals (such as body language) that you are not interested in talking to other people. Finally, you mentioned a desire to be more assertive in certain situations.

Patient: That pretty much sums it up.

Teaching Specific Social Skills

Before beginning social skills training, we highly recommend that patients purchase or borrow the second edition of the self-help book, *Messages: The Communication Skills Book* (McKay et al., 1995). This book covers all aspects of communication, including those that are often problematic for people with social phobia, such as listening and self-disclosure, nonverbal communication, assertiveness, conflict and negotiation, making contact, interviewing, and public speaking. This book also doubles as a text for therapists who are interested in learning more about training their patients to communicate better. The book is highly structured and offers numerous illustrations, examples, and exercises for the reader to try.

In the remainder of this section, we will discuss skills related to nonverbal communication, casual conversation, and assertive communication. Many of the suggestions in these sections are based on recommendations from *Messages*. We recommend referring to this book for additional ideas. There are also a number of other good books that are readily available in the self-help or business sections in many bookstores. We have listed several in Appendix C of this book.

Nonverbal communication

There are a number of ways in which people send nonverbal signals that they are unwilling to communicate openly. Exhibit 6.10 lists examples of nonverbal behaviors that suggest open (e.g., trusting and interested) and closed (e.g., defensive, untrusting, and uninterested) styles of communication.

Keep in mind that there are cultural differences with respect to the meaning of various nonverbal behaviors (McKay et al., 1995; Sue, 1990).

Exhibit 6.10
Nonverbal Behaviors That Suggest Open and Closed Styles
of Communication

Examples of Open Nonverbal Behaviors
- Leaning forward or standing close to another person
- Maintaining eye contact
- Speaking at a volume that is easily heard by others
- Keeping arms uncrossed
- Keeping hands open
- Smiling warmly

Examples of Closed Nonverbal Behaviors
- Leaning back or standing far away from another person
- Avoiding eye contact
- Speaking quietly
- Crossing arms
- Clenching fists
- Maintaining a serious facial expression

For example, although a lack of eye contact is more likely to be seen as a sign of shyness or social anxiety in some cultures, other cultures are more likely to view avoidance of eye contact as a sign of respect. Cultural differences have also been reported with respect to how people interpret smiling, silences during conversations, and volume and tone during speech.

As was reviewed by McKay et al. (1995), there are also gender differences with respect to nonverbal communication. It can be helpful to educate patients regarding the possibility that different people may interpret their nonverbal communication styles in different ways. However, despite possible differences in the styles of communication between men and women and across cultures, there is still a great degree of variability among people within particular cultures and genders. Therefore, it is important to guard against relying on cultural and gender stereotypes when communicating with others or making assumptions about how others interpret one's own nonverbal behaviors.

Conversation skills

People with social phobia may have difficulties with several different aspects of casual conversation, including listening to the other person, disclosing information about themselves, and keeping conversations going. McKay et al. (1995) listed 12 different reasons why people sometimes do not listen during conversations. Of these, 5 are especially relevant in social phobia:

1. comparing oneself to the other individual (e.g., "I am not as smart as he is," "She is more attractive than I am")

2. filtering what the other person is saying (e.g., paying attention only to parts of the conversation that support one's fear that the other person is being critical or judgmental)
3. rehearsing what to say next (e.g., practicing how to respond to the other individual's comments rather than listening to what the other person is actually saying)
4. derailing the conversation (e.g., changing the subject to a more comfortable topic)
5. placating the other person (e.g., agreeing with the other individual regardless of what he or she says, in order to avoid potential conflict)

Not listening during a conversation can make the speaker feel as though the listener is distracted and uninterested in communicating. McKay et al. (1995) have suggested a number of strategies for ensuring active listening during a conversation. First, they recommended that the individual maintain eye contact during the conversation. Second, they suggested that the individual convey his or her understanding of the conversation by periodically paraphrasing statements made by the other person and showing empathy for the other person's feelings and experiences. Paraphrasing will indicate that the individual is interested in the conversation. Finally, they recommended that the individual ask for clarification when information is unclear during a conversation.

People with social phobia may also benefit from practicing disclosing information about themselves and expressing their ideas, during role-play simulations and real-life exposure practices. Self-disclosure and the expression of thoughts and feelings will help patients to foster more intimate relationships and improve their communication. McKay et al. (1995) described four main types of expression: observations and facts (e.g., "It is hot outside," "It is almost lunch time"), thoughts and opinions (e.g., "He always seems uptight around the boss," "Buying a dog was the right thing to do"), feelings ("I was angry when you did not phone me," "I am very excited about my trip to Europe"), and needs and desires (e.g., "Would you mind taking a shorter lunch today?; I could really use your help with some work," "I would love to have dinner with you tonight").

Good communication should include statements that fit clearly into one of these four categories of expression. Communication can be undermined when messages are mixed or indirect. For example, the statement "You have no problem remembering to call people when it is important to you" may be an indirect way of saying "You did not call me" (observation), and "I felt hurt when I did not receive your call" (feeling). In addition to being direct, good communication should be clear (e.g., the individual should not ask a question when he or she means to make a statement, avoid focusing on too many things at once, distinguish between observations and opinions, make sure that the nonverbal aspects of the communication are congruent with the verbal statement, and be clear about his or her wants and feelings) and immediate (e.g., do not wait 2 weeks to let someone know that something he or she had said was hurtful).

For people who have difficulty keeping conversations going (e.g., making small talk), trying to use open-ended questions can help keep a conversation alive for longer. Consider the following conversation between two people who have just met at a mutual friend's wedding reception.

> **Peter:** So, are you a friend of the bride or the groom?
> **Jon:** The groom.
> **Peter:** How long have you known him?
> **Jon:** About 3 years.
> **Peter:** Oh. Are you enjoying the music?
> **Jon:** It's okay. How about you?
> **Peter:** It's okay.

Note that Peter and Jon are asking closed-ended questions that are easily answered with a single word or phrase. As a result, the conversation is simply a series of short questions and answers. If they had chosen to use open-ended questions (e.g., those that cannot be answered easily with a "yes," "no," or other single word or phrase), the conversation might have developed more. Here is an example of the same conversation with more open-ended questions.

> **Peter:** So, are you a friend of the bride or the groom?
> **Jon:** The groom.
> **Peter:** How did you meet him?
> **Jon:** About 3 years ago, we were roommates in college.
> **Peter:** Oh. What was that like?
> **Jon:** Actually, it was great. He is a bit messy, but we had some really good times. I met a lot of new friends through him as well. How do you know him?
> **Peter:** I actually never met the groom until today. I am friends with the bride, but I live on the other side of the country, so we never get to see one another.

To summarize, there are a number of strategies that patients can use to improve their conversation skills. Among those discussed in this section are learning to listen, learning to express oneself directly and clearly, and learning to use open-ended questions to facilitate conversation when making small talk.

Assertiveness training

McKay et al. (1995) described three different communication styles. *Aggressive communication* involves expressing ones feelings, needs, or wants at the expense of other people's feelings, needs, and wants. This style of responding has the effect of closing the channels of communication and can result in hurt feelings, grudges, anger, and alienation from the other person. An example of an aggressive way of asking someone to socialize is the statement, "If you cared about me and were not so selfish, you would invite me to get together more often."

The opposite of aggressive communication is *passive communication*. This communication style puts other people's wants, needs, and feelings ahead of one's own. Needs and desires are often communicated indirectly or not at all, and the individual may expect other people to know what he or she wants despite having not provided the information in a direct way. Passive communications are often said with a quiet voice, with frequent pauses and hesitations. Like aggressive responses, passive responses close the channels of communication and can lead a person to feel hurt and resentful. Repeatedly responding in a passive way can also put someone at risk for responding aggressively in the future. An example of a passive way of inviting someone to socialize is the statement, "We should get together sometime."

In contrast to aggressive and passive styles of communicating, *assertive communication* takes into account one's own feelings, needs, and wants, as well as those of the other person. Assertive communication has many of the features of good communication described earlier, including a tendency to be direct, clear, and immediate. An assertive statement (particularly if the purpose of the statement is to get someone else to change his or her behavior) should include a person's observations regarding the situation, his or her feelings in response to the situation, and a description of how he or she would like things to change. In addition, assertive communication should include active listening to the other person's perspective (e.g., trying to hear and understand the other person's point of view, validating the other person's feelings, asking for clarification, etc.). Although assertive communication does not guarantee that a person will get his or her own way, relative to aggressive and passive styles of communication, assertive statements are more likely to keep the channels of communication open and to maximize the chances of reaching a mutually satisfactory resolution. An example of an assertive way to invite someone to socialize is the statement, "Would you like to see a movie this weekend?"

CONCLUSION

In this chapter we provide a step-by-step overview of exposure-based treatments for people with phobic disorders, as well as ideas for social skills training with individuals suffering from social phobia. This chapter should improve the reader's understanding of how to present the rationale for exposure and social skills training to clients and prepare him or her to use some of these techniques with individuals suffering from PD, agoraphobia, social phobia, or specific phobia. The forms and handouts from this chapter (as well as the other chapters from this book) may be copied freely by purchasers of this volume and may be distributed to patients and clients. At first, it may seem that there is a lot to remember when working with these strategies. We recommend that clinicians bring notes into the session, if some of these strategies are new, and to consider asking patients to take notes when being presented with new information.

In the next chapter we describe cognitive strategies for changing phobic thinking. Typically, these techniques are taught before beginning exposure, particularly when treating PD or social phobia. Once exposure begins, cognitive restructuring can provide patients with a context in which to interpret their experiences during exposure practices.

7

COGNITIVE STRATEGIES

In this chapter we provide an overview of how cognitive strategies can be used to change phobic thinking. We borrowed heavily from classic writings on the cognitive treatment of phobic disorders (e.g., Beck et al., 1985), as well as from more recent books and chapters that address the topic (e.g., Beck, 1995; Burns, 1989; Craske & Barlow, 1993; Greenberger & Padesky, 1995; Wells, 1997). We begin with a discussion of how to present to the patient the rationale for cognitive therapy, including a discussion of the underlying assumptions. Next, we review strategies that can be used to help patients to identify their anxious beliefs and predictions and provide an overview of the cognitive distortions and information-processing biases that are most often seen in people with phobic disorders. This is followed by a comprehensive section outlining specific strategies for challenging phobic thinking, including education, examining the evidence, challenging catastrophic thinking, rational self-statements, perspective thinking, cost–benefit analysis, and behavioral experiments. We conclude with sections on the use of diaries and monitoring forms in cognitive therapy, common mistakes to avoid, and troubleshooting. As with the other chapters in Part 2 of this book, this chapter includes examples of a number of different handouts and forms that can be copied freely and shared with patients.

THE RATIONALE FOR COGNITIVE THERAPY

As is discussed in chapter 5, structured cognitive therapy is an important component of psychological treatments for panic disorder (PD), with or without agoraphobia, and social phobia. These strategies are usually taught early in treatment, before the exposure-based techniques. By learning to change their anxious thoughts, individuals are often able to enter feared situations more easily and are able to interpret their experiences in these situations in a less negative way. Cognitive techniques are less often used in a formal or structured way when treating people with specific phobias; however, cognitive methods can still be used informally to help patients with specific phobias to cope with their fear during exposure practices.

The process of cognitive therapy includes several steps. At the beginning, the therapist should share with the patient the general assumptions and principles of cognitive therapy. These include the assumption that fear and other negative emotions have their root in negative thinking patterns. In addition, the importance of setting goals, structuring sessions, and completing homework should be emphasized. As with exposure homework (see chapter 6), there appears to be a relationship between compliance with cognitive restructuring homework assignments and outcome of cognitive therapy (Neimeyer & Feixas, 1990).

After the rationale for treatment is conveyed to the patient, early cognitive therapy sessions tend to focus on helping the patient to identify fearful thoughts, assumptions, and information-processing biases. The nature of cognitive distortions is discussed and examples are provided for the patient. Once the patient has become proficient at identifying his or her fearful thoughts, the treatment shifts to helping the patient change his or her phobic patterns of thinking. Usually, cognitive strategies are used as part of a comprehensive cognitive–behavioral therapy (CBT) protocol.

Assumptions and Principles of Cognitive Therapy

Although cognitive therapy is often conducted differently across settings and psychological problems, there are four assumptions and principles that are shared among cognitive therapists.

The role of cognitive appraisal in emotion

The role of cognitive appraisal in determining emotional states has been a topic of debate among psychologists for some time. Although some theorists assume that emotions can occur automatically, without cognitive appraisal (e.g., Zajonc, 1980, 1984), others have argued that cognitive appraisal is a necessary precursor to any emotional state (e.g., Lazarus, 1982).

In general, cognitive therapy is based on an assumption that our negative emotions are often, if not always, influenced by our thoughts, assumptions, beliefs, predictions, and information-processing biases. It is not the events in our lives that we react to with fear, but rather our interpretation of these events. In the case of anxiety and fear, the anxious belief is often a prediction that some negative event or dangerous consequence is likely to occur.

According to the theory underlying cognitive therapy, the assumptions that underlie anxiety and fear may often be outside of a person's awareness. In other words, many patients may not be able to articulate the specific anxious predictions on which their fear is based. For example, individuals with PD often experience their panic attacks as occurring out of the blue, without any particular trigger, and sometimes report being unaware of what they are thinking in the moment that the panic attack begins. They may report that there are no negative thoughts associated with their panic attacks, and they may insist that they simply do not like the feelings associated with panic.

Nevertheless, an assumption of cognitive therapy is that there are predictions or anxious thoughts underlying fear and anxiety. If the person simply did not "like the feeling" associated with panic, a panic attack would be like any other form of intense discomfort (e.g., a headache or a bad rash)—uncomfortable but not scary. The fact that the emotion of fear accompanies the experience of panic is thought to be evidence that the patient's assumptions and predictions are of a fearful nature. Cognitive therapy assumes that with practice, the patient can become more adept at identifying his or her fearful cognitions.

The role of guided discovery

An assumption of cognitive therapy is that it is best to guide the patient to new ways of thinking using Socratic questioning rather than didactic instruction. So, rather than simply telling the patient that a particular feared consequence is unlikely, it is recommended that the patient be guided to come to this conclusion on his or her own, through a series of questions designed to examine the evidence supporting and contradicting the anxious prediction.

The importance of setting goals

Although setting goals is often not done in traditional insight-oriented psychotherapies, this process is an essential component of cognitive therapy (as well as behavioral therapies). Goals are typically set before treatment begins and may be revised as treatment progresses. Setting goals has several advantages. First, it provides a means to measure whether treatment is working and when treatment should end. Without identifying the goals of

Exhibit 7.1
Examples of Treatment Goals in Cognitive Therapy for Phobic Disorders

Panic Disorder With Agoraphobia
- To no longer experience panic attacks unexpectedly or in agoraphobic situations
- To be able to travel by airplane comfortably
- To return to work full-time
- To be able to drive to the mall and shop comfortably for several hours

Social Phobia
- To attend meetings at work on a regular basis
- To have friends over for dinner with no more than mild discomfort
- To date several times per month
- To have less rigid standards for my behavior (e.g., to be willing to look foolish at times)

Specific Phobia
- To be able to visit friends who live in apartment buildings and sit on the balcony
- To drive in the left lane on busy highways
- To be able to enter a pet store and look at a snake for 10 minutes
- To sit by my living room window during a thunderstorm, with only minimal fear

treatment, it is impossible to know whether the therapy has been successful. In addition, particular therapeutic techniques are often selected on the basis of the goals of treatment. Finally, knowing the goals of therapy makes it easier for the patient and therapist to stay on track. The patient should be taught that the goal of cognitive therapy is not simply to think positive thoughts instead of negative thoughts. Rather, the goal is to replace unrealistic thoughts with more balanced and realistic predictions and assumptions. Examples of additional appropriate treatment goals are provided in Exhibit 7.1.

The importance of setting an agenda and structure for the session

Cognitive therapy sessions tend to be quite structured, compared with those in other forms of psychotherapy. Each session typically begins with setting an agenda for the meeting. The agenda should be set collaboratively with the patient, although in more structured treatment protocols, there may be less flexibility in the agenda, particularly early in the treatment when there are specific tasks that need to be completed at each session. Regardless, the agenda should be discussed at the beginning of the session, and the patient should have an opportunity to add items that might be relevant. Setting an agenda will help the patient and therapist to manage their time more effectively. An agenda for a typical cognitive therapy session is provided in Exhibit 7.2.

Exhibit 7.2
Structure of a Typical Cognitive Therapy Session

1. Setting the agenda for the session
2. Discussion of the patient's functioning in the previous week
3. Review of the patient's homework for the previous week
4. Psychoeducation (e.g., introduction to cognitive biases)
5. Application of cognitive therapy techniques (e.g., cognitive restructuring, hypothesis testing, etc.—may also occur during the earlier discussion and review of homework)
6. Assigning new homework

STRATEGIES FOR ELICITING PHOBIC BELIEFS AND ASSUMPTIONS

A number of techniques may be used to elicit the patient's phobic beliefs and assumptions. The most commonly used method is to simply ask the patient a series of open-ended questions, such as those listed in chapter 4 (Exhibit 4.4). These questions can be framed in the context of hypothetical situations (e.g., "What is the worst thing that might happen if you were to fly in an airplane?" "What are you afraid will happen if you have a panic attack in a movie theatre?") or actual episodes of anxiety (e.g., "During your recent flight to Florida, what were you thinking might happen?" "What did you think it meant when your friend did not return your telephone call?).

It is best to ask the patient for specific fearful predictions, assumptions, and interpretations (e.g., "When you are feeling anxious at a party, what are you afraid will happen?") rather than asking for more general thoughts (e.g., When you are feeling anxious at a party, what are your thoughts?"). General questions are more likely to elicit thoughts that do not lend themselves to restructuring (e.g., "I want to leave" and "I can cope with this situation") rather than specific anxious predictions (e.g., "People will think I am boring").

Strategies for Patients Who Have Difficulty Identifying Cognitions

Some patients may have difficulty identifying their fearful thoughts. In some cases, the fear may have been present for so long that the thoughts are well rehearsed, occur quickly, and occur automatically. In other cases, the fact that the patient avoids the situation on a regular basis may prevent the thought from entering his or her conscious awareness. There are a number of strategies that may used to help patients to identify their anxious thoughts.

Sometimes the thoughts can be elicited indirectly by presenting hypothetical scenarios that control for key variables. For example, to determine whether a patient's fear of flying is related to having a panic attack, the therapist might ask, "Would you still be afraid of getting on an airplane if you had a guarantee that you would not experience a panic attack?" Or, to determine whether an agoraphobic patient's fear of crowds is related to the possibility of scrutiny by others, the therapist could ask, "Would you still be afraid to be in a crowd if you knew for sure that nobody was aware of you?"

Paying attention to shifts in affect during the treatment session can also help the therapist to identify negative beliefs (Wells, 1997). For example, when a patient appears fearful or anxious, the therapist can ask the patient to describe his or her emotional state and to identify the assumptions and thoughts underlying the emotional shift. It may be easier for patients to identify their thoughts during an episode of anxiety or fear than when they are not especially anxious. In fact, the therapist can take advantage of this principle by eliciting phobic thoughts during exposure to the phobic object or situation (e.g., using a behavioral approach test or role-play exercise).

Finally, if a patient is unable to identify his or her fearful thoughts in response to open-ended questions, it may be helpful to provide for patients a list of common phobic beliefs and assumptions and ask them the extent to which they agree with each prediction or assumption on the list. Examples of phobic thoughts that are often held by patients are listed in Exhibit 7.3.

Exhibit 7.3
Common Beliefs Among People With Phobic Disorders

Panic Disorder With or Without Agoraphobia
- A racing heart is a sign that I am having a heart attack
- Dizziness is a sign that I am about to faint
- Feeling unreal or detached is a sign that I am going to go crazy
- If my panic attack is too intense, I will lose control
- My panic attack will last forever unless I take medication or escape from the situation
- If I don't leave the situation when I feel panicky, my fear will spiral out of control
- The elevator will get stuck when I am on it
- If people see me panicking, they will think I am crazy
- I cannot speak clearly when I am having a panic attack
- I must be with my spouse so that I can get help in the event of a panic attack
- I always must have a plan in place in case I need to escape or leave a situation early
- If I continue to have panic attacks, I will develop a serious illness in the future
- I have a physical illness (e.g., heart disease, vestibular dysfunction) that my doctor has not yet identified

Social Phobia
- It is important that everybody likes me
- If my boss doesn't like me, I will get fired
- If I am not liked by a particular person, I am unlikable
- If someone rejects me, I deserve it

(continued)

Exhibit 7.3
(*Continued*)

Social Phobia (*Continued*)
- People find me unattractive
- I will look incompetent if I speak to my boss
- People will become angry with me if I make a mistake
- People are untrustworthy and nasty
- People should always be interested in what I say
- People should not look at me the wrong way
- I should be able to hide my anxiety symptoms
- If my hands shake at work, it will be a disaster
- Anxiety is a sign of weakness
- I should not appear anxious
- It is awful to blush, shake, or sweat in front of others
- People can tell when I am anxious
- I will not be able to speak if I am too anxious

Specific Phobia: Animals
- I could not manage having a spider crawl on me
- If I get too close to a dog, it will attack me
- I will lose control and embarrass myself if encounter a cat
- Snakes are slimy and disgusting to touch
- Bees can tell that I am afraid of them

Specific Phobia: Heights
- If I am in a high place, I will be drawn to the ledge and I may jump
- I will lose my balance and fall
- If I stand too close to the railing on a balcony, someone will accidentally push me over
- The structure of the bridge is unstable

Specific Phobia: Storms
- If I sit near the window during a storm, I am likely to be struck by lightning
- There is a high chance of being struck by lightning during a storm
- It is safer to stay home if there is a risk of a thunderstorm

Specific Phobia: Injections
- Injections are painful
- I will faint if I have blood drawn
- The doctor will think I am an idiot when she sees how scared I am
- The needle will break off in my arm

Specific Phobia: Flying
- Plane crashes are relatively common
- The pilot has been drinking or is too tired to be flying the airplane
- The fact that the flight attendants always review the safety features of the airplane is evidence that something could easily go wrong
- A turbulent flight is more likely to crash than a smooth flight
- Airplane safety is poor because of inadequate maintenance of the aircraft

Specific Phobia: Enclosed Places
- If I am in a closet (or elevator, tunnel, small room, etc.) for too long, I will run out of air
- I will suffocate if I am stuck in a closed place
- If the elevator gets stuck, I will never get out

COGNITIVE DISTORTIONS AND
INFORMATION-PROCESSING BIASES

Often, popular books on cognitive therapy (e.g., Burns, 1989) describe comprehensive lists of *cognitive distortions* that underlie fear, anxiety, and other negative emotions. In our opinion, the thinking styles in these lists overlap considerably with one another, and patients often find it difficult to decide whether a particular thought is an example of one distortion or another. Instead, we tend to emphasize a relatively small number of anxious cognitive styles (summarized over the next few pages) that are broader in scope and subsume a range of anxious and fearful thoughts. Admittedly, however, even the thinking styles listed here do not necessarily represent distinct, nonoverlapping categories.

Furthermore, when presenting this information to patients, we prefer not to use the term cognitive distortion, because it implies that the patient is thinking incorrectly and differently from everyone else. This could serve to reinforce the patient's belief that he or she is inferior, strange, or different. Instead, we use terms such as *biased thinking* and *anxious thinking,* and we emphasize the fact that almost everyone engages in these styles of thinking from time to time. In addition, we suggest that the extent to which this occurs can affect the frequency and intensity with which a person experiences fear and anxiety.

Arbitrary Inference

Arbitrary inferences are conclusions that are drawn with little or no supporting evidence. An example is the belief that one is going to faint during a panic attack despite never having fainted before. Another example is the belief, held by some spider-phobic individuals, that a spider can tell when a person is frightened of spiders. In social phobia, people often interpret ambiguous social cues (e.g., a person who seems uninterested) as confirming their anxious beliefs (e.g., the person does not like me).

A number of distortions described by other authors may actually be thought of as examples of arbitrary inference. For example, *probability overestimations* (Craske & Barlow, 1993) are instances in which an individual overestimates the likelihood of some negative event occurring. A related distortion, known as *mind reading* (Burns, 1989), is also a form of arbitrary inference, in which people (e.g., with social phobia) assume incorrectly that other people are reacting negatively to them, despite a lack of supporting evidence. *Personalization* (Burns, 1989) is third example of arbitrary inference, in which people take more responsibility for a particular event than they ought to. For instance, a person with social phobia may assume that he or she is to blame if a restaurant server is rude, whereas in reality many different factors (in addition to the patient's behavior) contributed to the server's reactions.

Selective Abstraction

Selective abstraction involves paying too much attention to some types of information (usually information that confirms one's anxious beliefs) and ignoring other more important and relevant types of information. For example, a patient with PD who is afraid of having a heart attack while exercising may selectively recall stories of young people who died suddenly while exercising and ignore statistics showing that regular exercise protects people from having heart attacks. Similarly, a person with a specific phobia of flying may pay more attention to occasional news stories about airline crashes than to statistics showing that plane crashes are very rare. An individual with social phobia may pay more attention to a negative or neutral comment from another person (e.g., "you look tired today") than a positive comment or compliment (e.g., "you look nice today").

Catastrophic Thinking

Catastrophic thinking (also called *catastrophizing*) involves assuming that a particular event or consequence would be unmanageable if it were to occur. Examples include such thoughts as "It would be unmanageable to faint in a public place," "I could not manage having a spider on me," "I could not cope with panicking at a baseball game," and "It would be terrible to lose my train of thought during a presentation." Thinking catastrophically about the phobic object or situation is common among most individuals with phobic disorders.

All-or-Nothing Thinking

This style of thinking is common among people who are particularly perfectionistic and hold excessively high, rigid standards regarding their behavior. Statements that include words such as "always," "never," "should," or "must" may reflect all-or-nothing thinking. For example, an individual with social phobia may believe that it is unforgivable to show even mild signs of anxiety or to make a small error during a presentation.

Biased Information Processing

As is reviewed in chapters 1–3, individuals with phobic disorders selectively attend to threat-related information and selectively recall information that is consistent with their phobias. These cognitive biases have a number of clinical implications. First, patients are especially likely to notice evidence supporting their fearful beliefs. For example, an individual with PD is more likely to notice certain physical symptoms than is another individual who is not particularly frightened of bodily sensations. Similarly, a person with a spider phobia is likely to be the first person to find a spider when there is one in the room. An individual with a fear of speaking in public is likely to notice the people in the audience who seem bored, uninterested, or overly critical.

Second, people with phobic disorders may be more likely than others to recall events that support their phobic beliefs or even to distort their recollections in a direction that is consistent with their anxious predictions. For example, is reviewed in chapter 3, people with spider and snake fears tend to overestimate the amount of activity by a feared animal that they have seen previously. Similarly, people with social phobia may be more likely than nonphobic individuals to recall particular episodes of being teased in high school.

Core Beliefs and Negative Cognitive Schemas

In recent years, a number of authors (e.g., Beck, 1995; Padesky, 1994; Young, 1994) have emphasized the importance of addressing deeper cognitive structures (e.g., core beliefs, schemas, and underlying assumptions) that maintain negative thinking. Although the emphasis on deeper cognitive structures has been more pronounced among people who study depression, it is relevant to phobic disorders as well. According to J.S. Beck (1995), core beliefs are one's most central beliefs about the self (e.g., "I am incompetent"), other people (e.g., "other people cannot be trusted"), and the world (e.g., "the world is a dangerous place"). A.T. Beck (1964) differentiated between schemas (i.e., cognitive structures within the mind) and core beliefs (i.e., the specific content of schemas).

In contrast, Padesky (1994) used the terms *core belief* and *schema* interchangeably. However, she distinguished between core beliefs, underlying assumptions, and automatic thoughts. As was described earlier, core beliefs (schemas) are *stable beliefs* about the self, other people, or the world. Underlying assumptions are *conditional beliefs* about the self, the world, or the future (e.g., "If I look anxious, people will lose respect for me"). Finally, automatic thoughts are transient beliefs that flow automatically in and out of one's mind. Automatic thoughts are often related to a specific situation (e.g., "I will make a fool of myself during the presentation," "I will have a panic attack at the mall").

One strategy that is sometimes used to elicit core beliefs is the *downward arrow technique*. This strategy involves continuing to ask questions about the meaning of each fearful belief that the patient reports until the core beliefs underlying the patient's anxious interpretations are uncovered. The following clinical vignette provides an illustration with a college professor who is anxious when lecturing. Note that initially the patient reports a fear of having his hands shake during a lecture. However, with additional questioning, it becomes clear that the patient has a number of more basic beliefs, including the core beliefs that anxiety is a sign of weakness and the conditional belief that respect from others ultimately depends on his ability to control his anxiety symptoms.

> **Patient:** I was particularly anxious during my lecture last Tuesday.
> **Therapist:** What were you afraid might happen when you were feeling anxious?
> **Patient:** Mostly, I was afraid that people would notice my hands shaking when I was changing the overhead transparencies.
> **Therapist:** Why would that be a problem? What might it lead to?
> **Patient:** I guess I'm afraid that they will realize how anxious I am.
> **Therapist:** What would be bad about your students noticing that you are anxious?
> **Patient:** They will lose respect for me. If they think I am anxious when I am lecturing, they won't take me seriously. They will see me as weak.
> **Therapist:** What if the students don't take you seriously?
> **Patient:** They will laugh behind my back. I suppose they might even give me poor teaching evaluations at the end of the semester.
> **Therapist:** Why would that be a problem?
> **Patient:** Well, if I get too many poor teaching evaluations, I will never get promoted.
> **Therapist:** What if you don't get promoted? What would that mean about you?
> **Patient:** It would mean I'm inadequate in some way. I should be able to get promoted.
> **Therapist:** What will happen if you don't get promoted?
> **Patient:** People would lose respect for me for sure.
> **Therapist:** Who would lose respect for you?
> **Patient:** My colleagues especially. But maybe even my family and friends to some extent.
> **Therapist:** To summarize then, it seems as though one of the beliefs that may be contributing to your anxiety while lecturing is the belief that respect from your students and from those you care about depends on such things as your ability to get promoted, your teaching evaluations, and your ability to prevent your hands from shaking.

Once you have helped a patient to identify his or her anxious thoughts, the next step is to provide strategies for modifying phobic thinking. These are discussed in the next section.

STRATEGIES FOR CHANGING PHOBIC THINKING

Education

Education is an important component of cognitive therapy. During the early sessions, patients are provided with a cognitive model of their phobic condition as well as information about cognitive methods for overcoming their phobias. In addition, education regarding the nature of the phobic object or situation is often encouraged. For example, we recommend that people with animal phobias take steps to learn more about the animal that they fear. People who are convinced that flying is dangerous should be educated with respect to relevant statistics on the safety of flying. Patients who believe that a panic attack could lead to fainting should be provided with corrective information (i.e., that fainting tends not to occur during panic attacks). Education can include having the patient conduct library research (e.g., reading about snakes), providing the patient with corrective information, and siting research findings that are relevant to the patient's fear.

Examining the Evidence

People typically assume that their thoughts are correct. Cognitive therapy teaches patients to treat their beliefs as hypotheses or guesses about the way things are and to seek out evidence supporting and contradicting their phobic beliefs. Through this process, patients are taught to replace their anxious beliefs and predictions with more balanced and realistic thoughts. Examining the evidence includes a number of steps: (a) identifying anxious beliefs; (b) generating alternative explanations, predictions, or beliefs; (c) examining the evidence for the original belief and the alternative beliefs; and (d) choosing a more realistic interpretation or prediction. Exhibits 7.4, 7.5, and 7.6 provide examples for each step in the treatment of PD, social phobia, and specific phobia (claustrophobia), respectively.

Patients should be taught to ask themselves specific questions that are likely to help with the process of examining the evidence. Some examples of questions are as follows:

- Do I know for sure that my prediction will come true?
- What does my past experience tell me about the likelihood of my prediction coming true?
- Are there times when I have made the same prediction and it did not come true?
- Are there facts or statistics that can help me decide whether my prediction is likely to come true?

Exhibit 7.4
Steps for Examining the Evidence: An Illustration for
Panic Disorder and Agoraphobia

---

1. Identifying the Anxious Thought
   - I am dizzy because I am having a heart attack

2. Generating Alternative Beliefs
   - I am dizzy because I am feeling anxious
   - I am dizzy because I am paying attention to whether I am dizzy
   - I am dizzy because it is normal to be dizzy sometimes, for no apparent reason
   - I am dizzy because I am hungry
   - I am dizzy because I had too much to drink last night
   - I am dizzy because I have a mild viral infection (e.g., a cold or flu)
   - I am dizzy because of hormonal changes (e.g., I am premenstrual)
   - I am dizzy because I stood up too quickly
   - I am dizzy from running up the stairs too quickly

3. Examining the Evidence

   Evidence Supporting my Anxious Belief
   - I have heard that people get dizzy when they are having a heart attack; my heart is also pounding, which I think may be a sign of heart trouble
   - I imagine that this is what a heart attack feels like

   Evidence Supporting my Alternative Beliefs
   - I have none of the risk factors for heart disease; I am a 24-year-old woman, with normal blood pressure, normal cholesterol levels, and no family history of heart disease
   - I have had many medical tests, none of which has shown any problems
   - I have felt dizzy and thought that I was having a heart attack many times before, yet I have never had a heart attack
   - My dizziness has tended to be associated with my anxiety in the past
   - The more attention I pay to my dizziness, the worse it usually gets
   - Generally, people are more likely to get dizzy for benign reasons than because they are having a heart attack

4. Choosing a More Realistic Belief
   - I am probably dizzy because I am anxious and paying extra attention to how I am feeling physically

---

- Are there other possible interpretations for this situation?
- How might another person interpret this situation?

Patients may find it useful to have questions such as these typed on a small index card so that they may be carried in a pocket or wallet.

Challenging Catastrophic Thinking

Recall that catastrophic thinking involves assuming that a particular outcome would be terrible and unmanageable if it were to occur. Undoing catastrophic thinking involves imagining the feared outcome and

Exhibit 7.5
Steps for Examining the Evidence: An Illustration for Social Phobia

1. Identifying the Anxious Thought
   - During my presentation, people will notice my blushing and think that I am strange

2. Generating Alternative Beliefs
   - Nobody will notice my blushing
   - Only a small number of people will notice my blushing
   - People who notice my blushing will think I am feeling hot
   - People who notice my blushing will think I am feeling unwell
   - People who notice my blushing will think I am feeling a bit anxious
   - It is normal to blush sometimes, so people will think nothing of it if they notice me blush

3. Examining the Evidence

   Evidence Supporting my Anxious Belief
   - I believe that my blushing is very extreme
   - In high school people teased me for blushing on a few occasions
   - I tend to notice when other people blush

   Evidence Supporting my Alternative Beliefs
   - I know a lot of people who blush easily and people don't seem to think they are strange
   - When I notice other people blushing, I don't think they are strange
   - Often people do not seem to have noticed me blush when I ask them if it was noticeable
   - When people have noticed my blushing, they haven't tended to treat me differently
   - The people in the audience know me well. I can't imagine that their opinions of me would change dramatically based on whether I blush during a single presentation

4. Choosing a More Realistic Belief
   - Some people may notice my blushing, but it's unlikely that they will think I'm strange

---

considering possible ways of coping with it, rather than emphasizing how terrible it would be. Questions to facilitate this process include, "What is the worst thing that could happen?" and "How could I cope with . . . if it did occur?" The following is a vignette illustrating how to challenge catastrophic thinking in social phobia.

> **Patient:** I am terrified of asking Tom (a coworker) to have lunch with me.
> **Therapist:** What might happen that is so terrifying?
> **Patient:** I'm afraid that he will say yes and that I will make a fool of myself during the lunch.

Exhibit 7.6
Steps for Examining the Evidence: An Illustration for Claustrophobia

1. Identifying the Anxious Thought
   - I will get stuck on the elevator and suffocate from a lack of fresh air

2. Generating Alternative Beliefs
   - I will not get stuck in the elevator
   - I may get stuck in the elevator, but I will not suffocate

3. Examining the Evidence

   Evidence Supporting my Anxious Belief
   - I know people who have been stuck on elevators
   - I feel breathless when I am in an enclosed place for more than a minute or two

   Evidence Supporting my Alternative Beliefs
   - I have never been stuck on an elevator before
   - I know many people who taken elevators several times per day over a period of years, and all but two people have never been stuck
   - Of the two people I know who have been stuck, both got out of the elevator in less than a half hour
   - I have never heard of anyone getting stuck on an elevator and never getting out
   - I have never heard of anyone ever running out of air on an elevator
   - If there is enough air for other people on the elevator, there is enough air for me

4. Choosing a More Realistic Belief
   - It is unlikely that I will be stuck on an elevator; however, if I am stuck, I will not run out of air and I will likely get out from the elevator after a brief time

---

Therapist: What does "making a fool of myself" mean? What would that look like?

Patient: I imagine that I would babble and not make any sense.

Therapist: What if that happened? What is the worst outcome that you imagine?

Patient: I guess he might think I am an idiot?

Therapist: What if he did think you were an idiot.

Patient: I wouldn't like it.

Therapist: Would it be manageable?

Patient: I guess it would be okay in the long run, but it would be uncomfortable during the lunch.

Therapist: What is so terrible about feeling uncomfortable?

Patient: I don't like to feel uncomfortable, but I suppose that nothing bad could happen as a result.

Therapist: In fact, it is possible that allowing yourself to feel uncomfortable during the lunch may help you to feel more comfortable in the long run.

Patient: That has happened for me before. It is often not until I stop trying so hard to feel calm that I actually start to feel better.

Rational Self-Statements

The use of rationale self-statements involves reminding oneself of alternative, nonanxious beliefs when one is feeling anxious or fearful. This strategy can be particularly helpful during exposure to situations in which it is not practical to go through all of the various steps for cognitive restructuring (e.g., identifying anxious thoughts, identifying alternative thoughts, examining the evidence, etc.). For example, during a panic attack triggered by a presentation, it may be helpful to remind oneself that "Regardless of whether people notice my panic symptoms, the presentation will be over soon and it won't matter anymore." Often, rational self-statements are initially derived through the process of Socratic questioning and written down to use again during future episodes of anxiety.

Rational self-statements should be realistic and believable. For example, it does not make sense for an agoraphobic patient to say "I will not have a panic attack at the movie theater" if he or she has frequently experienced panic attacks in theaters in the past. Rather, it might be helpful to remind oneself that "Even if a panic attack occurs, it will not lead to a heart attack or loss of control." Examples of other rational self-statements are provided in Exhibit 7.7.

Exhibit 7.7
Examples of Rational Self-Statements

Panic Disorder With Agoraphobia
- The worst thing that will happen during a panic attack is that I will feel uncomfortable
- If I stay long enough, my fear will eventually decrease
- Panic attacks never last forever
- I have already experienced my worst panic attack and lived through it

Social Phobia
- It would be manageable if some people didn't like me
- People are unlikely to be as unforgiving as I am with myself
- It is normal to look anxious during a job interview
- People often don't seem to notice my shaky hands

Specific Phobia
- It is not dangerous to have a common spider crawl on me
- The chances of dying in a plane crash are 1 in 10 million
- Most people are never struck by lightning
- Any pain that I experience at the dentist will only be for a short time

---

Perspective Taking

Taking another person's perspective is a useful way to challenge one's anxious thoughts. For example, a man who is phobic of flying may be able to see that the chances of the plane crashing are minimal when he imagines a friend in an airplane instead of himself. Similarly, a person who is fearful of having a panic attack in a crowded supermarket might see such an event as less catastrophic after imagining the consequences of a stranger having a panic attack in the store. The following is an example of how to use perspective taking to challenge anxious thoughts in social phobia.

> **Patient:** Even if one person at the party thinks I look anxious, that will be one person too many.
> **Therapist:** Why would it be a problem for someone to notice that you are anxious?
> **Patient:** I would look foolish because there is no reason for me to be anxious.
> **Therapist:** How would another person know that you are anxious?
> **Patient:** Probably because I would not be saying much.
> **Therapist:** Let's imagine for a moment that it is someone else (other than you) who is at the party and not feeling comfortable. What do you think other people would think if they noticed that the other person was relatively quiet?
> **Patient:** I suppose they might think she is shy.
> **Therapist:** Would that necessarily have a negative impact on the person's life?
> **Patient:** If she didn't care what other people thought, it wouldn't matter really.
> **Therapist:** Do you think that other people would find the person to be foolish?
> **Patient:** Probably not.
> **Therapist:** What if a few people did think the person was foolish or strange?
> **Patient:** As long as everyone didn't think that, it would be okay. I have some close friends who I care about very much who don't necessarily make a good impression on everyone. They still seem to get by just fine.

Cost–Benefit Analysis

Consider the following beliefs and assumptions: It is important for people to like me, it is important to look calm, I should not feel anxious while I am driving, I should always make a good impression on other people, and I need to be careful around high places. These beliefs are typical of people with certain phobic disorders; however, there is also some truth to each of these statements. In fact, most people probably hold these beliefs to some extent. It is difficult to determine whether thoughts such as these are true, because each of these statements is a subjective opinion. There are differences across individuals and across situations with respect to how strongly people hold these beliefs.

For thoughts such those just described, it can be helpful to discuss the costs and benefits of having the particular belief rather than whether the belief is true. For most people, the belief that "it is important to make a good impression on others" is a helpful belief to have. It motivates a person to dress nicely, get to work on time, be polite, and so forth. However, for some people, this belief may not be beneficial if it is held too intensely and inflexibly. For an individual who is constantly frightened of making mistakes or making a bad impression (e.g., a person with social phobia), performance in social situations may actually be impaired by such a belief. For an individual with social phobia, the costs of having such strict standards may outweigh the benefits, and it may be helpful in the long run to loosen one's standards regarding how important it is to make a good impression.

The goal of treatment is not to eliminate the beliefs that contribute to anxiety, but rather to bring them to a level that is helpful and no longer causing impairment. For example, rather than teaching a dog-phobic individual to have no fear around dogs, the goal of therapy should be to teach the patient to have a healthy respect for dogs so that he or she can be around dogs comfortably but still be able to identify situations in which there may be realistic danger.

Behavioral Experiments

Behavioral experiments can be used for a variety of purposes in cognitive therapy. Most commonly, they are used to demonstrate to patients that particular beliefs and assumptions are unfounded. For example, a patient with PD who is fearful of her legs collapsing during a panic attack in the mall might be asked to stand on one leg during an episode of panic to demonstrate that the feared outcome does not occur. Similarly, an individual with social phobia who is fearful of having shaky hands while drinking a glass of water might be encouraged to purposely let his hands shake and even to spill his water in order to learn that the consequences are manageable.

Behavioral experiments may also be used to demonstrate how cognitive processes influence symptoms of anxiety and fear. For example, the following experiment is designed to illustrate for a patient with PD how his or her attention to physical symptoms influences whether these symptoms are experienced. Ask the patient to scan his or her body until an itch is found somewhere on the surface of his or her skin. Usually, within a few seconds or minutes, the patient will notice an itch and may even scratch it. This experiment can be used to illustrate the relationship between one's tendency to look for particular bodily sensations and the likelihood of finding that particular sensation.

USING DIARIES AND MONITORING FORMS

We recommend that patients use diaries and monitoring forms to challenge their anxious thoughts. This is particularly important for patients with social phobia or PD, for whom systematic cognitive restructuring is typically an important component of treatment. In addition to providing the patient with a blank form to complete, it can be helpful to include an example of a completed form or written instructions for how to complete the form. Exhibits 7.8, 7.9, and 7.10 contain a blank version of a Cognitive Monitoring Form, a completed sample of the form (for PD), and a handout containing instructions for completing the form (for social phobia), respectively. Many other cognitive monitoring forms exist in various published sources (Beck, 1995; Burns, 1989; Greenberger & Padesky, 1995; Wells, 1997). They differ with respect to how much detail they provide, how easy they are to complete, and how relevant they are to anxiety-based concerns (versus depression or other negative emotions). We recommend having a range of different forms available and choosing the best form for a particular patient's needs.

MISTAKES IN COGNITIVE THERAPY

Although cognitive strategies appear to be useful for the treatment of people with phobic disorders, there are a number of errors often made by new therapists that can undermine the effectiveness of cognitive techniques.

Not Attending to the Patient's Emotions

Occasionally, therapists get caught up in the technical aspects of cognitive therapy and forget to attend to the patient's emotions during the therapy session. There are two points to remember here. First, the patient's emotions should not be discounted. In fact, the anxiety or fear reported by the patient make perfect sense when interpreted in the context of the phobic beliefs (e.g., it is no wonder that a patient with PD feels frightened if he or she believes that a heart attack is imminent). Second, there are times during therapy (e.g., if a patient is extremely distressed about a recent life event) when it may be more beneficial to provide support than to engage the patient in the technical aspects of cognitive restructuring. The therapist

Exhibit 7.8
Cognitive Monitoring Form

Situation	Initial Fear (0–100)	Fearful Thoughts and Predictions	Rational Responses and Countering	Outcome

Exhibit 7.9
Cognitive Monitoring Form (Example for Panic Disorder)

Situation	Initial Fear (0–100)	Fearful Thoughts and Predictions	Rational Responses and Countering	Outcome
Oct. 15: at work, in a crowded room. Feeling racing heart and dizziness.	85	I will faint if I stay here.	I have felt this way over 500 times before and have never fainted. In fact, I don't know anyone who has ever fainted from a panic attack. Besides, even if I did faint, I would only be unconscious for a short time. People would be concerned about me, but my embarrassment would pass.	My fear gradually decreased over a period of 15 minutes or so. I did not faint.
		My boss will notice that I'm anxious.	It is possible that my boss would not notice. There are over 50 people in the room. My boss is not even looking my way. Besides, even if my boss did notice, she would be understanding. Everyone gets anxious sometimes . . . even my boss.	I'm not sure whether my boss noticed my fear. She did not say anything to indicate that she noticed.

Exhibit 7.10
Instructions for Completing the Cognitive Monitoring Form (Social Phobia)

The purpose of this form is to help you to use the strategies for countering the thoughts, predictions, and assumptions that sometimes lead to anxiety and fear. This sheet is to be completed each time you experience an episode of social anxiety or a panicky feeling in front of others. (Complete the form either during or soon after the episode.)

Column 1: Situation

Record date and time. Describe the situation and triggers for your fear. Typical examples include

- Went to a meeting
- Person was watching me on the subway
- Ate lunch with a coworker
- I was blushing
- My hands shook in front of my boss
- Went to a party
- Had to do a presentation for class
- Was introduced to my sister's new boyfriend
- Went on a blind date

Column 2: Initial Fear

Rate your fear level before countering your fearful thoughts.

Column 3: Fearful Thoughts and Predictions

In this column list anxious thoughts that occur in response to the situation and triggers in column 1. Usually these thoughts will be predictions of danger, embarrassment, etc. Often these thoughts will be automatic or almost unconscious. It will take practice to identify anxious thoughts. Try to come up with very specific thoughts. Thoughts like "Something bad will happen" are too vague. Typical examples of thoughts include

- People will notice that I am nervous
- I will make a fool of myself
- People will think I am stupid
- People will see me for the idiot I am
- People will think I am ugly
- I will have to leave the situation
- I am incompetent
- I need to drink alcohol to feel comfortable
- People can tell how I am feeling
- Anxiety is a sign of weakness
- I will be viewed as boring
- People will not like me
- I will have nothing to say

Column 4: Rational Responses and Countering

Use countering strategies to challenge anxious and fearful thinking. For example, if you believe that other people will think you are incompetent if your hands shake, examine the evidence and try to identify other possible interpretations of the situation. You might ask yourself, "What else might people think?" or "Is it possible

(*continued*)

Exhibit 7.10
(*Continued*)

that people might not even notice?" or "What would I think of someone else if I saw his or her hands shaking?" As you realize that your predictions are unlikely to come true, you fear will decrease. Note that in some cases, your predictions may be realistic (e.g., "I will get anxious when I give a presentation" might be a realistic prediction for a person who usually gets anxious in this situation). If this is the case, there are still a number of questions that you can ask yourself to challenge your anxious beliefs: For example, "What is the worst that can happen", "If my prediction were true, why would that be a problem?" "What might it mean about me if my beliefs were true?" "How can I cope with the possibility of my prediction being true?" By asking yourself questions such as these, you will often conclude that even if the prediction were true, it would be manageable.

Column 5: Outcome

In this column, describe the outcome of your attempts to challenge your anxious thoughts. Did the challenging work? What did you conclude in the end regarding the accuracy of your anxious predictions?

---

should be sensitive to the patient's needs during the session and may even need to put cognitive therapy on hold for a few minutes or for an entire session or more, depending on the situation.

Telling the Patient What He or She Is Thinking

The therapist should not assume to know what a patient is thinking. The suspicion that a patient is experiencing a particular negative automatic thought or negative assumption should not be assumed correct until it is confirmed by the patient him- or herself. It is important for the therapist to ask and not tell the patient what he or she is thinking.

Arguing With the Patient

It is important that the therapy not turn into an argument about whether the patient's beliefs are true or false. If the therapist is not careful, cognitive therapy can sometimes begin to sound more like a prosecuting attorney cross-examining a witness than a therapist trying to help a patient. Instead, the patient and therapist should collaboratively discuss the ways in which particular thoughts may be exaggerations and together generate alternative beliefs and interpretations. The therapist should attempt to understand the patient's perspective regarding the feared object or situation and to help the patient to see the situation from other perspectives. It is also important to remember that the patient's beliefs are not always exaggerations. Some individuals with social phobia are rejected by others (e.g., perhaps as a function of social skills deficits). Similarly, some people with driving phobias are at increased risk for being in a car accident (e.g., as a function of poor driving skills).

For some patients, it may be necessary to remind the individual of the process of cognitive therapy and of why the therapist is asking certain questions. Some patients may be more likely to misinterpret therapeutic questioning as criticism. Rather than implying that a patient's beliefs are wrong, it is best to promote the idea that most situations can be viewed from multiple perspectives and that cognitive therapy involves exploring the range of possible interpretations and predictions before deciding whether a particular belief is appropriate.

Continuing a Nonproductive Line of Questioning

If a particular line of questioning is not leading to the desired outcome, it is important for the therapist to know when to quit and to move on to another topic. For example, despite the therapist's best efforts, a patient may be unwilling or unable to make a particular cognitive shift at a given moment. Or, a therapist may be having difficulty generating appropriate questions to challenge a particular belief. If a specific line of questioning is not working, it is okay to move on. In fact, repeatedly engaging the patient in nonproductive lines of questioning could compromise the therapeutic relationship and the patient's confidence in the treatment.

TROUBLESHOOTING

In this section are possible solutions for several problems that sometimes arise while conducting cognitive therapy for phobic disorders.

The Patient Cannot Identify Specific Cognitions

Sometimes, despite trying all of the strategies discussed in this chapter, a patient will find it very difficult to identify specific cognitions underlying his or her fear. First, be sure to exhaust all the possible different ways of asking the patient about his or her thoughts (e.g., "What was going through your mind at the time?" "What were you saying to your self?" "What did you expect to happen?" "Did you have any kind if internal dialogue?"). Sometimes asking questions in a different way will help to elicit a person's anxious thoughts.

The patient may have trouble articulating negative automatic thoughts if he or she holds these beliefs as facts and is unable to recognize them as interpretations. Also, early in treatment, patients may have difficulty distinguishing between feeling statements (e.g., "I felt terrified") and thought statements (e.g., "I thought I was going to die"). Sometimes, having the patient describe other aspects of the episode (e.g., triggers, situation, symptoms, and feelings) will give rise to some of the patient's thought processes. Or, instead of being asked to identify anxious thoughts, the patient may be asked whether he or she is aware of any images that go through his or her mind when confronted by the phobic object or situation. If all attempts at cognitive therapy fail, consider emphasizing behavioral strategies (e.g., exposure), which do not depend on the patient's being able to identify fearful thoughts.

The Patient Does Not Believe the Alternative Rational Thoughts

At the treatment, patients will often report that using the cognitive strategies seems artificial or contrived and that it is difficult to believe the alternative, rational beliefs. If this happens, the therapist should reassure the patient that cognitive change requires repeated practice of the cognitive restructuring exercises and may take some time. In addition, the therapist should be sure that the "hot cognition" rather than an ancillary thought or a rhetorical question has been accurately identified. If the thought being challenged is not the relevant thought, the process may not be helpful.

The therapists should ensure that the evidence for both sides of the issue is considered valid by the patient. If it is not, this may point to deeper levels of belief. If this is the case, it may be useful to examine in more detail the patient's anxious core beliefs. If nonanxious thoughts generated during cognitive restructuring are inconsistent with basic core beliefs, it may be necessary to address the core beliefs in addition to specific thoughts (see Padesky, 1994). Finally, the therapist may consider emphasizing behavioral strategies (e.g., exposure or behavioral experiments). Often real-life experience is the most powerful way to change anxious thoughts.

The Patient Is Too Anxious to Think Clearly

During the height of a panic attack or intense fear, patients will often report that they are too frightened to think clearly and therefore are unable to use the cognitive strategies when in the phobic situation. Patients should be encouraged to use the cognitive strategies during less anxiety-provoking exposure practices. They can also use the cognitive strategies before entering the phobic situation. This will help the patient to manage anticipatory anxiety and will also prepare the patient for being in the situation. Finally, the patient should be encouraged to use the cognitive strategies after leaving the phobic situation. This will help the patient to interpret the experience in a realistic and helpful way after the fact.

The Patient Will Not Complete the Cognitive Monitoring Forms

Some patients may be unwilling or unable to complete the cognitive monitoring forms. If this occurs, consider completing a form in session to record and challenge the patient's beliefs and ideas around using the form. Sometimes patients predict a lack of success (e.g., "this form won't work for me") or respond in a perfectionistic way (e.g., "my automatic thoughts aren't clear enough, I'll mess up this exercise"). If the person continues to have difficulty completing the forms, there are two options. First, try using a simpler monitoring form (e.g., a two-column form—with one column that includes that anxious thoughts and a second column for alternative thoughts). Alternatively, consider using the forms less frequently or dropping them entirely, particularly if the patient understands the cognitive strategies well enough to use them without the forms and the patient is able to recall the details of his or episodes of anxiety throughout the week.

CONCLUSION

In this chapter we provide an overview of the cognitive strategies that can be useful for combating phobic thinking, particularly in patients suffering from PD, agoraphobia, or social phobia. In specific phobias, cognitive therapy techniques are used informally, if at all. Note that cognitive therapy should not be viewed as an alternative to exposure-based treatments for these conditions. Rather, these strategies should be considered to be an adjunct to exposure. When cognitive techniques are used, they are typically introduced near the start of treatment, before beginning exposure. Cognitive therapy can boost a patient's confidence to confront a feared situation and provide a context in which to interpret his or her experiences during exposure practices.

8

PHARMACOLOGICAL AND PHYSICAL APPROACHES

In the first three chapters, we reviewed research regarding the efficacy of the available treatments for reducing the severity of the behavioral, cognitive, and emotional symptoms that are characteristic of phobic disorders. In this chapter, we review the practical aspects of prescribing medications for people suffering from panic disorder (PD) with agoraphobia (PDA) or without agoraphobia, social phobia, and specific phobia. Although this information will be especially relevant to professionals who prescribe medications, it will also be important for nonprescribing clinicians to be familiar with the material on pharmacotherapy. Throughout this chapter, generic names of medications are used. Trade names are provided the first time each drug is mentioned and again in Tables 8.1 and 8.4.

In addition, we have chosen to include other "physical" approaches to treatment in this chapter, including herbal preparations; health habits (e.g., diet, exercise, and sleep); applied tension for blood, injury, and injection phobias; and breathing retraining for PD. Although applied tension and breathing retraining are typically considered as behavioral treatments, they are similar to pharmacotherapy and other physical treatments in that they are designed to intervene at a physical level, or at least at the level of physical symptoms.

WHY NONPHYSICIANS NEED TO BE FAMILIAR WITH PHARMACOTHERAPY

Regardless of whether a clinician is permitted to prescribe medications, it is important that anyone who works with anxiety disorders be familiar with the basics regarding pharmacological treatments for these conditions. People who seek psychological treatments for PD or social phobia often present when they are already taking medications. The therapist should be aware of possible interactions between psychological and pharmacological treatments. Otherwise, the clinician may not know whether to attribute changes in the patient's symptoms to the psychological treatment or to the effects of the medication (e.g., therapeutic effects, side effects, withdrawal symptoms).

In addition, being familiar with the effects of pharmacotherapy will allow the therapist to determine when it is in the patient's best interests to be referred for treatment with medication. Knowledge about drug treatments will also facilitate effective communication with the prescribing physician about the pharmacological portion of the treatment, thereby promoting the development and implementation of a coordinated treatment plan that will best meet the patient's needs.

Finally, patients who are taking medications for phobic disorders sometimes receive treatment for the wrong condition, are prescribed inappropriate medications, or take drugs at dosages that are either too high or too low. Being aware of the guidelines for appropriate pharmacotherapy will help the therapist to identify cases in which a patient is not being treated in the most effective way. In these cases, it is important to obtain permission to discuss the treatment with the prescribing physician.

PREPARING FOR PHARMACOTHERAPY

In choosing between pharmacological and psychological treatments, the clinician should consider (a) the evidence relating to the efficacy of the various choices, (b) the suitability of each option for the particular patient, (c) the short-term and long-term costs of each approach, and (d his or her own skill in delivering each type of therapeutic intervention. If a medication is to be used, the prescribing clinician should also take into account the main actions of the drug, the indications for which it is approved, the side effect profile, the potential interaction with other medications, and the potential impact of any physical illness that the patient may be suffering.

Educating the Patient About Pharmacotherapy

Phobic disorders tend to be chronic, and most of the medications that are used in their treatment typically need to be taken for several months and sometimes even for years. Apart from a few instances (e.g., for discrete performance-related fears or specific phobias), medication will need to be taken daily and sometimes several times per day. Patients need to understand the rationale behind medication use and the detrimental effects of partial compliance in order to ensure that they comply for long periods of time with compounds that can be unpleasant to take.

Educating the patient about the therapeutic effects and the potential side effects of the available medications is an essential first step in helping the patient decide whether to take medication. Patients often need assistance in evaluating the costs and benefits of taking a particular medication. Taking the time to discuss fully the risks and benefits of pharmacotherapy will enhance patient compliance with the medication regimen.

Medications are easy to prescribe, they are readily available, and they demand little in the way of work from the patient. The most important benefit of medications is that they often offer a great deal of symptomatic relief for their approved indications. This relief usually occurs within a few weeks and continues for as long as the medication is taken at an appropriate dosage. Medications can be delivered in a primary care setting without need of a specialist's involvement and may provide very cost-effective treatment.

Despite these benefits, some patients with anxiety disorders are uncomfortable taking medications for their symptoms. Patients should be warned of the possible costs of starting pharmacotherapy. To start, they should be informed of the likelihood of possible side effects, particularly those involving sexual dysfunction, weight gain, and other symptoms that are likely to be a source of concern. In addition, medications can be costly, occasionally cause significant physical problems, may produce dependency, and are often associated with relapse following discontinuation. Many self-help groups, industry sources, pharmacists, self-help books, and web sites offer up-to-date information about the potential benefits and risks of all the commonly used medications. It is helpful to provide written information to patients about medication before starting treatment. In general, unless there is a crisis demanding immediate intervention, it is advisable to discuss the possible use of medications after a thorough assessment and then to allow the patient time at home to review his or her treatment options with family members and other social supports before instituting drug treatment.

Issues Related to Assessment

Although assessment is covered in chapter 4, there are several assessment-related issues that are particularly relevant to pharmacotherapy and are worth mentioning here. Before starting pharmacotherapy, it is essential to take a detailed history. The clinician should establish whether the patient has a history of substance abuse or dependence on illegal drugs, alcohol, or medications. Psychotropic medications often interact with other drugs and alcohol. If the patient is unwilling or unable to reduce or eliminate the use of other substances, treatment with medications may be contraindicated. In addition, a history of substance use disorders may put a patient at risk for becoming dependent on certain prescribed medications, particularly the benzodiazepines.

A complete medical history should also be taken. The clinician should be aware of any medical conditions that are present as well as any other medications that the patient is taking. Medications should be selected to avoid interactions with other drugs and to avoid causing side effects that may exacerbate the symptoms of a medical illness. If possible, a complete physical examination by a physician is a good idea. Finally, it is important to establish whether other forms of psychopathology are present. For example, if a patient is suffering from obsessive–compulsive disorder (OCD) in addition to PD, the clinician should consider treating the person with a selective serotonin reuptake inhibitor (SSRI), which is likely to help with both the PD symptoms and the OCD symptoms.

CHOOSING BETWEEN SHORT-TERM AND LONG-TERM TREATMENTS

Because of their chronicity, phobic disorders often require long-term treatment when medication is used. Antidepressants (the specific drugs are reviewed later in the chapter) are usually recommended as first-line treatments, particularly for PD and generalized social phobia. Although benzodiazepines also appear to be effective for treating these conditions (see chapters 1 and 2), they have fallen out of favor over the past few years because of their potential for abuse and the difficulty that patients sometimes have in stopping these medications after long term use. In addition, the non-benzodiazepine, anxiolytic buspirone (Buspar) is rarely used for treating phobic disorders because of its lack of established efficacy (see chapters 1 and 2).

In rare cases when medications are used for the management of specific phobias and discrete forms of social phobia (e.g., public speaking phobias), the pharmacological agents are usually taken for a very short period, usually just before encountering the phobic situation (e.g., when flying in an airplane, giving a speech, etc.). In these circumstances, the choice of medications is limited to benzodiazepines or sometimes a beta-adrenergic blocking medication, particularly for discrete performance-related fears. Typically, PD and generalized social phobia should not be treated on a short-term, as-needed basis.

SHORT-TERM MEDICATION TREATMENTS FOR PERFORMANCE-RELATED FEARS

Medication treatment for social phobia differs across subtypes of the disorder. Compared with generalized social phobia, discrete performance-related fears are usually a problem only in circumstances that occur predictably and somewhat infrequently (e.g., when speaking in front of a group). Therefore, performance-based fears are often treated intermittently or on an as-needed basis. The choice of treatment is usually between a beta-adrenergic blocking agent, such as propanalol (Inderal), and a short-acting benzodiazepine, such as lorazepam. In either case, a single low dose of the chosen medication is given approximately 30 minutes before the phobic situation is encountered.

Beta-Blockers

Propanalol and other beta-blocking agents reduce the peripheral manifestations of anxiety. The major contraindication to their use is the presence of asthma. A single dose of 5 to 10 mg taken orally 20 to 30 minutes before the anxiety-producing event is usually sufficient to reduce feelings of shakiness and palpitations. It is advisable to have the patient take a trial dose at home when there is no threat so that he or she can predict the response to the drug's effects in the phobic situation. Although many orchestral performers take propanalol regularly, the events that trigger performance anxiety are relatively infrequent for most people. Propanalol is not very effective for reducing anxiety in generalized social phobia and is thus not recommended for that condition. In fact, even for treating performance-related fears, most of the outcome research was conducted in the 1970s, using representative groups of musicians, actors, and people who speak in front of groups (see Antony & Barlow, 1997). It is not clear whether participants in these early studies would have been diagnosed with social phobia according to the current criteria in the *Diagnostic and Statistical Manual of Mental Disorders, 4th Edition* (*DSM-IV*; American Psychiatric Association, 1994).

Benzodiazepines

Benzodiazepines can also be used on an as-needed basis in single doses if the phobic anxiety is experienced infrequently. The most useful benzodiazepines are those that are absorbed quickly and have a relatively short elimination half-life. Alprazolam (Xanax) and lorazepam (Ativan) are suitable, and so is diazepam (Valium), despite its long elimination half-life. The medication is given as a single dose of the lowest amount available 20 to 30 minutes before the task is anticipated. Alprazolam 0.25 mg, lorazepam 0.5 to 1 mg, or diazepam 2.5 to 5 mg is usually sufficient. Lorazepam is available in a sublingual preparation that has very rapid onset of action and can be taken 10 minutes before encountering the phobic situation.

The main side effects of benzodiazepines are sedation and unsteadiness, and they may also cause disinhibition. In addition, benzodiazepines interact with alcohol. Therefore it is very important to warn people who are taking a benzodiazepine for performance anxiety at a public function (e.g., being the best man at a wedding) not to drink any alcohol before or after taking the medication. As with the beta-blockers, it is advisable to have the patient take a test dose a few days before the event. Only a small supply of medication should be prescribed (e.g., enough for 5 to 10 events). Any escalation in the dose or in the frequency of use should be treated as a warning that the patient may be at risk for abusing the drug. For such patients, an alternative treatment should be used. Benzodiazepines should not be taken, particularly in high doses, before any task requiring a high level of motor skill, for example, when driving.

Short-acting drugs can be used on an as-needed basis to help a person through a difficult situation when there is insufficient time to use cognitive–behavioral therapy (CBT) or if the patient is not interested in pursuing CBT. They can also be used in the initial stages of exposure therapy if the patient refuses to enter a feared situation without some guarantee of feeling relatively calm. Although anxiolytics are sometimes difficult to discontinue following chronic use, this is less often a problem when they are taken infrequently to reduce anxiety in a particular situation.

Some experts have raised concerns that anxiolytic medication may interfere with the effects of exposure. These concerns stem from predictions based on learning and information-processing theories (see Craske, 1999, pp. 160–164), animal research demonstrating that medications can interfere with the effects of exposure (see Gray, 1987), and studies showing that benzodiazepines can impair memory (e.g., Curran et al., 1994). Despite these concerns, there is little evidence in humans that using low doses of medications in the initial stages of exposure for phobic disorders prevents behavioral or cognitive change from occurring. If medications are used at the beginning of behavioral treatment, however, we recommend that as the patient becomes more comfortable with exposure, the medication gradually be discontinued.

SHORT-TERM MEDICATION TREATMENTS FOR SPECIFIC PHOBIA

Despite the relative absence of studies investigating the use of medications for specific phobias, there is considerable anecdotal evidence that benzodiazepines are sometimes effective for calming patients who are exposed to certain types of feared situations (e.g., air travel). Beta-blockers do not produce the calm feeling that occurs with benzodiazepines and are typically not used to treat specific phobias.

The occasional use of benzodiazepines for flight phobia, before surgery in an individual with a blood or injury phobia, or before encountering an unavoidable and predictable claustrophobic experience (e.g., magnetic resonance imaging) is permissible. However, benzodiazepines should not become the main method of treatment if the person is having frequent exposure to these situations. For specific phobias, behavioral therapies should be the first-line treatment, and medications should be used only as an adjunct to psychological treatment, if at all. Recommended benzodiazepine dosages for specific phobias are similar to those used in performance-related fears.

LONG-TERM MEDICATION TREATMENT FOR PHOBIC DISORDERS

Antidepressants

As is reviewed in chapters 1 and 2, long-term treatment with antidepressants has been shown to be effective for treating generalized social phobia and PD (with and without agoraphobia). However, the effects of antidepressants are often delayed for as long as 4 to 6 weeks, making them unsuitable for as-needed use. When the decision is made to treat generalized social phobia or PD with antidepressants, the patient has to understand that the treatment will be necessary for at least 6 months and frequently longer. Consistent, daily use is essential in order to obtain the benefit of the drug. The management of compliance is a central focus of longer term treatment of the anxiety disorders.

Generalized social phobia

The SSRIs such as paroxetine (Paxil) and sertraline (Zoloft), monoamine oxidase inhibitors (MAOIs) such as phenelzine (Nardil), and reversible inhibitors of monoamine oxidase (RIMAs) such as moclobemide (Manerix) are the main agents used for treating generalized social phobia. The evidence regarding the efficacy of these medications is reviewed in chapter 2. Although controlled clinical trials do not exist for all five SSRIs, it is likely that they are all about equally effective. However, individual patients may respond better to one drug over another, and it is often difficult to predict in advance which is likely to have the strongest benefits. Additionally, although venlafaxine (Effexor) and nefazodone (Serzone) have not been subjected to double-blind clinical trials, there is evidence from small case series that they are also effective for patients suffering from generalized social phobia (see chapter 2). As reviewed in chapter 2, evidence regarding moclobemide for generalized social phobia has been mixed. Generally, as reviewed in chapter 2, the tricyclic antidepressants (TCAs), such as imipramine (Tofranil), do not appear to be particularly useful for treating social phobia.

Currently, the best first-line medication treatment for generalized social phobia is an SSRI. As reviewed in chapter 2, paroxetine, fluvoxamine (Lovox), and sertraline have been demonstrated to be more effective than placebo in a limited number of controlled trials. Fluoxetine (Prozac) and citalopram have some evidence of efficacy in uncontrolled open trials. At the time that this chapter was written, paroxetine was the only SSRI to have an approved indication for generalized social phobia (i.e., social anxiety disorder, as it is referred to in the paroxetine trials). In the United Kingdom, moclobemide is approved as a treatment for social phobia.

Panic disorder with and without agoraphobia

As is the case with social phobia, controlled trials have shown the SSRIs to be effective for treating PD, and several of these drugs (e.g., paroxetine and sertraline) are officially indicated for treating panic. There are also numerous trials supporting the use of TCAs such as clomipramine (Anafranil) and imipramine, as well as venlafaxine. Open-label trials with nefazodone suggest that this medication may also be effective for decreasing panic-related symptoms. Controlled trials with nefazodone for PD are currently under way. A review of pharmacotherapy studies of PD may be found in chapter 1.

Dosages, side effects, and drug interactions

When treating people with generalized social phobia or PD, the SSRIs are used in the same dose range as they are for the management of major depression (see Table 8.1). However, the initial dosage should usually be quite low for anxious patients, particularly those with PD. SSRIs are generally well tolerated, but they do have side effects that can be troublesome. The most common side effects are nausea and stomach upset, agitation, and

Table 8.1
Dose Ranges for Antidepressants in the Treatment of Social Phobia and
Panic Disorder (With or Without Agoraphobia)

Generic name	Brand name	Starting dose	Daily dose
Selective Serotonin Reuptake Inhibitors (SSRIs)			
paroxetine	Paxil	10 mg	40–60 mg
fluvoxamine	Luvox	50 mg	150–300 mg
sertraline	Zoloft	50 mg	100–200 mg
fluoxetine	Prozac	10–20 mg	20–60 mg
citalopram	Celexa	10 mg	20–60 mg
Other Antidepressants			
imipramine	Tofranil	10–25 mg	100–250 mg
clomipramine	Anafranil	25–50 mg	100–250 mg
phenelzine	Nardil	15–30 mg	30–75 mg
moclobemide	Manerix	200–300 mg	450–600 mg
venlafaxine	Effexor	37.5–75 mg	150–225 mg
nefazodone	Serzone	100–200 mg	300–500 mg

Note. The SSRIs and monoamine oxidase inhibitors (e.g., phenelzine) appear to be effective for both social phobia and PD (with and without agoraphobia). Tricyclic antidepressants (e.g., imipramine and clomipramine) have been shown to be useful for treating PD but not social phobia. More research is needed regarding the effectiveness of venlafaxine and nefazodone, although initial findings are promising. Findings regarding moclobemide for social phobia have been mixed, and more research is needed regarding the effectiveness of moclobemide as a treatment for panic. Brand names listed in this table are for the United States and Canada and may differ in other countries.

headache. They often cause weight gain with long-term treatment, although citalopram (Celexa) may be an exception. Also, in higher doses, the SSRIs tend to produce sexual dysfunction (e.g., delayed or failure to achieve orgasm or impaired sexual arousal) in both sexes. It is advisable to start SSRI treatment in anxious patients with a low dose because of the possibility of causing agitation. Anxious patients find this feeling to be very unpleasant, and a proportion discontinue the medication very early in treatment because of this particular adverse effect. Side effects and drug interactions for the SSRIs and other antidepressants are provided in Table 8.2.

Other practical aspects of antidepressant treatment

The phases of medication treatment are summarized in Table 8.3. These stages include the assessment phase, initiation of the drug, dose escalation (also known as *titration*), drug maintenance phase, drug discontinuation, and, occasionally, the treatment of symptom recurrence or relapse. As is indicated in Table 8.3, each of these phases is associated with particular tasks to which the clinician should attend.

Apart from the evidence from controlled trials, choosing a particular medication for a given patient should take into account a number of factors,

Table 8.2
Side Effects and Interactions of Antidepressants

Drug Class	Common Side Effects	Interactions
Selective serotonin reuptake inhibitors (SSRIs)	nausea, anorexia, insomnia, nervousness, agitation, sweating, sexual dysfunction	coadministration of MAOIs is contraindicated. Also, CY-P450 drugs
Tricyclic antidepressants (TCAs)	dry mouth, blurred vision, constipation, tachycardia, urinary hesitancy, hypotension, sedation, weight gain; clomipramine in high dose increases seizure risk	MAOIs, antiarrhythmics, antihypertensives
Monoamine-oxidase inhibitors (MAOIs)	hypotension, edema, insomnia	SSRIs, TCAs, tyramine-containing foods, sympathomimetics
Moclobemide	insomnia, nausea	SSRIs, antihypertensives, antipsychotics, sympathomimetics, excessive tyramine
Venlafaxine	nausea, dizziness, dry mouth; blood pressure increase at higher doses	MAOIs, CY-P450
Nefazodone	dizziness, dry mouth, drowsiness	benzodiazepines, antihypertensives

Table 8.3
Phases of Medication Treatment

Phase	Specific Tasks	Comments
Assessment	baseline measures physical assessment obtain information regarding previous medications, their effectiveness, and their side effects	respond to patient's concerns about taking medications
Initiation	begin with low doses have frequent contact attend to allergic or otherwise unusual responses, side effects, etc.	anxious patients tend to respond to higher starting doses with agitation frequent contact, by telephone, alleviates anticipatory anxiety
Dose escalation	measure symptom improvement using patient diaries, interview, and self-report measures track side effects	dose escalation is usually accomplished easily after dose initiation
Maintenance	monitor compliance with steady dose continue to assess gains and side effects consider introducing other treatments (e.g., cognitive–behavioral therapy) if there is only a partial response to medication	choose as low a dose as possible while maintaining benefit
Discontinuation	choose timing of discontinuation carefully do not discontinue medications too quickly assess for the possibility of symptom recurrence or withdrawal symptoms	continue treatment for at least 6 months before slowly fading the dose
Relapse	assess for possible triggers for relapse resume treatment or switch to a new treatment	if relapse occurs during or after discontinuation, consider resuming the same medication or switching to a different treatment if relapse occurs while taking a particular medication, consider switching to a different drug class or adding cognitive–behavioral therapy

including evidence from previous treatment, family history of response to a particular medication, the presence of comorbid conditions, whether the patient is taking other medications, the cost of the medication, the side effects of the medications, and variations among medications with respect to their metabolism and mechanisms of action (e.g., half-life). It is usual to begin treatment with an SSRI. However, there is no evidence that any particular drug is superior to any other within the same class of antidepressants. In other words, any SSRI is as likely to be as effective as any other SSRI. Although SSRIs are expensive, they tend to be better tolerated than TCAs and MAOIs. In addition, although there is no evidence of SSRIs being more effective than other types of antidepressants for treating people with panic disorder, SSRIs appear to be more effective than TCAs for treating people with generalized social phobia.

The main advantage of SSRIs over other classes of antidepressant is in the side effect profiles and toxicity. Tricyclic antidepressants interfere with cardiac conduction and are much more dangerous in overdose than are the SSRIs. It is advisable to obtain an EKG recording before starting TCA therapy and to monitor cardiac function serially as the dose increases. Blood levels taken 1 week or more after the last dose change can be very helpful in monitoring compliance and in preventing the patient from being exposed to a potentially toxic dose range. Clomipramine increases the risk of seizures at higher doses (i.e., 250 mg and above).

Fluoxetine has a very long half-life, as does its metabolite norfluoxetine. This means that it takes several weeks for the drug to reach a steady state in the plasma and many weeks for the drug to be cleared from the body following discontinuation. It is therefore difficult for the clinician to determine the effects of changing the dosage. In addition, if the drug has to be stopped, there may need to be a delay prior to starting another medication. Fluoxetine and paroxetine blood levels increase proportionately more at higher doses than at lower doses. This may lead to a greater chance of interaction with other medications as the dose of these SSRIs is increased. The SSRIs, apart from fluoxetine, all have half-lives of 15–30 hours, reach steady state in a few days, and are cleared quickly (Janicak, Davies, Preskorn, & Ayd, 1997, p. 303). Sertraline and citalopram have linear pharmacokinetics, so changes in blood level are predictable from dose changes. With increasing age, paroxetine and fluoxetine produce higher blood levels compared with those produced in a younger person by the same dose.

Most patients tolerate SSRIs well. However, as the dose increases, so does the likelihood of dropping out from treatment. It is important to wait for the dose to take effect rather than to push the dose higher too quickly. Lower doses are associated with fewer adverse effects, and there is little evidence that high doses provide significantly greater benefit than do lower doses for most patients.

The question of how long the treatment should last is important, but unfortunately there is little evidence available to guide that decision when treating people with phobic disorders. Treatment for at least 12 weeks is necessary to determine the potential degree of change due to any particular drug. Treatment for 6 to 12 months is usual for the first episode of treatment, followed by a slow tapering of the medication. During the medication treatment phase, the patient should also receive CBT, if possible, in order to augment the effects of the medication and to build some protection against possible relapse when the drug is discontinued. For example, recent findings from a long-term treatment study with imipramine showed that a significant minority of patients relapse after discontinuing long-term treatment (Mavissakalian & Perel, 1999).

Care needs to be taken in discontinuing paroxetine, because of its short half-life. There have been accounts of a flu-like illness occurring following rapid withdrawal. Fluvoxamine, sertraline, and citalopram can be discontinued slowly, usually without encountering any problems. Fluoxetine is cleared so slowly that the main difficulty occurs when switching the patient to another medication. With a switch to an MAOI, the patient should wait at least 5 weeks after the use of fluoxetine before the MAOI can be started.

Benzodiazepines

Long-term, daily use of benzodiazepines, particularly alprazolam and clonazepam (Klonapin; Rovotril), has been shown to reduce panic attacks and anticipatory anxiety in people suffering from PD as well as to reduce the symptoms of social phobia. In addition, benzodiazepines can be used as adjunctive therapy to antidepressants if the level of anxiety or agitation remains troublesome. Treatment is initiated with a low dose of alprazolam or clonazepam (see Table 8.4). The main advantage of benzodiazepines over other pharmacological and psychological treatments is that the onset of action is very rapid. Panic attacks can be aborted within 15 to 20 minutes, and after a few days, frequent panic attacks may be brought under control. Caution has to be taken with patients who exhibit very frequent, long-lasting panic attacks that are almost always uncued and not in response to particular situations. A minority of these patients may be suffering from episodes of emotional dyscontrol that could be secondary to an Axis II (dramatic cluster) condition rather than PD. Clinicians should be cautious before prescribing benzodiazepines to such a patient.

In most people suffering from PD (with or without agoraphobia), the panic attacks reduce markedly within 1 to 2 weeks (Ballenger et al., 1988) and tend to remain in partial or full remission as long as the medication is continued (Rickels, Schweizer, Weiss, & Zavodnick, 1992). Benzodiazepines produce tolerance in that the effect of a steady dose may diminish over

Table 8.4
Benzodiazepines in the Treatment of Social Phobia and Panic Disorder (With or Without Agoraphobia)

Generic name	Brand name	Dose range	Typical side effects	Comments
Alprazolam	Xanax	0.25 mg tid–qid up to 6 mg daily	drowsiness, reduced concentration, unsteadiness, amnesia, physical dependence, interdose rebound	Contraindicated if history of drug or alcohol abuse. Discontinue slowly. Seizure risk during discontinuation. Use lower doses in elderly patients.
Clonazepam	Klonapin Rivotril	0.25–0.5 mg bid up to 6 mg daily	drowsiness, reduced concentration, unsteadiness, amnesia, physical dependence, interdose rebound	Contraindicated if history of drug or alcohol abuse. Discontinue slowly. Seizure risk during discontinuation. Use lower doses in elderly patients.

Note. bid–twice daily; tid = three times daily; qid = four times daily. Controlled trials have shown that alprazolam and clonazepam are both effective for the short-term treatment of PD and social phobia. Brand names listed in this table are for the United States and Canada and may differ in other countries.

time. Although there is concern that the dose may continue to escalate, evidence from naturalistic studies (Romach et al., 1992) shows that the majority of users either maintain a steady dose or reduce the total daily dose themselves.

However, some patients may respond to the initial relief from the anxiety symptoms with a rapid self-administered escalation of their benzodiazepine dose. Therefore, the initial prescription for benzodiazepines should be restricted and without repeats, and the patient should be seen weekly until the effects of the medication can be fully assessed. It is important to keep accurate track of the amount of benzodiazepines consumed each day. Benzodiazepines should be taken on a predetermined schedule and not used in response to changes in the patient's level of anxiety. Patients should be given only enough medication to be used according to the prescribed schedule.

Clonazepam has a longer half-life than alprazolam and can be taken twice a day. Alprazolam requires doses three or four times each day and therefore may lead to more as-needed use. Concern arises in those patients in whom low-dose benzodiazepine (i.e., 2 mg or less of alprazolam or clonazepam daily) is insufficient to produce a marked decrease in panic frequency. As the dose is increased, so are the side effects of sedation, ataxia, and memory impairment. The risk of these side effects is greater in the elderly, which may increase the probability of falling and causing fractures.

The major difficulty in using benzodiazepines is the discontinuation phase. Reductions in dose are followed rapidly by increases in anxiety and often by the return of panic attacks. Discontinuation must be carried out slowly. Abrupt discontinuation produces a return of the panic attacks, which can be more severe than the initial episode for which the patient sought treatment (Pecknold et al., 1988). Severe insomnia and agitation frequently follow rapid dose reduction, and there is the potential for withdrawal seizures, although their occurrence is rare. It is most helpful if at the beginning of benzodiazepine treatment the patient has the expectation that the medication will be stopped at some time. Frequent attempts should be made to reduce the dose during therapy. Furthermore, discontinuing benzodiazepines is often more successful if done in combination with CBT (Bruce et al., 1995; Otto et al., 1993; Spiegel et al., 1994).

HERBAL REMEDIES FOR PHOBIC DISORDERS

Many patients who present for treatment are likely to be taking herbal remedies for their anxiety. Commonly used herbal preparations include St. John's wort, kava, ginkgo, Valerian root, and ginseng. With very few exceptions, such as the use of St. John's wort for depression (Kim, Streltzer,

& Goebert, 1999; Philipp, Kohnen, & Hiller, 1999), evidence supporting the use of herbal remedies for phobic disorders, or other psychological disorders for that matter, is sparse (Wong, Smith, & Boon, 1998). There is currently no evidence that any herbal remedies work better than (or even as well as) traditional medications for phobic disorders.

Furthermore, very little is known about the safety of these remedies or the extent to which they interact with traditional medications. Because some of these herbs are believed to affect neurotransmitter function (e.g., St. John's wort is thought to affect serotonergic function), clinicians should ask patients whether they are taking any herbal remedies before prescribing new medications. Patients should also be warned about possible interactions between medications and herbal remedies (see Wong et al., 1998, for a review). Controlled trials using herbal preparations for anxiety disorders are currently underway. In the coming years, more information regarding the safety and efficacy of these treatments will be available.

IMPROVING HEALTH HABITS

There is reason to assume that health habits may have an impact on anxiety symptoms, particularly in people suffering from PD (Roy-Byrne & Uhde, 1988). For example, there is evidence that compared with people in the general population, individuals with PD are more likely to smoke (Amering et al., 1999; Breslau & Klein, 1999), are sensitive to the effects of caffeine (Beck & Berisford, 1992; Lee, Flegel, Greden, & Cameron, 1988), and are more likely to avoid physical exercise (Broocks et al., 1997), perhaps because of increased likelihood of experiencing panic-related sensations (Cameron & Hudson, 1986; Schwartz, 1989). Clinically, some people with PD also report poor sleep habits, partly related to a fear of having a panic attack while sleeping or before going to sleep. For example, some patients avoid going to sleep until they are exhausted, so that they are likely to fall asleep more quickly, with less time and mental energy to focus on their physical feelings while lying in bed.

Despite findings suggesting that health habits can affect anxiety, there is very little research on the impact of improving health habits on the symptoms of phobic disorders. In one controlled study, the effects of physical exercise, clomipramine, and placebo for the treatment of PD were compared (Broocks et al., 1998). Although exercise was not as effective as clomipramine, it did lead to more significant symptom reduction compared with placebo. In addition, some authors have suggested that aerobic exercise may be a useful addition to standard treatments for anxiety (Hays, 1999; Martinsen, 1993).

We recommend that clinicians routinely ask patients about their health habits. Patients who smoke or who consume excessive amounts of caffeine or alcohol should be warned about the relationship between these drugs and anxiety. Patients who have poor sleep habits should be taught strategies for improving their sleep (e.g., Morin, 1993). Finally, patients should also be encouraged to exercise regularly. This is particularly important for individuals with PD who are frightened of the feelings associated with exercise (see chapter 6).

APPLIED TENSION FOR BLOOD-INJURY-INJECTION PHOBIA

As is reviewed in chapter 3, blood, injury, and injection phobias are often associated with fainting during exposure to the phobic situation. Fainting is triggered by a sudden drop in systolic and diastolic blood pressure, accompanied by reduced heart rate and a reduction in muscle tone. Over the past 20 years, a number of case reports (e.g., Kozak & Montgomery, 1981; Öst & Sterner, 1987) and controlled studies (e.g., Hellström et al., 1996; Öst, Fellenius, & Sterner, 1991) have shown that teaching patients to systematically tense the muscles of the body in the presence of blood- and injection-related stimuli raises blood pressure, prevents fainting, and ultimately helps them to overcome their phobias.

The protocol for applied tension involves a number of steps (Antony, Craske, & Barlow, 1995; Öst & Sterner, 1987). Initially, the patient is taught to use the tension exercises outside of the phobic situation. After mastering the technique, he or she is taught to use the exercises during exposure to blood- and injection-related situations. By the end of treatment, the patient should be able to encounter the phobic situation comfortably without the applied tension exercises.

Description of the Tensing Procedure

Initially, the patient should be sitting in a comfortable chair. Next, the patient should be instructed to tense all of the muscles in his or her body, including those in the arms, torso, legs, and face. The tension should be held for 10 or 15 seconds, until there is a "rush" or a "warm feeling" in the head. At this point, the patient should release the tension and let his or her body return to its normal state for 20 to 30 seconds. This tension–relaxation cycle should be repeated five times for a given practice session. It may be instructive to demonstrate for the patient the effect of the tension exercises on blood pressure. If you have access to equipment for measuring blood pressure, try taking a reading immediately before and after the tension exercise.

At the beginning of treatment, the patient should be encouraged to practice the exercises five different times throughout the day (with each practice including 5 tension–relaxation cycles). A week of practice should be enough for the patient to have perfected the procedure. If the patient develops headaches during the practices, he or she should be encouraged to decrease the strength of the tension or decrease the frequency of the practices. If patients have a medical condition that could be affected by the procedure (e.g., hypertension), he or she should consult a physician before using the tension exercises.

Applied Tension: Combining the Tension Exercises with Exposure

Once the patient has mastered the tension exercises, he or she should be encouraged to use the exercises during exposure practices, beginning with items that are relatively low on his or her exposure hierarchy (see chapter 6). The tension exercises may be used immediately before or during exposure to blood- or injection-related images or situations. As each situation in the hierarchy becomes more manageable, the patient should be encouraged to move on to more difficult situations.

If the patient is frightened of receiving injections or blood tests, he or she may be required to keep one arm relaxed so that the needle can be inserted. For such cases, the patient should practice tensing all parts of the body except for his or her "needle arm." Or some medical technicians may ask the patient to flex the arm just before blood is drawn, so that the veins are more accessible. In such cases, it may not be necessary to relax the arm during the procedure.

Once the patient is able to confront the previously feared situations with minimal anxiety, he or she should discontinue the tension exercises. After the fear has decreased, many individuals are able to be in situations involving blood or needles without fainting. If the feelings of faintness return or are still present, the patient should be encouraged to begin using the applied tension exercises again when exposed to problematic situations.

BREATHING RETRAINING FOR PANIC DISORDER

As is reviewed in chapter 1, instruction in breathing retraining (BRT) is often included as a component of CBT for PD and agoraphobia. Despite the popularity of this procedure, we recommend that BRT *not* be included on a routine basis for the treatment of PD (although in some cases, as will be described, it may be appropriate to include this procedure). We prefer not to use this procedure for three reasons. First (see chapter 1), there is no empirical evidence that CBT with BRT is any more effective than the same treatment without BRT (Schmidt et al., in press). Furthermore, some investigators (e.g., Hibbert & Chan, 1989) have shown few significant differences between BRT and a credible placebo with respect to their effects on decreasing panic symptomatology. In fact, in a comprehensive review of the literature on BRT, Garssen, de Ruiter, and van Dyck (1992) concluded that BRT probably works by providing patients with a distraction and a sense of control. In short, the research suggests that BRT adds no benefit over and above the effects of the other CBT strategies that are typically used to treat PD. In fact, Schmidt et al. (in press) suggested that the addition of BRT may have detrimental effects for some individuals.

A second reason why we prefer not to use BRT is that the standard treatment for PD and agoraphobia already includes a number of specific interventions (e.g., psychoeducation, cognitive restructuring, situational exposure, and interoceptive exposure), each of which requires intensive practice. Adding BRT increases the risk that patients will not have the time to master any of the procedures at a level necessary to use them effectively. By including a smaller number of strategies, patients have more of an opportunity to learn to use each one properly.

Finally, in our opinion, the BRT procedures are philosophically at odds with the other cognitive and behavioral strategies. Whereas the cognitive and exposure-based strategies are designed to teach the patient that the panic symptoms are not dangerous and that it does not matter whether he or she experiences them, BRT is designed to provide symptom relief. In other words, BRT could be viewed as a form of symptom avoidance.

Although we have reservations about the use of BRT, there are several conditions under which it may be useful to use this procedure. First, if a patient frequently hyperventilates (this can be assessed by asking the patient or by observing the patient during the treatment sessions), then it may be helpful to teach the procedures for slowing down his or her breathing. Second, if a patient specifically asks to be taught to use BRT, it may be reasonable to teach the breathing exercises because the patient's expectations can have a powerful effect on treatment outcome. Third, BRT may be an option for patients who refuse to practice exposure strategies without having a coping strategy that they can use when in feared situations.

When BRT is used with a particular individual, the patient should be informed that for long-term success, it is important to learn strategies that target the fear of physical sensations (e.g., cognitive restructuring and exposure) rather than relying exclusively on strategies designed for the relief of physical symptoms (e.g., BRT or pharmacotherapy). In addition, it should be noted that although there are studies that have included BRT as a component of treatment for PD and agoraphobia, empirically validated treatment protocols for social phobia and specific phobia have tended not to include BRT.

Instructions for Breathing Retraining

The description of the BRT procedures in this section is adapted from Craske and Barlow's (1993) protocol for treating PD. Typically, BRT is taught early in the protocol, over two sessions, with continuing homework practices throughout the duration of the treatment. At the initial BRT session, the patient undergoes a voluntary hyperventilation challenge to illustrate the role of overbreathing in causing panic sensations. This is followed by education regarding the physiological basis of hyperventilation and, finally, teaching the patient to attend to his or her breathing and to breathe in a relaxed way, initially without changing his or her breathing rate. After a week of practicing the technique at home, the exercise is refined at the next session, at which time the patient is taught to slow down his or her breathing. Over the remaining weeks, the patient is encouraged to try the BRT exercises in increasingly anxiety-provoking situations. We will now consider each of these steps in more detail.

Voluntary hyperventilation challenge

As a demonstration of how hyperventilation can contribute to panic symptoms, patients are asked to stand up and breathe quickly and deeply for 90 seconds, as if they were blowing up a large balloon or air mattress. Patients should be encouraged to continue the challenge for the full 90 seconds, although if they need to stop earlier, they will probably still benefit from the demonstration. Following the challenge, the patient should sit down and wait until the symptoms have subsided. Then the therapist should ask the patient to describe the symptoms experienced, the level of fear achieved during the challenge, and the extent to which the experience was similar to his or her naturally occurring panic attacks.

Although most patients will respond to the challenge with fear, some are not fearful during the challenge, for a number of reasons. First, the symptoms triggered by the challenge may not be relevant to some patients. In addition, the extent to which the patient associates the therapist and the therapist's office with safety can affect the patient's response to the challenge. Finally, unlike naturally occurring, unexpected panic attacks, any symptoms that occur during the hyperventilation challenge have an obvious cause and therefore may not be feared by some patients. If a patient does not respond fearfully to the hyperventilation challenge, he or she may still benefit from the BRT instruction.

Education regarding the physiology of hyperventilation

After the hyperventilation challenge, the therapist should engage the patient in a brief discussion of the physiology of hyperventilation. Although

- The normal breathing rate while at rest is about 10 to 14 breaths per minute.
- Hyperventilation is defined as breathing too quickly and deeply for the body's needs at a given point in time.
- Intense emotions (e.g., fear), life stress, or habit can cause an individual to overbreathe.
- Overbreathing can be intense for a short period of time (e.g., during a panic attack) or more subtle, over longer periods (e.g., due to chronic life stress or mild habitual overbreathing).
- Hyperventilation causes carbon dioxide levels in the blood to drop, which in turn produces a drop in the acid level of the blood. It is these two changes that ultimately produce many of the symptoms that occur during hyperventilation (e.g., dizziness, breathlessness, unreality, increased heart rate). Other symptoms (e.g., chest tightness, sweating) are caused by the fact that hyperventilation is physically demanding on the body, like exercise.
- Behaviors such as sighing and yawning may trigger uncomfortable symptoms in people who tend to hyperventilate chronically, by dumping large amounts of carbon dioxide in a short period.
- Although the symptoms produced by hyperventilation are uncomfortable, they are not dangerous. In fact, the symptoms are designed to help prepare the body for escape when it is confronted by a threat.

Craske and Barlow (1993) have provided a very detailed description of the physiology, we typically highlight only several key points, which are summarized in Exhibit 8.1.

Teaching the controlled breathing exercises

Initially, patients should be instructed to breathe through their nose, using their diaphragm rather than their chest muscles. During diaphragmatic breathing, the bottom part of the chest should expand more during inhalations than should the top part of the chest. It may be helpful to have the patient put one hand on the top half of the chest and the other hand about two to three inches below the first hand. If the person is breathing diaphragmatically, the bottom hand should move more than the top hand as the patient breathes in and out. Initially, it may be easier for the patient to do the exercise while lying on his or her back than while sitting up.

Once the patient is able to breathe from the diaphragm, he or she should be instructed to mentally count each inhalation and to think the word *relax* during each exhalation (e.g., 1–inhale, *relax*–exhale; 2–inhale, *relax*–exhale; 3–inhale, *relax*–exhale; etc.). After reaching 10 breaths, the patient should return to 1 and start the counting again. During exhalations, the patient should let go of any tensions in the body as he or she mentally repeats the word *relax*. The counting and relaxation should help the patient to focus on his or her breathing during the exercise. Initially, the patient should not try to change the rate of his or her breathing. Rather, the exercise should focus on continuing to breathe diaphragmatically and counting the breaths.

At the end of the session, the patient should be instructed to practice the breathing exercises twice per day over the next week, for 10 minutes each time. At the next session, the therapist should review the patient's progress with the breathing control exercises. Initially, patients often have trouble breathing from the diaphragm. Additional instruction and practice in diaphragmatic breathing should be provided if necessary. In addition, some patients may find that their anxiety increases during the practices. Because the exercises focus the patient's attention on his or her body, they may lead to increased anxiety, particularly if uncomfortable physical sensations are noticed. With practice, this problem should subside as the patient gets used to the procedure.

Slowing down the patient's breathing

After reviewing the patient's progress during the first week, the next step is to have the patient slow his or her breathing until the inhalation–exhalation cycle takes about 6 seconds to complete. The patient should continue to practice the slower breathing for 10 minutes twice per day over the coming weeks. Initially, the practices should occur in safe and relaxing environments.

Combining BRT with exposure exercises

Over time, the patient will become more and more proficient at using the BRT exercises. As treatment progresses, the patient should be encouraged to try the exercises in increasingly anxiety-provoking situations (e.g., while driving, while shopping in a supermarket, etc.).

APPENDIX A
SOURCES FOR ASSESSMENT
MATERIALS

STRUCTURED AND SEMISTRUCTURED
DIAGNOSTIC INTERVIEWS[1]

Anxiety Disorders Interview Schedule for DSM-IV (ADIS-IV)

Psychological Corporation
Harcourt Brace & Company
555 Academic Court
San Antonio, TX 78204-2498

phone: 800-211-8378 (US); 800-387-7278 (Canada)
web: www.psychcorp.com

Composite International Diagnostic Interview (CIDI)

American Psychiatric Press, Inc.
1400 K Street, NW
Washington, DC 20005

phone: 800-368-5777
fax: 202-789-2648
web: www.appi.org

---

[1] Please note that many of the instruments and scales listed in the Appendixes will be published along with detailed descriptions in a forthcoming volume scheduled to be published in 2001: Antony, M.M., Orsillo, S.M., & Roemer, L. (Eds.). (in press). *Practitioner's guide to empirically-based measures of anxiety*. New York: Kluwer Academic/Plenum.

Mini International Neuropsychiatric Interview (MINI)

Department of Psychiatry
University of South Florida
3515 East Fletcher Ave.
Tampa, FL 33613

phone: 813-974-4544
fax: 813-974-4575
web: www.medical-outcomes.com

Primary Care Evaluation of Mental Disorders (PRIME-MD)
Patient Health Questionnaire (PHQ)

Biometrics Research Department, Unit 74
New York State Psychiatric Institute
722 West 168th St.
New York, NY 10032

phone: 212-543-5524
fax: 212-543-5525

Structured Clinical Interview for DSM-IV (SCID-IV)

Research Version:
Biometrics Research Department, Unit 74
New York State Psychiatric Institute
722 West 168th St.
New York, NY 10032

phone: 212-543-5524
fax: 212-543-5525

Clinician's Version:
American Psychiatric Press, Inc.
1400 K Street, NW
Washington, DC 20005

phone: 800-368-5777
fax: 202-789-2648
web: www.appi.org

Computerized Version:
Multi-Health Systems, Inc.
908 Niagara Falls Blvd.
North Tonawanda, NY 14120-2060

phone: 800-456-3003 (US); 800-268-6011 (Canada)
web: www.mhs.com

MEASURES FOR PANIC DISORDER AND AGORAPHOBIA

Agoraphobia Scale

Öst, L.-G. (1990). The Agoraphobia Scale: An evaluation of its reliability and validity. *Behaviour Research and Therapy, 28,* 323–329.

Agoraphobic Cognitions Questionnaire (ACQ)

Schutte, N.S., & Malouff, J.M. (1995). *Sourcebook of adult assessment strategies.* New York: Plenum Press.

Fischer, J., & Corcoran, K.J. (1994). Measures for clinical practice: Vol. 2. Adults. New York: Free Press.

Agoraphobic Cognitions Scale (ACS)

Hoffart, A., Friis, S., & Martinsen, E.W. (1992). Assessment of fear of fear among agoraphobic patients: The Agoraphobic Cognitions Scale. *Journal of Psychopathology and Behavioral Assessment, 14,* 175–187.

Agoraphobic Self-Statements Questionnaire (ASQ)

van Hout, W.J.P.J., Emmelkamp, P.M.G., Koopmans, P.C., Bögels, S.M., & Bouman, T.K. (in press). Assessment of self-statements in agoraphobic situations: Construction and psychometric evaluations of the Agoraphobic Self-Statements Questionnaire (ASQ). *Journal of Anxiety Disorders.*

Albany Panic and Phobia Questionnaire (APPQ)

Rapee, R.M., Craske, M.G., & Barlow, D.H. (1994/1995). Assessment instrument for panic disorder that includes fear of sensation-producing activities: The Albany Panic and Phobia Questionnaire. *Anxiety, 1,* 114–122.

Anxiety Sensitivity Index (ASI)

IDS Publishing
P.O. Box 389
Worthington, OH 43085

phone: 614-885-2323

Anxiety Sensitivity Index—Expanded Version

Dr. Steven Taylor
Department of Psychiatry
University of British Columbia
Vancouver, BC, Canada

Taylor, S., & Cox, B.J. (1998). An expanded Anxiety Sensitivity Index: Evidence for a hierarchic structure in a clinical sample. *Journal of Anxiety Disorders, 12,* 463–483.

Anxiety Sensitivity Profile (ASP)

Taylor, S., & Cox, B.J. (1998). Anxiety Sensitivity: Multiple dimensions and hierarchic structure. *Behaviour Research and Therapy, 36,* 37–51.

Body Sensations Interpretation Questionnaire (BSIQ)

Clark, D.M., Salkovskis, P.M., Öst, L.-G., Breitholtz, E., Koeler, K.A., Westling, B.E., Jeavons, A., & Gelder, M. (1997). Misinterpretation of body sensations in panic disorder. *Journal of Consulting and Clinical Psychology, 65,* 203–213.

Body Sensations Questionnaire (BSQ)

Schutte, N.S., & Malouff, J.M. (1995). *Sourcebook of adult assessment strategies.* New York: Plenum Press.

Fischer, J., & Corcoran, K.J. (1994). *Measures for clinical practice: Vol. 2. Adults.* New York: Free Press.

Body Vigilance Scale (BVS)

Schmidt, N.B., Lerew, D.R., & Trakowski, J.H. (1997). Body vigilance in panic disorder: Evaluating attention to bodily perturbations. *Journal of Consulting and Clinical Psychology, 65,* 214–220.

Brief Panic Disorder Screen (BPDS)

Apfeldorf, W.J., Shear, M.K., Leon, A.C., & Portera, L. (1994). A brief screen for panic disorder. *Journal of Anxiety Disorders, 8,* 71–78.

Catastrophic Cognitions Questionnaire (CCQ)

Dr. Tian P. S. Oei
Department of Psychology
University of Queensland
Australia

Khawaja, N.G., & Oei, T.P.S. (1992). Development of a catastrophic cognition questionnaire. *Journal of Anxiety Disorders, 6,* 305–318.

Fear Questionnaire (FQ)

Marks, I.M, & Mathews, A.M. (1979). Brief standard self-rating for phobic patients. *Behaviour Research and Therapy, 17,* 263–267.

Schutte, N.S., & Malouff, J.M. (1995). *Sourcebook of adult assessment strategies.* New York: Plenum Press.

Fischer, J., & Corcoran, K.J. (1994). *Measures for clinical practice: Vol. 2. Adults.* New York: Free Press.

Mobility Inventory for Agoraphobia (MI)

Chambless, D.L., Caputo, G.C., Jasin, S.E., Gracely, E.J., & Williams, C. (1985). The Mobility Inventory for Agoraphobia. *Behaviour Research and Therapy, 23*, 35–44.

Schutte, N.S., & Malouff, J.M. (1995). *Sourcebook of adult assessment strategies*. New York: Plenum Press.

Fischer, J., & Corcoran, K.J. (1994). *Measures for clinical practice: Vol. 2. Adults*. New York: Free Press.

NIMH Panic Questionnaire

Dr. Thomas W. Uhde
Department of Psychiatry,
Wayne State University
Detroit, MI

Scupi, B.S., Maser, J.D., & Uhde, T.W. (1992). The National Institute of Mental Health Panic Questionnaire: An instrument for assessing clinical characteristics of panic disorder. *Journal of Nervous and Mental Disease, 180*, 566–572.

Panic and Agoraphobia Scale (PAS)

Hogrefe & Huber Publishers
P.O. Box 2487
Kirkland, WA 98083-2487

phone: 425-820-1500
fax: 425-823-8324 (US); 416-482-6339 (Canada)
web: www.hhpub.com

Bandelow, B. (1995). Assessing the efficacy of treatments for panic disorder and agoraphobia: II. The Panic and Agoraphobia Scale. *International Clinical Psychopharmacology, 10*, 73–81.

Panic Appraisal Inventory (PAI)

Dr. Michael J. Telch
Department of Psychology
University of Texas at Austin
Austin, TX

Feske, U., & de Beurs, E. (1997). The Panic Appraisal Inventory: Psychometric properties. *Behaviour Research and Therapy, 35*, 875–882.

Panic Attack Cognitions Questionnaire (PACQ)

Fischer, J., & Corcoran, K.J. (1994). *Measures for clinical practice: Vol. 2. Adults*. New York: Free Press.

Panic Attack Questionnaire—Revised (PAQ-R)

Dr. Brian J. Cox
Department of Psychiatry
University of Manitoba
Winnipeg, Canada

Norton, G.R., Dorward, J., & Cox, B.J. (1986). Factors associated with panic attacks in nonclinical subjects. *Behavior Therapy, 17,* 239–252.

Panic Attack Symptoms Questionnaire (PASQ)

Fischer, J., & Corcoran, K.J. (1994). *Measures for clinical practice: Vol. 2. Adults.* New York: Free Press.

Panic Disorder Self-Report (PDSR)

Dr. Michelle G. Newman
Department of Psychology
Penn State University
University Park, PA

Panic Disorder Severity Scale (PDSS)

Dr. M. Katherine Shear
Western Psychiatric Institute and Clinic
Pittsburgh, PA

Shear, M.K., Brown, T.A., Barlow, D.H., Money, R., Sholomskas, D.E., Woods, S.W., Gorman, J.M., & Papp, L.A. (1997). Multicenter collaborative panic disorder severity scale. *American Journal of Psychiatry, 154,* 1571–1575.

Texas Safety Maneuver Scale (TSMS)

Kamphuis, J.H., & Telch, M.J. (1998). Assessment of strategies to manage or avoid perceived threats among panic disorder patients: The Texas Safety Maneuver Scale (TSMS). *Clinical Psychology and Psychotherapy, 5,* 177-186.

MEASURES FOR SOCIAL PHOBIA AND SOCIAL ANXIETY

Brief Social Phobia Scale (BSPS)

Davidson, J.R.T., Potts, N.L.S., Richichi, E.A., Ford, S.M., Krishnan, R.R., Smith, R.D., & Wilson, W. (1991). The Brief Social Phobia Scale. *Journal of Clinical Psychiatry, 52*(Suppl. 11), 48–51.

Fear of Negative Evaluation Scale (FNE)

Watson, D., & Friend, R. (1969). Measurement of social-evaluative anxiety. *Journal of Consulting and Clinical Psychology, 33,* 448–457.

Fischer, J., & Corcoran, K.J. (1994). *Measures for clinical practice: Vol. 2. Adults.* New York: Free Press.

Fear Questionnaire (FQ)

Marks, I.M., & Mathews, A.M. (1979). Brief standard self-rating for phobic patients. *Behaviour Research and Therapy, 17,* 263–267.

Schutte, N.S., & Malouff, J.M. (1995). *Sourcebook of adult assessment strategies.* New York: Plenum Press.

Fischer, J., & Corcoran, K.J. (1994). *Measures for clinical practice: Vol. 2. Adults.* New York: Free Press.

Index of Social Phobia Improvement

Turner, S.M., Beidel, D.C., & Wolff, P.L. (1994). A composite measure to determine improvement following treatment for social phobia: The Index of Social Phobia Improvement. *Behaviour Research and Therapy, 32,* 471–476.

Liebowitz Social Anxiety Scale (LSAS)

Heimberg, R.G., Horner, K.J., Safren, S.A., Brown, E.J., Schneier, F.R., & Liebowitz, M.R. (1999). Psychometric properties of the Liebowitz Social Anxiety Scale. *Psychological Medicine, 29,* 199–212.

Personal Report of Confidence as a Speaker (PRCS)

Paul, G. (1966). *Insight versus desensitization in psychotherapy: An experiment in anxiety reduction.* Palo Alto, CA: Stanford University Press.

Social Avoidance and Distress Scale (SADS)

Watson, D., & Friend, R. (1969). Measurement of social-evaluative anxiety. *Journal of Consulting and Clinical Psychology, 33,* 448–457.

Fischer, J., & Corcoran, K.J. (1994). *Measures for clinical practice: Vol. 2. Adults.* New York: Free Press.

Social Cognitions Questionnaire (SCQ)

Dr. Edna Foa
Department of Psychiatry
University of Pennsylvania
Philadelphia, PA

Social Interaction Anxiety Scale (SIAS)

Mattick, R.P., & Clarke, J.C. (1998). Development and validation of measures of social phobia scrutiny fear and social interaction anxiety. *Behaviour Research and Therapy, 36,* 455–470.

Social Phobia and Anxiety Inventory (SPAI)

Multi-Health Systems, Inc.
908 Niagara Falls Blvd.
North Tonawanda, NY 14120-2060

phone: 800-456-3003 (US); 800-268-6011 (Canada)
web: www.mhs.com

Social Phobia Inventory (SPIN)

Dr. Jonathan Davidson
Department of Psychiatry
Duke University Medical School
Durham, NC

Connor, K.M., Davidson, J.R.T., Churchill, E., Sherwood, A., Foa, E.B., & Weisler, R.H. (in press). Psychometric properties of the Social Phobia Inventory (SPIN): A new self-rating scale. *British Journal of Psychiatry.*

Social Phobia Scale (SPS)

Mattick, R.P., & Clarke, J.C. (1998). Development and validation of measures of social phobia scrutiny fear and social interaction anxiety. *Behaviour Research and Therapy, 36,* 455–470.

MEASURES FOR SPECIFIC PHOBIA

Acrophobia Questionnaire (AC)

Dr. David C. Cohen
Department of Psychology
California State University
Bakersfield, CA

Cohen, D.C. (1977). Comparison of self-report and overt-behavioral procedures for assessing acrophobia. *Behavior Therapy, 8,* 17–23.

Blood-Injection Symptom Scale (BISS)

Page, A.C., Bennett, K.S., Carter, O., smith, J., & Woodmore, K. (1997). The Blood-Infection Symptom Scale (BISS). Assessing a structure of phobic symptoms elicited by blood and injections. *Behaviour Research and Therapy, 35,* 457–464.

Claustrophobia General Cognitions Questionnaire (CGCQ)

Febbraro, G.A.R., & Clum, G.A. (1995). A dimensional analysis of claustrophobia. *Journal of Psychopathology and Behavioral Assessment, 17,* 335–351.

Claustrophobia Questionnaire (CQ)

Radomsky, A.S., Rachman, S., Thordarson, D.S., McIsaac, H.K., & Teachman, B.A. (in press). The Claustrophobia Questionnaire (CLQ). *Journal of Anxiety Disorders*.

Claustrophobia Situations Questionnaire (CSQ)

Febbraro, G.A.R., & Clum, G.A. (1995). A dimensional analysis of claustrophobia. *Journal of Psychopathology and Behavioral Assessment, 17*, 335–351.

Dental Anxiety Inventory (DAI)

Stouthard, M.E.A., Hoogstraten, J., & Mellenbergh, G.J. (1995). A study on the convergent and discriminant validity of the Dental Anxiety Inventory. *Behaviour Research and Therapy, 33*, 589–595.

Dental Cognitions Questionnaire (DCQ)

de Jongh, A., Muris, P., Schoenmakers, N., & Horst, G.T. (1995). Negative cognitions of dental phobics: Reliability and validity of the Dental Cognitions Questionnaire. *Behaviour Research and Therapy, 33*, 507–515.

Dental Fear Survey (DFS)

Schutte, N.S., & Malouff, J.M. (1995). *Sourcebook of adult assessment strategies*. New York: Plenum Press.

Fischer, J., & Corcoran, K.J. (1994). *Measures for clinical practice: Vol. 2. Adults*. New York: Free Press.

Fear of Spiders Questionnaire (FSQ)

Szymanski, J., & O'Donohue, W. (1995). Fear of Spiders Questionnaire. *Journal of Behavior Therapy and Experimental Psychiatry, 26*, 31–34.

Fear Questionnaire (FQ)

Marks, I.M., & Mathews, A.M. (1979). Brief standard self-rating for phobic patients. *Behaviour Research and Therapy, 17*, 263–267.

Schutte, N.S., & Malouff, J.M. (1995). *Sourcebook of adult assessment strategies*. New York: Plenum Press.

Fischer, J., & Corcoran, K.J. (1994). *Measures for clinical practice: Vol. 2. Adults*. New York: Free Press.

Fear Survey Schedule (FSS-II)

Geer, J.H. (1965). The development of a scale to measure fear. *Behaviour Research and Therapy, 3*, 45–53.

Fear Survey Schedule (FSS-III)

Wolpe, J., & Lang, P.J. (1964). A fear survey schedule for use in behaviour therapy. *Behaviour Research and Therapy, 2,* 27–30.

Medical Fear Survey (MFS)

Dr. Ronald A. Kleinknecht
Department of Psychology
Western Washington University
Bellingham, WA

Kleinknecht, R.A., Kleinknecht, E.E., Sawchuk, C., Lee, T., & Lohr, J. (1999). The Medical Fear Survey: Psychometric properties. *The Behavior Therapist, 22,* 109–119.

Mutilation Questionnaire (MQ)

Snake Questionnaire (also called the *Snake Anxiety Questionnaire*)

Dr. Rafael Klorman
Department of Psychology
University of Rochester
Rochester, NY

Klorman, R., Hastings, J., Weerts, T., Melamed, B.G., & Lang, P. (1974). Psychometric description of some specific-fear questionnaires. *Behavior Therapy, 5,* 401–409.

Spider Phobia Beliefs Questionnaire (SPBQ)

Arntz, A., Lavy, E., van den Berg, G., & van Rijsoort, S. (1993). Negative beliefs of spider phobics: A psychometric evaluation of the Spider Phobia Beliefs Questionnaire. *Advances in Behaviour Research and Therapy, 15,* 257–277.

Spider Phobia Questionnaire (SPQ)

Watts, F.N., & Sharrock, R. (1984). Questionnaire dimensions of spider phobia. *Behaviour Research and Therapy, 22,* 575–580.

Spider Phobia Questionnaire–Extended Version

Barker, H.J., & Edelmann, R.J. (1987). Questionnaire dimension of spider phobia: A replication and extension. *Personality and Individual Differences, 8,* 737–739.

Spider Questionnaire (SPQ)

Dr. Rafael Klorman
Department of Psychology
University of Rochester
Rochester, NY

Klorman, R., Hastings, J., Weerts, T., Melamed, B.G., & Lang, P. (1974). Psychometric description of some specific-fear questionnaires. *Behavior Therapy*, 5, 401–409

MEASURES FOR OTHER RELEVANT DIMENSIONS

Beck Anxiety Inventory (BAI)

Beck Depression Inventory (2nd ed.) (BDI-2)

Psychological Corporation
Harcourt Brace & Company
555 Academic Court
San Antonio, TX 78204-2498

phone: 800-211-8378 (US); 800-387-7278 Canada)
web: www.psychcorp.com

Depression Anxiety Stress Scales (DASS)

The Psychological Foundation of Australia
Room 1017A, Level 10
Mathews Building
University of New South Wales
Sydney 2052 Australia

phone: 02-385-3038
fax: 02-385-3641
web: www.psy.unsw.edu.au/DASS/
e-mail: p.lovibond@unsw.edu.au

Illness Intrusiveness Rating Scale (IIRS)

Dr. Gerald M. Devins
Centre for Addiction and Mental Health
Clarke Division
Toronto, Ontario, Canada

Antony, M.M., Roth, D., Swinson, R.P., Huta, V., & Devins, G.M. (1998). Illness intrusiveness in individuals with panic disorder, obsessive compulsive disorder, or social phobia. *Journal of Nervous and Mental Disease*, 186, 311–315.

Frost Multidimensional Perfectionism Scale (FMPS, Frost et al., 1990)

Fischer, J., & Corcoran, K.J. (1994). *Measures for clinical practice: Vol. 2. Adults*. New York: Free Press.

Multidimensional Perfectionism Scale (MPS, Hewitt, Flett, Turnbull-Donovan, & Mikail, 1991)

Dr. Paul L. Hewitt
Department of Psychology
University of British Columbia
Vancouver, Canada

Hewitt, P.L., Flett, G.L., Turnbull-Donovan, W., & Mikail, S.F. (1991). The Multidimensional Perfectionism Scale: Reliability, validity, and psychometric properties in psychiatric samples. *Psychological Assessment: A Journal of Consulting and Clinical Psychology, 3,* 464–468.

State–Trait Anxiety Inventory (STAI)

Mind Garden
P.O. Box 60669
Palo Alto, CA 94306

phone: 415-424-8493

Multi-Health Systems Inc.
908 Niagara Falls Blvd.
North Tonawanda, NY 14120-2060

phone: 800-456-3003 (US); 800-268-6011 (Canada)
web: www.mhs.com

APPENDIX B
RECOMMENDED READINGS FOR CLINICIANS

PANIC DISORDER WITH AND WITHOUT AGORAPHOBIA

Barlow, D. H., & Brown, T. A. (1996). Psychological treatments for panic disorder and panic disorder with agoraphobia. In M. R. Mavissakalian & R. F. Prien (Eds.), *Long-term treatments of anxiety disorders* (pp. 221–240). Washington, DC: American Psychiatric Press.

Clark, D.M. (1996). Panic disorder: From theory to therapy. In P.M. Salkovskis (Ed.), *Frontiers of cognitive therapy* (pp. 318–344). New York: Guilford Press.

Clark, D.M. (1997). Panic disorder and social phobia. In D.M. Clark & C.G. Fairburn (Eds.), *Science and practice of cognitive behaviour therapy* (pp. 119–153). New York: Oxford University Press.

Mavissakalian, M. R. (1996). Antidepressant medications for panic disorder. In M. R. Mavissakalian & R. F. Prien (Eds.), *Long-term treatments of anxiety disorders* (pp. 221–240). Washington, DC: American Psychiatric Press.

McNally, R. J. (1994). *Panic disorder: A critical analysis.* New York: Guilford Press.

Rachman, S., & Maser, J.D. (1988). *Panic: Psychological perspectives.* Hillsdale, NJ: Erlbaum.

Rosenbaum, J.F., & Pollack, M.H. (1998). *Panic disorder and its treatment.* New York: Marcel Dekker.

Shear, M.K. (1997). Panic disorder with and without agoraphobia. In A. Tasman, J. Kay, & J.A. Lieberman (Eds.), *Psychiatry* (pp. 1020–1036). Philadelphia: W.B. Saunders.

Swinson, R. P., & Cox, B. J. (1996). Benzodiazepine treatment for panic disorders. In M. R. Mavissakalian & R. F. Prien (Eds.), *Long-term treatments of anxiety disorders* (pp. 221–240). Washington, DC: American Psychiatric Press.

Practical Treatment Manuals for Clinicians

Barlow, D.H., & Cerny, J.A. (1988). *Psychological treatment of panic.* New York: Guilford Press.

Bouman, T.K., & Emmelkamp, P.M.G. (1996). Panic disorder and agoraphobia. In V.B. Van Hasselt & M. Hersen (Eds.), *Sourcebook of psychological treatment manuals for adult disorders* (pp. 23–63). New York: Plenum Press.

Craske, M.G., & Barlow, D.H. (1993). Panic disorder and agoraphobia. In D.H. Barlow (Ed.), *Clinical handbook of psychological disorders* (2nd ed., pp. 1–47). New York: Guilford Press.

Craske, M.G., Barlow, D. H., & Meadows, E.A. (2000). *Mastery of your anxiety and panic, third edition (MAP-3). Therapist guide.* San Antonio TX: Psychological Corporation.

Otto, M.W., Jones, J.C., Craske, M.G., & Barlow, D.H. (1996). *Stopping anxiety medication: Panic control therapy for benzodiazepine discontinuation* (therapist guide). San Antonio, TX: Psychological Corporation.

Zuercher-White, E. (1997). *Treating panic disorder and agoraphobia: A step by step clinical guide.* Oakland, CA: New Harbinger.

Zuercher-White, E. (1999). *Overcoming panic disorder and agoraphobia* (therapist protocol). Oakland, CA: New Harbinger.

Video Resources

Clark, D.M. (1998). *Cognitive therapy for panic disorder* (video tape). APA Psychotherapy Videotape Series. Washington, DC: American Psychological Association.

Rapee, R.M. (1999). Fight or flight? Overcoming panic and agoraphobia (video tape). New York: Guilford Publications.

SOCIAL PHOBIA

Antony, M.M. (1997). Assessment and treatment of social phobia. *Canadian Journal of Psychiatry, 42,* 826–834.

Antony, M.M., & Barlow, D.H. (1997). Social and specific phobias. In A. Tasman, J. Kay, & J.A. Lieberman (Eds.), *Psychiatry* (pp. 1037–1059). Philadelphia: W.B. Saunders.

Beidel, D.C., & Turner, S.M. (1998). *Shy children, phobic adults: Nature and treatment of social phobia.* Washington, DC: American Psychological Association.

Chambless, D.L., & Hope, D.A. (1996). Cognitive approaches to the psychopathology and treatment of social phobia. In P.M. Salkovskis (Ed.), *Frontiers of cognitive therapy* (pp. 345–382). New York: Guilford Press.

Clark, D.M. (1997). Panic disorder and social phobia. In D.M. Clark & C.G. Fairburn (Eds.), *Science and practice of cognitive behaviour therapy* (pp. 119-153). New York: Oxford University Press.

Heimberg, R.G., Liebowitz, M.R., Hope, D.A., & Schneier, F.R. (Eds.). (1995). *Social phobia: Diagnosis, assessment, and treatment.* New York: Guilford Press.

Schmidt, L.A., & Schulkin, J. (Eds.). (1999). *Extreme fear, shyness and social phobia: Origins, biological mechanisms, and clinical outcomes.* New York: Oxford University Press.

Stein, M.B. (Ed.). (1995). *Social phobia: Clinical and research perspectives.* Washington, DC: American Psychiatric Press.

Turner, S.M., Cooley-Quille, M.R., & Beidel, D.C. (1996). Behavioral and pharmacological treatment for social phobia. In M.R. Mavissakalian & R.F. Prien (Eds.), *Long-term treatments of anxiety disorders* (pp. 343–372). Washington, DC: American Psychiatric Press.

Practical Treatment Manuals for Clinicians

Hope, D.A., & Heimberg, R.G. (1993). Social phobia and social anxiety. In D.H. Barlow (Ed.), *Clinical handbook of psychological disorders* (2nd ed., pp. 99–136). New York: Guilford Press.

Rapee, R.M., & Sanderson, W.C. (1998). *Social phobia: Clinical application of evidence-based psychotherapy.* Northvale, NJ: Jason Aronson.

Scholing, A., Emmelkamp, P.M.G., & Van Oppen, P. (1996). Cognitive–behavioral treatment of social phobia. In V.B. Van Hasselt & M. Hersen (Eds.), *Sourcebook of psychological treatment manuals for adult disorders* (pp. 123–177). New York: Plenum Press.

Video Resources

Rapee, R.M. (1999). *I think they think . . . Overcoming social phobia* (videotape). New York: Guilford Press.

SPECIFIC PHOBIA

Antony, M.M., & Barlow, D.H. (1997). Social and specific phobias. In A. Tasman, J. Kay, & J.A. Lieberman (Eds.), *Psychiatry* (pp. 1037–1059). Philadelphia: W.B. Saunders.

Davey, G.C.L. (1997). *Phobias: A handbook of theory, research and treatment.* New York: Wiley.

Öst, L. -G. (1996). Long term effects of behavior therapy for specific phobia. In M. R. Mavissakalian & R. F. Prien (Eds.), *Long-term treatments of the anxiety disorders* (pp. 121–170). Washington, DC: American Psychiatric Press.

Practical Treatment Manuals for Clinicians

Antony, M. M., & Barlow, D. H. (1998). Specific phobia. In V. E. Caballo (Ed.), *Handbook of cognitive behavioural treatments for psychological disorders* (pp. 1–22). Oxford, UK: Pergamon Press.

Bourne, E.J. (1998). *Overcoming specific phobia: A hierarchy and exposure-based protocol for the treatment of all specific phobias* (therapist protocol). Oakland, CA: New Harbinger.

Bruce, T.J., & Sanderson, W.C. (1998). *Specific phobias: Clinical applications of evidence-based psychotherapy.* Northvale, NJ: Jason Aronson.

Craske, M.G., Antony, M.M., & Barlow, D.H. (1997). *Mastery of your specific phobia: Therapist guide.* San Antonio, TX: Psychological Corporation.

ANXIETY DISORDERS AND COGNITIVE BEHAVIOR THERAPY (GENERAL)

Andrews, G., Crino, R., Hunt, C., Lampe, L., & Page, A. (1994). *The treatment of anxiety disorders: Clinician's guide and patient manuals.* New York: Cambridge University Press.

Barlow, D.H. (1988). *Anxiety and its disorders: The nature and treatment of anxiety and panic.* New York: Guilford Press.

Barlow, D.H. (Ed.). (1993). *Clinical handbook of psychological disorders* (2nd ed.). New York: Guilford Press.

Barlow, D.H., Esler, J.L., & Vitali, A.E. (1998). Psychosocial treatments for panic disorders, phobias, and generalized anxiety disorder. In P.E. Nathan & J.M. Gorman (Eds.), *A guide to treatments that work* (pp. 288–318). New York: Oxford University Press.

Beck, A.T., & Emery, G. (1985). *Anxiety disorders and phobias: A cognitive perspective.* New York: Basic Books.

Beck, A.T., Wright, F.D., Newman, C.F., & Liese, B.S. (1993). *Cognitive therapy with inpatients.* New York: Guilford Press.

Beck, J.S. (1995). *Cognitive therapy: Basics and beyond.* New York: Guilford Press.

Clark, D.M., & Fairburn, C.G. (Eds.). (1997). *Science and practice of cognitive behaviour therapy.* New York: Oxford University Press.

Craig, K.D., & Dobson, K.S. (Eds.). (1995). *Anxiety and depression in adults and children.* Thousand Oaks, CA: Sage Publications.

Craske, M.G. (1999). *Anxiety disorders: Psychological approaches to theory and treatment.* Boulder, CO: Westview Press.

Hawton, K., Salkovskis, P.M., Kirk, J., & Clark, D.M. (1989). *Cognitive behaviour therapy for psychiatric problems: A practical guide.* New York: Oxford University Press.

Leahy, R. (Ed.). (1997). *Practicing cognitive therapy: A guide to interventions.* Northvale, NJ: Jason Aronson.

Mavissakalian, M.R., & Prien, R.F. (Eds.). (1996). *Long-term treatments of anxiety disorders*. Washington, DC: American Psychiatric Press.

Persons, J.B. (1990). *Cognitive therapy in practice: A case formulation approach*. New York: Norton.

Rapee, R.M. (Ed.). (1996). *Current controversies in the anxiety disorders*. New York: Guilford Press.

Roth, W.T. (1997). *Treating anxiety disorders*. San Francisco, CA: Jossey-Bass.

Roy-Byrne, P.P., & Cowley, D.S. (1998). Pharmacological treatment of panic, generalized anxiety, and phobic disorders. In P.E. Nathan & J.M. Gorman (Eds.), *A guide to treatments that work* (pp. 319–338). New York: Oxford University Press.

Salkovskis, P.M. (Ed.). (1996). *Frontiers of cognitive therapy*. New York: Guilford Press.

Van Hasselt, V.B., & Hersen, M. (Eds.). (1996). *Sourcebook of psychological treatment manuals for adult disorders*. New York: Plenum Press.

Wells, A. (1997). *Cognitive therapy of anxiety disorders: A practice manual and conceptual guide*. New York: Wiley.

APPENDIX C
RECOMMENDED READINGS FOR CONSUMERS

PANIC DISORDER AND AGORAPHOBIA

Craske, M.G., & Barlow, D.H. (2000). *Mastery of your anxiety and panic, third edition (MAP-3): Client workbook.* San Antonio, TX: Psychological Corporation.

Craske, M.G., & Barlow, D.H. (2000). *Mastery of your anxiety and panic, third edition (MAP-3): Client workbook for agoraphobia.* San Antonio, TX: Psychological Corporation.

Otto, M.W., Pollack, M.H., & Barlow, D.H. (1996). *Stopping anxiety medication: Panic control therapy for benzodiazepine discontinuation: Client workbook.* San Antonio, TX: Psychological Corporation.

Rachman, S., & de Silva, P. (1996). *Panic disorder: The facts.* New York: Oxford University Press.

Wilson, R.R. (1996). *Don't panic: Taking control of anxiety attacks* (rev. ed.). New York: Harper Perennial.

Zuercher-White, E. (1997). *An end to panic: Breakthrough techniques for overcoming panic disorder* (2nd ed.). Oakland, CA: New Harbinger.

Zuercher-White, E. (1999). *Overcoming panic disorder and agoraphobia: Client manual.* Oakland, CA: New Harbinger.

SPECIFIC PHOBIAS

Antony, M.M., Craske, M.G., & Barlow, D.H. (1995). *Mastery of your specific phobia: Client workbook.* San Antonio TX: Psychological Corporation.

Bourne, E.J. (1998). *Overcoming specific phobia: A hierarchy and exposure-based protocol for the treatment of all specific phobias: Client manual.* Oakland, CA: New Harbinger.

Brown, D. (1996). *Flying without fear.* Oakland, CA: New Harbinger.

Hartman, C., & Huffaker, J.S. (1995). *The fearless flyer: How to fly in comfort and without trepidation.* Portland, OR: Eighth Mountain Press.

SOCIAL PHOBIA

Antony, M.M., & Swinson, R.P. (2000). *Shyness and social anxiety workbook: Proven, step-by-step techniques for overcoming your fear.* Oakland, CA: New Harbinger.

Desberg, P. (1996). *No more butterflies: Overcoming shyness, stage fright, interview anxiety, and fear of public speaking.* Oakland, CA: New Harbinger.

Hope, D.A., Heimberg, R.G., Juster, H.R., & Turk, C.L. (2000). *Managing social anxiety.* San Antonio, TX: Psychological Corporation.

Markway, B.G., Carmin, C.N., Pollard, C.A., & Flynn, T. (1992). *Dying of embarrassment: Help for social anxiety and phobia.* Oakland, CA: New Harbinger.

Marshall, J.R. (1994). *Social phobia: From shyness to stage fright.* New York, NY: BasicBooks.

Rapee, R.M. (1998). *Overcoming shyness and social phobia: A step-by-step guide.* Northvale, NJ: Jason Aronson.

Robin, M.W., & Balter, R. (1995). *Performance anxiety.* Holbrook, MA: Adams Publishing.

Schneier, F., & Welkowitz, L. (1996). *The hidden face of shyness: Understanding and overcoming social anxiety.* New York: Avon Books.

Perfectionism

Antony, M.M., & Swinson, R.P. (1998). *When perfect isn't good enough: Strategies for coping with perfectionism.* Oakland, CA: New Harbinger.

Communication and Social Skills

Browne, J. (1997). *Dating for dummies.* Foster City, CA: IDG Books.

Davidson, J. (1997). *The complete idiot's guide to assertiveness.* New York: Alpha Books.

Dorio, M. (1997). *The complete idiot's guide to the perfect interview.* New York: Alpha Books.

Hopson, B., & Scally, M. (1993). *Assertiveness: A positive process.* San Diego, CA: Pfeiffer/Mercury Books.

Hopson, B., & Scally, M. (1993). *Communication skills to inspire confidence.* San Diego: Pfeiffer/Mercury Books.

Kennedy, J.L. (1996). *Job interviews for dummies.* Foster City, CA: IDG Books.

Krannish, C.R., & Krannish, R.L. (1998). *Interview for success: A practical guide to increasing job interviews, offers, and salaries* (7th ed.). Manassas Park, VA: Impact Publications.

Kroeger, L. (1997). *The complete idiot's guide to successful business presentations.* New York: Alpha Books.

Kushner, M. (1996). *Successful presentations for dummies.* Foster City, CA: IDG Books.

McKay, M., Davis, M., & Fanning, P. (1995). *Messages: The communications skills book* (2nd ed.). Oakland, CA: New Harbinger.

Michelli, D. (1997). *Successful assertiveness.* Haupauge, NY: Barron's Educational Series, Inc.

Pincus, M. (1999). *Interview strategies that lead to job offers.* Haupauge, NY: Barron's Educational Series.

Rozakis, L. (1996). *The complete idiot's guide to speaking in public with confidence.* New York: Alpha Books.

Tessina, T. (1998). *The unofficial guide to dating again.* New York: MacMillan.

Wilson, R.F. (1997). *Conducting better job interviews.* Haupauge, NY: Barron's Educational Series.

ANXIETY DISORDERS AND COGNITIVE BEHAVIOR THERAPY (GENERAL)

Bourne, E.J. (1995). *The anxiety and phobia workbook* (2nd ed.). Oakland, CA: New Harbinger.

Burns, D.D. (1999). *The feeling good handbook* (rev. ed.). New York: Plume.

Butler, G., & Hope, T. (1995). *Managing your mind: The mental fitness guide.* New York: Oxford University Press.

Davis, M., Eshelman, E.R., & McKay, M. (1995). *The relaxation and stress reduction workbook* (4th ed.). Oakland, CA: New Harbinger.

Greenberger, D., & Padesky, C.A. (1995). *Mind over mood: A cognitive therapy treatment manual for clients.* New York: Guilford Press.

McKay, M., Davis, M., & Fanning, P. (1997). *Thoughts and feelings: Taking control of your moods and your life* (2nd ed.). Oakland, CA: New Harbinger.

APPENDIX D
NATIONAL AND INTERNATIONAL ORGANIZATIONS, INTERNET RESOURCES, STATISTICAL INFORMATION, AND OTHER TREATMENT RESOURCES[1]

This appendix contains resources for clinicians and professionals, including the following:

- Information on national and international organizations with an interest in phobic disorders and their treatment
- Internet and World Wide Web sites with information on phobic disorders
- Statistics that can be used for the treatment of specific phobias, including safety statistics regarding driving, thunderstorms, flying, and drowning
- Information on programs that treat fear of flying
- Contact information for a company that sells live spiders and insects (Carolina Biological Supply Company)
- Popular movies that depict scenes of blood, surgery, animals, vomiting, and heights (for the exposure-based treatment of specific phobias)

---

[1]Compiled by Karen Rowa and Martin M. Antony

Note that contact information (especially web site addresses) changes frequently. The information in this appendix was up-to-date at the time that it was written.

NATIONAL ORGANIZATIONS: NORTH AMERICA

Agoraphobic Foundation of Canada
PO Box 132
Chomeday
Laval, Quebec
Canada H7W 4K2

phone: 450-688-4726

American Psychiatric Association
Division of Public Affairs
Attention: Marcia Bennett
Dept. NASD, 1400 K St. NW
Washington, DC 20005

phone: 202-682-6000
email: mbennett@psych.org

- Referrals for psychiatrists

American Psychological Association
Office of Public Affairs
750 First St., NE
Washington, DC 20002-4242

phone: 202-336-5700; 800-964-2000 (referral line)
email: public.affairs@apa.org
web: www.apa.org

- Listings of state or provincial psychological associations that can provide psychologist referrals

Anxiety Disorders Association of America
11900 Parklawn Dr., Suite 100
Rockville, MD 20852

phone: 301-231-9350
fax: 301-231-7392
email: anxdis@aol.com
web: www.adaa.org

- Newsletter
- Information on support groups in the United States, Canada, South Africa, and Australia

- Names of professionals who treat anxiety disorders in the United States, Canada, and elsewhere
- Book catalog

Association for the Advancement of Behavior Therapy (AABT)
305 Seventh Ave.–16th Floor
New York, NY 10001-6008

phone: 212-647-1890 or 1-800-685-AABT
fax: 212-647-1865
email: mailback@aabt.org (under subject header insert "menu")
web: www.aabt.org/aabt

- Names of professionals who treat anxiety disorders
- Information and brochures on specific phobias and social phobia

ENcourage Connection
ENcourage Newsletter
13610 North Scottsdale Rd.
Suite 10-126
Scottsdale, AZ 85254

web: www.encourageconnection.com

- Newsletter on anxiety, panic, and agoraphobia
- Resources and information

Freedom From Fear
308 Seaview Ave.
Staten Island, NY 10305

phone: 718-351-1717
fax: 718-667-8893
email: fffnadsd@aol.com

- Information
- Newsletter
- Information on support groups

National Anxiety Foundation
3135 Custer Dr.
Lexington, KY 40517-4001

phone: 606-272-7166
web: www.lexington-on-line.com

- Information packages
- Names of professionals who treat anxiety disorders in the United States, Africa, China, and France

Australia

Anxiety Disorders Foundation
PO Box 492
Fullerton, South Australia 5063

phone: 08-8373-2258
fax: 08-8373-2090

- Information
- Support services

Anxiety Disorders Foundation of Australia (NSW Branch)
PO Box 6198
Shopping World
North Sydney, New South Wales 2060
Australia

phone: 016-282-897
fax: 02-9716 0416
email: adfa@crufad.unsw.edu.au
web: www.ocs.mq.edu.au/~abaillie/adfa.html

- Information
- Newsletter
- Names of anxiety disorder clinics and individual therapists who specialize in anxiety in Australia

New South Wales Association for Mental Health
  (General Mental Health Services)
60–62 Victoria Rd.
Gladesville, New South Wales 2111
Australia

- NSW Mental Health Information Services
  phone: 02-9816-5688 or 1800-674-200 (local toll-free)
  fax: 02-9816-4056
  email: nswamh@gpo.com.au
- Mental Health Information for Rural and Remote Australia
  phone: 02-9879-5341 or 1300-785-005 (local toll-free)
  fax: 02-9816-4056
  email: mhirra@gpo.com.au
- Information services
- Referrals to treatment or support services
- Resource centre with lending services for association members

Panic and Anxiety Disorders Foundation of Western Australia (PADWA)
PO Box 130
Nedlands, Western Australia 6909

- Information
- Support services

Belgium

Fobex

phone: 089-30-65-19
email: fobex@hotmail.com
web: http://gallery.uunet.be/FOBEX/index.htm

- Treatment services for anxiety disorders

France

Association Francaise de Therapie Comportementale et Cognitive
100 rue de la Sante
75674 Paris Cedex, France

phone: 01-45-88-35-28
fax: 01-45-89-55-66

- Referrals for cognitive-behavioral therapists

Association Francophone de Formation et de Recherche en Therapie Comportementale et Cognitive (AFFORTHECC)
10 Ave. Gantin
74150 Rumilly, France

phone: 04-50-01-49-80
fax: 04-50-64-58-46
email: afforthecc@aol.com

- Referrals for cognitive-behavioral therapists

South Africa

The South African Depression and Anxiety Disorders Support Group
PO Box 650301
Benmore, 2010, South Africa

phone: 27-11-884-1797; 0800-11-83-92 or 0800-11-92-83 (help line)
fax: 27-1-884-0625
email: anxiety@iafrica.com
web: www.anxiety.org.za

- Referrals for support groups
- Names of medical professionals who specialize in anxiety disorders

- Newsletter
- Anxiety book list

Spain

Asociación Espanola de Terapia Cognitivo Conductual Social
Apartado de Correos 8221
28080 Madrid, Spain

phone: +34-91-5411672 (also fax)

Asociación Psicologica Iberoamericana de Clinica y Salud (APICSA)
Apartado de Correos 1245
18080 Granada
Spain

phone: +34-902-117486 (also fax)
email: apicsa@ibm.net

Sociedad para el Estudio de la Ansiedad y el Estres (SEAS)
Facultad de Psicologia, Buzón 23
Universidad Complutense de Madrid
Campus de Somosaguas
28223 Madrid, Spain

email: seas@psi.ucm.es

United Kingdom

British Psychological Society
St. Andrews House
48 Princess Rd. East
Leicester LE1 7DR, United Kingdom

phone: 0116-254-9658
email: enquiry@bps.org.uk
web: www.bps.org.uk

- The web page contains a list of chartered psychologists and their specialty areas

No Panic
93 Brands Farm Way
Randlay, Telford, Shropshire
TF3 2JQ
United Kingdom

phone: 0-19-52-59-00-05; 0-19-52-59-05-45 (help line)
fax: 0-19-52-27-09-62
web: www.iop.bpmf.ac.uk/home/depts/psychiat/nursing/nopanic.htm

- Agoraphobia Resource Page: www.cstone.net/users/maybell/agora.htm
- Anxieties.com: www.anxieties.com/home.htm
- Anxiety and Panic Book Store: www.wellnessbooks.com/anxiety
- Anxiety and Panic Internet Resource: www.algy.com/anxiety/index.shtml
- *Anxiety Disorders and Their Treatment: A Critical Review of the Evidence-Based Literature*, by M.M. Antony and R.P. Swinson (Health Canada, 1996): www.hc-sc.gc.ca/hppb/mentalhealth/pdfs/anxiety_review.pdf
- Anxiety Disorders Association of America: www.adaa.org
- Anxiety Disorders Cyberpsych Penpals: www.cyberpsych.org/cgi-bin/penpals.pl
- Anxiety Network International: www.anxietynetwork.com
- Anxiety Relief Center (Bristol-Myers Squibb): www.anxiety-relief.com
- Anxiety-Panic.com (internet links): anxiety-panic.com/default.cfm
- Canadian Network for Mood and Anxiety Treatments (CANMAT): www.canmat.org
- CBT website: www.cognitivetherapy.com
- DIRECT–Anxiety Information Centre: www.fhs.mcmaster.ca/direct/anxiety/anxiety.html
- Doctors Guide to Anxiety Disorders Information and Resources: www.pslgroup.com/anxiety.htm
- Fear of Flying: www.anxieties.com/7Flying/summary.htm
- Fear of Flying: www1.nb.sympatico.ca/healthyway/HEALTHYWAY/feature_fly1.html
- Internet Mental Health: www.mentalhealth.com
- National Anxiety Foundation: www.lexington-on-line.com/naf.html
- NIMH Anxiety Disorders Education Program: www.nimh.nih.gov/anxiety
- Paxil Anxiety Disorders Page: www.panicattack.com
- Shyness Home Page: www.shyness.com
- Social Anxiety Network: www.social-anxiety-network.com
- Social Phobia / Social Anxiety Association: www.socialphobia.org
- Spider Homepage (excellent exposure materials for people with spider phobias): www.powerup.com.au/~glen/spideri.htm

alt.support.anxiety-panic
alt.support.shyness
alt.support.social-phobia

STATISTICS TO BE USED
DURING PSYCHOEDUCATION
IN TREATMENT OF SPECIFIC PHOBIAS

Phobias of Driving: American Statistics

- In 1996 there were 41,907 fatalities in the United States caused by motor vehicle accidents. (Source: U.S. Department of Transportation)
- Using an estimate of the United States' population of 272 million, the percentage of the population that had fatal car accidents in 1996 was 0.0154% or 1.54 per 10,000.
- 41% of the people killed in car accidents died in alcohol-related crashes.
- fewer than 1% of total crashes resulted in death.
- 56% of fatal crashes involved one vehicle.

Phobias of Driving: Canadian Statistics

- In 1997 there were 3,064 fatalities in Canada caused by motor vehicle accidents. (Source: Transport Canada)
- Using an estimate of Canada's population as 30 million, the percentage of the population that had fatal car accidents in 1997 was 0.0102% or 1 in 10,000.
- In Ontario, the fatality rate was 1.4 per 100,000 vehicles in 1997.
- In 1994 there were 3,260 fatalities in Canada caused by motor vehicle accidents. (Source: Office of Highway Information Management, U.S. Government)
- The fatality rate was 0.66 per 100 million kilometers. This rate is lower than that in the U.S. (0.95), Mexico (9.44), U.K. (0.78), Sweden (0.88), Germany (1.69), France (1.82), and Japan (1.55).
- Using an estimate of Canada's population as 30 million, the percentage of the population that had fatal car accidents in 1994 was 0.01% or 1 in 10,000.

- In Ontario, there are 1,700 deaths annually caused by car accidents. (Source: Jack Davidson, Toronto Star, 1998)
- In Canada, the majority of accidents in 1997 occurred during clear weather and daylight. (Source: Transport Canada)
- A large minority of accidents occurred after dark.

Storm and Lightning Phobias

- The chance of being stuck by lightning in one year is 2.8 million to 1. (Source: STATS and National Center for Health Statistics, 1990)
- Factors that affect this statistic: geography (probability in U.S. is higher than in South Africa and Singapore and lower in U.K.), climate (tropical climates with frequent thunderstorms have a higher probability), activities (golfers have a higher probability).
- States with the highest number of fatalities caused by lightning (in descending order): Florida, Michigan, Texas, New York, Tennessee. (Source: National Lightning Safety Institute)
- Four or more people are injured nonfatally for every fatality. (Source: STATS and British Medical Journal)
- The chance of being fatally struck by lightning is 1 in 1.9 million. (Source: National History Museum of Los Angeles County, Massachusetts Institute of Technology, University of California at Berkeley)
- Locations of fatalities caused by lightning over 35 years. (Source: National Lightning Safety Institute):
  - 27% open fields and recreation areas (not golf)
  - 14% under trees (not golf)
  - 8% water related (boating, fishing, swimming)
  - 5% golf
  - 3% heavy-machinery related
  - 2.4% telephone related
  - 0.7% radio, transmitter, and antenna related
- 2,000 thunderstorms are in progress at any given moment. (Source: OMNI magazine)
- There is a flash of lightning every 20 seconds in a typical thunderstorm. (Source: OMNI magazine)

Air Travel Phobias

- Odds of dying in plane crash are 1 in 500,000 (based on flying 100,000 miles per year in a commercial jet). (Source: STATS)

- Odds of dying in a commercial airline are 1 in 10 million. (Source: National History Museum of Los Angeles County, Massachusetts Institute of Technology, University of California at Berkeley)
- Odds of being killed by a plane on the ground are 1 in 25,000,000. (Source: STATS)
- There are 66,000 successful commercial flights every day in Canada and the United States. (Source: Jack Davidson, *Toronto Star*, 1998)
- Over 200,000 aircraft take off and land every day in the U.S. (Source: *New York Times*, 1998)
- Each year in the 1990s has seen approximately 25 million takeoffs and landings of commercial airlines in the U.S. (Source: *New York Times*, 1998)
- Aircraft accidents receive 8100% more media coverage than do the same number of deaths caused by cancer, heart disease, guns, or cars. (Source: Jack Davidson, *Toronto Star*, 1998)
- In 1997 there were 2,001 aviation accidents and 375 fatalities in the United States. (Source: National Airspace System)
- The majority of accidents were caused by pilot deviations.
- Fatal accident rate is 0.87 per 100,000 flight hours.
- In the United States in 1991 the total accident rate was 5.31 per 100,000 flight hours, and the fatal accident rate was 1.09 per 100,000 flight hours. (Source: National Transportation Safety Board)
- For large air carriers, the total accident rate was 0.22 per 100,000 flight hours and the fatal accident rate was 0.03 per 100,000 flight hours.
- In the United States in 1996, the percentage of transportation fatalities caused by any type of aviation travel was 1.4%. (Source: U.S. Department of Transportation)
- For air carriers, the percentage was 0.9%.

Drowning Phobias

- In Canada in 1994, 729 people died as a result of drowning, suffocation, or choking. (Source: Reform Party website: www.reform.ca/garrypress/morttab.html)
- In the United States in 1996, 4,631 people died as a result of drowning or submersion. (Source: Center for Disease Control and Prevention website: www.cdc.gov/ncipc/osp/mortdata.htm)

PROGRAMS TO OVERCOME FEAR OF FLYING

Avserve Canada–Fear of Flying Treatment
  (offered in association with Air Canada)
5014 New St., Suite 130
Burlington, Ontario L7L 6E8
Canada

phone: 905-639-4343
information lines: Toronto: 416-323-5520
                  Vancouver: 604-643-5622
                  Montreal: 514-422-4499

- 5-week course conducted by a psychologist and pilot. Course includes relaxation training, information and education on airplanes and flying, use of flight simulators and parked aircraft, and a round-trip graduation flight.

Fear of Flying Clinic (Seattle)
15127 N.E. 24th, Suite 211
Redmond, WA 98052-5547

phone: 206-772-1122
email: fofc@scn.com
web: www.scn.org/health/fofc

- seminars offered in the fall and spring
- seminars run over 2 weekends with optional graduation flight
- clients work with female pilots and a behavioral counselor

Flight to Freedom (associated with American Airlines)
2407 Crockett Court
Grapevine, TX 76051

phone: 817-424-5108
fax: 817-421-7361
email: F2Freedom@aol.com
web: www.fearofflying.net

- weekend seminars in Dallas/Fort Worth area providing relaxation and coping skills, information about flying, use of parked aircraft, graduation flight
- audiocassette program

Freedom From Fear of Flying
Capt. T.W. Cummings, Director
2021 Country Club Prado
Coral Gables, FL 33134

phone: 305-261-7042

- audiocassettes (one that simulates a flight) and information booklets are available
- 3-day seminars offered around the U.S. with an optional graduation flight
- seminars include information about flying, the fear cycle, deep-breathing exercises, and aircraft tours

USAir Fearful Flyer Program
PO Box 15410
Pittsburgh, PA 15237

phone: 412-366-8112

- 2-day course with a therapist and USAir captain
- graduation flight
- program runs out of Rochester, Baltimore, Philadelphia, Pittsburgh, and one alternating location

Wings—Freedom to Fly (associated with Northwest/KLM)
2600 Lone Oak Point
Eagan, MN 55121

phone: 612-726-7733
fax: 612-726-6132
email: wings@natco.com
web: www.nwa.com/services/bustrav/wings.shtml

- weekend course providing techniques to manage fears, information about flying, and graduation flight
- program runs out of Detroit, Minneapolis, and Memphis

PURCHASING LIVE SPIDERS AND INSECTS

Carolina Biological Supply Company
2700 York Rd.
Burlington, NC 27215-3398

phone: 910-584-0381
fax: 910-584-3399

VIDEOS, MOVIES, AND TELEVISION PROGRAMS THAT MAY BE USED FOR SPECIFIC-PHOBIA EXPOSURE

Blood, Injection, and Surgery Phobias

- *The Operation Show* (The Learning Channel)
- *Trauma: Life in the ER* (The Learning Channel)
- *Philadelphia*
- *The Doctor*
- *Rush*
- *Trainspotting*
- *Drugstore Cowboy*

Animal Phobias

- *Raiders of the Lost Ark* (snakes)
- *Arachnophobia* (spiders)
- *101 Dalmations* (live-action version) (dogs)
- *Beethoven* (dogs)
- *Microcosmos* (insects)
- *The Lost Boys* (maggots/bugs)

Vomit Phobias

- *Stand by Me*
- *Monty Python's The Meaning of Life*
- *The Exorcist*
- *Dying Young*
- *City of Angels*
- *He Got Game*
- *Fear and Loathing in Las Vegas*

Height Phobias

- *Cliffhanger*
- *True Lies*

REFERENCES

Abelson, J. L., & Curtis, G. C. (1989). Cardiac and neuroendocrine responses to exposure therapy in height phobics: Desynchrony within the "physiological response system." *Behaviour Research and Therapy, 27,* 561–567.

Abene, M. V., & Hamilton, J. D. (1998). Resolution of fear of flying with fluoxetine treatment. *Journal of Anxiety Disorders, 12,* 599–603.

Acierno, R. E., Hersen, M., & van Hasselt, V. B. (1993). Interventions for panic disorder: A critical review of the literature. *Clinical Psychology Review, 13,* 561–578.

Adler, C. M., Craske, M. G., & Barlow, D. H. (1987). Relaxation-induced panic (RIP): When resting isn't peaceful. *Integrative Psychiatry, 5,* 94–112.

Akutagawa, D. (1956). *A study in construct validity of the psychoanalytic concept of latent anxiety and test of a projection distance hypothesis.* Unpublished doctoral dissertation, University of Pittsburgh.

Albano, A. M., DiBartolo, P. M., Heimberg, R. G., & Barlow, D. H. (1995). Children and adolescents: Assessment and treatment. In R. G. Heimberg, M. R. Liebowitz, D. A. Hope, & F. R. Schneier (Eds.), *Social phobia: Diagnosis, assessment, and treatment* (pp. 387–425). New York: Guilford Press.

Alden, L. E., & Wallace, S. T. (1995). Social phobia and social appraisal in successful and unsuccessful social interactions. *Behaviour Research and Therapy, 33,* 497–505.

Al-Kubaisy, T., Marks, I. M., Logsdail, S., Marks, M. P., Lovell, K., Sungur, M., & Araya, R. (1992). Role of exposure homework in phobia reduction: A controlled study. *Behavior Therapy, 23,* 599–621.

Allgulander, C. (1999). Paroxetine in social anxiety disorder: A randomized placebo-controlled study. *Acta Psychiatrica Scandinavica, 100,* 193–198.

Altamura, A. C., Pioli, R., Vitto, M., & Mannu, P. (1999). Venlafaxine in social phobia: A study in selective serotonin reuptake inhibitor non-responders. *International Clinical Psychopharmacology, 14,* 239–245.

American Psychiatric Association. (1980). *Diagnostic and statistical manual of mental disorders* (3rd ed.). Washington, DC: Author.

American Psychiatric Association. (1987). *Diagnostic and statistical manual of mental disorders* (3rd ed., rev.). Washington, DC: Author.

American Psychiatric Association (1991). DSM-IV options book: Work in progress. Washington, DC: Author.

American Psychiatric Association. (1994). *Diagnostic and statistical manual of mental disorders* (4th ed.). Washington, DC: Author.

American Psychiatric Association. (1998). Practice guidelines for the treatment of patients with panic disorder. *American Journal of Psychiatry, 155*(Suppl.), 1–34.

Amering, M., Bankier, B., Berger, P., Griengl, H., Windhaber, J., & Katschnig, H. (1999). Panic disorder and cigarette smoking behavior. *Comprehensive Psychiatry, 40,* 35–38.

Amering, M., Katschnig, H., Berger, P., Windhaber, J., Baischer, W., & Dantendorfer, K. (1997). Embarrassment about the first panic attack predicts agoraphobia in panic disorder patients. *Behaviour Research and Therapy, 35,* 517–521.

Amir, N., Coles, M. E., Rutigliano, P., & Foa, E. B. (1997, November). *Implicit and explicit memory bias in social phobia.* Paper presented at the meeting of the Association for Advancement of Behavior Therapy, Miami, FL.

Amir, N., McNally, R. J., Riemann, B. C., Burns, J., Lorenz, M., & Mullen, J. T. (1996). Suppression of the emotional stroop effect by increased anxiety in patients with social phobia. *Behaviour Research and Therapy, 34,* 945–948.

Amir, N., McNally, R. J., Riemann, B. C., & Clements, C. (1996). Implicit memory bias for threat in panic disorder: Application of the "white noise" paradigm. *Behaviour Research and Therapy, 34,* 157–162.

Andrews, G., Stewart, G., Allen, R., & Henderson, A. S. (1990). The genetics of six neurotic disorders: A twin study. *Journal of Affective Disorders, 19,* 23–29.

Antony, M. M. (1997). Assessment and treatment of social phobia. *Canadian Journal of Psychiatry, 42,* 826–834.

Antony, M. M., & Barlow, D. H. (1996). Emotion theory as a framework for explaining panic attacks and panic disorder. In R. M. Rapee (Ed.), *Current controversies in the anxiety disorders* (pp. 55–76). New York: Guilford Press.

Antony, M. M., & Barlow, D. H. (1997). Social and specific phobias. In A. Tasman, J. Kay, & J. A. Lieberman (Eds.), *Psychiatry* (pp. 1037–1059). Philadelphia: W. B. Saunders.

Antony, M. M., & Barlow, D. H. (1998). Specific phobia. In V. E. Caballo (Ed.), *Handbook of cognitive behavioural treatments for psychological disorders* (pp. 1–22). Oxford, UK: Pergamon Press.

Antony, M. M., Bieling, P. J., Cox, B. J., Enns, M. W., & Swinson, R. P. (1998). Psychometric properties of the 42-item and 21-item versions of the Depression Anxiety Stress Scales (DASS) in clinical groups and a community sample. *Psychological Assessment, 10,* 176–181.

Antony, M. M., Brown, T. A., & Barlow, D. H. (1997a). Heterogeneity among specific phobia types in DSM-IV. *Behaviour Research and Therapy, 35,* 1089–1100.

Antony, M. M., Brown, T. A., & Barlow, D. H. (1997b). Response to hyperventilation and 5.5% CO_2 inhalation of subjects with types of specific phobia, panic disorder, or no mental disorder. *American Journal of Psychiatry, 154,* 1089–1095.

Antony, M. M., Brown, T. A., Craske, M. G., Barlow, D. H., Mitchell, W. B., & Meadows, E. A. (1995). Accuracy of heart beat estimation in panic disorder, social phobic and non-anxious controls. *Journal of Anxiety Disorders, 9,* 355–371.

Antony, M. M., Craske, M. G., & Barlow, D. H. (1995). *Mastery of your specific phobia: Client manual.* San Antonio, TX: Psychological Corporation.

Antony, M. M., Downie, F., & Swinson, R. P. (1998). Diagnostic issues and epidemiology in obsessive compulsive disorder. In R. P. Swinson, M. M. Antony, S. Rachman, & M. A. Richter (Eds.), *Obsessive-compulsive disorder: Theory, research, and treatment* (pp. 3–32). New York: Guilford Press.

Antony, M. M., Leeuw, I., Ing, N., & Swinson, R. P. (1998, November). *Effect of distraction and coping style on in vivo exposure treatment for specific phobia of spiders.* Paper presented at the meeting of the Association for Advancement of Behavior Therapy, Washington, DC.

Antony, M. M., Meadows, E. A., Brown, T. A., & Barlow, D. H. (1994). Cardiac awareness before and after cognitive–behavioral treatment for panic disorder. *Journal of Anxiety Disorders, 8,* 341–350.

Antony, M. M., Moras, K., Meadows, E. A., Di Nardo, P. A., Utech, J. E., & Barlow, D. H. (1994). The diagnostic significance of the functional impairment and subjective distress criterion: An illustration with the DSM-III-R anxiety disorders. *Journal of Psychopathology and Behavioral Assessment, 16,* 253–263.

Antony, M. M., Orsillo, S. M., & Roemer, L. (Eds.) (in press) *Practitioner's guide to empirically-based measures of anxiety.* New York: Kluwer Academic/Plenum.

Antony, M. M., Purdon, C. L., Huta, V., & Swinson, R. P. (1998). Dimensions of perfectionism across the anxiety disorders. *Behaviour Research and Therapy, 36,* 1143–1154.

Antony, M. M., Roth, D., Swinson, R. P., Huta, V., & Devins, G. M. (1998). Illness intrusiveness in individuals with panic disorder, obsessive compulsive disorder, or social phobia. *Journal of Nervous and Mental Disease, 186,* 311–315.

Antony, M. M., & Swinson, R. P. (1996). *Anxiety disorders and their treatment: A critical review of the evidence-based literature.* Ottawa, Ontario: Health Canada.

Antony, M. M., & Swinson, R. P. (1998). *When perfect isn't good enough: Strategies for coping with perfectionism.* Oakland, CA: New Harbinger.

Antony, M. M., & Swinson, R. P. (1999). *Panic Frequency Questionnaire.* Unpublished scale. St. Joseph's Hospital, Hamilton, Ontario, Canada.

Antony, M. M., & Swinson, R. P. (2000a). [Comorbid conditions in anxiety disorders]. Unpublished data, St. Joseph's Hospital, Hamilton, Ontario, Canada.

Antony, M. M., & Swinson, R. P. (2000b). *Shyness and social anxiety workbook: Proven, step-by-step techniques for overcoming your fear.* Oakland, CA: New Harbinger.

Apfeldorf, W. J., Shear, M. K., Leon, A. C., & Portera, L. (1994). A brief screen for panic disorder. *Journal of Anxiety Disorders, 8,* 71–78.

Arntz, A. (1993). Endorphins stimulate approach behaviour, but do not reduce subjective fear: A pilot study. *Behaviour Research and Therapy, 31,* 403–405.

Arntz, A., Lavy, E., van den Berg, G., & van Rijsoort, S. (1993). Negative beliefs of spider phobics: A psychometric evaluation of the Spider Phobia Beliefs Questionnaire. *Advances in Behaviour Research and Therapy, 15,* 257–277.

Arntz, A., & van den Hout, M. (1996). Psychological treatment of panic disorder without agoraphobia: Cognitive therapy versus applied relaxation. *Behaviour Research and Therapy, 34,* 113–121.

Arrindell, W. A. (1980). Dimensional structure and psychopathology correlates of the Fear Survey Schedule (FSS-III) in a phobic population: A factorial definition of agoraphobia. *Behaviour Research and Therapy, 18,* 229–242.

Arrindell, W. A. (1993). The fear of fear concept: Stability, retest artefact and predictive power. *Behaviour Research and Therapy, 31,* 139–148.

Arrindell, W. A., Cox, B. J., van der Ende, J., & Kwee, M. G. T. (1995). Phobic dimensions: II. Cross-national confirmation of the multidimensional structure underlying the Mobility Inventory (MI). *Behaviour Research and Therapy, 33,* 711–724.

Arrindell, W. A., Kolk, A. M., Pickersgill, M. J., & Hageman, W. J. J. M. (1993). Biological sex, sex role orientation, masculine sex role stress, dessimulation and self-reported fears. *Advances in Behaviour Research and Therapy, 15,* 103–146.

Arrindell, W. A., Pickersgill, M. J., Merckelbach, H., Ardon, A. M., & Cornet, F. C. (1991). Phobic dimensions: III. Factor analytic approaches to the study of common phobic fears: An updated review of findings obtained with adult subjects. *Advances in Behaviour Research and Therapy, 13,*73–130.

Asmundson, G. J. G., Sandler, L. S., Wilson, K. G., & Norton, G. R. (1993). Panic attacks and interoceptive acuity for cardiac sensations. *Behaviour Research and Therapy, 31,* 193–197.

Asmundson, G. J. G., Sandler, L. S., Wilson, K. G., & Walker, J. R. (1992). Selective attention toward physical threat in patients with panic disorder. *Journal of Anxiety Disorders, 6,* 295–303.

Asmundson, G. J. G., & Stein, M. B. (1994a). Selective processing of social threat in patients with generalized social phobia: Evaluation using a dot-probe paradigm. *Journal of Anxiety Disorders, 8,* 107–117.

Asmundson, G. J. G., & Stein, M. B. (1994b). Triggering the false suffocation alarm in panic disorder patients by using a voluntary breath-holding procedure. *American Journal of Psychiatry, 151,* 264–266.

Asmundson, G. J. G., & Stein, M. B. (1994/1995). Dot-probe evaluation of cognitive processing biases in patients with panic disorder: A failure to replicate and extend. *Anxiety, 1,* 123–128.

Baker, B. L., Cohen, D. C., & Saunders, J. T. (1973). Self-directed desensitization for acrophobia. *Behaviour Research and Therapy, 11*, 79–89.

Bakish, D., Hooper, C. L., Filteau, M. -J., Charbonneau, Y., Fraser, G., West, D. L., Thibaudeau, C., & Raine, D. (1996). A double-blind placebo-controlled trial comparing fluvoxamine and imipramine in the treatment of panic disorder with or without agoraphobia. *Psychopharmacology Bulletin, 32*, 135–141.

Bakker, A., van Balkom, A. J. L. M., Spinhoven, P., Blaauw, B. M. J. W., & van Dyck, R. (1998). Follow-up on the treatment of panic disorder with or without agoraphobia: A quantitative review. *Journal of Nervous and Mental Disease, 186*, 414–419.

Ballenger, J. C., Burrows, G. D., DuPont, R. L., Lesser, I. M., Noyes, R., Jr., Pecknold, J. C., Rifkin, A., & Swinson, R. (1988). Alprazolam in panic disorder and agoraphobia: Results from a multicenter trial. *Archives of General Psychiatry, 45*, 413–422.

Ballenger, J. C., Wheadon, D. E., Steiner, M., Bushnell, W., & Gergel, I. P. (1998). Double-blind, fixed-dose, placebo-controlled study of paroxetine in the treatment of panic disorder. *American Journal of Psychiatry, 155*, 36–42.

Bandelow, B. (1995). Assessing the efficacy of treatments for panic disorder and agoraphobia: II. The Panic and Agoraphobia Scale. *International Clinical Psychopharmacology, 10*, 73–81.

Bandelow, B. (1999). *Panic and Agoraphobia Scale (PAS) manual.* Seattle, WA: Hogrefe & Huber.

Bandelow, B., Brunner, E., Broocks, A., Beinroth, D., Hajak, G., Pralle, L., & Rüther, E. (1998). The use of the Panic and Agoraphobia Scale in a clinical trial. *Psychiatry Research, 77*, 43–49.

Bandelow, B., Hajak, G., Holzrichter, S., Kunert, H. J., & Rüther, E. (1995). Assessing the efficacy of treatments for panic disorder and agoraphobia: I. Methodological problems. *International Clinical Psychopharmacology, 10*, 83–93.

Barker, H. J., & Edelmann, R. J. (1987). Questionnaire dimension of spider phobia: A replication and extension. *Personality and Individual Differences, 8*, 737–739.

Barlow, D. H. (1988). *Anxiety and its disorders: The nature and treatment of anxiety and panic.* New York: Guilford Press.

Barlow, D. H., & Brown, T. A. (1996). Psychological treatments for panic disorder and panic disorder with agoraphobia. In M. R. Mavissakalian & R. F. Prien (Eds.), *Long-term treatments of anxiety disorders* (pp. 221–240). Washington, DC: American Psychiatric Press.

Barlow, D. H., Brown, T. A., & Craske, M. G. (1994). Definitions of panic attacks and panic disorder in DSM-IV: Implications for research. *Journal of Abnormal Psychology, 103*, 553–564.

Barlow, D. H., & Craske, M. G. (1994). *Mastery of your anxiety and panic: II. Client workbook.* San Antonio, TX: Psychological Corporation.

Barlow, D. H., Craske, M. G., Cerny, J. A., & Klosko, J. S. (1989). Behavioral treatment of panic disorder. *Behavior Therapy, 20*, 261–282.

Barlow, D.H., Gorman, J.M., Shear, M.K., & Woods, S.W. (2000). A randomized controlled trial of cognitive-behavioral treatment vs. imipramine and their combination for panic disorder: Primary outcome results. *Journal of the American Medical Association, 283,* 2529–2536.

Barlow, D. H., O'Brien, G. T., & Last, C. G. (1984). Couples treatment of agoraphobia. *Behavior Therapy, 15,* 41–58.

Barsky, A. J., Cleary, P. D., Sarnie, M. K., & Ruskin, J. N. (1994). Panic disorder, palpitations, and the awareness of cardiac activity. *Journal of Nervous and Mental Disease, 182,* 63–71.

Başoğlu, M., Marks, I. M., Kiliç, C., Brewin, C. R., & Swinson, R. P. (1994). Alprazolam and exposure for panic disorder with agoraphobia: Attribution of improvement to medication predicts subsequent relapse. *British Journal of Psychiatry, 164,* 652–659.

Bates, L. W., McGlynn, F. D., Montgomery, R. W., & Mattke, T. (1996). Effects of eye-movement desensitization versus no treatment on repeated measures of fear of spiders. *Journal of Anxiety Disorders, 6,* 555–569.

Beauclair, L., Fontaine, R., Annable, L., Holobow, N., & Chouinard, G. (1994). Clonazepam in the treatment of panic disorder: A double-blind, placebo-controlled trial investigating the correlation between clonazepam concentrations in plasma and clinical response. *Journal of Clinical Psychopharmacology, 14,* 111–118.

Bebchuk, J. M., & Tancer, M. E. (1999). Neurobiology of social phobia. *CNS Spectrums, 4*(11), 42–48.

Bech, P., & Angst, J. (1996). Quality of life and social phobia. *International Clinical Psychopharmacology, 11*(Suppl. 3), 97–100.

Beck, A. T. (1964). Thinking and depression: II. Theory and therapy. *Archives of General Psychiatry, 10,* 561–571.

Beck, A. T., Emery, G., & Greenberg, R. L. (1985). *Anxiety disorders and phobias: A cognitive perspective.* New York: Basic Books.

Beck, A. T., & Steer, R. A. (1990). *Beck Anxiety Inventory manual.* San Antonio, TX: Psychological Corporation.

Beck, A. T., Steer, R. A., & Brown, G. K. (1996). *Beck Depression Inventory: Second edition manual.* San Antonio, TX: Psychological Corporation.

Beck, J. G., & Berisford, M. A. (1992). The effects of caffeine on panic patients: Response components of anxiety. *Behavior Therapy, 23,* 405–422.

Beck, J. G., Ohtake, P. J., & Shipherd, J. C. (1999). Exaggerated anxiety is not unique to CO_2 in panic disorder: A comparison of hypercapnic and hypoxic challenges. *Journal of Abnormal Psychology, 108,* 473–482.

Beck, J. G., Stanley, M. A., Baldwin, L. E., Deagle, E. A., III, & Averill, P. (1994). Comparison of cognitive therapy and relaxation training for panic disorder. *Journal of Consulting and Clinical Psychology, 62,* 818–826.

Beck, J. G., & Zebb, B. J. (1994). Behavioral assessment and treatment of panic disorder: Current status, future directions. *Behavior Therapy, 25,* 581–611.

Beck, J. S. (1995). *Cognitive therapy: Basics and beyond.* New York: Guilford Press.

Becker, E., Rinck, M., & Margraf, J. (1994). Memory bias in panic disorder. *Journal of Abnormal Psychology, 103,* 396–399.

Beidel, D. C., Borden, J. W., Turner, S. M., & Jacob, R. G. (1989). The Social Phobia and Anxiety Inventory: Concurrent validity with a clinic sample. *Behaviour Research and Therapy, 27,* 573–576.

Beidel, D. C., Turner, S. M., & Cooley, M. R. (1993). Assessing reliable and clinically significant change in social phobia: Validity of the Social Phobia and Anxiety Inventory. *Behaviour Research and Therapy, 31,* 331–337.

Beidel, D. C., Turner, S. M., & Fink, C. M. (1996). Assessment of childhood social phobia: Construct, convergent, and discriminative validity of the Social Phobia and Anxiety Inventory for Children (SPAI-C). *Psychological Assessment, 8,* 235–240.

Beidel, D. C., Turner, S. M., & Morris, T. L. (1995). A new inventory to assess childhood social anxiety and phobia: The Social Phobia and Anxiety Inventory for Children. *Psychological Assessment, 7,* 73–79.

Beidel, D. C., Turner, S. M., Stanley, M. A., & Dancu, C. V. (1989). The Social Phobia and Anxiety Inventory: Concurrent and external validity. *Behavior Therapy, 20,* 417–427.

Beitman, B. D., Basha, I., Flaker, G., DeRosear, L., Mukerji, V., & Lamberti, J. (1987). Non-fearful panic disorder: Panic attacks without fear. *Behaviour Research and Therapy, 25,* 487–492.

Beitman, B. D., Kushner, M., Lamberti, J. W., & Mukerji, V. (1990). Panic disorder without fear in patients with angiographically normal coronary arteries. *Journal of Nervous and Mental Disease, 178,* 307–312.

Bekker, M. H. J. (1996). Agoraphobia and gender: A review. *Clinical Psychology Review, 16,* 129–146.

Bell, C. J., & Nutt, D. J. (1998). Serotonin and panic. *British Journal of Psychiatry, 172,* 465–471.

Benca, R., Matuzas, W., & Al-Sadir, J. (1986). Social phobia, MVP, and response to imipramine [letter]. *Journal of Clinical Psychopharmacology, 6,* 50–51.

Bieling, P. J., Antony, M. M., & Swinson, R. P. (1998). The State–Trait Anxiety Inventory, Trait Version: Structure and content re-examined. *Behaviour Research and Therapy, 36,* 777–788.

Binik, Y. M., Chowanec, G. D., & Devins, G. M. (1990). Marital role strain, illness intrusiveness, and their impact on marital and individual adjustment in end-stage renal disease. *Psychology and Health, 4,* 245–257.

Bisaga, A., Katz, J. L., Antonini, A., Wright, E., Margouleff, C., Gorman, J. M., & Eidelberg, D. (1998). Cerebral glucose metabolism in women with panic disorder. *American Journal of Psychiatry, 155,* 1178–1183.

Black, D. W., Wesner, R., Bowers, W., & Gabel, J. (1993). A comparison of fluvoxamine, cognitive therapy, and placebo in the treatment of panic disorder. *Archives of General Psychiatry, 50,* 44–50.

Blanchard, J. J., & Brown, S. B. (1998). Structured diagnostic interview schedules. In C. R. Reynolds (Ed.), *Comprehensive clinical psychology: Vol. 3. Assessment* (pp. 97–130). New York: Elsevier Science.

Bland, K., & Hallam, R. S. (1981). Relationship between response to graded exposure and marital satisfaction in agoraphobics. *Behaviour Research and Therapy, 19,* 335–338.

Bland, R. C., Orn, H., & Newman, S. C. (1988). Lifetime prevalence of psychiatric disorders in Edmonton. *Acta Psychiatrica Scandinavica, 77*(Suppl. 338), 24–32.

Boone, M. L., McNeil, D. W., Masia, C. L., Turk, C. L., Carter, L. E., Ries, B. J., & Lewin, M. R. (1999). Multimodal comparisons of social phobia subtypes and avoidant personality disorder. *Journal of Anxiety Disorders, 13,* 271–292.

Booth, R., & Rachman, S. (1992). The reduction of claustrophobia: I. *Behaviour Research and Therapy, 30,* 207–221.

Botella, C., & García-Palacios, A. (1999). The possibility of reducing therapist contact and total length of therapy in the treatment of panic disorder. *Behavioural and Cognitive Psychotherapy, 27,* 231–247.

Bouchard, S., Gauthier, J., LaBerge, B., French, D., Pelletier, M. -H., & Godbout, C. (1996). Exposure versus cognitive restructuring in the treatment of panic disorder with agoraphobia. *Behaviour Research and Therapy, 34,* 213–224.

Bourdon, K. H., Boyd, J. H., Rae, D. S., Burns, B. J., Thompson, J. W., & Locke, B. Z. (1988). Gender differences in phobias: Results of the ECA community study. *Journal of Anxiety Disorders, 2,* 227–241.

Bourne, E. J. (1998a). *Overcoming specific phobia: A hierarchy and exposure-based protocol for the treatment of all specific phobias (client manual).* Oakland, CA: New Harbinger.

Bourne, E. J. (1998b). *Overcoming specific phobia: A hierarchy and exposure-based protocol for the treatment of all specific phobias (therapist protocol).* Oakland, CA: New Harbinger.

Bourque, P., & Ladouceur, R. (1980). An investigation of various performance-based treatments with acrophobics. *Behaviour Research and Therapy, 18,* 161–170.

Bouwer, C., & Stein, D. J. (1998). Use of the selective serotonin reuptake inhibitor citalopram in the treatment of generalized social phobia. *Journal of Affective Disorders, 49,* 79–82.

Boyer, W. (1994). Serotonin uptake inhibitors are superior to imipramine in alleviating panic attacks: A meta-analysis. In G. Darcourt, J. Mendlewicz, & N. Brunello (Eds.), *Current therapeutic approaches to panic and other anxiety disorders* (vol. 8, pp. 55–60). Basel, Switzerland: S. Kargar Publishers, Inc.

Bradwejn, J. (1995). Cholecystokinin and panic disorder. In J. Bradwejn & E. Vasar (Eds.), *Cholecystokinin and anxiety: From neuron to behavior* (pp. 73–86). Austin, TX: R. G. Landes.

Bradwejn, J., & Koszycki, D. (1994). Imipramine antagonism of the panicogenic effects of cholecystokinin tetrapeptide in panic disorder patients. *American Journal of Psychiatry, 151,* 261–263.

Breitholtz, E., Westling, B. E., & Öst, L. -G. (1998). Cognitions in generalized anxiety disorder and panic disorder. *Journal of Anxiety Disorders, 12,* 567–577.

Breslau, N., & Klein, D. F. (1999). Smoking and panic attacks: An epidemiologic investigation. *Archives of General Psychiatry, 56,* 1141–1147.

Brewer, C. (1972). Beneficial effect of beta-adrenergic blockade on "exam nerves." *Lancet, 2,* 435.

Broocks, A., Bandelow, B., Pekrun, G., George, A., Meyer, T., Bartmann, U., Hillmer-Vogel, U., & Ruether, E. (1998). Comparison of aerobic exercise, clomipramine, and placebo in the treatment of panic disorder. *American Journal of Psychiatry, 155,* 603–609.

Broocks, A., Meyer, T. F., Bandelow, B., George, A., Bartmann, U., Ruether, E., & Hillmer-Vogel, U. (1997). Exercise avoidance and impaired endurance capacity in patients with panic disorder. *Neuropsychobiology, 36,* 182–187.

Brown, D. (1996). *Flying without fear.* Oakland, CA: New Harbinger.

Brown, E. J., Heimberg, R. G., & Juster, H. R. (1995). Social phobia subtypes and avoidant personality disorder: Effect on severity of social phobia, impairment, and outcome of cognitive behavioral treatment. *Behavior Therapy, 26,* 467–486.

Brown, E. J., Turovsky, J., Heimberg, R., Juster, H. R., Brown, T. A., & Barlow, D. H. (1997). Validation of the Social Interaction Anxiety Scale and Social Phobia Scale across the anxiety disorders. *Psychological Assessment, 9,* 21–27.

Brown, T. A., Antony, M. M., & Barlow, D. H. (1995). Diagnostic comorbidity in panic disorder: Effect on treatment outcome and course of comorbid diagnoses following treatment. *Journal of Consulting and Clinical Psychology, 63,* 408–418.

Brown, T.A., & Cash, T.F. (1989). The phenomenon of panic in nonclinical populations: Further evidence and methodological considerations. *Journal of Anxiety Disorders, 3,* 139-148.

Brown, T. A., Chorpita, B. F., Korotitsch, W., & Barlow, D. H. (1997). Psychometric properties of the Depression Anxiety Stress Scales (DASS) in clinical samples. *Behaviour Research and Therapy, 35,* 79–89.

Brown, T. A., & Deagle, E. A. (1992). Structured interview assessment of nonclinical panic. *Behavior Therapy, 23,* 75–85.

Brown, T. A., Di Nardo, P., & Barlow, D. H. (1994). *Anxiety Disorders Interview Schedule for DSM-IV (Lifetime Version).* San Antonio, TX: Psychological Corporation.

Brown, T. M., Black, B., & Uhde, T. W. (1994). The sleep architecture of social phobia. *Biological Psychiatry, 35,* 420–421.

Bruce, T. J., & Sanderson, W. C. (1998). *Specific phobias: Clinical applications of evidence-based psychotherapy.* Northvale, NJ: Jason Aronson.

Bruce, T. J., Spiegel, D. A., Gregg, S. F., & Nuzzarello, A. (1995). Predictors of alprazolam discontinuation with and without cognitive behavior therapy in panic disorder. *American Journal of Psychiatry, 152,* 1156–1160.

Bruch, M. A., & Heimberg, R. G. (1994). Differences in perceptions of parental and personal characteristics between generalized and nongeneralized social phobics. *Journal of Anxiety Disorders, 8,* 155–168.

Buigues, J., & Vallejo, J. (1987). Therapeutic response to phenelzine in patients with panic disorder and agoraphobia with panic attacks. *Journal of Clinical Psychiatry, 48,*55–59.

Burke, K. C., Burke, J. D., Regier, D. A., & Rae, D. S. (1990). Age at onset of selected mental disorders in five community populations. *Archives of General Psychiatry, 47,* 511–518.

Burns, D. D. (1989). *The feeling good handbook.* New York: Plume.

Butler, G., Cullington, A., Munby, M., Amies, P., & Gelder, M. (1984). Exposure and anxiety management in the treatment of social phobia. *Journal of Consulting and Clinical Psychology, 52,* 642–650.

Bystritsky, A., Rosen, R., Suri, R., & Vapnik, T. (1999). Pilot open-label study of nefazodone in panic disorder. *Depression and Anxiety, 10,* 137–139.

Cahill, S. P., Carrigan, M. H., & Frueh, B. C. (1999). Does EMDR work? And if so, why? A critical review of controlled outcome and dismantling research. *Journal of Anxiety Disorders, 13,* 5–33.

Cameron, C. M. (1997). Information-processing approaches to phobias. In G. C. L. Davey (Ed.), *Phobias: A handbook of theory, research and treatment* (pp. 397–414). New York: Wiley.

Cameron, O. G., & Hudson, C. J. (1986). Influence of exercise on anxiety level in patients with anxiety disorders. *Psychosomatics, 27,* 720–723.

Carducci, B. J., & Zimbardo, P. G. (1995, November/December). Are you shy? *Psychology Today,* pp. 34–40, 64, 66, 68, 70, 78, 82.

Carlin, A. S., Hoffman, H. G., & Weghorst, S. (1997). Virtual reality and tactile augmentation in the treatment of spider phobia: A case report. *Behaviour Research and Therapy, 35,* 153–158.

Carr, J. E. (1996). Neuroendocrine and behavioral interaction in exposure treatment of phobic avoidance. *Clinical Psychology Review, 16,* 1–15.

Carter, C. S., Fawcett, J., Hertzman, M., Papp, L. A., Jones, W., Patterson, W. M., Swinson, R. P., Weise, C. C., Maddock, R. J., Denahan, A. Q., & Liebowitz, M. (1995). Adinazolam-SR in panic disorder with agoraphobia: Relationship of daily dose to efficacy. *Journal of Clinical Psychopharmacology, 56,* 202–210.

Carter, M. M., Hollon, S. D., Carson, R., & Shelton, R. C. (1995). Effects of a safe person on induced distress following a biological challenge in panic disorder with agoraphobia. *Journal of Abnormal Psychology, 104,* 156–163.

Cavallini, M. C., Perna, G., Caldirola, D., & Bellodi, L. (1999). A segregation study of panic disorder in families of panic patients responsive to the 35% CO_2 challenge. *Biological Psychiatry, 46,* 815–820.

Cerny, J. A., Barlow, D. H., Craske, M. G., & Himadi, W. G. (1987). Couples treatment of agoraphobia: A two-year follow-up. *Behavior Therapy, 18,* 401–415.

Chaleby, K. (1987). Social phobia in Saudis. *Social Psychiatry, 22,* 167–170.

Chaleby, K., & Ziady, G. (1988). Mitral valve prolapse and social phobia. *British Journal of Psychiatry, 152,* 280–281.

Chambless, D. L., Caputo, G. C., Bright, P., & Gallagher, R. (1984). Assessment of "fear of fear" in agoraphobics: The Body Sensations Questionnaire and the Agoraphobic Cognitions Questionnaire. *Journal of Consulting and Clinical Psychology, 52,* 1090–1097.

Chambless, D. L., Caputo, G. C., Jasin, S. E., Gracely, E. J., & Williams, C. (1985). The Mobility Inventory for Agoraphobia. *Behaviour Research and Therapy, 23,* 35–44.

Chambless, D. L., & Gracely, E. J. (1989). Fear of fear and the anxiety disorders. *Cognitive Therapy and Research, 13,* 9–20.

Chambless, D. L., Renneberg, B., Goldstein, A., & Gracely, E. J. (1992). MCMI-diagnosed personality disorders among agoraphobic outpatients: Prevalence and relationship to severity and treatment outcome. *Journal of Anxiety Disorders, 6,* 193–211.

Chambless, D. L., & Steketee, G. (1999). Expressed emotion and behavior therapy outcome: A prospective study with obsessive–compulsive and agoraphobic outpatients. *Journal of Consulting and Clinical Psychology, 67,* 658–665.

Chambless, D. L., Tran, G. Q., & Glass, C. R. (1997). Predictors of response to cognitive–behavioral treatment for social phobia. *Journal of Anxiety Disorders, 11,* 221–240.

Chang, S. C. (1997). Social anxiety (phobia) and East Asian culture. *Depression and Anxiety, 5,* 115–120.

Charney, D. S., Heninger, G. R., & Breier, A. (1984). Noradrenergic function in panic anxiety: Effects of yohimbine in healthy subjects and patients with agoraphobia and panic disorder. *Archives of General Psychiatry, 41,* 751–763.

Chartier, M. J., Hazen, A. L., & Stein, M. B. (1998). Lifetime patterns of social phobia: A retrospective study of the course of social phobia in a non-clinical population. *Depression and Anxiety, 7,* 113–121.

Chen, Y. -W., & Dilsaver, S. C. (1995). Comorbidity of panic disorder in bipolar illness: Evidence from the Epidemiologic Catchment Area Survey. *American Journal of Psychiatry, 152,* 280–282.

Clark, D. M. (1986). A cognitive approach to panic. *Behaviour Research and Therapy, 24,* 461–470.

Clark, D. M. (1988). A cognitive model of panic attacks. In S. Rachman & J. D. Maser (Eds.), *Panic: Psychological perspectives* (pp. 71–89). Hillsdale, NJ: Erlbaum.

Clark, D. B., & Agras, W. S. (1991). The assessment and treatment of performance anxiety in musicians. *American Journal of Psychiatry, 148,* 598–605.

Clark, D. M., Salkovskis, P. M., Hackmann, A., Middleton, H., Anastasiades, P., & Gelder, M. (1994). A comparison of cognitive therapy, applied relaxation and imipramine in the treatment of panic disorder. *British Journal of Psychiatry, 164,* 759–769.

Clark, D. M., Salkovskis, P. M., Hackmann, A., Wells, A., Ludgate, J., & Gelder, M. (1999). Brief cognitive therapy for panic disorder: A randomized controlled trial. *Journal of Consulting and Clinical Psychology, 67,* 583–589.

Clark, D. M., Salkovskis, P. M., Öst, L. -G., Breitholtz, E., Koehler, K. A., Westling, B. E., Jeavons, A., & Gelder, M. (1997). Misinterpretation of body sensations in panic disorder. *Journal of Consulting and Clinical Psychology, 65,* 203–213.

Clark, D. M., & Wells, A. (1995). A cognitive model of social phobia. In R. G. Heimberg, M. R. Liebowitz, D. A. Hope, & F. R. Schneier (Eds.), *Social phobia: Diagnosis, assessment, and treatment* (pp. 69–93). New York: Guilford Press.

Cloitre, M., Cancienne, J., Heimberg, R. G., Holt, C. S., & Liebowitz, M. (1995). Memory bias does not generalize across anxiety disorders. *Behaviour Research and Therapy, 33,* 305–307.

Cloitre, M., Heimberg, R. G., Holt, C. S., & Liebowitz, M. R. (1992). Reaction time to threat stimuli in panic disorder and social phobia. *Behaviour Research and Therapy, 30,* 609–617.

Cloitre, M., Shear, M. K., Cancienne, J., & Zeitlin, S. B. (1994). Implicit and explicit memory for catastrophic associations to body sensation words in panic disorder. *Cognitive Therapy and Research, 18,* 225–240.

Clum, G. A., Broyles, S., Borden, J., & Watkins, P. L. (1990). Validity and reliability of the Panic Attack Symptoms and Cognitions Questionnaires. *Journal of Psychopathology and Behavioral Assessment, 12,* 233–245.

Cohen, A. S., Barlow, D. H., & Blanchard, E. B. (1985). Psychophysiology of relaxation-associated panic attacks. *Journal of Abnormal Psychology, 94,* 96–101.

Cohen, D. C. (1977). Comparison of self-report and overt-behavioral procedures for assessing acrophobia. *Behavior Therapy, 8,* 17–23.

Coldwell, S. E., Getz, T., Milgrom, P., Prall, C. W., Spadafora, A., & Ramsey, D. S. (1998). CARL: A LabVIEW 3 computer program for conducting exposure therapy for the treatment of dental injection fear. *Behaviour Research and Therapy, 36,* 429–441.

Coles, M. E., Amir, N., Kozak, M. J., & Foa, E. B. (1997, November). *Enhanced ability to forget socially relevant material in social phobia: Use of the directed forgetting paradigm.* Paper presented at the meeting of the Association for Advancement of Behavior Therapy, Miami, FL.

Connor, K. M., Davidson, J. R. T., Churchill, L. E., Sherwood, A., Foa, E., & Weisler, R. H. (2000). Psychometric properties of the Social Phobia Inventory (SPIN): A new self-rating scale. *British Journal of Psychiatry, 176,* 379–386.

Connor, K. M., Davidson, J. R. T., Churchill, E., Tupler, L. A., Sherwood, A., Foa, E. B., & Weisler, R. H. (1999, June). *Psychometric properties of the Social Phobia Inventory (SPIN): A new self-rating scale.* Paper presented at the meeting of the National Institute of Mental Health, New Clinical Drug Evaluation Unit, Boca Raton, FL.

Connor, K. M., Kobak, K., Churchill, E., Potts, N. L. S., Katzelnick, D., & Davidson, J. R. T. (1999, September). *The Mini–SPIN: A brief screening instrument for social phobia*. Paper presented at the meeting of the European College of Neuropsychopharmacology, London, UK.

Constans, J. I., Penn, D. L., Ihen, G. H., & Hope, D. A. (1999). Interpretive biases for ambiguous stimuli in social anxiety. *Behaviour Research and Therapy, 37*, 643–651.

Cottraux, J., Note, I. D., Cungi, C., Legeron, P., Heim, F., Chneiweiss, L., Bernard, G., & Bouvard, M. (1995). A controlled study of cognitive behaviour therapy with buspirone or placebo in panic disorder with agoraphobia. *British Journal of Psychiatry, 167*, 635–641.

Coupland, N. J., & Nutt, D. J. (1995). Neurobiology of anxiety and panic. In J. Bradwejn & E. Vasar (Eds.), *Cholecystokinin and anxiety: From neuron to behavior* (pp. 1–32). Austin, TX: R. G. Landes.

Cowley, D. S., Ha, E. H., & Roy-Byrne, P. P. (1997). Determinants of pharmacologic treatment failure in panic disorder. *Journal of Clinical Psychiatry, 58*, 555–561.

Cox, B. J., Cohen, E., Direnfeld, D. M., & Swinson, R. P. (1996). Does the Beck Anxiety Inventory measure anything beyond panic attack symptoms? *Behaviour Research and Therapy, 34*, 949–954.

Cox, B. J., Direnfeld, D. M., Swinson, R. P., & Norton, G. R. (1994). Suicidal ideation and suicide attempts in panic disorder and social phobia. *American Journal of Psychiatry, 151*, 882–887.

Cox, B. J., Endler, N. S., Lee, P. S., & Swinson, R. P. (1992). A meta-analysis of treatments for panic disorder with agoraphobia: Imipramine, alprazolam, and in vivo exposure. *Journal of Behavior Therapy and Experimental Psychiatry, 23*, 175–182.

Cox, B. J., Endler, N. S., & Swinson, R. P. (1995). An examination of levels of agoraphobic severity in panic disorder. *Behaviour Research and Therapy, 33*, 57–62.

Cox, B. J., Norton, G. R., & Swinson, R. P. (1992). *Panic Attack Questionnaire—Revised*. Toronto, Ontario, Canada: Clarke Institute of Psychiatry.

Cox, B. J., Norton, G. R., Swinson, R. P., & Endler, N. S. (1990). Substance abuse and panic-related anxiety: A critical review. *Behaviour Research and Therapy, 28*, 385–393.

Cox, B. J., Parker, J. D. A., & Swinson, R. P. (1996). Confirmatory factor analysis of the Fear Questionnaire with social phobia patients. *British Journal of Psychiatry, 168*, 497–499.

Cox, B. J., Ross, L., Swinson, R. P., & Direnfeld, D. M. (1998). A comparison of social phobia outcome measures in cognitive–behavioral group therapy. *Journal of Behavior Modification, 22*, 285–297.

Cox, B. J., & Swinson, R. P. (1994). Overprediction of fear in panic disorder with agoraphobia. *Behaviour Research and Therapy, 32*, 735–739.

Cox, B. J., & Swinson, R. P. (1995). Assessment and measurement. In M. B. Stein (Ed.), *Social phobia: Clinical and research perspectives* (pp. 261–291). Washington, DC: American Psychiatric Press.

Cox, B. J., Swinson, R. P., Kuch, K., & Reichman, J. T. (1993). Dimensions of agoraphobia assessed by the Mobility Inventory. *Behaviour Research and Therapy, 31*, 427–431.

Cox, B. J., Swinson, R. P., Parker, J. D., Kuch, K., & Reichman, J. T. (1993). Confirmatory factor analysis of the Fear Questionnaire in panic disorder with agoraphobia. *Psychological Assessment, 5*, 235–237.

Cox, B. J., Swinson, R. P., & Shaw, B. F. (1991). Value of the Fear Questionnaire in differentiating agoraphobia and social phobia. *British Journal of Psychiatry, 159*, 842–845.

Craske, M. G. (1991). Phobic fear and panic attacks: The same emotional states triggered by different cues? *Clinical Psychology Review, 11*, 599–620.

Craske, M. G. (1999). *Anxiety disorders: Psychological approaches to theory and treatment.* Boulder, CO: Westview Press.

Craske, M. G., Antony, M. M., & Barlow, D. H. (1997). *Mastery of your specific phobia: Therapist guide.* San Antonio, TX: Psychological Corporation.

Craske, M. G., & Barlow, D. H. (1988). A review of the relationship between panic and avoidance. *Clinical Psychology Review, 8*, 667–685.

Craske, M. G., & Barlow, D. H. (1989). Nocturnal panic. *Journal of Nervous and Mental Disease, 177*, 160–167.

Craske, M. G., & Barlow, D. H. (1993). Panic disorder and agoraphobia. In D. H. Barlow (Ed.), *Clinical handbook of psychological disorders* (2nd ed.) (pp. 1–47). New York: Guilford Press.

Craske, M. G., & Barlow, D. H. (1994). *Agoraphobia supplement to the MAP II Program (client workbook).* San Antonio TX: Psychological Corporation.

Craske, M. G., Brown, T. A., & Barlow, D. H. (1991). Behavioral treatment of panic disorder: A two-year follow-up. *Behavior Therapy, 22*, 289–304.

Craske, M. G., Bunt, R., Rapee, R. M., & Barlow, D. H. (1991). Perceived control and controllability during in vivo exposure: Spider phobics. *Journal of Anxiety Disorders, 5*, 285–292.

Craske, M. G., Maidenberg, E., & Bystritsky, A. (1995). Brief cognitive–behavioral versus nondirective therapy for panic disorder. *Journal of Behavior Therapy and Experimental Psychiatry, 26*, 113–120.

Craske, M. G., Meadows, E. A., & Barlow, D. H. (1994). *Mastery of your anxiety and panic: II. Therapist guide.* San Antonio TX: Psychological Corporation.

Craske, M. G., Mohlman, J., Yi, J., Glover, D., & Valeri, S. (1995). Treatment of claustrophobias and snake/spider phobias: Fear of arousal and fear of context. *Behaviour Research and Therapy, 33*, 197–203.

Craske, M. G., & Rachman, S. J. (1987). Return of fear: Perceived skill and heart rate responsivity. *British Journal of Clinical Psychology, 26*, 187–199.

Craske, M. G., Rapee, R. M., & Barlow, D. H. (1988). The significance of panic-expectancy for individual patterns of avoidance. *Behavior Therapy, 19*, 577–592.

Craske, M. G., & Rowe, M. K. (1997). Nocturnal panic. *Clinical Psychology: Science and Practice, 4*, 153–174.

Craske, M. G., Sanderson, W. C., & Barlow, D. H. (1987). The relationships among panic, fear, and avoidance. *Journal of Anxiety Disorders, 1*, 153–160.

Craske, M. G., & Sipsas, A. (1992). Animal phobias versus claustrophobias: Exteroceptive versus interoceptive cues. *Behaviour Research and Therapy, 30*, 569–581.

Craske, M. G., Street, L., & Barlow, D. H. (1989). Instructions to focus upon or distract from internal cues during exposure treatment of agoraphobic avoidance. *Behaviour Research and Therapy, 27*, 663–672.

Craske, M. G., Street, L. L., Jayaraman, J., & Barlow, D. H. (1991). Attention versus distraction during in vivo exposure: Snake and spider phobias. *Journal of Anxiety Disorders, 5*, 199–211.

Cross-National Collaborative Panic Study, Second Phase Investigators. (1992). Drug treatment of panic disorder. *British Journal of Psychiatry, 160*, 191–202.

Crowe, R. R., Noyes, R., Samuelson, S., Wesner, R., & Wilson, R. (1990). Close linkage between panic disorder and α-haptoglobin excluded in 10 families. *Archives of General Psychiatry, 47*, 377–380.

Curran, H. V., Bond, A., O'Sullivan, G., Bruce, M., Marks, I., Lelliot, P., Shine, P., & Lader, M. (1994). Memory functions, alprazolam and exposure therapy: A controlled longitudinal study of agoraphobia with panic disorder. *Psychological Medicine, 24*, 969–976.

Curtis, G. C., Hill, E. M., & Lewis, J. A. (1990). *Heterogeneity of DSM-III-R simple phobia and the simple phobia/agoraphobia boundary: Evidence from the ECA study.* (Report to the DSM-IV Anxiety Disorders Workgroup). Ann Arbor: University of Michigan.

Curtis, G. C., Himle, J. A., Lewis, J. A., & Lee, Y. (1989). *Specific situational phobias: Variant of agoraphobia?* (Report to the DSM-IV Anxiety Disorders Workgroup). Ann Arbor: University of Michigan.

Curtis, G. C., Magee, W. J., Eaton, W. W., Wittchen, H. -U., & Kessler, R. C. (1998). Specific fears and phobias: Epidemiology and classification. *British Journal of Psychiatry, 173*, 212–217.

Daiuto, A. D., Baucom, D. H., Epstein, N., & Dutton, S. S. (1998). The application of behavioral couples therapy to the assessment and treatment of agoraphobia: Implications of empirical research. *Clinical Psychology Review, 18*, 663–687.

Davey, G. C. L. (1989). Dental phobias and anxieties: Evidence for conditioning processes in the acquisition and modulation of a learned fear. *Behaviour Research and Therapy, 27*, 51–58.

Davey, G. C. L. (1997a). A conditioning model of phobias. In G. C. L. Davey (Ed.), *Phobias: A handbook of theory, research and treatment* (pp. 301–322). New York: Wiley.

Davey, G. C. L. (Ed.). (1997b). *Phobias: A handbook of theory, research and treatment.* New York: Wiley.

Davidson, J. R. T. (1998). *Social Phobia Inventory (SPIN).* Unpublished scale, Duke University Medical School, Durham, NC.

Davidson, J. R., Beitman, B., Greist, J. H., Maddock, R. J., Lewis, C. P., Sheridan, A. Q., Carter, C., Krishnan, K. R., Liebowitz, M. R., & Haack, D. G. (1994). Adinazolam sustained-release treatment of panic disorder: A double-blind study. *Journal of Clinical Psychopharmacology, 14,* 255–263.

Davidson, J. R. T., Miner, C. M., de Veaugh-Geiss, J., Tupler, L. A., Colket, J. T., & Potts, N. L. S. (1997). The Brief Social Phobia Scale: A psychometric evaluation. *Psychological Medicine, 27,* 161–166.

Davidson, J. R. T., Potts, N., Richichi, E., Krishnan, R., Ford, S. M., Smith, R., & Wilson, W. H. (1993). Treatment of social phobia with clonazepam and placebo. *Journal of Clinical Psychopharmacology, 13,* 423–428.

Davidson, J. R. T., Potts, N. L. S., Richichi, E. A., Ford, S. M., Krishnan, R. R., Smith, R. D., & Wilson, W. (1991). The Brief Social Phobia Scale. *Journal of Clinical Psychiatry, 52*(Suppl. 11), 48–51.

de Beurs, E., Chambless, D. L., & Goldstein, A. J. (1997). Measurement of panic disorder by a modified panic diary. *Depression and Anxiety, 6,* 133–139.

de Beurs, E., van Balkom, A. J., Lange, A., Koele, P., & van Dyke, R. (1995). Treatment of panic disorder with agoraphobia: Comparison of fluvoxamine, placebo, and psychological panic management combined with exposure and of exposure in vivo alone. *American Journal of Psychiatry, 152,* 683–691.

de Beurs, E., van Dyck, R., Lange, A., & van Balkom, A. J. (1995). Perceived upbringing and its relationship to treatment outcome in agoraphobia. *Clinical Psychology and Psychotherapy, 2,* 78–85.

de Cristofaro, M. T. R., Sessarego, A., Pupi, A., Biondi, F., & Faravelli, C. (1993). Brain perfusion abnormalities in drug-naïve lactate-sensitive panic patients: A SPECT study. *Biological Psychiatry, 33,* 505–512.

de Jong, G. M., & Bouman, T. K. (1995). Panic disorder: A baseline period. Predictability of agoraphobic avoidance behavior. *Journal of Anxiety Disorders, 9,* 185–199.

de Jong, P. J., Andrea, H., & Muris, P. (1997). Spider phobia in children: Disgust and fear before and after treatment. *Behaviour Research and Therapy, 35,* 559–562.

de Jong, P. J., Mayer, B., & van den Hout, M. (1997). Conditional reasoning and phobic fear: Evidence for a fear-confirming reasoning pattern. *Behaviour Research and Therapy, 35,* 507–516.

de Jong, P. J., van den Hout, M., & Merckelbach, H. (1995). Covariation bias and return of fear. *Behaviour Research and Therapy, 33,* 211–213.

de Jong, P. J., Weertman, A., Horselenberg, R., & van den Hout, M. (1997). Deductive reasoning and pathological anxiety: Evidence for a relatively strong "belief bias" in phobic subjects. *Cognitive Therapy and Research, 21,* 647–662.

de Jongh, A., Broeke, E. T., & Renssen, M. R. (1999). Treatment of specific phobias with eye movement desensitization and preprocessing (EMDR): Protocol, empirical status and conceptual issues. *Journal of Anxiety Disorders, 13*, 69–85.

de Jongh, A., Muris, P., Horst, G. T., van Zuuren, F., Schoenmakers, N., & Makkes, P. (1995). One-session cognitive treatment of dental phobia: Preparing dental phobics for treatment by restructuring negative cognitions. *Behaviour Research and Therapy, 33*, 947–954.

de Jongh, A., Muris, P., Schoenmakers, N., & Ter Horst, G. T. (1995). Negative cognitions of dental phobics: Reliability and validity of the Dental Cognitions Questionnaire. *Behaviour Research and Therapy, 33*, 507–515.

de Ruiter, C., Rijken, H., Garssen, B., & Kraaimaat, F. (1989). Breathing retraining, exposure and a combination of both, in the treatment of panic disorder with agoraphobia. *Behaviour Research and Therapy, 27*, 647–655.

de Silva, P., & Rachman, S. (1984). Does escape behaviour strengthen agoraphobic avoidance? A preliminary study. *Behaviour Research and Therapy, 22*, 87–91.

DeMartinis, N. A., Schweizer, E., & Rickels, K. (1996). An open-label trial of nefazodone in high comorbidity panic disorder. *Journal of Clinical Psychiatry, 57*, 245–248.

den Boer, J. A., & Westenberg, H. G. M. (1991). Do panic attacks reflect an abnormality in serotonin receptor subtypes? *Human Psychopharmacology, 6*, S25–30.

Denholtz, M. S., & Mann, E. T. (1975). An automated audiovisual treatment of phobias administered by non–professionals. *Journal of Behavior Therapy and Experimental Psychiatry, 6*, 111–115.

Devins, G. M., Binik, Y. M., Hutchinson, T. A., Hollomby, D. J., Barré, P. E., & Guttman, R. D. (1983). The emotional impact of end-stage renal disease: Importance of patients' perceptions of intrusiveness and control. *International Journal of Psychiatry in Medicine, 13*, 327–343.

Devins, G. M., Edworthy, S. M., Guthrie, N. G., Martin, L. (1992). Illness intrusiveness in rheumatoid arthritis: Differential impact on depressive symptoms over the adult lifespan. *Journal of Rheumatology, 19*, 709–715.

Devins, G. M., Mandin, H., Hons, R. B., Burgess, E. D., Klassen, J., Taub, K., Schorr, S., Letourneau, P. K., & Buckle, S. (1990). Illness intrusiveness and quality of life in end-stage renal disease: Comparison and stability across treatment modalities. *Health Psychology, 9*, 117–142.

Devins, G. M., Seland, T. P., Klein, G., Edworthy, S. M., Saary, M. J. (1993). Stability and determinants of psychosocial well-being in multiple sclerosis. *Rehabilitation Psychology, 38*, 11–26.

Di Nardo, P., Brown, T., A., & Barlow, D. H. (1994). *Anxiety Disorders Interview Schedule for DSM-IV.* San Antonio, TX: Psychological Corporation.

Di Nardo, P. A., Guzy, L. T., Jenkins, J. A., Bak, R. M., Tomasi, S. F., & Copland, M. (1988). Etiology and maintenance of dog fears. *Behaviour Research and Therapy, 26*, 241–244.

Di Nardo, P. A., Moras, K., Barlow, D. H., Rapee, R. M., & Brown, T. A. (1993). Reliability of DSM-III-R anxiety disorder categories: Using the Anxiety Disorders Interview Schedule-Revised (ADIS-R). *Archives of General Psychiatry, 50,* 251–256.

Di Nardo, P. A., O'Brien, G. T., Barlow, D. H., Waddell, M. T., & Blanchard, E. B. (1983). Reliability of DSM-III anxiety disorder categories using a new structured interview. *Archives of General Psychiatry, 40,* 1070–1074.

Diaferia, G., Sciuto, G., Perna, G., Bernardeschi, L., Battaglia, M., Rusmini, S., & Bellodi, L. (1993). DSM-III-R personality disorders in panic disorder. *Journal of Anxiety Disorders, 7,* 153–161.

Dunner, D. L., Ishiki, D., Avery, D. H., Wilson, L. G., & Hyde, T. S. (1986). Effect of alprazolam and diazepam on anxiety and panic attacks in panic disorder: A controlled study. *Journal of Clinical Psychiatry, 47,* 458–460.

Eaton, W. W., Dryman, A., & Weissman, M. M. (1991). Panic and phobia. In L. N. Robins & D. A. Regier (Eds.), *Psychiatric disorders in America: The Epidemiological Catchment Area Study* (pp. 155–179). New York: The Free Press.

Eaton, W. W., Kessler, R. C., Wittchen, H. U., & Magee, W. J. (1994). Panic and panic disorder in the United States. *American Journal of Psychiatry, 115,* 413–420.

Edelman, R. E., & Chambless, D. L. (1993). Compliance during sessions and homework in exposure-based treatment of agoraphobia. *Behaviour Research and Therapy, 31,* 767–773.

Edelman, R. E., & Chambless, D. L. (1995). Adherence during sessions and homework in cognitive–behavioral group treatment of social phobia. *Behaviour Research and Therapy, 33,* 573–577.

Ehlers, A. (1995). A 1-year prospective study of panic attacks: Clinical course and factors associated with maintenance. *Journal of Abnormal Psychology, 104,* 164–172.

Ehlers, A., & Breuer, P. (1992). Increased cardiac awareness in panic disorder. *Journal of Abnormal Psychology, 101,* 371–382.

Ehlers, A., & Breuer, P. (1995). Selective attention to physical threat in subjects with panic attacks and specific phobias. *Journal of Anxiety Disorders, 9,* 11–31.

Ehlers, A., Breuer, P., Dohn, D., & Fiegenbaum, W. (1995). Heartbeat perception and panic disorder: Possible explanations for discrepant findings. *Behaviour Research and Therapy, 33,* 69–76.

Ehlers, A., Hofmann, S. G., Herda, C. A., & Roth, W. T. (1994, October–December). Clinical characteristics of driving phobia. *Journal of Anxiety Disorders, 8,* 323–339.

Ehlers, A., & Margraf, J. (1989). The psychophysiological model of panic attacks. In P. M. G. Emmelkamp, W. T. A. M. Everaerd, F. W. Kraaimaat, & M. J. M. van Son (Eds.), *Fresh perspectives on anxiety disorders* (pp. 1–29). Amsterdam: Swets & Zeitlinger.

Ehlers, A., Margraf, J., Davies, S., & Roth, W. T. (1988). Selective processing of threat cues in subjects with panic attacks. *Cognition and Emotion, 2*, 201–219.

Emmelkamp, P. M., Mersch, P. P., Vissia, E., & van Der Helm, M. (1985). Social phobia: A comparative evaluation of cognitive and behavioral interventions. *Behaviour Research and Therapy, 23*, 365–369.

Emmelkamp, P. M. G., & Wessels, H. (1975). Flooding in imagination vs. flooding in vivo: A comparison with agoraphobics. *Behaviour Research and Therapy, 13*, 7–15.

Emmelkamp, P. M. G., Van Dyck, R., Bitter, M., Heins, R., Onstein, E. J., & Eisen, B. (1992). Spouse-aided therapy with agoraphobia. *British Journal of Psychiatry, 160*, 51–56.

Eskin, E., Orsillo, S. M., Heimberg, R. G., Holt, C. S., & Liebowitz, M. R. (1991, November). *Gender effects on social phobic fear and avoidance.* Paper presented at the meeting of the Association for Advancement of Behavior Therapy, New York, NY.

Ettigi, P., Meyerhoff, A. S., Chirban, J. T., Jacobs, R. J., & Wilson, R. R. (1997). The quality of life and employment in panic disorder. *Journal of Nervous and Mental Disease, 185*, 368–372.

Everaerd, W. T. A. M., Rijken, H. M., & Emmelkamp, P. M. G. (1973). A comparison of "flooding" and "successive approximation" in the treatment of agoraphobia. *Behaviour Research and Therapy, 11*, 105–117.

Fahlén, T., Nilsson, H. L., Borg, K., Humble, M., & Pauli, U. (1995). Social phobia: The clinical efficacy and tolerability of the monoamine oxidase-A and serotonin uptake inhibitor Brofaromine. *Acta Psychiatrica Scandinavica, 92*, 351–358.

Faravelli, C., & Pallanti, S. (1989). Recent life events and panic disorder. *American Journal of Psychiatry, 146*, 622–626.

Faravelli, C., Pallanti, S., Biondi, F., Paterniti, S., & Scarpato, M. A. (1992). Onset of panic disorder. *American Journal of Psychiatry, 149*, 827–828.

Faravelli, C., Paterniti, S., & Scarpato, A. (1995). 5-year prospective, naturalistic follow-up study of panic disorder. *Comprehensive Psychiatry, 36*, 271–277.

Fava, G. A., Grandi, S., & Canestrari, R. (1988). Prodromal symptoms in panic disorder with agoraphobia. *American Journal of Psychiatry, 145*, 1564–1567.

Febbraro, G. A. R., & Clum, G. A. (1995). A dimensional analysis of claustrophobia. *Journal of Psychopathology and Behavioral Assessment, 17*, 335–351.

Febbraro, G. A. R., Clum, G. A., Roodman, A. A., & Wright, J. H. (1999). The limits of bibliotherapy: A study of the differential effectiveness of self-administered interventions in individuals with panic attacks. *Behavior Therapy, 30*, 209–222.

Feske, U., & Chambless, D. L. (1995). Cognitive behavioral versus exposure only treatment for social phobia: A meta-analysis. *Behavior Therapy, 26*, 695–720.

Feske, U., & de Beurs, E. (1997). The Panic Appraisal Inventory: Psychometric properties. *Behaviour Research and Therapy, 35*, 875–882.

Fiegenbaum, W. (1988). Long-term efficacy of ungraded versus graded massed exposure in agoraphobics. In I. Hand & H. -U. Wittchen (Eds.), *Panic and phobias 2: Treatments and variables affecting course and outcome* (pp. 83–88). New York: Springer-Verlag.

First, M. B., Spitzer, R. L., Gibbon, M., & Williams, J. B. W. (1996). *Structured Clinical Interview for DSM-IV Axis I Disorders—Patient Edition* (SCID-I/P, Version 2.0). New York: Biometrics Research Department, New York State Psychiatric Institute.

Flynn, T. M., Taylor, P., & Pollard, C. A. (1992). Use of mobile phones in the behavioral treatment of driving phobias. *Journal of Behavior Therapy and Experimental Psychiatry, 23*, 299–302.

Foa, E. B., Blau, J. S., Prout, M., & Latimer, P. (1977). Is horror a necessary component of flooding (implosion)? *Behaviour Research and Therapy, 15*, 397–402.

Foa, E. B., Franklin, M. E., Perry, K. J., & Herbert, J. D. (1996). Cognitive biases in generalized social phobia. *Journal of Abnormal Psychology, 105*, 433–439,

Foa, E. B., Jameson, J. S., Turner, R. M., & Payne, L. L. (1980). Massed versus spaced exposure sessions in the treatment of agoraphobia. *Behaviour Research and Therapy, 18*, 333–338.

Foa, E. B., & Kozak, M. J. (1986). Emotional processing of fear: Exposure to corrective information. *Psychological Bulletin, 99*, 20–35.

Foa, E. B., & Rothbaum, B. O. (1998). *Treating the trauma of rape: Cognitive behavioral therapy for PTSD.* New York: Guilford Press.

Foa, E. B., & Wilson, R. (1991). *Stop obsessing! How to overcome your obsessions and compulsions.* New York: Bantam Books.

Fredrikson, M., Annas, P., Fischer, H., & Wik, G. (1996). Gender and age differences in the prevalence of specific fears and phobias. *Behaviour Research and Therapy, 26*, 241–244.

Fredrikson, M., Wik, G., Greitz, T., Eriksson, L., Stone-Elander, S., Ericson, K., & Sedvall, G. (1993). Regional cerebral blood flow during experimental phobic fear. *Psychophysiology, 30*, 126–130.

Freshman, M., Amir, N., Foa, E. B., & Clark, D. (1997, November). *The psychometric properties of the Social Cognitions Questionnaire (SCQ).* Paper presented at the meeting of the Association for Advancement of Behavior Therapy, Miami Beach, FL.

Friedman, S., Jones, J. C., Chernen, L., & Barlow, D. H. (1992). Suicidal ideation and suicide attempts among patients with panic disorder: A survey of two outpatient clinics. *American Journal of Psychiatry, 149*, 680–685.

Frost, R. O., Heimberg, R. G., Holt, C. S., Mattia, J. L., & Neubauer, A. L. (1993). A comparison of two measures of perfectionism. *Personality and Individual Differences, 14*, 119–126.

Frost, R. O., Marten, P., Lahart, C., & Rosenblate, R. (1990). The dimensions of perfectionism. *Cognitive Therapy and Research, 14*, 449–468.

Fydrich, T., Chambless, D. L., Perry, K. J., Buergener, F., & Beazley, M. B. (1998). Behavioral assessment of social performance: A rating system for social phobia. *Behaviour Research and Therapy, 36,* 995–1010.

Fyer, A. J., Mannuzza S., Chapman, T. F., Liebowitz, M. R., & Klein, D. F. (1993). A direct interview family study of social phobia. *Archives of General Psychiatry, 50,* 286–293.

Fyer, A. J., Mannuzza, S., Chapman, T. F., Lipsitz, J., Martin, L. Y., & Klein, D. F. (1996). Panic disorder and social phobia: Effects of comorbidity on familial transmission. *Anxiety, 2,* 173–178.

Fyer, A. J., Mannuzza, S., Gallops, M. S., Martin, L. Y., Aaronson, C., Gorman, J. M., Liebowitz, M. R., & Klein, D. F. (1990). Familial transmission of simple phobias and fears. *Archives of General Psychiatry, 47,* 252–256.

Fyer, A. J., Mannuzza, S., Martin, L. Y., Gallops, M. S., Endicott, J., Schleyer, B., Gorman, J., Liebowitz, M. R., & Klein, D. F. (1989). Reliability of anxiety assessment: II. Symptom assessment. *Archives of General Psychiatry, 46,* 1102–1110.

Galbaud du Fort, G., Newman, S. C., & Bland, R. C. (1993). Psychiatric comorbidity and treatment seeking: Sources of selection bias in the study of clinical populations. *Journal of Nervous and Mental Disease, 181,* 467–474.

Garssen, B., de Ruiter, C., & van Dyck, R. (1992). Breathing retraining: A rational placebo? *Clinical Psychology Review, 12,* 141–153.

Garvey, M., Noyes, R., & Cook, B. (1990). Comparison of panic disordered patients with high versus low MHPG. *Journal of Affective Disorders, 20,* 7–12.

Gauthier, J., & Marshall, W. L. (1977). The determination of optimal exposure to phobic stimuli in flooding therapy. *Behaviour Research and Therapy, 15,* 403–410.

Geer, J. H. (1965). The development of a scale to measure fear. *Behaviour Research and Therapy, 3,* 45–53.

Gelernter, C. S., Uhde, T. W., Cimbolic, P., Arnkoff, D. B., Vittone, B. J., & Tancer, M. E. (1991). Cognitive–behavioral and pharmacological treatments of social phobia: A controlled study. *Archives of General Psychiatry, 48,* 938–945.

George, L. K., Hughes, D. C., & Blazer, D. G. (1986). Urban/rural differences in the prevalence of anxiety disorders. *American Journal of Social Psychiatry, 6,* 249–258.

George, M. S., & Ballenger, J. C. (1992). The neuroanatomy of panic disorder: The emerging role of the right parahippocampal region. *Journal of Anxiety Disorders, 6,* 181–188.

Gerdes, T., Yates, W. R., & Clancy, G. (1995). Increasing identification and referral of panic disorder over the past decade. *Psychosomatics, 36,* 480–486.

Getka, E. J., & Glass, C. R. (1992). Behavioral and cognitive–behavioral approaches to the reduction of dental anxiety. *Behavior Therapy, 23,* 433–448.

Gilboa-Schechtman, E., Freshman, M., Amir, N., & Foa, E. B. (1997, November). *Have I seen this face before? Memory for facial expressions in generalized social phobics*. Paper presented at the meeting of the Association for Advancement of Behavior Therapy, Miami, FL.

Gitin, N. M., Herbert, J. D., & Schmidt, C. (1996, November). *One-session in vivo exposure for odontophobia*. Paper presented at the meeting of the Association for Advancement of Behavior Therapy, New York, NY.

Goddard, A. W., & Charney, D. S. (1998). SSRIs in the treatment of panic disorder. *Depression and Anxiety, 8*(Suppl. 1), 114–120.

Goisman, R. M., Goldenberg, I., Vasile, R. G., & Keller, M. B. (1995). Comorbidity of anxiety disorders in a multicenter anxiety study. *Comprehensive Psychiatry, 36*, 303–311.

Goisman, R. M., Warshaw, M. G., & Keller, M. B. (1999). Psychosocial treatment prescriptions for generalized anxiety disorder, panic disorder, and social phobia, 1991–1996 (1999). *American Journal of Psychiatry, 156*, 1819–1821.

Goisman, R. M., Warshaw, M. G., Steketee, G. S., Fierman, E. J., Rogers, M. P., Goldenberg, I., Weinshenker, N. J., Vasile, R. G., & Keller, M. B. (1995). DSM-IV and the disappearance of agoraphobia without a history of panic disorder: New data on a controversial diagnosis. *American Journal of Psychiatry, 152*, 1438–1443.

Goldstein, A. J., & Chambless, D. L. (1978). A reanalysis of agoraphobia. *Behavior Therapy, 9*, 47–59.

Goldstein, R., Weissman, M. M., Adams, P. B., Horwath, E., Lish, J. D., Charney, D., Woods, S. W., Sobin, C., & Wickramaratne, P. J. (1994). Psychiatric disorders in relatives of probands with panic disorder and/or major depression. *Archives of General Psychiatry, 51*, 383–394.

Gorman, J. M., Liebowitz, M. R., Fyer, A. J., Campeas, R., & Klein, D. F. (1985). Treatment of social phobia with atenolol. *Journal of Clinical Psychopharmacology, 5*, 298–301.

Gorman, J. M., Liebowitz, M. R., Fyer, A. J., & Stein, J. (1989). A neuroanatomical hypothesis for panic disorder. *American Journal of Psychiatry, 146*, 148–161.

Gould, R. A., Buckminster, S., Pollack, M. H., Otto, M. W., & Yap, L. (1997). Cognitive–behavioral and pharmacological treatment for social phobia: A meta-analysis. *Clinical Psychology: Science and Practice, 4*, 291–306.

Gould, R. A., & Clum, G. A. (1995). Self-help plus minimal therapist contact in the treatment of panic disorder: A replication and extension. *Behavior Therapy, 26*, 533–546.

Gould, R. A., Clum, G. A., & Shapiro, D. (1993). The use of bibliotherapy in the treatment of panic: A preliminary investigation. *Behavior Therapy, 24*, 241–252.

Graham, J., & Gaffan, E. A. (1997). Fear of water in children and adults: Etiology and familial effects. *Behaviour Research and Therapy, 35*, 91–108.

Gray, J. A. (1987). Interactions between drugs and behavior therapy. In H. J. Eysenck & I. Martin (Eds.), *Theoretical foundations of behavior therapy* (pp. 433–447). New York: Plenum Press.

Greenberger, D., & Padesky, C. A. (1995). *Mind over mood: A cognitive therapy treatment manual for clients.* New York: Guilford Press.

Griez, E., & Schruers, K. (1998). Experimental pathophysiology of panic. *Journal of Psychosomatic Research, 45,* 493–503.

Gunther, L. M., Denniston, J. C., & Miller, R. R. (1998). Conducting exposure treatment in multiple contexts can prevent relapse. *Behaviour Research and Therapy, 36,* 75–91.

Habke, A. M., Hewitt, P. L., Norton, G. R., & Asmundson, G. (1997). The Social Phobia and Social Interaction Anxiety Scales: An exploration of the dimensions of social anxiety and sex differences in structure and relations with pathology. *Journal of Psychopathology and Behavioral Assessment, 19,* 21–39.

Hackmann, A., Surawy, C., & Clark, D. M. (1998). Seeing yourself through others' eyes: A study of spontaneously occurring images in social phobia. *Behavioural and Cognitive Psychotherapy, 26,* 3–12.

Hafner, R. J. (1984). The marital repercussions of behavior therapy for agoraphobia. *Psychotherapy, 21,* 530–542.

Haidt, J., McCauley, C., & Rozin, P. (1994). Individual differences in sensitivity to disgust: Scale sampling seven domains of disgust elicitors. *Personality and Individual Differences, 16,* 701–713.

Hand, I., LaMontagne, Y., & Marks, I. M. (1974). Group exposure (flooding) in vivo for agoraphobics. *British Journal of Psychiatry, 124,* 588–602.

Harris, L. M., & Menzies, R. G. (1996). Origins of specific fears: A comparison of associative and nonassociative accounts. *Anxiety, 2,* 248–250.

Hartley, L. R., Ungapen, S., Dovie, I., & Spencer, D. J. (1983). The effect of beta-adrenergic blocking drugs on speakers' performance and memory. *British Journal of Psychiatry, 142,* 512–517.

Harvey, J. M., Richards, J. C., Dziadosz, T., & Swindell, A. (1993). Misinterpretations of ambiguous stimuli in panic disorder. *Cognitive Therapy and Research, 17,* 235–248.

Haw, J., & Dickerson, M. (1998). The effects of distraction on desensitization and reprocessing. *Behaviour Research and Therapy, 36,* 765–769.

Hayes, S. C., Barlow, D. H., & Nelson-Gray, R. O. (1999). *The scientist–practitioner: Research and accountability in the age of managed care* (2nd ed.). New York: Allyn & Bacon.

Hays, K. F. (1999). *Working it out: Using exercise in psychotherapy.* Washington, DC: American Psychiatric Association.

Hazen, A. L., & Stein, M. B. (1995). Clinical phenomenology and comorbidity. In M. B. Stein (Ed.), *Social phobia: clinical and research perspectives* (pp. 3–42). Washington, DC: American Psychiatric Press.

Hecker, J. E., Losee, M. C., Fritzler, B. K., & Fink, C. M. (1996). Self-directed versus therapist-directed cognitive behavioral treatment for panic disorder. *Journal of Anxiety Disorders, 10,* 253–265.

Heide, F. J., & Borkovec, T. D. (1983). Relaxation-induced anxiety: Paradoxical anxiety enhancement due to relaxation training. *Journal of Consulting and Clinical Psychology, 51*, 171–182.

Heide, F. J., & Borkovec, T. D. (1984). Relaxation-induced anxiety: Mechanisms and theoretical implications. *Behaviour Research and Therapy, 22*, 1–12.

Heimberg, R. G. (1994). Cognitive assessment strategies and the measurement of outcome of treatment for social phobia. *Behaviour Research and Therapy, 32*, 269–280.

Heimberg, R. G., Dodge, C. S., Hope, D. A., Kennedy, C. R., & Zollo, L. J. (1990). Cognitive behavioral group treatment for social phobia: Comparison with a credible placebo control. *Cognitive Therapy and Research, 14*, 1–23.

Heimberg, R. G., & Holt, C. S. (1989). *The issue of subtypes in the diagnosis of social phobia: A report to the social phobia subworkgroup for DSM-IV.* Unpublished manuscript. Albany, NY: Department of Psychology, University at Albany, State University of New York.

Heimberg, R. G., Holt, C. S., Schneier, F. R., Spitzer, R. L., & Liebowitz, M. R. (1993). The issue of subtypes in the diagnosis of social phobia. *Journal of Anxiety Disorders, 7*, 249–269.

Heimberg, R. G., Horner, K. J., Safren, S. A., Brown, E. J., Schneier, F. R., & Liebowitz, M. R. (1999). Psychometric properties of the Liebowitz Social Anxiety Scale. *Psychological Medicine, 29*, 199–212.

Heimberg, R. G., & Juster, H. R. (1995). Cognitive–behavioral treatments: Literature review. In R. G. Heimberg, M. R. Liebowitz, D. A. Hope, & F. R. Schneier (Eds.), *Social phobia: Diagnosis, assessment, and treatment* (pp. 261–301). New York: Guilford Press.

Heimberg, R. G., Liebowitz, M. R., Hope, D. A., Schneier, F. R., Holt, C. S., Welkowitz, L. A., Juster, H. R., Campeas, R., Bruch, M. A., Cloitre, M., Fallon, B., & Klein, D. F. (1998). Cognitive–behavioural group treatment versus phenelzine in social phobia: 12 week outcome. *Archives of General Psychiatry, 55*, 1133–1141.

Heimberg, R.G., Makris, G.S., Juster, H.R., Öst, L.-G., & Rapee, R.M. (1997). Social phobia: A preliminary cross-national comparison. *Depression and Anxiety, 5*, 130-133.

Heimberg, R. G., Mennin, D. S., & Jack, M. S. (1999). Computer-assisted rating scales for social phobia: Reliability and validity may not be what they appear. *Depression and Anxiety, 9*, 44–45.

Heimberg, R. G., Salzman, D. G., Holt, C. S., & Blendell, K. A. (1993). Cognitive–behavioral group treatment for social phobia: Effectiveness at five-year follow-up. *Cognitive Therapy and Research, 17*, 325–339.

Hellström, K., Fellenius, J., & Öst, L. -G. (1996). One versus five sessions of applied tension in the treatment of blood phobia. *Behaviour Research and Therapy, 34*, 101–112.

Hellström, K., & Öst, L. -G. (1995). One-session therapist directed exposure vs. two forms of manual directed self-exposure in the treatment of spider phobia. *Behaviour Research and Therapy, 33*, 959–965.

Hellström, K., & Öst, L. -G. (1996). Prediction of outcome in the treatment of specific phobia: A cross-validation study. *Behaviour Research and Therapy, 34*, 403–411.

Henderson, L., & Zimbardo, P. (1998). Shyness. In H.S. Friedman (Ed.), *Encyclopedia of mental health* (*vol. 3*, pp. 497–509). San Diego, CA: Academic Press.

Henriksson, M. M., Isometsä, E. T., Kuoppasalmi, K. I., Heikkinen, M. E., Marttunen, M. J., & Lönnqvist, J. K. (1996). Panic disorder and completed suicide. *Journal of Clinical Psychiatry, 57*, 275–281.

Herbert, J. D., Bellack, A. S., & Hope, D. A. (1991). Concurrent validity of the Social Phobia and Anxiety Inventory. *Journal of Psychopathology and Behavioral Assessment, 13*, 357–368.

Hewitt, P. L., & Flett, G. L. (1991). Perfectionism in the self and social contexts: Conceptualization, assessment, and association with psychopathology. *Journal of Personality and Social Psychology, 60*, 456–470.

Hewitt, P. L., Flett, G. L., Turnbull-Donovan, W., & Mikail, S. F. (1991). The Multidimensional Perfectionism Scale: Reliability, validity, and psychometric properties in psychiatric samples. *Psychological Assessment: A Journal of Consulting and Clinical Psychology, 3*, 464–468.

Hibbert, G. A., & Chan, M. (1989). Respiratory control: Its contribution to the treatment of panic attacks. A controlled study. *British Journal of Psychiatry, 154*, 232–236.

Himle, J. A., McPhee, K., Cameron, O. J., & Curtis, G. C. (1989). Simple phobia: Evidence for heterogeneity. *Psychiatry Research, 28*, 25–30.

Hoffart, A. (1995). A comparison of cognitive and guided mastery therapy of agoraphobia. *Behaviour Research and Therapy, 33*, 423–434.

Hoffart, A. (1997). Interpersonal problems among patients suffering from panic disorder with agoraphobia before and after treatment. *British Journal of Medical Psychology, 70*, 149–157.

Hoffart, A. (1998). Cognitive and guided mastery therapy of agoraphobia: Long-term outcome and mechanisms of change. *Cognitive Therapy and Research, 22*, 195–207.

Hoffart, A., Due-Madsen, J., Lande, B., Gude, T., Bille, H., & Torgersen, S. (1993). Clomipramine in the treatment of agoraphobic inpatients resistant to behavioral therapy. *Journal of Clinical Psychiatry, 54*, 481–487.

Hoffart, A., Friis, S., & Martinsen, E. W. (1992). Assessment of fear of fear among agoraphobic patients: The Agoraphobic Cognitions Scale. *Journal of Psychopathology and Behavioral Assessment, 14*, 175–187.

Hoffart, A., & Martinsen, E. W. (1990). Exposure-based integrated vs. pure psychodynamic treatment of agoraphobic inpatients. *Psychotherapy, 27*, 210–218.

Hofmann, S. G., Bufka, L. F., & Barlow, D. H. (1999). Panic provocation procedures in the treatment of panic disorder: Early perspectives and case studies. *Behavior Therapy, 30,* 305–317.

Hofmann, S. G., Ehlers, A., & Roth, W. T. (1995). Conditioning theory: A model of the etiology of public speaking anxiety? *Behaviour Research and Therapy, 33,* 567–571.

Holle, C., Neely, J. H., & Heimberg, R. G. (1997). The effects of blocked versus random presentation and semantic relatedness of stimulus words on response to a modified Stroop task among social phobics. *Cognitive Therapy and Research, 21,* 681–697.

Hollifield, M., Katon, W., Skipper, B., Chapman, T., Ballenger, J. C., Mannuzza, S., & Fyer, A. J. (1997). Panic disorder and quality of life: Variables predictive of functional impairment. *American Journal of Psychiatry, 154,* 766–772.

Hope, D.A., Heimberg, R.G., Juster, H.R., & Turk, C.L. (2000). *Managing social anxiety.* San Antonio, TX: The Psychological Corporation.

Holt, C. S., Heimberg, R. G., Hope, D. A., & Liebowitz, M. R. (1992). Situational domains of social phobia. *Journal of Anxiety Disorders, 6,* 63–77.

Hope, D. A., Heimberg, R., G., & Bruch, M. A. (1995). Dismantling cognitive–behavioral group therapy for social phobia. *Behaviour Research and Therapy, 33,* 637–650.

Hope, D. A., Rapee, R. M., Heimberg, R. G., & Dombeck, M. J. (1990). Representations of self in social phobia: Vulnerability to social threat. *Cognitive Therapy and Research, 14,* 177–189.

Hornig, C. D., & McNally, R. J. (1995). Panic disorder and suicide attempt: A reanalysis of data from the Epidemiologic Catchment Area study. *British Journal of Psychiatry, 167,* 76–79.

Horwath, E., Adams, P., Wickramaratne, P., Pine, D., & Weissman, M. M. (1997). Panic disorder with smothering symptoms: Evidence for increased risk in first-degree relatives. *Depression and Anxiety, 6,* 147–153.

Horwath, E., Johnson, J., & Hornig, C. D. (1993). Epidemiology of panic disorder in African-Americans. *American Journal of Psychiatry, 150,* 465–469.

Horwath, E., Lish, J. D., Johnson, J., Hornig, C. D., & Weissman, M. M. (1993). Agoraphobia without panic: Clinical reappraisal of an epidemiological finding. *American Journal of Psychiatry, 150,* 1496–1501.

Howard, W. A., Murphy, S. M., & Clarke, J. C. (1983). The nature and treatment of fear of flying: A controlled investigation. *Behavior Therapy, 14,* 557–567.

Hsu, A., Sandbrand, D., Nazarian, M., Hurtado, L., Yocum, M., & Craske, M. G. (1997, November). *Does cognitive change predict treatment outcome for nocturnal panic?: A preliminary analysis.* Paper presented at the meeting of the Association for Advancement of Behavior Therapy, Miami Beach, FL.

Hugdahl, K., & Öst, L. -G. (1985). Subjectively rated physiological and cognitive symptoms in six different clinical phobias. *Personality and Individual Differences, 6,* 175–188.

International Multicenter Clinical Trial Group on Moclobemide in Social Phobia. (1997). Moclobemide in social phobia: A double-blind, placebo-controlled clinical study. *European Archives of Psychiatry and Clinical Neurosciences, 247,* 71–80.

Ito, L. M., Noshirvani, H., Başoğlu, M., & Marks, I. M. (1996). Does exposure to internal cues enhance exposure to external cues in agoraphobia with panic? *Psychotherapy and Psychosomatics, 65,* 24–28.

Izard, C. E. (Ed.) (1977). *Human emotions.* New York: Plenum Press.

James, I. M., Burgoyne, W., & Savage, I. T. (1983). Effect of pindolol on stress-related disturbances of musical performance: Preliminary communication. *Journal of the Royal Society of Medicine, 76,* 194–196.

Janicak, P. G., Davies, J. M., Preskorn S. H., & Ayd, F. . J. (1997). *Principles and practice of psychopharmacotherapy* (2nd ed.). Baltimore, MD: Williams and Wilkins.

Jansson, L., Jerremalm, A., & Öst, L. -G. (1986). Follow-up of agoraphobic patients treated with exposure in vivo or applied relaxation. *British Journal of Psychiatry, 149,* 486–490.

Jefferson, J. W. (1997). Antidepressants in panic disorder. *Journal of Clinical Psychiatry, 58*(Suppl. 2), 20–24.

Jerremalm, A., Jansson, L., & Öst, L. -G. (1986a). Cognitive and physiological reactivity and the effects of different behavioral methods in the treatment of social phobia. *Behaviour Research and Therapy, 24,* 171–180.

Jerremalm, A., Jansson, L., & Öst, L. -G. (1986b). Individual response patterns and the effects of different behavioral methods in the treatment of dental phobia. *Behaviour Research and Therapy, 24,* 587–596.

Jerremalm, A., Johansson, J., & Öst, L. -G. (1980). Applied relaxation as a self-control technique for social phobia. *Scandinavian Journal of Behavioral Therapy, 9,* 35–43.

Johnson, J., Weissman, M. M., & Klerman, G. L. (1990). Panic disorder, comorbidity, and suicide attempts. *Archives of General Psychiatry, 47,* 805–808.

Johnston, D. G., Troyer, I. E., & Whitsett, S. F. (1988). Clomipramine treatment of agoraphobic women: An eight-week controlled trial. *Archives of General Psychiatry, 45,* 453–459.

Jones, M. K., Whitmont, S., & Menzies, R. G. (1996). Danger expectancies and insight in spider phobia. *Anxiety, 2,* 179–185.

Juster, H. R., Heimberg, R. G., Frost, R. O., Holt, C. S., Mattia, J. I., & Faccenda, K. (1996). Social phobia and perfectionism. *Personality and Individual Differences, 21,* 403–410.

Kamphuis, J.H., & Telch, M.J. (1998). Assessment of strategies to manage or avoid perceived threats among panic disorder patients: The Texas Safety Maneuver Scale (TSMS). *Clinical Psychology and Psychotherapy, 5,* 177-186.

Karno, M., Golding, J. M., Burnam, M. A., Hough, R. L., Escobar, J. I., Wells, K. M., & Boyer, R. (1989). Anxiety disorders among Mexican Americans and non-Hispanic Whites in Los Angeles. *Journal of Nervous and Mental Disease*, 177, 202–209.

Katerndahl, D. A., & Realini, J. P. (1997a). Comorbid psychiatric disorders in subjects with panic attacks. *Journal of Nervous and Mental Disease*, 185, 669–674.

Katerndahl, D. A., & Realini, J. P. (1997b). Quality of life and panic-related work disability in subjects with infrequent panic and panic disorder. *Journal of Clinical Psychiatry*, 58, 153–158.

Katzelnick, D. J., Kobak, K. A., Greist, J. H., Jefferson, J. W., Mantle, J. M., & Serlin, R. C. (1995). Sertraline for social phobia: A double-blind, placebo-controlled crossover study. *American Journal of Psychiatry*, 152, 1368–1371.

Keijsers, G. P. J., Hoogduin, C. A. L., & Schaap, C. P. D. R. (1994). Prognostic factors in the behavioral treatment of panic disorder with and without agoraphobia. *Behavior Therapy*, 25, 689–708.

Kelsey, J. E. (1995). Venlafaxine in social phobia. *Psychopharmacology Bulletin*, 31, 767–771.

Kenardy, J., Oei, T. P. S., & Evans, L. (1990). Neuroticism and age of onset for agoraphobia with panic attacks. *Journal of Behavior Therapy and Experimental Psychiatry*, 21, 193–197.

Kenardy, J., & Taylor, C. B. (1999). Expected versus unexpected panic attacks: A naturalistic prospective study. *Journal of Anxiety Disorders*, 13, 435–445.

Kendler, K. S., Karkowski, L. M., & Prescott, C. A. (1999). Fear and phobias: Reliability and heritability. *Psychological Medicine*, 29, 539–553.

Kendler, K. S., Neale, M. C., Kessler, R. C., Heath, A. C., & Eaves, L. J. (1992). The genetic epidemiology of phobias in women: The interrelationship of agoraphobia, social phobia, situational phobia, and simple phobia. *Archives of General Psychiatry*, 39, 273–281.

Kendler, K. S., Neale, M. C., Kessler, R. C., Heath, A. C., & Eaves, L. J. (1993). Panic disorder in women: A population-based study. *Psychological Medicine*, 23, 397–406.

Kessler R. C., McGonagle K. A., Zhao S., Nelson, C. B., Hughes, M., Eshleman, S., Wittchen H. -U., & Kendler, K. (1994). Lifetime and 12-month prevalence of DSM-III-R psychiatric disorders in the United States: Results from the National Comorbidity Survey. *Archives of General Psychiatry*, 51, 8–19.

Kessler, R. C., Stang, P., Wittchen, H. -U., Stein, M., & Walters, E. E. (1999). Lifetime co-morbidities between social phobia and mood disorders in the U.S. National Comorbidity Survey. *Psychological Medicine*, 29, 555–567.

Kessler, R. C., Stein, M. B., & Berglund, P. (1998). Social phobia subtypes in the national comorbidity study. *American Journal of Psychiatry*, 155, 613–619.

Keyl, P. M., & Eaton, W. W. (1990). Risk factors for the onset of panic disorder and other panic attacks in a prospective, population-based study. *American Journal of Epidemiology*, 131, 301–311.

Khawaja, N. G., & Oei, T. P. S. (1992). Development of a catastrophic cognition questionnaire. *Journal of Anxiety Disorders, 6,* 305–318.

Kim, H. L., Streltzer, J., & Goebert, D. (1999). St. John's Wort for depression: A meta-analysis of well-defined clinical trials. *Journal of Nervous and Mental Disease, 187,* 532–538.

Kindt, M., & Brosschot, J. F. (1997). Phobia-related cognitive bias for pictorial and linguistic stimuli. *Journal of Abnormal Psychology, 106,* 644–648.

King, R. J., Mefford, I. N., & Wang, C. (1986). CSF dopamine levels correlate with extraversion in depressed patients. *Psychiatric Research, 19,* 305–310.

Klein, D. F. (1964). Delineation of two drug responsive anxiety syndromes. *Psychopharmacologia, 5,* 397–408.

Klein, D. F. (1981). Anxiety reconceptualized. In D. F. Klein & J. Rabkin (Eds.), *Anxiety: New research and changing concepts* (pp. 235–263). New York: Raven Press.

Klein, D. F. (1993). False suffocation alarms, spontaneous panics, and related conditions: An integrative hypothesis. *Archives of General Psychiatry, 50,* 306–317.

Klein, D. F. (1994). Testing the suffocation false alarm theory of panic disorder. *Anxiety, 1,* 1–7.

Klein, D. F., & Fink, M. (1962). Psychiatric reaction patterns to imipramine. *American Journal of Psychiatry, 119,* 432–438.

Klein, D. F., & Gorman, J. M. (1987). A model of panic and agoraphobic development. *Acta Psychiatrica Scandinavica, 76,* 87–95.

Kleinknecht, R. A. (1992). The Mutilation Questionnaire for assessing blood/injury fear and phobia. *The Behavior Therapist, 15,* 66–67.

Kleinknecht, R. A. (1993). Rapid treatment of blood and injection phobias with eye movement desensitization. *Journal of Behavior Therapy and Experimental Psychopathology, 24,* 211–217.

Kleinknecht, R.A., & Bernstein, D.A. (1978). The assessment of dental fear. *Behavior Therapy, 9,* 626-634.

Kleinknecht, R. A., Dinnel, D. L., Kleinknecht, E. E., Hiruma, N., & Harada, N. (1997). Cultural factors in social anxiety: A comparison of social phobia symptoms and Taijin Kyofusho. *Journal of Anxiety Disorders, 11,* 157–177.

Kleinknecht, R. A., Kleinknecht, E. E., Sawchuk, C., Lee, T., & Lohr, J. (1999). The Medical Fear Survey: Psychometric properties. *The Behavior Therapist, 22,* 109–119.

Kleinknecht, R. A., Kleinknecht, E. E., & Thorndike, R. M. (1997). The role of disgust and fear in blood and injection-related fainting symptoms: A structural equation model. *Behaviour Research and Therapy, 35,* 1075–1087.

Kleinknecht, R. A., & Thorndike, R. M. (1990). The Mutilation Questionnaire as a predictor of blood/injury fear and fainting. *Behaviour Research and Therapy, 28,* 429–437.

Kleinknecht, R. A., Thorndike, R. M., & Walls, M. M. (1996). Factorial dimensions and correlates of blood, injury, injection and related medical fears: Cross-validation of the Medical Fear Survey. *Behaviour Research and Therapy, 34,* 323–331.

Kleinknecht, R.A., Tolin, D.F., Lohr, J.M., & Kleinknecht, E.E. (1996, November). *Relationships between blood injury fears, disgust sensitivity, and vasovagal fainting in two independent samples.* Paper presented at the meeting of the Association for Advancement of Behavior Therapy, New York, NY.

Klerman, G. L., & Weissman, M. M. (1993). *New applications of interpersonal psychotherapy.* Washington, DC: American Psychiatric Press.

Klieger, D. M. (1987). The Snake Anxiety Questionnaire as a measure of ophidophobia. *Educational and Psychological Measurement, 47,* 449–459.

Klieger, D. M. (1994). A new approach to the measurement of ophidophobia. *Personality and Individual Differences, 16,* 505–508.

Klieger, D. M., & Franklin, M. E. (1993). Validity of the Fear Survey Schedule in phobia research: A laboratory test. *Journal of Psychopathology and Behavioral Assessment, 15,* 207–217.

Klorman, R., Hastings, J., Weerts, T., Melamed, B. G., & Lang, P. (1974). Psychometric description of some specific-fear questionnaires. *Behavior Therapy, 5,* 401–409.

Knott, V., Bakish, D., Lusk, S., & Barkely, J. (1997). Relaxation-induced EEG alterations in panic disorder patients. *Journal of Anxiety Disorders, 11,* 365–376.

Knowles, J. A., Fyer, A. J., Vieland, V. J., Weissman, M. M., Hodge, S. E., Heiman, G. A., Haghighi, F., de Jesus, G. M., Rassnick, H., Preud'homme-Rivelli, X., Austin, T., Cunjak, J., Mick, S., Fine, L. D., Woodley, K. A., Das, K., Maier, W., Adams, P. B., Freimer, N. B., Klein, D. F., & Gilliam, T. C. (1998). Results of a genome-wide genetic screen for panic disorder. *American Journal of Medical Genetics, 81,* 139–147.

Kobak, K. A., Schaettle, S. C., Greist, J. H., Jefferson, J. W., Katzelnick, D. J., & Dottl, S. L. (1998). Computer-administered rating scales for social anxiety in a clinical drug trial. *Depression and Anxiety, 7,* 97–104.

Kozak, M. J., & Montgomery, G. K. (1981). Multimodal behavioral treatment of recurrent injury-scene elicited fainting (vasodepressor syncope). *Behavioural Psychotherapy, 9,* 316–321.

Kramer, M. S., Cutler, N. R., Ballenger, J. C., Patterson, W. M., Mendels, J., Chenault, A., Shrivastava, R., Matzura-Wolfe, D., Lines, C., & Reines, S. (1995). A placebo-controlled trial of L-365,260, a CCKB antagonist, in panic disorder. *Society of Biological Psychiatry, 37,* 462–466.

Kroeze, S., & van den Hout, M. A. (1998). No superior perception of hyperventilatory sensations in panic disorder. *Behaviour Research and Therapy, 36,* 285–295.

Krystal, J. H., Woods, S. W., Hill, C. L., & Charney, D. S. (1991). Characteristics of panic attack subtypes: Assessment of spontaneous panic, situational panic, and limited symptoms. *Comparative Psychiatry, 32,* 474–480.

Kushner, M. G., & Beitman, B. D. (1990). Panic attacks without fear: An overview. *Behaviour Research and Therapy, 28,* 469–479.

Kushner, M. G., Sher, K. J., & Beitman, B. D. (1990). The relations between alcohol problems and the anxiety disorders. *American Journal of Psychiatry, 147,* 685–695.

Kwon, S. -M., Evans, L., & Oei, T. P. S. (1990). Factor structure of the Mobility Inventory for Agoraphobia: A validation study with Australian samples of agoraphobic patients. *Journal of Psychopathology and Behavioral Assessment, 12,* 365–374.

Laberge, B., Gauthier, J. G., Côté, G., Plamondon, J., & Cormier, H. J. (1993). Cognitive–behavioral therapy of panic disorder with secondary major depression: A preliminary investigation. *Journal of Consulting and Clinical Psychology, 61,* 1028–1037.

Landy, F. J., & Gaupp, L. A. (1971). A factor analysis of the FSS-III. *Behaviour Research and Therapy, 9,* 89–93.

Lang, A. J., & Craske, M. G. (2000). Manipulations of exposure-based therapy to reduce return of fear: A replication. *Behaviour Research and Therapy, 38,* 1–12.

Lang, P. J. (1985). The cognitive psychophysiology of emotion: Fear and anxiety. In A. H. Tuma & J. D. Maser (Eds.), *Anxiety and the anxiety disorders* (pp. 131–170). Hillsdale, NJ: Erlbaum.

Lang, P. J. (1988). Fear, anxiety, and panic: Context, cognition, and visceral arousal. In S. Rachman & J. D. Maser (Eds.), *Panic: Psychological perspectives* (pp. 219–236). Hillsdale, NJ: Erlbaum.

Lang, P. J., & Lazovik, A. D. (1963). The experimental desensitization of an animal phobia. *Journal of Abnormal and Social Psychology, 66,* 519–525.

Lavy, E., van den Hout, M., & Arntz, A. (1993a). Attentional bias and facilitated escape: A pictorial test. *Advances in Behaviour Research and Therapy, 15,* 279–289.

Lavy, E., van den Hout, M., & Arntz, A. (1993b). Attentional bias and spider phobia: Conceptual and clinical issues. *Behaviour Research and Therapy, 31,* 17–24.

Lazarus, R. S. (1982). Thoughts on the relations between emotion and cognition. *American Psychologist, 37,* 1019–1024.

Leary, M. R., & Kowalski, R. M. (1995). The self-presentation model of social phobia. In R. G. Heimberg, M. R. Liebowitz, D. A. Hope, & F. R. Schneier (Eds.), *Social phobia: Diagnosis, assessment, and treatment* (pp. 94–112). New York: Guilford Press.

Lee, M. A., Flegel, P., Greden, J. F., & Cameron, O. G. (1988). Anxiogenic effects of caffeine on panic and depressed patients. *American Journal of Psychiatry, 145,* 632–635.

Leon, A. C., Portera, L., & Weissman, M. M. (1995). The social costs of anxiety disorders. *British Journal of Psychiatry, 166*(Suppl. 27), 19–22.

Lesser, I. M., Rubin, R. T., Pecknold, J. C., Rifkin, A., Swinson, R. P., Lydiard, R. B., Burrows, G. D., Noyes, R., & DuPont, R. L. (1988). Secondary depression in panic disorder and agoraphobia: I. Frequency, severity, and response to treatment. *Archives of General Psychiatry, 45,* 437–443.

Leung, A. W., & Heimberg, R. G. (1996). Homework compliance, perceptions of control, and outcome of cognitive behavioral treatment of social phobia. *Behaviour Research and Therapy, 34,* 423–432.

Leung, A. W., Heimberg, R. G., Holt, C. S., & Bruch, M. A. (1994). Social anxiety and perception of early parenting among American, Chinese American, and social phobic samples. *Anxiety, 1,* 80–89.

Levine, B. A., & Wolpe, J. (1980). In vivo desensitization of a severe driving phobia through radio contact. *Journal of Behavior Therapy and Experimental Psychiatry, 11,* 281–282.

Lewinsohn, P. M., Zinbarg, R., Seeley, J. R., Lewinsohn, M., & Sack, W. H. (1997). Lifetime comorbidity among anxiety disorders and between anxiety disorders and other mental disorders in adolescents. *Journal of Anxiety Disorders, 11,* 377–394.

Lewis, M. H., Gariepy, J., & Devaud, L. L. (1989, December). *Dopamine and social behavior: A mouse model of "timidity."* Paper presented at the meeting of the American College of Neuropsychopharmacology, Maui, Hawaii.

Ley, R. (1987). Panic disorder: A hyperventilation interpretation. In L. Michelson & L. M. Ascher (Eds.), *Anxiety and stress disorders: Cognitive–behavioral assessment and treatment* (pp. 191–212). New York: Guilford Press.

Ley, R. (1994). The "suffocation alarm" theory of panic attacks: A critical commentary. *Journal of Behavior Therapy and Experimental Psychiatry, 25,* 269–273.

Liddell, A., Locker, D., & Burman, D. (1991). Self-reported fears (FSS-II) of subjects aged 50 years and over. *Behaviour Research and Therapy, 29,* 105–112.

Liddell, A., & Lyons, M. (1978). Thunderstorm phobias. *Behaviour Research and Therapy, 16,* 306–308.

Lidren, D. M., Watkins, P. L., Gould, R. A., Clum, G. A., Asterino, M., & Tulloch, H. L. (1994). A comparison of bibliotherapy and group therapy in the treatment of panic disorder. *Journal of Consulting and Clinical Psychology, 62,* 865–869.

Liebowitz, M. R. (1987). Social phobia. *Modern Problems in Pharmacopsychiatry, 22,* 141–173.

Liebowitz, M. R., Fyer, A. J., Gorman, J. M., Campeas, R., & Levin, A. (1986). Phenelzine in social phobia. *Journal of Clinical Psychopharmacology, 6,* 93–98.

Liebowitz, M. R., Fyer, A. J., Gorman, J. M., Dillon, D., Appleby, I. L., Levy, G., Anderson, S., Levitt, M., Palij, M., Davies, S. O., & Klein, D. F. (1984). Lactate provocation of panic attacks: I. Clinical and behavioral findings. *Archives of General Psychiatry, 41,* 764–770.

Liebowitz, M.R., Fyer, A.J., Gorman, J.M., Dillon, D., Davies, S., Stein, J.M., Cohen, B.S., & Klein, D.F. (1985). Specificity of lactate infusions in social phobia versus panic disorders. *American Journal of Psychiatry, 142,* 947–950.

Liebowitz, M. R., Gorman, J. M., Fyer, A. J., Campeas, R., Levin, A. P., & Sandberg, D. (1988). Pharmacotherapy of social phobia: An interim report of a placebo-controlled comparison of phenelzine and atenolol. *Journal of Clinical Psychiatry, 49,* 252–257.

Liebowitz, M. R., Heimberg, R. G., Schneier, F. R., Hope, D. A., Davies, S., Holt, C. S., Goetz, D., Juster, H. R., Lin, S. -H., Bruch, M. A., Marshall, R. D., & Klein, D. F. (1999). Cognitive–behavioral group therapy versus phenelzine in social phobia: Long-term outcome. *Depression and Anxiety, 10,* 89–98.

Liebowitz, M. R., Schneier, F., Campeas, R., Hollander, E., Hatterer, J., & Fyer, A. J. (1992). Phenelzine vs atenolol in social phobia: A placebo-controlled comparison. *Archives of General Psychiatry, 49,* 290–300.

Lipsitz, J. D., Markowitz, J. C., Cherry, S., & Fyer, A. J. (1999). Open trial of interpersonal psychotherapy for the treatment of social phobia. *American Journal of Psychiatry, 156,* 1814–1816.

Liss, A., Antony, M. M., Purdon, C. L., & Swinson, R. P. (1999, November). *Psychoeducation versus group therapy for social phobia: Preliminary findings.* Paper presented at the meeting of the Association for Advancement of Behavior Therapy, Toronto, Canada.

Loerch, B., Graf-Morgenstern, M., Hautzinger, M., Schlegel, S., Hain, C., Sandmann, J, & Benkert, O. (1999). Randomized placebo-controlled trial of moclobemide, cognitive–behavioural therapy and their combination in panic disorder and agoraphobia. *British Journal of Psychiatry, 174,* 205–212.

Lohr, J. M., Lilienfeld, S. O., Tolin, D. F., & Herbert, J. D. (1999). Eye movement desensitization and reprocessing: An analysis of specific versus non-specific treatment factors. *Journal of Anxiety Disorders, 13,* 185–207.

Lohr, J. M., Tolin, D. F., & Kleinknecht, R. A. (1995). Eye movement desensitization of medical phobias: Two case studies. *Journal of Behavior Therapy and Experimental Psychiatry, 26,* 141–151.

Lohr, J. M., Tolin, D. F., & Kleinknecht, R. A. (1996). An intensive design investigation of eye movement desensitization and reprocessing of claustrophobia. *Journal of Anxiety Disorders, 10,* 73–88.

Lohr, J. M., Tolin, D. F., & Lilienfeld, S. O. (1998). Efficacy of eye movement desensitization and reprocessing: Implications for behavior therapy. *Behavior Therapy, 29,* 123–156.

Londborg, P. D., Wolkow, R., Smith, W. T., DuBoff, E., England, D., Ferguson, J., Rosenthal, M., & Weise, C. (1998). Sertraline in the treatment of panic disorder. *British Journal of Psychiatry, 173,* 54–60.

Lopatka, C. L. (1989). *The role of unexpected events in avoidance.* Unpublished master's thesis, University at Albany, State University of New York.

Lott, M., Greist, J. H., Jefferson, J. W., Kobak, K. A., Katzelnick, D. J., Katz, R. J., & Schaettle, S. C. (1997). Brofaromine for social phobia: A multicenter, placebo-controlled, double blind study. *Journal of Clinical Psychopharmacology, 17,* 255–260.

Lovibond, S. H., & Lovibond, P. F. (1995). *Manual for the Depression Anxiety Stress Scales* (2nd ed.). Sydney, Australia: The Psychology Foundation of Australia.

Lundh, L. -G., Czyzykow, S., & Öst, L. -G. (1997). Recognition bias for safe faces in panic disorder with agoraphobia. *Behaviour Research and Therapy, 36,* 323–337.

Lundh, L. -G., & Öst, L. -G. (1996). Recognition bias for critical faces in social phobics. *Behaviour Research and Therapy, 34,* 787–794.

Lundh, L. -G., & Öst, L. -G. (1997). Explicit and implicit memory bias in social phobia. The role of subdiagnostic type. *Behaviour Research and Therapy, 35,* 305–317.

Lundh, L. -G., Thulin, U., Czyzykow, S., & Öst, L. -G. (1998). Explicit and implicit memory bias in panic disorder with agoraphobia. *Behaviour Research and Therapy, 35,* 1003–1014.

Magee, W. J., Eaton, W. W., Wittchen, H. -U., McGonagle, K. A., & Kessler, R. C. (1996). Agoraphobia, simple phobia, and social phobia in the national comorbidity survey. *Archives of General Psychiatry, 53,* 159–168.

Mahone, E. M., Bruch, M. A., & Heimberg, R. G., (1993). Focus of attention and social anxiety: The role of negative self-thoughts and perceived positive attributes of the other. *Cognitive Therapy and Research, 17,* 209–224.

Maidenberg, E., Chen, E., Craske, M., Bohn, P., & Bystritsky, A. (1996). Specificity of attentional bias in panic disorder and social phobia. *Journal of Anxiety Disorders, 10,* 529–541.

Maier, W., Roth, M., Buller, R., Argyle, N., Rosenberg, R., Brandon, S., & Benkert, O. (1991). Agoraphobia in panic disorder: An indicator of the severity of panic disorder or a distinct diagnostic entity? *Psychiatric Annals, 21,* 374–381.

Mannuzza, S., Aronowitz, B., Chapman, T., Klein, D. F., & Fyer, A. J. (1992). Panic disorder and suicide attempts. *Journal of Anxiety Disorders, 6,* 261–274.

Mannuzza, S., Chapman, T. F., Klein, D. F., & Fyer, A. J. (1994/1995). Familial transmission of panic disorder: Effect of major depression comorbidity. *Anxiety, 1,* 180–185.

Mannuzza, S., Fyer, A. J., Martin, L. Y., Gallops, M. S., Endicott, J., Gorman, J., Liebowitz, M. R., & Klein, D. F. (1989). Reliability of anxiety assessment: I. Diagnostic agreement. *Archives of General Psychiatry, 46,* 1093–1101.

Mannuzza, S., Schneier, F. R., Chapman, T. F., Liebowitz, M. R., Klein, D. F., & Fyer, A. J. (1995). Generalized social phobia: Reliability and validity. *Archives of General Psychiatry, 52,* 220–237.

Mansell, W., Clark, D. M., Ehlers, A., & Chen, Y. -P. (1999). Social anxiety and attention away from emotional faces. *Cognition and Emotion, 13,* 673–690.

Marchione, K. E., Michelson, L., Greenwald, M., & Dancu, C. (1987). Cognitive behavioral treatment of agoraphobia. *Behaviour Research and Therapy, 25,* 319–328.

Markowitz, J. C. (1998). *Interpersonal psychotherapy.* Washington, DC: American Psychiatric Press.

Marks, I. M. (1987a). Behavioral aspects of panic disorder. *American Journal of Psychiatry, 144,* 1160–1165.

Marks, I. M. (1987b). *Fears, phobias, and rituals.* New York: Oxford University Press.

Marks, I. M., & Mathews, A. M. (1979). Brief standard self-rating for phobic patients. *Behaviour Research and Therapy, 17,* 263–267.

Marks, M. P. Başoğlu, M. Al-Kubaisy, T. Sengün, S., & Marks, I. M. (1991). Are anxiety symptoms and catastrophic cognitions directly related? *Journal of Anxiety Disorders, 5,* 247–254.

Marks, I. M., & Gelder, M. G. (1966). Different ages of onset in varieties of phobia. *American Journal of Psychiatry, 123,* 218–221.

Marks, I. M., Swinson, R. P., Başoğlu, M., Kuch, K., Noshirvani, H., O'Sullivan, G., Lelliott, P. T., Kirby, M., McNamee, G., Sengun, S., & Wickwire, K. (1993). Alprazolam and exposure alone and combined in panic disorder with agoraphobia: A controlled study in London and Toronto. *British Journal of Psychiatry, 162,* 776–787.

Markway, B. G., Carmin, C. N., Pollard, C. A., & Flynn, T. (1992). *Dying of embarrassment: Help for social anxiety and phobia.* Oakland, CA: New Harbinger.

Marshall, W. L., Bristol, D., & Barbaree, H. E. (1992). Cognitions and courage in the avoidance behavior of acrophobics. *Behaviour Research and Therapy, 30,* 463–470.

Martel, F. L., Hayward, C., Lyons, D. M., Sanborn, K., Varady, S., & Schatzberg, A. F. (1999). Salivary cortisol levels in socially phobic adolescent girls. *Depression and Anxiety, 10,* 25–27.

Martinsen, E. W. (1993). Therapeutic implications of exercise for clinically anxious and depressed patients. *International Journal of Sport Psychology, 24,* 185–199.

Mathews, A., & MacLeod, C. (1985). Selective processing of threat cues in anxiety states. *Behaviour Research and Therapy, 23,* 563–569.

Mattia, J. I., Heimberg, R. G., & Hope, D. A. (1993). The revised Stroop color-naming task in social phobics. *Behaviour Research and Therapy, 31,* 305–313.

Mattick, R. P., & Clarke, J. C. (1998). Development and validation of measures of social phobia scrutiny fear and social interaction anxiety. *Behaviour Research and Therapy, 36,* 455–470.

Mattick, R. P., & Peters, L. (1988). Treatment of severe social phobia: Effects of guided exposure with and without cognitive restructuring. *Journal of Consulting and Clinical Psychology, 56,* 251–260.

Mattick, R. P., Peters, L., & Clarke, J. C. (1989). Exposure and cognitive restructuring for social phobia: A controlled study. *Behavior Therapy, 20,* 3–23.

Mavissakalian, M. (1986). The Fear Questionnaire: A validity study. *Behaviour Research and Therapy, 24,* 83–85.

Mavissakalian, M. R. (1996a). Antidepressant medications for panic disorder. In M. R. Mavissakalian & R. F. Prien (Eds.), *Long-term treatments of anxiety disorders* (pp. 221–240). Washington, DC: American Psychiatric Press.

Mavissakalian, M. R. (1996b). Phenomenology of panic attacks: Responsiveness of individual symptoms to imipramine. *Journal of Clinical Psychopharmacology, 16,* 233–237.

Mavissakalian, M. R., & Perel, J. M (1989). Imipramine dose–response relationship in panic disorder with agoraphobia: Preliminary findings. *Archives of General Psychiatry, 46,* 127–131.

Mavissakalian, M. R., & Perel, J. M (1992). Protective effects of imipramine mainte-nance treatment in panic disorder with agoraphobia. *American Journal of Psychiatry, 149,* 1053–1057.

Mavissakalian, M. R., & Perel, J. M. (1995). Imipramine treatment of panic disorder with agoraphobia: Dose ranging and plasma level–response relationships. *American Journal of Psychiatry, 152,* 673–682.

Mavissakalian, M. R., & Perel, J. M (1999). Long-term maintenance and discontinu-ation of imipramine therapy in panic disorder with agoraphobia. *Archives of General Psychiatry, 56,* 821–827.

McGlynn, F. D., McNeil, D. W., Gallagher, S. L., & Vrana, S. (1987). Factor structure, stability, and internal consistency of the Dental Fear Survey. *Behavioral Assessment, 9,* 57–66.

McGlynn, F. D., Rose, M. P., & Jacobson, N. (1995). Effects of control and attentional instructions on arousal and fear during exposure to phobia-cue stimuli. *Journal of Anxiety Disorders, 9,* 451–461.

McGlynn, F. D., Rose, M. P., & Lazarte, A. (1994). Control and attention during exposure influence arousal and fear among insect phobias. *Journal of Behavior Modification, 18,* 371–388.

McKay, M., Davis, M, & Fanning, P. (1995). *Messages: The communications skills book* (2nd ed.). Oakland, CA: New Harbinger.

McKay, M., Rogers, P. D., & McKay, J. (1989). *When anger hurts: Quieting the storm within.* Oakland, CA: New Harbinger.

McLean, P. D., Woody, S., Taylor, S., & Koch, W. J. (1998). Comorbid panic disorder and major depression: Implications for cognitive–behavioural therapy. *Journal of Consulting and Clinical Psychology, 66,* 240–247.

McNally, R. J. (1994). *Panic disorder: A critical analysis.* New York: Guilford Press.

McNally, R. J. (in press). On eye movements and animal magnetism: A reply to Greenwald's defense of EMDR. *Journal of Anxiety Disorders.*

McNally, R. J., Amir, N., Louro, C. E., Lukach, B. M., Riemann, B. C., & Calamari, J. E. (1994). Cognitive processing of ideographic emotional information in panic disorder. *Behaviour Research and Therapy, 32,* 119–122.

McNally, R. J., Foa, E. B., & Donnell, C. D. (1989). Memory bias for anxiety information in patients with panic disorder. *Cognition and Emotion, 3,* 27–44.

McNally, R. J., Hornig, C. D., & Donnell, C. D. (1995). Clinical versus non-clinical panic: A test of suffocation false alarm theory. *Behaviour Research and Therapy, 33,* 127–131.

McNally, R. J., Hornig, C. D., Otto, M. W., & Pollack, M. H. (1997). Selective encoding of threat in panic disorder: Application of a dual priming paradigm. *Behaviour Research and Therapy, 35,* 543–549.

McNally, R. J., & Louro, C. E. (1992). Fear of flying in agoraphobia and simple phobia: Distinguishing features. *Journal of Anxiety Disorders, 6,* 319–324.

McNally, R. J., Riemann, B. C., & Kim, E. (1990). Selective processing of threat cues in panic disorder. *Behaviour Research and Therapy, 28,* 407–412.

McNally, R. J., & Steketee, G. S. (1985). The etiology and maintenance of severe animal phobias. *Behaviour Research and Therapy, 23*, 431–435.

McNeil, D. W., Ries, B. J., Taylor, L. J., Boone, M. L., Carter, L. E., Turk, C. L., & Lewin, M. R. (1995). Comparison of social phobia subtypes using Stroop tests. *Journal of Anxiety Disorders, 9*, 47–57.

McNeil, D. W., Ries, B. J., & Turk, C. L. (1995). Behavioral assessment: Self-report, physiology, and overt behavior. In R. G. Heimberg, M. R. Liebowitz, D. A. Hope, & F. R. Schneier (Eds.), *Social phobia: Diagnosis, assessment, and treatment* (pp. 202–231) New York: Guilford Press.

Mellman, T. A., & Uhde, T. W. (1989a). Electroencephalographic sleep in panic disorder: A focus on sleep-related panic attacks. *Archives of General Psychiatry, 46*, 178–184.

Mellman, T. A., & Uhde, T. W. (1989b). Sleep panic attacks: New clinical findings and theoretical implications. *American Journal of Psychiatry, 146*, 1204–1207.

Menzies, R. G., & Clarke, J. C. (1993a). A comparison of in vivo and vicarious exposure in the treatment of childhood water phobia. *Behaviour Research and Therapy, 31*, 9–15.

Menzies, R. G., & Clarke, J. C. (1993b). The etiology of fear of heights and its relationship to severity and individual response patterns. *Behaviour Research and Therapy, 31*, 355–365.

Menzies, R. G., & Clarke, J. C. (1993c). The etiology of childhood water phobia. *Behaviour Research and Therapy, 31*, 499–501.

Menzies, R. G., & Clarke, J. C. (1995a). Danger expectancies and insight in acrophobia. *Behaviour Research and Therapy, 33*, 215–221.

Menzies, R. G., & Clarke, J. C. (1995b). The etiology of acrophobia and its relationship to severity and individual response patterns. *Behaviour Research and Therapy, 33*, 795–803.

Menzies, R. G., & Clarke, J. C. (1995c). The etiology of phobias: A non-associative account. *Clinical Psychology Review, 15*, 23–48.

Menzies, R. G., & Harris, L. M. (1997). Mode of onset in evolutionary-relevant and evolutionary-neutral phobias: Evidence from a clinical sample. *Depression and Anxiety, 5*, 134–136.

Merckelbach, H., Arntz, A., Arrindell, W. A., & de Jong, P. J. (1992). Pathways to spider phobia. *Behaviour Research and Therapy, 30*, 543–546.

Merckelbach, H., Arntz, A., & de Jong, P. (1991). Conditioning experiences and spider phobics. *Behaviour Research and Therapy, 29*, 333–335.

Merckelbach, H., & de Jong, P. J. (1997). Evolutionary models of phobias. In G. C. L. Davey (Ed.), *Phobias: A handbook of theory, research and treatment* (pp. 323–348). New York: Wiley.

Merckelbach, H., de Jong, P. J., Arntz, A., & Schouten, E. (1993). The role of evaluative learning and disgust sensitivity in the etiology and treatment of spider phobia. *Advances in Behaviour Research and Therapy, 15*, 243–255.

Merckelbach, H., de Jong, P. J., Muris, P., & van den Hout, M. A. (1996). The etiology of specific phobias: A review. *Clinical Psychology Review, 16,* 337–361.

Merckelbach, H., Kenemans, J. L., Dijkstra, A., & Schouten, E. (1993). No attentional bias for pictoral stimuli in spider-fearful subjects. *Journal of Psychopathology and Behavioral Assessment, 15,* 197–206.

Merckelbach, H., & Muris, P. (1997). The etiology of childhood spider phobia. *Behaviour Research and Therapy, 35,* 1031–1034.

Merckelbach, H., Muris, P., de Jong, P. J., & de Jongh, A. (1999). Disgust sensitivity, blood-injection-injury fear, and dental anxiety. *Clinical Psychology and Psychotherapy, 6,* 279–285.

Merckelbach, H., Muris, P., & Schouten, E. (1996). Pathways to fear in spider phobic children. *Behaviour Research and Therapy, 34,* 935–938.

Mersch, P. P. (1995). The treatment of social phobia: The differential effectiveness of exposure in vivo and an integration of exposure in vivo, rational emotive therapy and social skills training. *Behaviour Research and Therapy, 33,* 259–269.

Mersch, P. P., Emmelkamp, P. M., Bögels, S. M., & van der Sleen, J. (1989). Social phobia: Individual response patterns and the effects of behavioral and cognitive interventions. *Behaviour Research and Therapy, 27,* 421–434.

Mersch, P. P., Emmelkamp, P. M., & Lips, C. (1991). Social phobia: Individual response patterns and long-term effects of behavioral and cognitive interventions. A follow-up study. *Behaviour Research and Therapy, 29,* 357–362.

Michelson, D., Lydiard, R. B., Pollack, M. H., Tamura, R. N., Hoog, S. L., Tepner, R., Demitrack, M. A., & Tollefson, G. D. (1998). Outcome assessment and clinical improvement in panic disorder: Evidence from a randomized controlled trial of fluoxetine and placebo. The Fluoxetine Panic Disorder Study Group. *American Journal of Psychiatry, 155,* 1570–1577.

Michelson, L. K., Marchione, K. E., Greenwald, M., Testa, S., & Marchione, N. J. (1996). A comparative study of panic disorder with agoraphobia: The relative and combined efficacy of cognitive therapy, relaxation training, and therapist-assisted exposure. *Journal of Anxiety Disorders, 10,* 297–330.

Michelson, L., Mavissakalian, M., & Marchione, K. (1988). Cognitive, behavioral, and psychophysiological treatments of agoraphobia: A comparative outcome investigation. *Behavior Therapy, 19,* 97–190.

Mineka, S., Davidson, M., Cook, M., & Keir, R. (1984). Observational conditioning of fear in rhesus monkeys. *Journal of Abnormal Psychology, 93,* 355–372.

Mineka, S., Mystkowski, J. L., Hladek, D., & Rodriguez, B. I. (1999). The effects of changing contexts on return of fear following exposure therapy for spider fear. *Journal of Consulting and Clinical Psychology, 67,* 599–604.

Moore, R., & Brødsgaard, I. (1994). Group therapy compared with individual desensitization for dental anxiety. *Community Dentistry and Oral Epidemiology, 22,* 258–262.

Moras, K., Di Nardo, P. A., Brown, T. A., & Barlow, D. H. (1994). *Comorbidity, functional inpairment, and depression among the DSM-III-R anxiety disorders.*

Unpublished manuscript. Center for Stress and Anxiety Disorders, State University of New York–Albany.

Morgan, H., & Raffle, C. (1999). Does reducing safety behaviours improve treatment response in patients with social phobia? *Australia and New Zealand Journal of Psychiatry, 33,* 503–510.

Morin, C. M. (1993). *Insomnia: Psychological assessment and management.* New York: Guilford Press.

Moroz, G., & Rosenbaum, J. F. (1999). Efficacy, safety, and gradual discontinuation of clonazepam in panic disorder: A placebo-controlled, multicenter study using optimized dosages. *Journal of Clinical Psychiatry, 60,* 604–612.

Mountz, J. M., Modell, J. G., Wilson, M. W., Curtis, G. C., Lee, M. A., Schmaltz, S., & Kuhl, D. E. (1989). Positron emission tomographic evaluation of cerebral blood flow during state anxiety in simple phobia. *Archives of General Psychiatry, 46,* 501–504.

Mowrer, O. H. (1939). Stimulus response theory of anxiety. *Psychological Review, 46,* 553–565.

Mulkens, S., de Jong, P. J., Dobbelaar, A., & Bögels, S. M. (1999). Fear of blushing: Fearful preoccupation irrespective of facial coloration. *Behaviour Research and Therapy, 37,* 1119–1128.

Mulkens, S. A. N., de Jong, P. J., & Merckelbach, H. (1996). Disgust and spider phobia. *Journal of Abnormal Psychology, 105,* 464–468.

Munjack, D. J., Bruns, J., Baltazar, P. L., Brown, R., Leonard, M., Nagy, R., Koek, R., Crocker, B., & Schafer, S. (1991). A pilot study of buspirone in the treatment of social phobia. *Journal of Anxiety Disorders, 5,* 87–98.

Muris, P., Mayer, B., & Merckelbach, H. (1998). Trait anxiety as a predictor of behaviour therapy outcome in spider phobia. *Behavioural and Cognitive Psychotherapy, 26,* 87–91.

Muris, P., & Merckelbach, H. (1995). Treating spider phobia with eye-movement desensitization and reprocessing: Two case reports. *Journal of Anxiety Disorders, 9,* 439–449.

Muris, P., & Merckelbach, H. (1996). A comparison of two spider phobia questionnaires. *Journal of Behavior Therapy and Experimental Psychiatry, 27,* 241–244.

Muris, P., Merckelbach, H., & Collaris, R. (1997). Common childhood fears and their origins. *Behaviour Research and Therapy, 35,* 929–937.

Muris, P., Merckelbach, H., Holdrinet, I., & Sijsenaar, M. (1998). Treating phobic children: Effects of EMDR versus exposure. *Journal of Consulting and Clinical Psychology, 66,* 193–198.

Muris, P., Merckelbach, H., van Haaften, H., & Mayer, B. (1997). Eye movement desensitization and reprocessing versus exposure in vivo: A single-session crossover study of spider-phobic children. *British Journal of Psychiatry, 171,* 82–86.

Muris, P., Schmidt, H., & Merckelbach, H. (1999). The structure of specific phobia symptoms among children and adolescents. *Behaviour Research and Therapy, 37,* 863–868.

Muris, P., Steerneman, P., Merckelbach, H., & Meesters, C. (1996). The role of parental fearfulness and modeling in children's fear. *Behaviour Research and Therapy, 34*, 265–268.

Myers, J. K., Weissman, M. M., Tischler, G. L., Holzer, C. E., Leaf, P. J., Orvaschel, H., Anthony, J. C., Boyd, J. H., Burke, J. D., Kramer, M., & Stoltzman, R. (1984). Six-month prevalence of psychiatric disorders in three communities. *Archives of General Psychiatry, 41*, 959–967.

Nair, N. P. V., Bakish, D., Saxena, B., Amin, M., Schwartz, G., & West, T. E. G. (1996). Comparison of fluvoxamine, imipramine, and placebo in the treatment of outpatients with panic disorder. *Anxiety, 2*, 192–198.

Neale, M.C., Walters, E.E., Eaves, L.J., Kessler, R.C., Heath, A.C., & Kendler, K.S. (1994). Genetics of blood-injury fears and phobias: A population-based twin study. *American Journal of Medical Genetics, 54*, 326-334.

Neimeyer, R. A., & Feixas, G. (1990). The role of homework and skill acquisition in the outcome of group cognitive therapy for depression. *Behavior Therapy, 21*, 281–292.

Nelissen, I., Muris, P., & Merckelbach, H. (1995). Computerized exposure and in vivo exposure treatments of spider fear in children: Two case reports. *Journal of Behavior Therapy and Experimental Psychiatry, 26*, 153–156.

Neron, S., Lacroix, D., & Chaput, Y. (1995). Group vs. individual cognitive behaviour therapy in panic disorder: An open clinical trial with a six month follow-up. *Canadian Journal of Behavioural Sciences, 27*, 379–392.

Nesse, R. M. (1987). An evolutionary perspective on panic disorder and agoraphobia. *Ethology and Sociobiology, 8*, 73S–83S.

Nesse, R. M., Curtis, G. C., Thyer, B. A., McCann, D. S., Huber-Smith, M. J., & Knopf, R. F. (1985). Endocrine and cardiovascular responses during phobic anxiety. *Psychosomatic Medicine, 47*, 320–332.

Newman, M. G., Hofmann, S. G., Trabert, W., Roth, W. T., & Taylor, C. B. (1994). Does behavioral treatment of social phobia lead to cognitive changes? *Behavior Therapy, 25*, 503–517.

Newman, M. G., Kenardy, J., Herman, S., & Taylor, C. B. (1997). Comparison of palmtop-computer-assisted brief cognitive–behavioral treatment to cognitive–behavioral treatment for panic disorder. *Journal of Consulting and Clinical Psychology, 65*, 178–183.

Newman, M. G., Zuelig, A. R., & Kachin, K. E. (1998, November). *The reliability and validity of the Panic Disorder Self-Report (PDSR): A new measure of panic disorder.* Paper presented at the meeting of the Association for Advancement of Behavior Therapy, Washington, DC.

Nordahl, T. E., Stein, M. B., Benkelfat, C., Semple, W. E., Andreason, P., Zametkin, A., Uhde, T. W., & Cohen, R. M. (1998). Regional cerebral metabolic asymmetries replicated in an independent group of patients with panic disorders. *Biological Psychiatry, 44*, 998–1006.

Norton, G. R., Cox, B. J., & Malan, J. (1992). Nonclinical panickers: A critical review. *Clinical Psychology Review, 12*, 121–139.

Norton, G. R., Dorward, J., & Cox, B. J. (1986). Factors associated with panic attacks in nonclinical subjects. *Behavior Therapy, 17,* 239–252.

Norton, G. R., Harrison, B., Hauch, J., & Rhodes, L. (1985). Characteristics of people with infrequent panic attacks. *Journal of Abnormal Psychology, 94,* 216–221.

Norton, G. R., McLeod, L., Guertin, J., Hewitt, P. L., Walker, J. R., & Stein, M. B. (1996). Panic disorder or social phobia: Which is worse? *Behaviour Research and Therapy, 34,* 273–276.

Norton, G. R., Norton, P. J., Walker, J. R., Cox, B. J., & Stein, M. B. (1999). A comparison of people with and without nocturnal panic attacks. *Journal of Behavior Therapy and Experimental Psychiatry, 30,* 37–44.

Norton, G. R., Pidlubny, S. R., & Norton, P. J. (1999). Prediction of panic attacks and related variables. *Behavior Therapy, 30,* 319–330.

Noyes, R., Moroz, G., Davidson, J. R. T., Liebowitz, M. R., Davidson, A., Siegel, J., Bell, J., Cain, J. W., Curlik, S. M., Kent, T. A., Lydiard, R. B., Mallinger, A. G., Pollack, M. H., Rapaport, M., Rasmussen, S. A., Hedges, D., Schweizer, E., & Uhlenhuth, E. H. (1997). Moclobemide in social phobia: A controlled dose–response trial. *Journal of Clinical Psychopharmacology, 17,* 247–254.

Nunn, J. D., Stevenson, R. J., & Whalan, G. (1984). Selective memory effects in agoraphobic patients. *British Journal of Clinical Psychology, 23,* 195–201.

Nutt, D., & Lawson, C. (1992). Panic attacks: A neurochemical overview of models and mechanisms. *British Journal of Psychiatry, 160,* 165–178.

Nutt, D. J. (1989). Altered central α–adrenoceptor sensitivity in panic disorder. *Archives of General Psychiatry, 46,* 165–169.

O'Brien, T. P., & Kelley, J. E. (1980). A comparison of self-directed and therapist-directed practice for fear reduction. *Behaviour Research and Therapy, 18,* 573–579.

O'Sullivan, G. H., Noshirvani, H., Başoğlu, M., Marks, I. M., Swinson, R., Kuch, K., & Kirby, M. (1994). Safety and side effects of alprazolam: Controlled study in agoraphobia with panic disorder. *British Journal of Psychiatry, 165,* 79–86.

O'Sullivan, G. H., Swinson, R., Kuch, K., Marks, I. M., Başoğlu, M., & Noshirvani, H. (1996). Alprazolam withdrawal symptoms in agoraphobia with panic disorder: Observations from a controlled Anglo–Canadian study. *Journal of Psychopharmacology, 10,* 101–109.

Oehrberg, S., Christiansen, P. E., Behnke, K., Borup, A. L., Severin, B., Soegaard, J., Calberg, H., Judge, R., Ohrstrom, J. K., Manniche, P. M. (1995). Paroxetine in the treatment of panic disorder: A randomised, double-blind, placebo-controlled study. *British Journal of Psychiatry, 167,* 374–379.

Oei, T. P. S., Kenna, D., & Evans, L. (1991). The reliability, validity, and utility of the SAD and FNE scales for anxiety disorder patients. *Personality and Individual Differences, 12,* 111–116.

Oei, T. P. S., Moylan, A., & Evans, L. (1991). Validity and clinical utility of the Fear Questionnaire for anxiety-disorder patients. *Psychological Assessment: A Journal of Consulting and Clinical Psychology, 3,* 391–397.

Oosterbaan, D. B., van Balkom, A. J. L. M, Spinhoven, P., van Oppen, P., & van Dyck, R. (1998). *Cognitive therapy versus moclobemide in social phobia: A controlled study*. Manuscript submitted for publication.

Osberg, J. W. (1981). The effectiveness of applied relaxation in the treatment of speech anxiety. *Behavior Therapy, 12*, 723–729.

Osman, A., Gutierrez, P. M., Barrios, F. X., Kopper, B. A., & Chiros, C. E. (1998). The Social Phobia and Social Interaction Anxiety Scales: Evaluation of psychometric properties. *Journal of Psychopathology and Behavioral Assessment, 20*, 249–264.

Öst, L. -G. (1985). Ways of acquiring phobias and outcome of behavioural treatment. *Behaviour Research and Therapy, 23*, 683–689.

Öst, L. -G. (1987a). Age of onset of different phobias. *Journal of Abnormal Psychology, 96*, 223–229.

Öst, L. -G. (1987b). Applied relaxation: Description of a coping technique and review of controlled studies. *Behaviour Research and Therapy, 25*, 397–409.

Öst, L. -G. (1988a). Applied relaxation vs. progressive relaxation in the treatment of panic disorder. *Behaviour Research and Therapy, 26*, 13–22.

Öst, L. -G. (1988b). Applied relaxation: Description of an effective coping technique. *Scandinavian Journal of Behavioural Therapy, 17*, 83–96.

Öst, L. -G. (1989). One-session treatment for specific phobias. *Behaviour Research and Therapy, 27*, 1–7.

Öst, L. -G. (1990). The Agoraphobia Scale: An evaluation of its reliability and validity. *Behaviour Research and Therapy, 28*, 323–329.

Öst, L. -G. (1992). Blood and injection phobia: Background and cognitive, physiological, and behavioral variables. *Journal of Abnormal Psychology, 101*, 68–74.

Öst, L. -G. (1996a). Long term effects of behavior therapy for specific phobia. In M. R. Mavissakalian & R. F. Prien (Eds.), *Long-term treatments of the anxiety disorders* (pp. 121–170). Washington, DC: American Psychiatric Press.

Öst, L. -G. (1996b). One-session group treatment for spider phobia. *Behaviour Research and Therapy, 34*, 707–715.

Öst, L. -G. (1997). Rapid treatment of specific phobias. In G. C. L. Davey (Ed.), *Phobias: A handbook of theory, research and treatment* (pp. 227–246). New York: Wiley.

Öst, L. -G., Brandberg, M., & Alm, T. (1997). One versus five sessions of exposure in the treatment of flying phobia. *Behaviour Research and Therapy, 35*, 987–996.

Öst, L. -G. Fellenius, J., & Sterner, U. (1991). Applied tension, exposure in vivo, and tension-only in the treatment of blood phobia. *Behaviour Research and Therapy, 29*, 561–574.

Öst, L. -G., Ferebee, I., & Furmark, T. (1997). One-session group therapy of spider phobia: Direct versus indirect treatments. *Behaviour Research and Therapy, 35*, 721–732.

Öst, L. -G., Jerremalm, A., & Johansson, J. (1981). Individual response patterns and the effects of different behavioral methods in the treatment of social phobia. *Behaviour Research and Therapy, 19*, 1–16.

Öst, L. -G., Johansson, J., & Jerremalm, A. (1982). Individual response patterns and the effects of different behavioral methods in the treatment of claustrophobia. *Behaviour Research and Therapy, 20*, 445–460.

Öst, L. -G., Lindahl, I. -L., Sterner, U., & Jerremalm, A. (1984). Exposure in vivo vs. applied relaxation in the treatment of blood phobia. *Behaviour Research and Therapy, 22*, 205–216.

Öst, L. -G., Salkovskis, P. M., & Hellström, K. (1991). One-session therapist directed exposure vs. self-exposure in the treatment of spider phobia. *Behavior Therapy, 22*, 407–422.

Öst, L. -G., & Sterner, U. (1987). Applied tension: A specific behavioral method for treatment of blood phobia. *Behaviour Research and Therapy, 25*, 25–29.

Öst, L. -G., & Westling, B. E. (1995). Applied relaxation vs. cognitive behavioral therapy in the treatment of panic disorder. *Behaviour Research and Therapy, 33*, 145–158.

Öst, L. -G., Westling, B. E., & Hellström, K. (1993). Applied relaxation, exposure in vivo and cognitive methods in the treatment of panic disorder with agoraphobia. *Behaviour Research and Therapy, 31*, 383–394.

Otto, M. W., Jones, J. C., Craske, M. G., & Barlow, D. H. (1996). *Stopping anxiety medication: Panic control therapy for benzodiazepine discontinuation* (therapist guide). San Antonio, TX: Psychological Corporation.

Otto, M. W., Pollack, M. H., & Barlow, D. H. (1996). *Stopping anxiety medication: panic control therapy for benzodiazepine discontinuation* (client workbook). San Antonio, TX: Psychological Corporation.

Otto, M. W., Pollack, M. H., Penava, S. J., & Zucker, B. G. (1999). Group cognitive–behavior therapy for patients failing to respond to pharmacotherapy for panic disorder: A clinical case series. *Behaviour Research and Therapy, 37*, 763–770.

Otto, M. W., Pollack, M. H., Sachs, G. S., Reiter, S. R., Meltzer-Brody, S., Rosenbaum, J. F. (1993). Discontinuation of benzodiazepine treatment: Efficacy of cognitive–behavioral therapy for patients with panic disorder. *American Journal of Psychiatry, 150*, 1485–1490.

Padesky, C. A. (1994). Schema change processes in cognitive therapy. Cognitive change processes in cognitive therapy. *Cognitive Psychology and Psychotherapy, 1*, 267–278.

Page, A. C. (1994). Blood-injection phobia. *Clinical Psychology Review, 14*, 443–461.

Page, A. C., Bennett, K. S., Carter, O., Smith, J., & Woodmore, K. (1997). The Blood–Injection Symptom Scale (BISS). Assessing a structure of phobic symptoms elicited by blood and injections. *Behaviour Research and Therapy, 35*, 457–464.

Page, A. C., & Martin, N. G. (1998). Testing a genetic structure of blood-injury-injection fears. *American Journal of Medical Genetics, 81*, 377–384.

Pande, A. C., Davidson, J. R., Jefferson, J. W., Janney, C. A., Katzelnick, D. J., Weisler, R. H., Greist, J. H., & Sutherland, S. M. (1999). Treatment of social phobia with gabapentin: A placebo-controlled study. *Journal of Clinical Psychopharmacology, 19*, 341–348.

Pande, A. C., Greiner, M., Adams, J. B., Lydiard, R. B., & Pierce, M. W. (1999). Placebo-controlled trial of the CCK-B antagonist CI-988, in panic disorder. *Biological Psychiatry, 46*, 860–862

Pantalon, M. V., & Lubetkin, B. S. (1995). Use and effectiveness of self-help books in the practice of cognitive and behavioral therapy. *Cognitive and Behavioral Practice, 2*, 213–228.

Papp, L. A., Klein, D. F., Martinez, J., Schneier, F., Cole, R., Liebowitz, M. R., Hollander, E., Fyer, A. J., Jordan, F., & Gorman, J. M. (1993). Diagnostic and substance specificity of carbon-dioxide-induced panic. *American Journal of Psychiatry, 150*, 250–257.

Papp, L. A., Schneier, F. R., Fyer, A. J., Liebowitz, M. R., Gorman, J. M., Coplan, J. D., Campeas, R., Fallon, B. A., & Klein, D. F. (1997). Clomipramine treatment of panic disorder: Pros and cons. *Journal of Clinical Psychiatry, 58*, 423–425.

Paul, G. (1966). *Insight versus desensitization in psychotherapy: An experiment in anxiety reduction.* Palo Alto, CA: Stanford University Press.

Pecknold, J., Luthe, L., Munjack, D., & Alexander, P. (1994). A double-blind, placebo-controlled, multi-center study with alprazolam and extended-release alprazolam in the treatment of panic disorder. *Journal of Clinical Psychopharmacology, 14*, 314–321.

Pecknold, J. C., Swinson, R. P., Kuch, K., & Lewis, C. P. (1988). Alprazolam in panic disorder and agoraphobia: Results from a multicenter trial. Discontinuation effects. *Archives of General Psychiatry, 45*, 429–436.

Penava, S. J., Otto, M. W., Maki, K. M., & Pollack, M. H. (1998). Rate of improvement during cognitive–behavioral group treatment for panic disorder. *Behaviour Research and Therapy, 36*, 665–673.

Perna, G., Caldirola, D., Arancio, C., & Bellodi, L. (1997). Panic attacks: A twin study. *Psychiatry Research, 66*, 69–71.

Perugi, G., Nassini, S., Lenzi, M., Simonini, E., Cassano, G. B., & McNair, D. M. (1994/1995). Treatment of social phobia with fluoxetine. *Anxiety, 1*, 282–286.

Peterson, R. A., & Heilbronner, R. L. (1987). The Anxiety Sensitivity Index: Construct validity and factor analytic structure. *Journal of Anxiety Disorders, 1*, 117–121.

Peterson, R. A., & Reiss, S. (1993). *Anxiety Sensitivity Index revised test manual.* Worthington, OH: IDS Publishing Corporation.

Philipp, M., Kohnen, R., & Hiller, K. -O. (1999). Hypericum extract versus imipramine or placebo in patients with moderate depression: Randomised multicentre study of treatment for eight weeks. *British Medical Journal, 319*, 1534–1539.

Phillips, G. C., Jones, G. E., Rieger, E. J., & Snell, J. B. (1997). Normative data for the Personal Report of Confidence as a Speaker. *Journal of Anxiety Disorders*, *11*, 215–230.

Pierce, K. A., & Kirkpatrick, D. R. (1992). Do men lie on fear surveys? *Behaviour Research and Therapy*, *30*, 415–418.

Pilkington, N. W., Antony, M. M., & Swinson, R. P. (1998, November). *Vigilance for autonomic and non-autonomic bodily sensations across the anxiety disorders and in non-clinical volunteers*. Paper presented at the meeting of the Association for Advancement of Behavior Therapy, Washington, DC.

Pitchot, W., Ansseau, M., Moreno, A. G., Hansenne, M., & von Frenckell, R. (1992). Dopaminergic function in panic disorder: Comparison with major and minor depression. *Biological Psychiatry*, *32*, 1004–1011.

Plomin, R. (1989). Environment and genes: Determinants of behavior. *American Psychologist*, *44*, 105–111.

Pohl, R. B., Wolkow, R. M., & Clary, C. M. (1998). Sertraline in the treatment of panic disorder: A double-blind multicenter trial. *American Journal of Psychiatry*, *155*, 1189–1195.

Pollack, M. H., Otto, M. W., Kaspi, S. P., Hammerness, P. G., & Rosenbaum, J. F. (1994). Cognitive behavior therapy for treatment-refractory panic disorder. *Journal of Clinical Psychiatry*, *55*, 200–205.

Pollack, M. H., Otto, M. W., Worthington, J. J., Manfro, G. G., & Wolkow, R. (1998). Sertraline in the treatment of panic disorder. *Archives of General Psychiatry*, *55*, 1010–1016.

Pollack, M. H., Worthington, J. J., Otto, M. W., Maki, K. M., Smoller, J. W., Manfro, G. G., Rudolph, R., & Rosenbaum, J. F. (1996). Venlafaxine for panic disorder: Results from a double-blind placebo-controlled study. *Psychopharmacology Bulletin*, *32*, 667–670.

Pollard, C. A., Bronson, S. S., & Kenney, M. R. (1989). Prevalence of agoraphobia without panic in clinical settings [letter]. *American Journal of Psychiatry*, *146*, 559.

Pollard, C. A., Henderson, J. G., Frank, M., & Margolis, R. B. (1989). Help-seeking patterns of anxiety disordered individuals in the general population. *Journal of Anxiety Disorders*, *3*, 131–138.

Pollard, C. A., Pollard, H. J., & Corn, K. J. (1989). Panic onset and major events in the lives of agoraphobics: A test of contiguity. *Journal of Abnormal Psychology*, *98*, 318–321.

Potts, N. L. S., Davidson, J. R. T., Krishnan, K. R. R., Doraiswamy, P. M., & Ritchie, J. C. (1991). Levels of urinary free cortisol in social phobia. *Journal of Clinical Psychiatry*, *52*(Suppl. 11), 41–42.

Poulton, R., Davies, S., Menzies, R. G., Langley, J. D., & Silva, P. A. (1998). Evidence for a non-associative model of the acquisition of a fear of heights. *Behaviour Research and Therapy*, *36*, 537–544.

Poulton, R., Menzies, R. G., Craske, M. G., Langley, J. D., & Silva, P. A. (1999). Water trauma and swimming experiences up to age 9 and fear of water at age 18: A longitudinal study. *Behaviour Research and Therapy, 37,* 39–48.

Prigatano, G. P., & Johnson, H. J. (1974). Autonomic nervous system changes associated with a spider phobic reaction. *Journal of Abnormal Psychology, 83,* 169–177.

Purdon, C. (1999). Thought suppression and psychopathology. *Behaviour Research and Therapy, 37,* 1029–1054.

Purdon, C., Antony, M. M., Monteiro, S., & Swinson, R. P. (in press). Social anxiety: Frequency in non-clinical individuals and influence on impressions of character features. *Journal of Anxiety Disorders.*

Purdon, C., Antony, M. M., & Swinson, R. P. (1999). Psychometric properties of the Frost et al. Multidimensional Perfectionism Scale in a clinical anxiety disorders sample. *Journal of Clinical Psychology, 55,* 1271–1286.

Rachman, S. (1976). The passing of the two-stage theory of fear and avoidance: Fresh possibilities. *Behaviour Research and Therapy, 14,* 125–131.

Rachman, S. (1977). The conditioning theory of fear-acquisition: A critical examination. *Behaviour Research and Therapy, 15,* 375–387.

Rachman, S. (1989). The return of fear: Review and prospect. *Clinical Psychology Review, 9,* 147–168.

Rachman, S., Craske, M. G., Tallman, K., & Solyom, C. (1984). Does escape behaviour strengthen agoraphobic avoidance? A replication. *Behavior Therapy, 17,* 366–384.

Rachman, S., & Cuk, M. (1992). Fearful distortions. *Behaviour Research and Therapy, 30,* 583–589.

Rachman, S., & Lopatka, C. (1988). Return of fear: Underlearning and overlearning. *Behaviour Research and Therapy, 26,* 99–104.

Rachman, S., Lopatka, C., & Levitt, K. (1988). Experimental analyses of panic: II. Panic patients. *Behaviour Research and Therapy, 26,* 33–40.

Rachman, S., Robinson, S., & Lopatka, C. (1987). Is incomplete fear reduction followed by a return of fear? *Behaviour Research and Therapy, 25,* 67–69.

Rachman, S., & Whittal, M. (1989a). The effect of an aversive event on the return of fear. *Behaviour Research and Therapy, 27,* 513–520.

Rachman, S., & Whittal, M. (1989b). Fast, slow and sudden reductions in fear. *Behaviour Research and Therapy, 27,* 613–620.

Radomsky, A. S., Rachman, S., Thordarson, D. S., McIsaac, H. K., & Teachman, B. A. (in press). The Claustrophobia Questionnaire (CLQ). *Journal of Anxiety Disorders.*

Raguram, R., & Bhide, A. V. (1985). Patterns of phobic neurosis: A retrospective study. *British Journal of Psychiatry, 147,* 557–560.

Raj, B. A., Corvea, M. H., & Dagon, E. M. (1993). The clinical characteristics of panic disorder in the elderly: A retrospective study. *Journal of Clinical Psychiatry, 54,* 150–155.

Rapaport, M. H., Wolkow, R. M., & Clary, C. M. (1998). Methodologies and outcomes from the sertraline multicenter flexible-dose trials. *Psychopharmacology Bulletin, 34*, 183–189.

Rapee, R. M. (1994a). Detection of somatic sensations in panic disorder. *Behaviour Research and Therapy, 32*, 825–831.

Rapee, R. M. (1994b). Failure to replicate a memory bias in panic disorder. *Journal of Anxiety Disorders, 8*, 291–300.

Rapee, R. M. (1995). Descriptive psychopathology of social phobia. In R. G. Heimberg, M. R. Liebowitz, D. A. Hope, & F. R. Schneier (Eds.), *Social phobia: Diagnosis, assessment, and treatment* (pp. 41–66). New York: Guilford Press.

Rapee, R. M. (1996). Information processing views of panic disorder. In R. M. Rapee (Ed.), *Current controversies in the anxiety disorders* (pp. 77–93). New York: Guilford Press.

Rapee, R. M. (1997). Perceived threat and perceived control as predictors of the degree of fear in physical and social situations. *Journal of Anxiety Disorders, 11*, 455–461.

Rapee, R. M. (1998). *Overcoming shyness and social phobia: A step-by-step guide.* Northvale, NJ: Jason Aronson.

Rapee, R. M., Brown, T. A., Antony, M. M., & Barlow, D. H. (1992). Response to hyperventilation and inhalation of 5.5% carbon dioxide-enriched air across the *DSM-III-R* anxiety disorders. *Journal of Abnormal Psychology, 101*, 538–552.

Rapee, R. M., Craske, M. G., & Barlow, D. H. (1994/1995). Assessment instrument for panic disorder that includes fear of sensation-producing activities: The Albany Panic and Phobia Questionnaire. *Anxiety, 1*, 114–122.

Rapee, R. M., & Heimberg, R. G. (1997). A cognitive–behavioral model of anxiety in social phobia. *Behaviour Research and Therapy, 35*, 741–756.

Rapee, R., Litwin, E. M., & Barlow, D. H. (1990). Impact of life events on subjects with panic disorder and on comparison subjects. *American Journal of Psychiatry, 147*, 640–644.

Rapee, R. M., & Lim, L. (1992). Discrepancy between self- and observer ratings of performance in social phobics. *Journal of Abnormal Psychology, 101*, 728–731.

Rapee, R. M., McCallum, S. L., Melville, L. F., Ravenscroft, H., & Rodney, J. M. (1994). Memory bias in social phobia. *Behaviour Research and Therapy, 32*, 89–99.

Rapee, R. M., & Melville, L. F. (1997). Recall of family factors in social phobia and panic disorder: Comparison of mother and offspring reports. *Depression and Anxiety, 5*, 7–11.

Rapee, R. M., & Sanderson, W. C. (1998). *Social phobia: Clinical application of evidence-based psychotherapy.* Northvale, NJ: Jason Aronson.

Rauch, S. L., Savage, C. R., Alpert, N. M., Miguel, E. C., Baer, L., Breiter, H. C., Fischman, A. J., Manzo, P. A., Moretti, C., & Jenike, M. A. (1995). A positron emission tomographic study of simple phobic symptom provocation. *Archives of General Psychiatry, 52*, 20–28.

Rees, C. S., Richards, J. C., & Smith, L. M. (1998). Medical utilisation and costs in panic disorder: A comparison with social phobia. *Journal of Anxiety Disorders, 12,* 421–435.

Regier, D. A., Kaelber, C. T., Rae, D. S., Farmer, M. E., Knauper, B., Kessler, R. C., & Norquist, G. S. (1998). Limitations of diagnostic criteria and assessment instruments for mental disorders: Implications for research and policy. *Archives of General Psychiatry, 55,* 109–115.

Reich, J., & Yates, W. (1988). A pilot study of treatment of social phobia with alprazolam. *American Journal of Psychiatry, 145,* 590–594.

Reiman, E. M., Fusselman, M. J., Fox, P. T., & Raichle, M. E. (1989). Neuroanatomical correlates of anticipatory anxiety. *Science, 243,* 1071–1073.

Reiman, E. M., Raichle, M. E., Robins, E., Mintun, M. A., Fusselman, M. J., Fox, P. T., Price, J. L., & Hackman, K. A. (1989). Neuroanatomical correlates of a lactate-induced anxiety attack. *Archives of General Psychiatry, 46,* 493–500.

Reiss, S., Peterson, R. A., Gursky, D. M., & McNally, R. J. (1986). Anxiety sensitivity, anxiety frequency and the prediction of fearfulness. *Behaviour Research and Therapy, 24,* 1–8.

Reiter, S. R., Pollack, M. H., Rosenbaum, J. F., & Cohen, L. S. (1990). Clonazepam for the treatment of social phobia. *Journal of Clinical Psychiatry, 51,* 470–471.

Renneberg, B., Chambless, D. L., & Gracely, E. J. (1992). Prevalence of SCID-diagnosed personality disorders in agoraphobic outpatients. *Journal of Anxiety Disorders, 6,* 111–118.

Richards, J. C., Edgar, L. V., & Gibbon, P. (1996). Cardiac acuity in panic disorder. *Cognitive Therapy and Research, 20,* 361–376.

Rickels, K., Schweizer, E., Weiss, S., & Zavodnick, S. (1992). Maintenance drug treatment for panic disorder: Short- and long-term outcome after drug taper. *Archives of General Psychiatry, 50,* 61–68.

Rijken, H., Kraaimaat, F., de Ruiter, C., & Garssen, B. (1992). A follow-up study on short-term treatment of agoraphobia. *Behaviour Research and Therapy, 30,* 63–66.

Riskind, J. H., Moore, R., & Bowley, L. (1995). The looming of spiders: The fearful perceptual distortion of movement and menace. *Behaviour Research and Therapy, 33,* 171–178.

Robins, L.N., Cottler, L., Bucholz, K., & Compton, W. (1995). *The Diagnostic Interview Schedule, Version IV.* Washington University School of Medicine, St. Louis, MO.

Robins, L. N., Helzer, J. E., Weissman, M. M., Orvaschel, H., Gruenberg, E., Burke, J. D., & Regier, D. A. (1984). Lifetime prevalence of specific psychiatric disorders in three sites. *Archives of General Psychiatry, 41,* 949–958.

Robins, L. N., & Regier, D. A. (Eds.). (1991). *Psychiatric disorders in America: The Epidemiologic Catchment Area Study.* New York: Free Press.

Robins, L. N., Wing, J., Wittchen, H. -U., Helzer, J. E., Babor, T. F., Burke, J., Farmer, A., Jablenski, A., Pickens, R., Regier, D. A., Sartorius, N., & Towle,

L. H. (1988). The Composite International, Diagnostic Interview: An epidemiological instrument suitable for use in conjunction with different diagnostic systems and in different cultures. *Archives of General Psychiatry, 45,* 1069–1077.

Rodriguez, B. I., & Craske, M. G. (1993). The effects of distraction during exposure to phobic stimuli. *Behaviour Research and Therapy, 31,* 549–558.

Rodriguez, B. I., & Craske, M. G. (1995). Does distraction interfere with fear reduction during exposure? A test among animal-fearful subjects. *Behavior Therapy, 26,* 337–349.

Rodriguez, B. I., Craske, M. G., Mineka, S., & Hladek, D. (1999). Context-specificity of relapse: Effects of therapist and environmental context on return of fear. *Behaviour Research and Therapy, 37,* 845–862.

Romach, M. K., Somer, G. R., Sobell, L. C., Sobell, M. B., Kaplan, H. L., & Sellers, E. M. (1992). Characteristics of long-term alprazolam users in the community. *Journal of Clinical Psychopharmacology, 12,* 316–321.

Rose, M. P., McGlynn, F. D., & Lazarte, A. (1995). Control and attention influence snake phobics' arousal and fear during laboratory confrontations with a caged snake. *Journal of Anxiety Disorders, 9,* 293–302.

Rosenbaum, J. F., Biederman, J., Hirshfeld, D. R., Bolduc, E. A., & Chaloff, J. (1991). Behavioral inhibition in children: A possible precursor to panic disorder or social phobia. *Journal of Clinical Psychiatry, 42*(Suppl.), 5–9.

Rosenbaum, J. F., Moroz, G., & Bowden, C. L. (1997). Clonazepam in the treatment of panic disorder with or without agoraphobia: A dose–response study of efficacy, safety, and discontinuance. *Journal of Clinical Psychopharmacology, 17,* 390–400.

Ross, H. E., Swinson, R., Larkin, E. J., & Doumani, S. (1994). Diagnosing comorbidity in substance abusers: Computer assessment and clinical validation. *Journal of Nervous and Mental Disease, 182,* 556–563.

Roth, D., Antony, M. M., & Swinson, R. P. (in press). Interpretations for anxiety symptoms in social phobia. *Behaviour Research and Therapy.*

Roth, D. A., Antony, M. M., & Swinson, R. P. (1999, November). *Symptom induction exercises in panic disorder.* Paper presented at the meeting of the Association for Advancement of Behavior Therapy, Toronto, Ontario, Canada.

Rothbaum, B. O., & Hodges, L. F. (1999). The use of virtual reality exposure in the treatment of anxiety disorders. *Journal of Behavior Modification, 23,* 507–525.

Rothbaum, B. O., Hodges, L. F., Kooper, R., Opdyke, D., Williford, J. S., & North, M. (1995a). Effectiveness of computer-generated (virtual reality) graded exposure in the treatment of acrophobia. *American Journal of Psychiatry, 152,* 626–628.

Rothbaum, B. O., Hodges, L. F., Kooper, R., Opdyke, D., Williford, J. S., & North, M. (1995b). Virtual reality graded exposure in the treatment of acrophobia: A case report. *Behavior Therapy, 26,* 547–554.

Rothbaum, B. O., Hodges, L. F., Watson, B. A., Kessler, G. D., & Opdyke, D. (1996). Virtual reality exposure therapy in the treatment of fear of flying: A case report. *Behaviour Research and Therapy, 34,* 477–481.

Rowa, K., Antony, M. M., Brar, S., & Swinson, R. P. (1999, November). *Psychological and medication treatments in panic disorder, obsessive–compulsive disorder, and social phobia.* Paper presented at the meeting of the Association for Advancement of Behavior Therapy, Toronto, Ontario, Canada.

Rowa, K., Antony, M.M., Brar, S., Summerfeldt, L.J., & Swinson, R.P. (in press). Treatment histories of patients with three anxiety disorders. *Depression and Anxiety.*

Rowe, M. K., & Craske, M. G. (1998a). Effects of an expanding-spaced vs. massed exposure schedule on fear reduction and return of fear. *Behaviour Research and Therapy, 36,* 701–717.

Rowe, M. K., & Craske, M. G. (1998b). Effects of varied-stimulus exposure training on fear reduction and return of fear. *Behaviour Research and Therapy, 36,* 719–734.

Roy-Byrne, P. P., Cowley, D. S., Greenblatt, D. J., Shader, R. I., & Hommer, D. (1990). Reduced benzodiazepine sensitivity in panic disorder. *Archives of General Psychiatry, 47,* 534–538.

Roy-Byrne, P. P., & Uhde, T. W. (1988). Exogenous factors in panic disorder: Clinical and research implications. *Journal of Clinical Psychiatry, 49,* 56–61.

Russell, J. L., Kushner, M. G., Beitman, B. D., & Bartels, K. M. (1991). Nonfearful panic disorder in neurology patients validated by lactate challenge. *American Journal of Psychiatry, 148,* 361–364.

Saboonchi, F., Lundh, L. -G., & Öst, L. -G. (1999). Perfectionism and self-consciousness in social phobia and panic disorder with agoraphobia. *Behaviour Research and Therapy, 37,* 799–808.

Safren, S. A., Heimberg, R. G., & Juster, H. R. (1996, November). *Expectancies of cognitive–behavioral group treatment for social phobia.* Paper presented at the meeting of the Association for Advancement of Behavior Therapy, New York, NY.

Safren, S. A., Turk, C. L., & Heimberg, R. G. (1998). Factor structure of the Social Interaction Anxiety Scale and Social Phobia Scale. *Behaviour Research and Therapy, 36,* 443–453.

Salaberria, K., & Echeburua, E. (1998). Long-term outcome of cognitive therapy's contribution to self-exposure in vivo to the treatment of generalized social phobia. *Journal of Behavior Modification, 22,* 262–284.

Salvator-Carulla, L., Segui, J., Fernandez-Cano, P., & Canet, J. (1995). Costs and offset effect in panic disorders. *British Journal of Psychiatry, 166*(Suppl. 27), 23–28.

Sanderson, A., & Carpenter, R. (1992). Eye movement desensitization versus image confrontation: A single-session crossover study of 58 phobic subjects. *Journal of Behavior Therapy and Experimental Psychiatry, 23,* 269–275.

Sanderson, W. C., Di Nardo, P. A., Rapee, R. M., & Barlow, D. H. (1990). Syndrome comorbidity in patients diagnosed with a DSM-III-R anxiety disorder. *Journal of Abnormal Psychology, 99,* 308–312.

Sanderson, W. C., Rapee, R. M., & Barlow, D. H. (1989). The influence of an illusion of control on panic attacks induced via inhalation of 5.5% carbon dioxide-enriched air. *Archives of General Psychiatry, 46,* 157–162.

Sawchuk, C. N., Lee, T. C., Tolin, D. F., & Lohr, J. M. (1997, November). *Generalized disgust sensitivity in blood–injection–injury phobia.* Paper presented at the meeting of the Association for Advancement of Behavior Therapy, Miami Beach, FL.

Sawchuk, C. N., Tolin, D. F., Lee, T. C., Lohr, J. M., & Kleinknecht (1998, November). *Relations between disgust sensitivity and contamination fears in specific phobia.* Paper presented at the meeting of the Association for Advancement of Behavior Therapy, Washington, DC.

Schlenker, B. R., & Leary, M. R. (1982). Social anxiety and self-presentation: A conceptualization and model. *Psychological Bulletin, 92,* 641–669.

Schmidt, L. A. (1999). Frontal brain electrical activity in shyness and sociability. *Psychological Science, 10,* 316–320.

Schmidt, N. B., Jacquin, K., & Telch, M. J. (1994). The overprediction of fear and panic in panic disorder. *Behaviour Research and Therapy, 32,* 701–707.

Schmidt, N. B., Lerew, D. R., & Jackson, R. J. (1999). Prospective evaluation of anxiety sensitivity in the pathogenesis of panic: Replication and extension. *Journal of Abnormal Psychology, 108,* 532–537.

Schmidt, N. B., Lerew, D. R., & Trakowski, J. H. (1997). Body vigilance in panic disorder: Evaluating attention to bodily perturbations. *Journal of Consulting and Clinical Psychology, 65,* 214–220.

Schmidt, N. B., Telch, M. J., & Jaimez, T. L. (1996). Biological challenge manipulation of PCO_2 levels. A test of Klein's (1993) suffocation alarm theory of panic. *Journal of Abnormal Psychology, 105,* 446–454.

Schmidt, N. B., Trakowski, J. H., & Staab, J. P. (1997). Extinction of panicogenic effects of a 35% CO_2 challenge in patients with panic disorder. *Journal of Abnormal Psychology, 106,* 630–638.

Schmidt, N. B., Woolaway-Bickel, K., Trakowski, J., Santiago, H., Storey, J., Koselka, M., & Cook, J. (in press). Dismantling cognitive behavioral treatment for panic disorder: Questioning the utility of breathing retraining. *Journal of Consulting and Clinical Psychology.*

Schmidt, S. M., Zoëga, T., & Crowe, R. R. (1993). Excluding linkage between panic disorder and the gamma-aminobutyric acid beta 1 receptor locus in five Icelandic pedigrees. *Acta Psychiatrica Scandinavica, 88,* 225–228.

Schneier, F. R., Goetz, D., Campeas, R., Fallon, B., Marshall, R., & Liebowitz, M. R. (1998). Placebo-controlled trial of moclobemide in social phobia. *British Journal of Psychiatry, 172,* 70–77.

Schneier, F. R., Heckelman, L. R., Garfinkel, R., Campeas, R., Fallon, B. A., Gitow, A., Street, L., Del Bene, D., & Liebowitx, M. R. (1994). Functional impairment in social phobia. *Journal of Clinical Psychiatry, 55*, 322–331.

Schneier, F. R., Johnson, J., Hornig, C. D., Liebowitz, M. R., & Weissman, M. M. (1992). Social phobia: Comorbidity and morbidity in an epidemiological sample. *Archives of General Psychiatry, 49*, 282–288.

Schneier, F. R., Saoud, J. B., Campeas, R., Fallon, B. A., Hollander, E., Coplan, J., & Liebowitz, M. R. (1993). Buspirone in social phobia. *Journal of Clinical Psychopharmacology, 13*, 251–256.

Scholing, A., & Emmelkamp, P. M. (1993a). Cognitive and behavioural treatments of fear of blushing, sweating, or trembling. *Behaviour Research and Therapy, 31*, 155–170.

Scholing, A., & Emmelkamp, P. M. (1993b). Exposure with and without cognitive therapy for generalized social phobia: Effects of individual and group treatment. *Behaviour Research and Therapy, 31*, 667–681.

Scholing, A., & Emmelkamp, P. M. G. (1996). Treatment of generalized social phobia: Results at long-term follow-up. *Behaviour Research and Therapy, 34*, 447–452.

Scholing, A., & Emmelkamp, P. M. G. (1999). Prediction of treatment outcome in social phobia: A cross-validation. *Behaviour Research and Therapy, 37*, 659–670.

Schutte, N. S., & Malouff, J. M. (1995). *Sourcebook of adult assessment strategies.* New York: Plenum Press.

Schwalberg, M. D., Barlow, D. H., Alger, S. A., & Howard, L. J. (1992). Comparison of bulimics, obese binge eaters, social phobics and individuals with panic disorder on comorbidity across the DSM-III-R anxiety disorders. *Journal of Abnormal Psychology, 101*, 675–681

Schwartz, C. E. (1989). Exercise and anxiety disorders. *American Journal of Psychiatry, 146*, 1357–1358.

Schweizer, E., Patterson, W., Rickels, K., & Rosenthal, M. (1993). Double-blind, placebo-controlled study of a once-a-day, sustained-release preparation of alprazolam for the treatment of panic disorder. *American Journal of Psychiatry, 150*, 1210–1215.

Schweizer, E., Pohl, R., Balon, R., Fox, I., Rickels, K., & Yeragani, V. K. (1990). Lorazepam vs. alprazolam in the treatment of panic disorder. *Pharmacopsychiatry, 23*, 90–93.

Schweizer, E., Rickels, K., Weiss, S., & Zavodnick, S. (1993). Maintenance drug treatment of panic disorder: Results of a prospective, placebo-controlled comparison of alprazolam and imipramine. *Archives of General Psychiatry, 50*, 51–60.

Scupi, B. S., Maser, J. D., & Uhde, T. W. (1992). The National Institute of Mental Health Panic Questionnaire: An instrument for assessing clinical characteristics of panic disorder. *Journal of Nervous and Mental Disease, 180*, 566–572.

Segal, D. L., Hersen, M., & van Hasselt, V. B. (1994). Reliability of the Structured Clinical Interview for DSM-III-R: An evaluative review. *Comprehensive Psychiatry, 35*, 316–327.

Shafran, R., Booth, R., & Rachman, S. (1993). The reduction of claustrophobia: II. Cognitive analyses. *Behaviour Research and Therapy, 31*, 75–85.

Shapiro, F. (1989). Eye movement desensitization: A new treatment for posttraumatic stress disorder. *Journal of Behavior Therapy and Experimental Psychiatry, 20*, 211–217.

Shapiro, F. (1999). Eye movement desensitization and reprocessing (EMDR) and the anxiety disorders: Clinical and research implications of an integrated psychotherapy treatment. *Journal of Anxiety Disorders, 13*, 35–67.

Sharp, D. M., Power, K. G., Simpson, R. J., Swanson, V., Moodie, E., Anstee, J. A., & Ashford, J. J. (1996). Fluvoxamine, placebo, and cognitive behaviour therapy used alone and in combination in the treatment of panic disorder and agoraphobia. *Journal of Anxiety Disorders, 10*, 219–242.

Shear, M. K., Brown, T. A., Barlow, D. H., Money, R., Sholomskas, D. E., Woods, S. W., Gorman, J. M., & Papp, L. A. (1997). Multicenter Collaborative Panic Disorder Severity Scale. *American Journal of Psychiatry, 154*, 1571–1575.

Shear, M. K., Cooper, A. M., Klerman, G. L., Busch, F. N., & Shapiro, T. (1993). A psychodynamic model of panic disorder. *American Journal of Psychiatry, 150*, 859–866.

Shear, M. K., Fyer, A. J., Ball, G., Josephson, S., Fitzpatrick, M., Gitlin, B., Frances, A., Gorman, J., Liebowitz, M., & Klein, D. (1991). Vulnerability to sodium lactate in panic disorder patients given cognitive–behavioral therapy. *American Journal of Psychiatry, 148*, 795–797.

Shear, M. K., & Maser, J. D. (1994). Standardized assessment for panic disorder research: A conference report. *Archives of General Psychiatry, 51*, 346–354.

Shear, M. K., Pilkonis, P. A., Cloitre, M., & Leon, A. C. (1994). Cognitive behavioral treatment compared with nonprescriptive treatment of panic disorder. *Archives of General Psychiatry, 51*, 395–401.

Shear, M. K., & Weiner, K. (1997). Psychotherapy for panic disorder. *Journal of Clinical Psychiatry, 58*(Suppl. 2), 38–45.

Sheehan, D. V., Lecrubier, Y., Sheehan, K. H., Amorim, P., Janavs, J., Weiller, E., Hergueta, T., Baker, R., & Dunbar, G. C. (1998). The Mini-International Neuropsychiatric Interview (MINI): The development and validation of a structured diagnostic psychiatric interview for DSM-IV and ICD-10. *Journal of Clinical Psychiatry, 59*(Suppl. 20), 22–33.

Sheehan, D. V., Raj, A. B., Harnett-Sheehan, K., Soto, S., & Knapp, E. (1993). The relative efficacy of high-dose buspirone and alprazolam in the treatment of panic disorder: A double-blind placebo-controlled study. *Acta Psychiatrica Scandinavica, 88*, 1–11.

Sheehan, D. V., Raj, A. B., Sheehan, K. H., & Soto, S. (1990). Is buspirone effective for panic disorder? *Journal of Clinical Psychopharmacology, 10*, 3–11.

Sheikh, J. I., & Swales, P. J. (1999). Treatment of panic disorder in older adults: A pilot study comparison of alprazolam, imipramine, and placebo. *International Journal of Psychiatry in Medicine, 29*, 107–117.

Siegel, L., Jones, W. C., & Wilson, J. O. (1990). Economic and life consequences experienced by a group of individuals with panic disorder. *Journal of Anxiety Disorders, 4*, 201–211.

Silove, D., Harris, M., Morgan, A., Boyce, P., Manicavasagar, V., Hadzi-Pavlovic, D., & Wilhelm, K. (1995). Is early separation anxiety a specific precursor of panic disorder–agoraphobia? A community study. *Psychological Medicine, 25*, 405–411.

Silove, D., Manicavasagar, V., Curtis, J., & Blaszczynski, A. (1996). Is early separation anxiety a risk factor for panic disorder? A critical review. *Comprehensive Psychiatry, 37*, 167–169.

Simpson, H. B., Schneier, F. R., Campeas, R. B., Marshall, R. D., Fallon, B. A., Davies, S., Klein, D. F., & Liebowitz, M. R. (1998). Imipramine in the treatment of social phobia. *Journal of Clinical Psychopharmacology, 18*, 132–135.

Simpson, H. B., Schneier, F. R., Marshall, R. D., Campeas, R. B., Vermes, D., Silvestre, J., Davies, S., & Liebowitz, M. R. (1998). Low-dose selegiline (L-deprenyl) in social phobia. *Anxiety and Depression, 7*, 126–129.

Skre, I., Onstad, S., Torgersen, S., & Kringlen, E. (1991). Higher interrater reliability for the structured clinical interview for DSM-III-R Axis I (SCID-I). *Acta Psychiatrica Scandinavica, 84*, 167–173.

Skre, I., Torgerson, O. S., Lygren, S., & Kringlen, E. (1993). A twin study of DSM-III-R anxiety disorders. *Acta Psychiatrica Scandinavica, 88*, 85–92.

Slavkin, SL., Holt, C. S., Heimberg, R. G., & Jaccard, J. J., Liebowitz, M. R. (1990, November). *The Liebowitz Social Phobia Scale: An exploratory analysis of construct validity.* Paper presented at the meeting of the Association for Advancement of Behavior Therapy, San Francisco, CA

Smari, J., Bjarnadottir, A., & Bragadottir, B. (1998). Social anxiety, social skills and expectancy/cost of negative social events. *Scandinavian Journal of Behavioural Therapy, 27*, 149–155.

Spence, S. H., Donovan, C., & Brechman-Toussaint, M. (1999). Social skills, social outcomes, and cognitive features of childhood social phobia. *Journal of Abnormal Psychology, 108*, 211–221.

Spiegel, D. A. (1998). Efficacy studies of alprazolam in panic disorder. *Psychopharmacology Bulletin, 34*, 191–195.

Spiegel, D. A., Bruce, T. J., Gregg, S. F., & Nuzzarello, A. (1994). Does cognitive behavior therapy assist slow-taper alprazolam discontinuation in panic disorder? *American Journal of Psychiatry, 151*, 876–881.

Spielberger, C. D. (1983). *Manual for the State–Trait Anxiety Inventory STAI (Form Y).* Palo Alto, CA: Mind Garden.

Spielberger, C. D., Gorsuch, R. L., Lushene, R., Vagg, P. R., & Jacobs, G. A. (1983). *Manual for the State–Trait Anxiety Inventory (Form Y).* Palo Alto, CA: Mind Garden.

Spitzer, R. L., Williams, J. B., Gibbon, M., & First, M. B. (1992). The structured clinical interview for DSM-III-R (SCID): I. History, rationale, and description. *Archives of General Psychiatry, 49*, 624–629.

Spitzer, R. L., Williams, J. B., Kroenke, K., Linzer, M., deGruy, F. V., Hahn, S. R., Brody, D., & Johnson, J. G. (1994). Utility of a new procedure for diagnosing mental disorders in primary care. The PRIME–MD 1000 study. *Journal of the American Medical Association, 272*, 1749–1756.

Sramek, J. J., Kramer, M. S., Reines, S., & Cutler, N. R. (1994/1995). Pilot study of a CCKB antagonist in patients with panic disorder: Preliminary findings. *Anxiety, 1*, 141–143.

Starcevic, V., Djordjevic, A., Latas, M., & Bogojevic, G. (1998). Characteristics of agoraphobia in women and men with panic disorder with agoraphobia. *Depression and Anxiety, 8*, 8–13.

Starcevic, V., Uhlenhuth, E. H., Kellner, R., & Pathak, D. (1993). Comorbidity in panic disorder: II. Chronology of appearance and pathogenic comorbidity. *Psychiatry Research, 46*, 285–293.

Stein, M. B. (1998). Medication treatments for panic disorder and social phobia. *Depression and Anxiety, 7*, 134–138.

Stein, M. B., Chartier, M. J., Hazen, A. L., Kozak, M. V., Tancer, M. E., Lander, S., Furer, P., Chubaty, D., & Walker, J. R. (1998). A direct-interview family study of generalized social phobia. *American Journal of Psychiatry, 155*, 90–97.

Stein, M. B., Delaney, S. M., Chartier, M. J., Kroft, C. D. L., & Hazen, A. L. (1995). [^{3}H] paroxetine binding to platelets of patients with social phobia: Comparison to patients with panic disorder and healthy volunteers. *Biological Psychiatry, 37*, 224–228.

Stein, M. B., Fyer, A. J., Davidson, J. R. T., Pollack, M. H., & Wiita, B. (1999). Fluvoxamine treatment of social phobia (social anxiety disorder): A double-blind, placebo-controlled study. *American Journal of Psychiatry, 156*, 756–760.

Stein, M. B., Huzel, L. L., & Delaney, S. M. (1993). Lymphocyte β-adrenoceptors in social phobia. *Biological Psychiatry, 34*, 45–50.

Stein, M. B., Liebowitz, M. R., Lydiard, R. B., Pitts, C. D., Bushnell, W., & Gergel, I. (1998). Paroxetine treatment of generalized social phobia (social anxiety disorder): A randomized controlled trial. *Journal of the American Medical Association, 280*, 708–713.

Stein, M. B., Walker, J. R., & Forde, D. R. (1994). Setting diagnostic thresholds for social phobia: Considerations from a community survey of social anxiety. *American Journal of Psychiatry, 151*, 408–412.

Stemberger, R. T., Turner, S. M., Beidel, D. C., & Calhoun, K. S. (1995). Social phobia: An analysis of possible developmental pathways. *Journal of Abnormal Psychology, 104*, 526–531.

Stern, R., & Marks, I. (1973). Brief and prolonged flooding: A comparison in agoraphobic patients. *Archives of General Psychiatry, 28*, 270–276.

Stopa, L., & Clark, D. M. (1993). Cognitive processes in social phobia. *Behaviour Research and Therapy, 31*, 255–267.

Stouthard, M. E. A., Hoogstraten, J., & Mellenbergh, G. J. (1995). A study on the convergent and discriminant validity of the Dental Anxiety Inventory. *Behaviour Research and Therapy, 33*, 589–595.

Stroop, J. R. (1935). Studies of interference in serial verbal reactions. *Journal of Experimental Psychology, 18*, 643–661.

Sue, D. W. (1990). Culture-specific strategies in counseling: A conceptual framework. *Professional Psychology: Research and Practice, 21*, 424–433.

Sullivan, G. M., Coplan, J. D., Kent, J. M., & Gorman, J. M. (1999). The noradrenergic system in pathological anxiety: A focus on panic with relevance to generalized anxiety and phobias. *Biological Psychiatry, 46*, 1205–1218.

Svebak, S., Cameron, A., & Levander, S. (1990). Clonazepam and imipramine in the treatment of panic attacks: A double-blind comparison of efficacy and side effects. *Journal of Clinical Psychiatry, 51*(Suppl.), 14–17.

Swinson, R. P. (1986). Reply to Kleiner. *The Behavior Therapist, 9*, 110–128.

Swinson, R. P., & Cox, B. J. (1996). Benzodiazepine treatment for panic disorders. In M. R. Mavissakalian & R. F. Prien (Eds.), *Long-term treatments of anxiety disorders* (pp. 221–240). Washington, DC: American Psychiatric Press.

Swinson, R. P., Cox, B. J., Shulman, I. D., Kuch, K., & Woszczyna, C. B. (1992). Medication use and the assessment of agoraphobic avoidance. *Behaviour Research and Therapy, 30*, 563–568.

Swinson, R. P., Cox, B. J., & Woszczyna, C. B. (1992). Use of medical services and treatment for panic disorder with agoraphobia and for social phobia. *Canadian Medical Association Journal, 147*, 878–883.

Swinson, R. P., Fergus, K. D., Cox, B. J., & Wickwire, K. (1995). Efficacy of telephone-administered behavioral therapy for panic disorder with agoraphobia. *Behaviour Research and Therapy, 33*, 465–469.

Swinson, R. P., Soulios, C., Cox, B. J., & Kuch, K. (1992). Brief treatment of emergency room patients with panic attacks. *American Journal of Psychiatry, 149*, 944–946.

Szymanski, J., & O'Donohue, W. (1995). Fear of Spiders Questionnaire. *Journal of Behavior Therapy and Experimental Psychiatry, 26*, 31–34.

Tancer, M. E. (1993). Neurobiology of social phobia. *Journal of Clinical Psychiatry, 54*(Suppl. 12), 26–30.

Tancer, M. E., Mailman, R. B., Stein, M. B., Mason, G. A., Carson, S. W., & Golden, R. N. (1994/1995). Neuroendocrine responsivity to monoaminergic system probes in generalized social phobia. *Anxiety, 1*, 216–223.

Tancer, M. E., Stein, M. B., Gelernter, C. S., & Uhde, T. W. (1990). The hypothalamic-pituitary-thyroid axis in social phobia. *American Journal of Psychiatry, 147*, 929–933.

Taylor, C. B., King, R., Margraf, J., Ehlers, A., Telch, M., Roth, W. T., & Agras, W. S. (1989). Use of medication and in vivo exposure in volunteers for panic disorder research. *American Journal of Psychiatry, 146*, 1423–1426.

Taylor, J. E., Deane, F. P., & Podd, J. V. (1999). Stability of driving fear acquisition pathways over one year. *Behaviour Research and Therapy, 37*, 927–939.

Taylor, S. (1996). Meta-analysis of cognitive behavioral treatment for social phobia. *Journal of Behavior Therapy and Experimental Psychiatry, 27*, 1–9.

Taylor, S., & Cox, B. J. (1998a). Anxiety Sensitivity: Multiple dimensions and hierarchic structure. *Behaviour Research and Therapy, 36,* 37–51.

Taylor, S., & Cox, B. J. (1998b). An expanded Anxiety Sensitivity Index: Evidence for a hierarchic structure in a clinical sample. *Journal of Anxiety Disorders, 12,* 463–483.

Taylor, S., Koch, W. J., & McNally, R. J. (1992). How does anxiety sensitivity vary across the anxiety disorders? *Journal of Anxiety Disorders, 6,* 249–259.

Taylor, S., Woody, S., Koch, W. J., McLean, P. D., & Anderson, K. W. (1996). Suffocation false alarms and efficacy of cognitive behavioral therapy for panic disorder. *Behavior Therapy, 27,* 115–126.

Taylor, S., Woody, S., Koch, W. J., McLean, P., Patterson, R. J., & Anderson, K. W. (1997). Cognitive restructuring in the treatment of social phobia: Efficacy and mode of action. *Journal of Behavior Modification, 21,* 487–511.

Teghtsoonian, R., & Frost, R. O. (1982). The effects of viewing distance on fear of snakes. *Journal of Behavior Therapy and Experimental Psychiatry, 13,* 181–190.

Telch, M. J. (1987). *The Panic Appraisal Inventory.* Unpublished manuscript, University of Texas, Austin.

Telch, M. J., Agras, W. S., Taylor, C. B., Roth, W. T., & Gallen, C. C. (1985). Combined pharmacological and behavioral treatment for agoraphobia. *Behaviour Research and Therapy, 23,* 325–335.

Telch, M. J., Brouillard, M., Telch, C. F., Agras, W. S., & Taylor, C. B. (1989). Role of cognitive appraisal in panic-related avoidance. *Behaviour Research and Therapy, 27,* 373–383.

Telch, M. J., Lucas, J. A., & Nelson, P. (1989). Nonclinical panic in college students: An investigation of prevalence and symptomatology. *Journal of Abnormal Psychology, 98,* 300–306.

Telch, M. J., Lucas, J. A., Schmidt, N. B., Hanna, H. H., Jaimez, T. L., & Lucas, R. A. (1993). Group cognitive–behavioral treatment of panic disorder. *Behaviour Research and Therapy, 31,* 279–287.

Teusch, L., Böhme, H., & Gastpar, M. (1997). The benefit of an insight-oriented and experiential approach on panic and agoraphobia symptoms. *Psychotherapy and Psychosomatics, 66,* 293–301.

Thorpe, S. J., & Salkovskis, P. M. (1997). Information processing in spider phobics: The Stroop colour naming task may indicate strategic but not automatic attentional bias. *Behaviour Research and Therapy, 35,* 131–144.

Thorpe, S. J., & Salkovskis, P. M. (1998a). Selective attention to real phobic and safety stimuli. *Behaviour Research and Therapy, 36,* 471–481.

Thorpe, S. J., & Salkovskis, P. M. (1998b). Studies on the role of disgust in the acquisition and maintenance of specific phobias. *Behaviour Research and Therapy, 36,* 877–893.

Thyer, B. A., & Himle, J. (1985). Temporal relationship between panic attack onset and phobic avoidance in agoraphobia. *Behaviour Research and Therapy, 23,* 607–608.

Thyer, B. A., Parish, R. T., Curtis, G. C., Nesse, R. M., Cameron, O. G. (1985). Ages of onset of DSM-III anxiety disorders. *Comprehensive Psychiatry, 26*, 113–122.

Tolin, D. F., Lohr, J. M., Lee, T. C., & Sawchuk, C. N. (1999). Visual avoidance in specific phobia. *Behaviour Research and Therapy, 37*, 63–70.

Tolin, D. F., Lohr, J. M., Sawchuk, C. N., & Lee, T. C. (1997). Disgust and disgust sensitivity in blood–injection–injury and spider phobia. *Behaviour Research and Therapy, 35*, 949–953.

Torgersen, S. (1979). The nature and origin of common fears. *British Journal of Psychiatry, 134*, 343-351.

Tran, G. Q., Haaga, D. A. F., & Chambless, D. L. (1997). Expecting that alcohol use will reduce social anxiety moderates the relation between social anxiety and alcohol assumption. *Cognitive Therapy and Research, 21*, 535–553.

Trower, P., & Gilbert, P. (1989). New theoretical conceptions of social anxiety and social phobia. *Clinical Psychology Review, 9*, 19–35.

Tsao, J.C.I., & Craske, M.G. (in press). Timing of treatment and return of fear: Effects of massed, uniform-, and expanding-spaced exposure schedules. *Behavior Therapy*.

Tseng, W. -S., Asai, M., Kitanishi, K., McLaughlin, D. G., & Kyomen, H. (1992). Diagnostic patterns of social phobia: Comparison in Tokyo and Hawaii. *Journal of Nervous and Mental Disease, 180*, 380–385.

Turgeon, L., Marchand, A., & Dupuis, G. (1998). Clinical features in panic disorder with agoraphobia: A comparison of men and women. *Journal of Anxiety Disorders, 12*, 539–553.

Turk, C.L., Fresco, D.M., & Heimberg, R.G. (1999). Cognitive behavior therapy. In M. Hersen & A.S. Bellack (Eds.), *Handbook of comparative treatments of adult disorders, 2nd edition* (pp. 287-316). New York, NY: John Wiley and Sons.

Turk, C. L., Heimberg, R. G., Orsillo, S. M., Holt, C. S., Gitow, A., Street, L. L., Schneier, F. R., & Liebowitz, M. R. (1998). An investigation of gender differences in social phobia. *Journal of Anxiety Disorders, 12*, 209–223.

Turner, S. M., Beidel, D. C., Cooley, M. R., & Woody, S. R. (1994). A multicomponent behavioral treatment for social phobia: Social effectiveness therapy. *Behaviour Research and Therapy, 32*, 381–390.

Turner, S. M., Beidel, D. C., & Dancu, C. V. (1996). *The Social Phobia and Anxiety Inventory Manual*. North Tonawanda, NY: Multi-Health Systems, Inc.

Turner, S. M., Beidel, D. C., Dancu, C. V., & Keys, D. J. (1986). Psychopathology of social phobia and comparison with avoidant personality disorder. *Journal of Abnormal Psychology, 95*, 389–394.

Turner, S. M., Beidel, D. C., Dancu, C. V., & Stanley, M. A. (1989). An empirically derived inventory to measure social fears and anxiety: The Social Phobia and Anxiety Inventory. *Psychological Assessment: A Journal of Consulting and Clinical Psychology, 1*, 35–40.

Turner, S. M., Beidel, D. C., Hersen, M., & Bellack, A. S. (1984). Effects of race on ratings of social skill. *Journal of Consulting and Clinical Psychology, 52*, 474–475.

Turner, S. M., Beidel, D. C., & Jacob, R. G. (1994). Social phobia: A comparison of behavior therapy and atenolol. *Journal of Consulting and Clinical Psychology, 62*, 350–358.

Turner, S. M., Beidel, D. C., & Wolff, P. L. (1994). A composite measure to determine improvement following treatment for social phobia: The Index of Social Phobia Improvement. *Behaviour Research and Therapy, 32*, 471–476.

Turner, S. M., Beidel, D. C., & Wolff, P. L. (1996). Is behavioral inhibition related to the anxiety disorers? *Clinical Psychology Review, 16*, 157–172.

Turner, S. M., Cooley-Quille, M. R., & Beidel, D. C. (1996). Behavioral and pharmacological treatment for social phobia. In M. R. Mavissakalian & R. F. Prien (Eds.), *Long-term treatments of anxiety disorders* (pp. 343–372). Washington, DC: American Psychiatric Press.

Turner, S. M., McCanna, M., & Beidel, D. C. (1987). Validity of the Social Avoidance and Distress and Fear of Negative Evaluation Scales. *Behaviour Research and Therapy, 25*, 113–115.

Turner, S. M., Stanley, M. A., Beidel, D. C., & Bond, L. (1989). The Social Phobia and Anxiety Inventory: Construct validity. *Journal of Psychopathology and Behavioral Assessment, 11*, 221–234.

Turner, S. M., Williams, S. L., Beidel, D. C., & Mezzich, J. E. (1986). Panic disorder and agoraphobia with panic attacks: Covariation along the dimensions of panic and agoraphobic fear. *Journal of Abnormal Psychology, 95*, 384–388.

Uhde, T. W. (1994). The anxiety disorders: Phenomenology and treatment of core symptoms and associated sleep disturbance. In M. Kryger, T. Roth, & W. Dement (Eds.), *Principles and practice of sleep medicine* (pp. 871–898). Philadelphia, PA: Saunders.

Uhde, T. W., Tancer, M. E., Gelernter, C. S., & Vittone, B. J. (1994). Normal urinary free cortisol and postdexamethasone cortisol in social phobia: Comparison to normal volunteers. *Journal of Affective Disorders, 30*, 155–161.

van Ameringen, M., Mancini, C., Oakman, J., & Collins, S. (1997, May). *Nefazodone in the treatment of social phobia.* Paper presented at the meeting of the American Psychiatric Association, San Diego, CA.

van Ameringen, M., Mancini, C., & Streiner, D. L. (1993). Fluoxetine efficacy in social phobia. *Journal of Clinical Psychiatry, 54*, 27–32.

van Ameringen, M., Mancini, C., Styan, G., & Donison D. (1991). Relationship of social phobia with other psychiatric illness. *Journal of Affective Disorders, 21*, 93–99

van Balkom, A. J. L. M., Bakker, A., Spinhoven, P., Blaauw, B. M. J. W., Smeenk, S., & Ruesink, B. (1997). A meta-analysis of the treatment of panic disorder with or without agoraphobia: A comparison of psychopharmacological, cognitive–behavioral, and combination treatments. *Journal of Nervous and Mental Disease, 185*, 510–516.

van Balkom, A. J. L. M., Nauta, M. C. E., & Bakker, A. (1995). Meta-analysis on the treatment of panic disorder with agoraphobia: Review and re-examination. *Clinical Psychology and Psychotherapy, 2,* 1014.

van den Hout, M., Arntz, A., & Hoekstra, R. (1994). Exposure reduced agoraphobia but not panic, and cognitive therapy reduced panic but not agoraphobia. *Behaviour Research and Therapy, 32,* 447–451.

van den Hout, M., Tenney, N., Huygens, K., & de Jong, P. (1997). Preconscious processing bias in specific phobia. *Behaviour Research and Therapy, 35,* 29–34.

van den Hout, M. A., van der Molen, G. M., Griez, E., Lousberg, H., & Nansen, A. (1987). Reduction of CO_2-induced anxiety in patients with panic attacks after repeated CO_2 exposure. *American Journal of Psychiatry, 144,* 788–791.

van der Does, A. J. W., Antony, M. M., Barsky, A. J., & Ehlers, A. (2000). Heartbeat perception in panic disorder: A re-analysis. *Behaviour Research and Therapy, 38,* 47–62.

van der Does, A. J. W., van Dyck, R., & Spinhoven, P. (1997). Accurate heartbeat perception in panic disorder: Fact and artefact. *Journal of Affective Disorders, 43,* 121–130.

van der Molen, G. M., van den Hout, M. A., Vroemen, J., Lousberg, H., & Griez, E. (1986). Cognitive determinants of lactate-induced anxiety. *Behaviour Research and Therapy, 24,* 677–680.

van Hout, W.J.P.J., Emmelkamp, P.M.G., Koopmans, P.C., Bögels, S.M., & Bouman, T.K. (in press). Assessment of self-statements in agoraphobic situations: Construction and psychometric evaluations of the Agoraphobic Self-Statements Questionnaire (ASQ). *Journal of Anxiety Disorders.*

van Velzen, C. J. M., Emmelkamp, P. M. G., & Scholing, A. (1997). The impact of personality disorders on behavioral treatment for social phobia. *Behaviour Research and Therapy, 35,* 889–900.

van Vliet, I. M., den Boer, J. A., & Westenberg, H. G. M. (1994). Psychopharmacological treatment of social phobia: A double blind placebo controlled study with fluvoxamine. *Psychopharmacology, 115,* 128–134.

van Vliet, I. M., den Boer, J. A., Westenberg, H. G. M., & Ho Pian, K. L. (1997). Clinical effects of buspirone in social phobia: A double-blind placebo-controlled study. *Journal of Clinical Psychiatry, 58,* 164–168.

van Vliet, I. M., den Boer, J. A., Westenberg, H. G. M., & Slaap, B. R. (1996). A double-blind comparative study of brofaromine and fluvoxamine in outpatients with panic disorder. *Journal of Clinical Psychopharmacology, 16,* 299–306.

Verburg, C., Griez, E., & Meijer, J. (1994). A 35% carbon dioxide challenge in simple phobias. *Acta Psychiatrica Scandinavica, 90,* 420–423.

Versiani, M., Nardi, A. E., Mundim, F. D., Alves, A. A., Liebowitz, M. R., & Amrein, R. (1992). Pharmacotherapy of social phobia: A controlled study with moclobemide and phenelzine. *British Journal of Psychiatry, 161,* 353–360.

Versiani, M., Nardi, A. E., Mundim, F. D., Pinto, S., Saboya, E., & Kovacs, R. (1996). The long-term treatment of social phobia with moclobemide. *International Clinical Psychopharmacology, 11*(Suppl. 3), 83–88.

Wade, A. G., Lepola, U., Koponen, H. J., Pedersen, V., & Pedersen, T. (1997). The effect of citalopram in panic disorder. *British Journal of Psychiatry, 170,* 549–553.

Wade, S. L., Monroe, S. M., & Michelson, L. K. (1993). Chronic life stress and treatment outcome in agoraphobia with panic attacks. *American Journal of Psychiatry, 150,* 1491–1495.

Walker, J. R., & Stein, M. B. (1995). Epidemiology. In M. B. Stein (Ed.), *Social phobia: Clinical and research perspectives* (pp. 189–228). Washington, DC: American Psychiatric Press.

Wardle, J., Hayward, P., Higgitt, A., Stabi, M., Blizard, R., & Gray, J. (1994). Effects of concurrent diazepam treatment on the outcome of exposure therapy in agoraphobia. *Behavior Research and Therapy, 32,* 203–215.

Ware, J., Jain, K., Burgess, I., & Davey, G. C. L. (1994). Disease-avoidance model: Factor analysis of common animal fears. *Behaviour Research and Therapy, 32,* 57–63.

Warshaw, M. G., Massion, A. O., Peterson, L. G., Pratt, L. A., & Keller, M. B. (1995). Suicidal behavior in patients with panic disorder: Retrospective and prospective data. *Journal of Affective Disorders, 34,* 235–247.

Watson, D., & Friend, R. (1969). Measurement of social-evaluative anxiety. *Journal of Consulting and Clinical Psychology, 33,* 448–457.

Watts, F. N., McKenna, F. P., Sharrock, R., & Trezise, L. (1986). Colour naming of phobia-related words. *British Journal of Psychology, 77,* 97–108.

Watts, F. N., & Sharrock, R. (1984). Questionnaire dimensions of spider phobia. *Behaviour Research and Therapy, 22,* 575–580.

Watts, F. N., Trezise, L., & Sharrock, R. (1986). Processing of phobic stimuli. *British Journal of Clinical Psychology, 25,* 253–259.

Wegner, D. M., Broome, A., & Blumberg, S. J. (1997). Ironic effects of trying to relax under stress. *Behaviour Research and Therapy, 35,* 11–21.

Weiller, E., Bisserbe, J. -C., Boyer, P., Lepine, J. -P., & Lecrubier, Y. (1996). Social phobia in general health care: An unrecognized undertreated disabling disorder. *British Journal of Psychiatry, 168,* 169–174.

Weissman, M. M., Bland, R. C., Canino, G. J., Greenwald, S., Lee, C. -K., Newman, S. C., Rubio-Stipec, M., & Wickramaratne, P. J. (1996). The cross-national epidemiology of social phobia: A preliminary report. *International Clinical Psychopharmacology, 11*(Suppl. 3), 9–14.

Weissman, M. M., Klerman, G. L., Markowitz, J. S., & Ouellette, R. (1989). Suicidal ideation and suicide attempts in panic disorder and attacks. *New England Journal of Medicine, 321,* 1209–1214.

Wells, A. (1997). *Cognitive therapy of anxiety disorders: A practice manual and conceptual guide.* New York: Wiley.

Wells, A., & Clark, D. M. (1997). Social phobia: A cognitive approach. In G. C. L. Davey (Ed.), *Phobias: A handbook of theory, research, and treatment* (pp. 3–26). New York: Wiley.

Wells, A., Clark, D. M., & Ahmad, S. (1998). How do I look with my minds eye: Perspective taking in social phobic imagery. *Behaviour Research and Therapy*, 36, 631–634.

Wells, A., Clark, D. M., Stopa, L., & Papageorgiou, C. (1999, September). *Assessment of thoughts and beliefs in social phobia: Development and properties of the Social Cognitions Questionnaire (SCQ)*. Paper presented at the meeting of the European Association of Behavioural and Cognitive Therapy, Dresden, Germany.

Wells, A., Clark, D. M., Salkovskis, P., Ludgate, J., Hackman, A., & Gelder, M. (1995). Social phobia: The role of in-situation safety behaviors in maintaining anxiety and negative beliefs. *Behavior Therapy*, 26, 153–161.

Wells, A., & Papageorgiou, C. (1998). Social phobia: Effects of external attention on anxiety, negative beliefs, and perspective taking. *Behavior Therapy*, 29, 357–370.

Wells, A., & Papageorgiou, C. (1999). The observer perspective: Biased imagery in social phobia, agoraphobia, and blood/injury phobia. *Behaviour Research and Therapy*, 37, 653–658.

Wessel, I., & Merckelbach, H. (1997). The impact of anxiety on memory for details in spider phobics. *Applied Cognitive Psychology*, 11, 223–231.

Wessel, I., & Merckelbach, H. (1998). Memory for threat-relevant and threat-irrelevant cues in spider phobics. *Cognitions and Emotion*, 12, 93–104.

Westling, B. E., & Öst, L. -G. (1993). Relationship between panic attack symptoms and cognitions in panic disorder patients. *Journal of Anxiety Disorders*, 7, 181–194.

Whitehead, W. E., Robinson, A., Blackwell, B., & Stutz, R. M. (1978). Flooding treatment of phobias: Does chronic diazepam increase effectiveness? *Journal of Behavior Therapy and Experimental Psychiatry*, 9, 219–225.

Widiger, T. A. (1992). Generalized social phobia versus avoidant personality disorder: A commentary on three studies. *Journal of Abnormal Psychology*, 101, 340–343.

Wilhelm, F. H., & Roth, W. T. (1996, November). *Acute and delayed effects of alprazolam on flight phobics during exposure*. Paper presented at the meeting of the Association for Advancement of Behavior Therapy, New York, NY.

Wilkinson, G., Balestrieri, M., Ruggeri, M., & Bellantuono, C. (1991). Meta-analysis of double-blind placebo-controlled trials of antidepressants and benzodiazepines for patients with panic disorders. *Psychological Medicine*, 21, 991–998.

Williams, J. B. W., Gibbon, M., First, M. B., Spitzer, R. L., Davis, M., Borus, J., Howes, M. J., Kane, J., Pope, H. G., Rounsaville, B., Wittchen, H. -U. (1992). The Structured Clinical Interview for DSM-III-R (SCID): II. Multisite test–retest reliability. *Archives of General Psychiatry*, 49, 630–636.

Williams, J. B., Spitzer, R. L., & Gibbon, M. (1992). International reliability of a diagnostic intake procedure for panic disorder. *American Journal of Psychiatry*, 149, 560–562.

Williams, K. E., & Chambless, D. L. (1990). The relationship between therapist characteristics and outcome of in vivo exposure treatment for agoraphobia. *Behavior Therapy, 21,* 111–116.

Wilson, G. D., & Priest, H. F. (1968). The principal components of phobic stimuli. *Journal of Clinical Psychology, 24,* 191.

Wilson, K. G., Sandler, L. S., & Asmundson, G. J. (1993). Fearful and non-fearful panic attacks in a student population. *Behaviour Research and Therapy, 31,* 407–411.

Wilson, K. G., Sandler, L. S., Asmundson, G. J. G., Larsen, D. K., & Ediger, J. M. (1991). Effects of instructional set on self-reports of panic attacks. *Journal of Anxiety Disorders, 5,* 43–63.

Winton, E. C., Clark, D. M., & Edelmann, R. J. (1995). Social anxiety, fear of negative evaluation and the detection of negative emotion in others. *Behaviour Research and Therapy, 33,* 193–196.

Wittchen, H.-U., & Beloch, E. (1996). The impact of social phobia on quality of life. *International Clinical Psychopharmacology, 11*(Suppl. 3), 15–23.

Wittchen, H.-U., Reed, V., & Kessler, R. C. (1998). The relationship of agoraphobia and panic in a community sample of adolescents and young adults. *Archives of General Psychiatry, 55,* 1017–1024.

Wittchen, H.-U., Stein, M. B., & Kessler, R. C. (1999). Social fears and social phobia in a community sample of adolescents and young adults: Prevalence, risk factors and comorbidity. *Psychological Medicine, 29,* 309–323.

Wlazlo, Z., Schroeder-Hartwig, K., Hand, I., Kaiser, G., & Münchau, N. (1990). Exposure in vivo vs. social skills training for social phobia: Long-term outcome and differential effects. *Behaviour Research and Therapy, 28,* 181–193.

Wolpe, J. (1958). *Psychotherapy by reciprocal inhibition.* Stanford, CA: Stanford University Press.

Wolpe, J., & Lang, P. J. (1964). A Fear Survey Schedule for use in behaviour therapy. *Behaviour Research and Therapy, 2,* 27–30.

Wolpe, J., & Rowan, V. C. (1988). Panic disorder: A product of classical conditioning. *Behaviour Research and Therapy, 26,* 441–450.

Wong, A. H. C., Smith, M., & Boon, H. S. (1998). Herbal remedies in psychiatric practice. *Archives of General Psychiatry, 55,* 1033–1044.

Woody, S. R. (1996). Effects of focus of attention on anxiety levels and social performance of individuals with social phobia. *Journal of Abnormal Psychology, 105,* 61–69.

World Health Organization. (1990). *Composite International Diagnostic Interview (CIDI): a) CIDI-interview (version 1.0), b) CIDI-user manual, c) CIDI-training manual, d) CIDI-computer programs.* Geneva: Author.

Yonkers, K. A., Zlotnick, C., Allsworth, J., Warshaw, M., Shea, T., & Keller, M. B. (1998). Is the course of panic disorder the same in women and men? *American Journal of Psychiatry, 155,* 596–602.

Young, J. E. (1994). *Cognitive therapy for personality disorders: A schema-focused approach* (rev. ed.). Sarasota, FL: Practitioner's Resource Press.

Zajonc, R. B. (1980). Feeling and thinking: Preferences need no inferences. *American Psychologist, 35,* 151–175.

Zajonc, R. B. (1984). On the primacy of affect. *American Psychologist, 39,* 117–123.

Zimbardo, P. G., Pilkonis, P. A., & Norwood, R. M. (1975). The social disease of shyness. *Psychology Today, 8,* 68–72.

Zinbarg, R. E., Barlow, D. H., & Brown, T. A. (1997). Hierarchical structure and general factor saturation of the Anxiety Sensitivity Index: Evidence and implications. *Psychological Assessment, 9,* 277–284.

Zoellner, L., Craske, M., Hussain, A., Lewis, M., & Echeveri, A. (1996, November). *Contextual effects of alprazolam during exposure therapy.* Paper presented at the meeting of the Association for Advancement of Behavior Therapy, New York, NY.

Zuercher-White, E. (1997a). *An end to panic: Breakthrough techniques for overcoming panic disorder* (2nd ed.). Oakland, CA: New Harbinger.

Zuercher-White, E. (1997b). *Treating panic disorder and agoraphobia: A step by step clinical guide.* Oakland, CA: New Harbinger.

Zvolensky, M. J., Eifert, G. H., Lejuez, C. W., & McNeil, D. W. (1999). The effects of offset control over 20% carbon-dioxide-enriched air on anxious responding. *Journal of Abnormal Psychology, 108,* 624–632.

Zvolensky, M. J., Lejuez, C. W., & Eifert, G. H. (1998). The role of offset control in anxious responding: An experimental test using repeated administrations of 20% carbon dioxide-enriched air. *Behavior Therapy, 29,* 193–209.

AUTHOR INDEX

Benca, R., 74
Bennett, K. S., 137
Berglund, P., 52
Berisford, M. A., 280
Bernstein, D. A., 137
Bhide, A. V., 85
Biederman, J., 61
Bieling, P. J., 147, 148, 222
Binik, Y. M., 149
Biondi, F., 16, 38
Bisaga, A., 38
Bisserbe, J.-C., 57
Bjarnadottir, A., 65
Blaauw, B. M. J. W., 45
Black, B., 67
Black, D. W., 43, 45
Blackwell, B., 102
Blanchard, E. B., 20,114
Blanchard, J. J., 109, 110
Bland, K., 40, 42
Bland, R. C., 54, 59
Blaszczynski, A., 22
Blau, J. S., 99
Blazer, D. G., 23
Blendell, K. A., 69
Blumberg, S. J., 204
Bögels, S. M., 63, 71, 135
Bogojevic, G., 24
Böhme, H., 42
Bohn, P., 30
Bolduc, E. A., 61
Bond, L., 145
Boon, H. S., 280
Boone, M. L., 66
Booth, R., 101
Borden, J., 136
Borden, J. W., 145
Borg, K., 73
Borkovec, T. D., 19, 20
Botella, C., 41
Bouchard, S., 40
Bouman, T. K., 16, 135
Bourdon, K. H., 22, 84, 86
Bourne, E. J., 171, 188
Bourque, P., 99, 205
Bouwer, C., 74
Bowden, C. L., 44
Bowers, W., 43
Bowley, L., 94
Boyer, P., 57
Boyer, W., 43

Bradwejn, J., 36
Bragadottir, B., 65
Brandberg, M., 99, 157
Brar, S., 4, 59
Brechman-Toussaint, M., 65
Breier, A., 35
Breitholtz, E., 27
Breslau, N., 280
Breuer, P., 29, 30, 31
Brewer, C., 75
Brewin, C. R., 46
Bright, P., 32
Bristol, D., 94
Broeke, E. T., 100
Bronson, S. S., 23
Broocks, A., 280
Broome, A., 204
Brosschot, J. F., 93
Brouillard, M., 16
Brown, D., 188
Brown, E. J., 71, 144, 145
Brown, G. K., 148
Brown, S. B., 109, 110
Brown, T. A., 19, 21, 30, 35, 39, 40, 42,
    58, 81, 96, 110, 111, 120, 137,
    148
Brown, T. M., 67
Broyles, S., 136
Brødsgaard, I., 99, 158
Bruce, T. J., 45, 152, 171, 279
Bruch, M. A., 56, 61, 64, 70
Bucholz, K., 54, 111
Buckminster, S., 77
Buergener, F., 66
Bufka, L. F., 211
Buigues, J., 43
Bunt, R., 198
Burgess, I., 83
Burgoyne, W., 75
Burke, J. D., 21
Burke, K. C., 21
Burman, D., 87
Burns, D. D., 172, 239, 246, 257
Burns, J., 62
Busch, F. N., 26
Bushnell, W., 43
Butler, G., 70
Bystritsky, A., 30, 42, 43

Cahill, S. P., 100
Caldirola, D., 37

Herda, C. A., 95
Herman, S., 208
Hersen, M., 39, 66, 114
Hewitt, P. L., 145, 148
Hibbert, G. A., 283
Hill, C. L., 18
Hill, E. M., 80
Hiller, K.-O., 280
Himadi, W. G., 41
Himle, J. A., 16, 80, 86, 87
Hirshfeld, D. R., 61
Hiruma, N., 56
Hladek, D., 203
Hodges, L. F., 207, 208
Hoekstra, R., 40
Hoffart, A., 24, 40, 42, 47, 135
Hoffman, H. G., 207
Hofmann, S. G., 60, 61, 70, 95, 211
Holdrinet, I., 100
Holle, C., 61
Hollifield, M., 24
Hollon, S. D., 36
Holobow, N., 44
Holt, C. S., 30, 50, 51, 52, 56, 62, 69,
        144, 148
Holzrichter, S., 136
Hommer, D., 35
Hoogduin, C. A. L., 41
Hoogstraten, J., 137
Hope, D. A., 51, 61, 64, 69, 70, 145
Ho Pian, K. L., 75
Horner, K. J., 144
Hornig, C. D., 17, 23, 26, 31, 35, 54
Horselenberg, R., 94
Horwath, E., 17, 23, 35
Howard, L. J., 58
Howard, W. A., 99
Hsu, A., 18
Hudson, C. J., 280
Hugdahl, K., 80
Hughes, D. C., 23
Humble, M., 73
Hussain, A., 103
Huta, V., 24, 60, 148
Huygens, K., 93
Huzel, L. L., 66
Hyde, T. S., 44

Ihen, G. H., 64
Ing, N., 203

Ishiki, D., 44
Ito, L. M., 40
Izard, C. E., 28

Jaccard, J. J., 144
Jack, M. S., 143, 144
Jackson, R. J., 22
Jacob, R. G., 75, 76, 145
Jacobs, G. A., 99
Jacobs, R. J., 24
Jacobson, N., 198
Jacquin, K., 32
Jaimez, T. L., 35
Jain, K., 83
James, I. M., 75
Jameson, J. S., 201
Janicak, P. G., 276
Jansson, L., 71, 101, 208
Jasin, S. E., 31
Jayaraman, J., 203
Jefferson, J. W., 42
Jerremalm, A., 71, 99, 101, 208
Johansson, J., 71, 99
Johnson, H. J., 98
Johnson, J., 17, 23, 26, 54
Johnston, D. G., 43
Jones, G. E., 141
Jones, J. C., 26, 152
Jones, M. K., 80, 94
Jones, W. C., 25
Juster, H. R., 56, 65, 69, 71, 72

Kachin, K. E., 136
Kaiser, G., 65
Kamphuis, J. H., 136
Karkowski, L. M., 37
Karno, M., 23
Kaspi, S. P., 46
Katerndahl, D. A., 16, 24, 26
Katzelnick, D. J., 74
Keijsers, G. P. J., 41, 42
Keir, R., 89
Keller, M. B., 4, 25, 26
Kelley, J. E., 206
Kellner, R., 26
Kenardy, J., 16, 21, 32, 208
Kendler, K. S., 37, 68, 97
Kenemans, J. L., 93
Kenna, D., 141
Kennedy, C. R., 69

Kenney, M. R., 23
Kent, J. M., 35
Kessler, G. D., 207
Kessler, R. C., 3, 4, 17, 22, 23, 37, 52, 54, 55, 58, 84
Keyl, P. M., 22
Keys, D. J., 66, 118
Khawaja, N. G., 135
Kiliç, C., 46
Kim, E., 30
Kim, H. L., 279
Kindt, M., 93
King, R. J., 67
Kirkpatrick, D. R., 86
Kitanishi, K., 56
Klein, D. F., 26, 33, 37, 42, 68, 75, 280
Kleinknecht, E. E., 56, 82, 83
Kleinknecht, R. A., 56, 82, 83, 100, 136, 137
Klerman, G. L., 26, 71
Klieger, D. M., 137, 146
Klorman, R., 136, 137
Klosko, J. S., 40
Knapp, E., 44
Knott, V., 20
Knowles, J. A., 37
Kobak, K. A., 143, 144, 146
Koch, W. J., 32, 35, 42
Koele, P., 45
Kohnen, R., 280
Kolk, A. M., 86
Koopmans, P. C., 135
Koponen, H. J., 43
Kopper, B. A., 144
Korotitsch, W., 148
Koszycki, D., 36
Kowalski, R. M., 59
Kozak, M. J., 62, 102, 203, 281
Kraaimaat, F., 39, 40
Kramer, M. S., 37
Kringlen, E., 68, 114
Krishnan, K. R. R., 66
Kroeze, S., 30
Kroft, C. D. L., 67
Krystal, J. H., 18
Kuch, K., 41, 44, 140
Kunert, H. J., 136
Kushner, M. G., 18, 19, 58
Kwee, M. G. T., 140

Kwon, S.-M., 140
Kyomen, H., 56

Laberge, B., 42
Lacroix, D., 157
Ladouceur, R., 99, 205
Lahart, C., 148
Lamberti, J. W., 18
LaMontagne, Y., 39
Landy, F. J., 87
Lang, A. J., 202
Lang, P. J., 28, 136, 137, 146
Lange, A., 42, 45
Langley, J. D., 91
Larkin, E. J., 111
Larsen, D. K., 20
Last, C. G., 41
Latas, M., 24
Latimer, P., 99
Lavy, E., 93, 95, 136
Lawson, C., 33
Lazarte, A., 198
Lazarus, R. S., 240
Lazovik, A. D., 146
Leary, M. R., 59, 60
Lecrubier, Y., 57
Lee, M. A., 280
Lee, P. S., 44
Lee, T. C., 83, 93
Lee, Y., 80
Leeuw, I., 203
Lejuez, C. W., 36
Leon, A. C., 25, 42, 138
Lepine, J.-P., 57
Lepola, U., 43
Lerew, D. R., 22, 135
Lesser, I. M., 25
Leung, A. W., 56, 72, 219
Levander, S., 44
Levin, A., 72
Levine, B. A., 208
Levitt, K., 32
Lewinsohn, M., 25
Lewinsohn, P. M., 25
Lewis, C. P., 44
Lewis, J. A., 80
Lewis, J. S., 80
Lewis, M., 103
Lewis, M. H., 67
Ley, R., 26, 34, 35

Pauli, U., 73
Payne, L. L., 201
Pecknold, J. C., 44, 279
Pedersen, T., 43
Pedersen, V., 43
Penava, S. J., 47, 157
Penn, D. L., 64
Perel, J. M., 36, 43, 277
Perna, G., 37
Perry, K. J., 64, 66
Perugi, G., 74
Peters, L., 70
Peterson, L. G., 26
Peterson, R. A., 32, 95, 135, 137, 138
Philipp, M., 280
Phillips, G. C., 141
Pickersgill, M. J., 86, 87
Pidlubny, S. R., 16
Pierce, K. A., 86
Pierce, M. W., 37
Pilkington, N. W., 29
Pilkonis, P. A., 42, 49
Pine, D., 35
Pioli, R., 74
Pitchot, W., 35
Plamondon, J., 42
Podd, J. V., 90
Pohl, R. B., 43
Pollack, M. H., 31, 43, 46, 47, 74, 75,
    77, 152, 157
Pollard, C. A., 21, 23, 57, 171, 208
Pollard, H. J., 21
Portera, L., 25, 138
Potts, N. L. S., 66
Poulton, R., 91
Pratt, L. A., 26
Prescott, C. A., 37
Preskorn, S. H., 276
Priest, H. F., 87
Prigatano, G. P., 98
Prout, M., 99
Pupi, A., 38
Purdon, C. L., 60, 63, 65, 148, 159, 204

Rachman, S. J., 32, 60, 61, 89, 90, 91,
    94, 101, 103, 104, 137, 162, 200
Radomsky, A. S., 137
Rae, D. S., 21
Raffle, C., 205
Raguram, R., 85
Raichle, M. E., 38

Raj, A. B., 44
Raj, B. A., 21, 22
Rapaport, M. H., 43
Rapee, R. M., 16, 21, 25, 27, 29, 30, 31,
    35, 36, 55, 56, 59, 60, 61, 62, 64,
    95, 114, 135, 171, 198
Rauch, S. L., 98
Ravenscroft, H., 62
Realini, J. P., 16, 24, 26
Reed, V., 17
Rees, C. S., 25
Regier, D. A., 17, 21, 86
Reich, J., 75
Reichman, J. T., 140
Reiman, E. M., 38
Reines, S., 37
Reiss, S., 32, 95, 135, 137, 138
Reiter, S. R., 75
Renneberg, B., 25
Renssen, M. R., 100
Rhodes, L., 20
Richards, J. C., 25, 29, 32
Rickels, K., 43, 44, 277
Rieger, E. J., 141
Riemann, B. C., 30, 31, 62
Ries, B. J., 62, 141
Rijken, H. M., 39, 40, 193
Rinck, M., 31
Riskind, J. H., 94
Ritchie, J. C., 66
Robins, L. N., 22, 54, 86, 110, 111
Robinson, A., 102
Robinson, S., 104
Rodney, J. M., 62
Rodriguez, B. I., 203
Roemer, L., 287
Rogers, P. D., 172
Romach, M. K., 279
Roodman, A. A., 41
Rose, M. P., 198
Rosen, R., 43
Rosenbaum, J. F., 44, 46, 61, 75
Rosenblate, R., 148
Rosenthal, M., 44
Ross, H. E., 111
Ross, L., 144
Roth, D., 24, 57, 63, 148, 211
Roth, W. T., 30, 45, 60, 70, 95, 103
Rothbaum, B. O., 193, 207, 208
Rowa, K., 4, 59
Rowan, V. C., 26

Rowe, M. K., 18, 168, 201, 202
Roy-Byrne, P. P., 35, 42, 280
Rozin, P., 82
Ruggeri, M., 42
Ruskin, J. N., 29
Russell, J. L., 19
Rüther, E., 136
Rutigliano, P., 62

Saboonchi, F., 65
Sack, W. H., 25
Safren, S. A., 72, 145
Salaberria, K., 70
Salkovskis, P. M., 83, 93, 99, 157, 206
Salvator-Carulla, 24
Salzman, D. G., 69
Samuelson, S., 37
Sanderson, A., 100
Sanderson, W. C., 16, 25, 36, 58, 88, 171
Sandler, L. S., 19, 20, 29, 30
Sarnie, M. K., 29
Saunders, J. T., 99
Savage, I. T., 75
Sawchuk, C. N., 83, 93
Scarpato, M. A., 16, 22
Schaap, C. P. D. R., 41
Schlenker, B. R., 59, 60
Schmidt, C., 99
Schmidt, H., 81
Schmidt, L. A., 67
Schmidt, N. B., 22, 32, 35, 36, 40, 135, 283
Schmidt, S. M., 37
Schneier, F. R., 52, 54, 55, 57, 67, 73, 74, 75
Schoenmakers, N., 137
Scholing, A., 70, 71, 156, 157
Schouten, E., 83, 92, 93
Schroeder-Hartwig, K., 65
Schruers, K., 35
Schwalberg, M. D., 58
Schwartz, C. E., 280
Schweizer, E., 43, 44, 277
Scupi, B. S., 135
Seeley, J. R., 25
Segal, D. L., 114
Segui, J., 24
Sengün, S., 32
Sessarego, A., 38
Shader, R. I., 35

Shafran, R., 101, 103
Shapiro, D., 41
Shapiro, F., 100
Shapiro, T., 26
Sharp, D. M., 45, 46
Sharrock, R., 93, 137
Shaw, B. F., 140
Shear, M. K., 26, 31, 36, 42, 45, 109, 136, 138, 152
Sheehan, D. V., 44, 111
Sheehan, K. H., 44
Sheikh, J. I., 44
Shelton, R. C., 36
Sher, K. J., 58
Shipherd, J. C., 35
Shulman, I. D., 140
Siegel, L., 25
Sijsenaar, M., 100
Silove, D., 22
Silva, P. A., 91
Simpson, H. B., 67, 73, 74
Sipsas, A., 80, 95
Skre, I., 68, 97, 114
Slaap, B. R., 43
Slavkin, S. L., 144
Smari, J., 65
Smith, J., 137
Smith, L. M., 25
Smith, M., 280
Snell, J. B., 141
Solyom, C., 200
Soto, S., 44
Soulios, C., 41
Spence, S. H., 65
Spencer, D. J., 75
Spiegel, D. A., 44, 45, 152, 279
Spielberger, C. D., 99, 147
Spinhoven, P., 29, 45, 73
Spitzer, R. L., 25, 52, 111, 114
Sramek, J. J., 37
Staab, J. P., 36
Stang, P., 58
Stanley, M. A., 40, 145
Starcevic, V., 24, 26
Steer, R. A., 147, 148
Steerneman, P., 91
Stein, D. J., 74
Stein, J., 33
Stein, M. B., 4, 18, 30, 35, 42, 52, 54, 55, 58, 62, 66, 67, 68, 74
Steiner, M., 43

SUBJECT INDEX

Automatic thoughts, 248
Avoidance patterns
    overt, 124–125, 166
    subtle, *126*, 166, 204
Avoidant personality disorder, 118
Avserve Canada–Fear of Flying Treatment (Air Canada program), 319
AWOPD. *See* Agoraphobia without history of panic disorder

BAI. *See* Beck Anxiety Inventory
BAT. *See* Behavioral approach test
BDI–2. *See* Beck Depression Inventory (2nd ed.)
Beck Anxiety Inventory (BAI), 147, 297
Beck Depression Inventory (2nd ed.) (BDI–2), 148, 297
Behavioral approach test (BAT), 108, 130–132
Behavioral assessment, 130–133
Behavioral component of panic, 163, 166–167
Behavioral experiments in cognitive therapy, 256–257
Behavioral treatments. *See* Applied tension; Breathing retraining; Cognitive-behavioral therapy; Exposure-based treatment; Psychological treatments, choice among
Belgium, organizations in, 313
Benzodiazepines, 268, 270–271
    See also Alprazolam; Anxiolytic medication; Diazepam; Lorazepam
    combined with antidepressants, 277
    contraindications for, *278*
    discontinuation phase and, 279
    dosages for, 270, 271, 277, *278*, 279
    exposure therapy and, 270–271
    long-term treatments and, 277–279
    panic disorder and, 42, 44, 45, 277–279, *278*
    short-term treatment with, 270–271
    side-effects of, 270, *278*, 279
    social phobias and, 74–75, 77, 269–271, 277–279, *278*
    specific phobias and, 271
Best Practices series (New Harbinger Publications), 171
Beta–blockers, 75, 269
Bibliotherapy, 171–172

Biological aspects of phobias. *See* Biological models; Family studies; Genetics research; Neurobiological research
Biological models, 32–35
BISS. *See* Blood–Injection Symptom Scale
Blood–injection–injury phobias, 80, 86, 87
    See also Medical phobias; Specific phobias
    applied tension and, 102, 281–282
    common phobic beliefs in, *245*
    disgust and, 82–83
    exposure resources and, *224*
    genetics and, 97
    pharmacotherapy and, 271
    prevalence of, 84, 86
    self-report measures for, *136*, *137*
Blood–Injection Symptom Scale (BISS), 294
Body Sensations Interpretation Questionnaire (BSIQ), 135, 290
Body Sensations Questionnaire (BSQ), 138–139, 290
Body vigilance, 29–30
Body Vigilance Scale (BVS), 135, 290
Brain imaging studies, 38, 97–98
Breathing retraining (BRT)
    nocturnal panic and, 18
    panic disorder and, 39, 40, 154, 155, 156, 282–286
    procedures in, 284–286
    social and specific phobias and, 283
Bridge phobias. *See* Height phobia; Situational phobia
Brief Panic Disorder Screen (PBDS), 138, 290
Brief Social Phobia Scale (BSPS), 143, 292
British Psychological Society, 314
Brofaromine (Consonar), 43, 73
BRT. *See* Breathing retraining
BSIQ. *See* Body Sensations Interpretation Questionnaire
BSPS. *See* Brief Social Phobia Scale
BSQ. *See* Body Sensations Questionnaire
Buspirone (Buspar), 268
    panic disorder and, 44
    social phobia and, 74, 75
BVS. *See* Body Vigilance Scale

Dental Cognitions Questionnaire (DCQ), 295

Dental Fear Survey (DFS), 295

Dental phobias, 101, *137*, 158

Depression, 115, 118
  standard measures for, 147–148, 297

Depression Anxiety Stress Scales (DASS), 135, 147–148, 297

Deracyn. *See* Adinazolam.

Development of phobias
  panic disorder and, 21–22
  social phobia and, 54–55, 60–61
  specific phobia and, 88–92

DFS. *See* Dental Fear Survey

Diagnostic and Statistical Manual of Mental Disorders (DSM–III;DSM–III–R;DSM–IV; APA)
  non-fearful panic, 18, 19
  panic attacks, 12, 15–16
  panic disorder, 12–13, 15–16, 22
  panic disorder with agoraphobia, 13, 15–16
  relationship between panic and agoraphobia, 15–17
  social phobia, 50–51, 53–54
  specific phobia, 79, 80–81, 84, 88
  types of phobias, 12–13

Diagnostic assessment, 109–121
  differential diagnosis, 112, 115–119
  semi-structured interviews, 109–112, 287–288
  structured interviews, 109–110, 287–288
  treatment decisions and, 119–121

Diagnostic criteria
  agoraphobia without history of panic disorder, 15
  panic attacks, 12
  panic disorder, 12–13
  panic disorder with agoraphobia, 13
  social phobia, 50–53
  specific phobia, 79–80

Diagnostic interviews
  semi-structured, 109–112, *111*, 113–114, 287–288
  structured, 109–110, 287–288

Diagnostic Interview Schedule (DIS–IV), 111

Diaries, 108, 132–133, 257
  See also Monitoring forms
  Panic Attack Diary (form), 132, *134*

Diazepam (Valium), 44, 102–103, 270

Disgust, and specific phobia, 82–83

Disgust sensitivity, measurement of, 82

Distraction, and exposure, 203–204

Dopamine, 67

Dot–probe task, 62

Downward arrow technique, 248–249

Driving phobias
  age of onset, 87
  assessment and, 129
  development models and, 89, 90
  exposure resources and, *224*
  PTSD and, 119
  statistics on, 316–317

Drowning phobias, statistics on, 318

Drug interactions
  antidepressants and, 273, *274*, 277
  herbal remedies and, 280

Duration of exposure, 200–201, 218, 227

ECA study. *See* Epidemiological Catchment Area study

Economic impacts
  agoraphobia and, 24–25
  panic disorder and, 24–25
  social phobia and, 57

Education of patient. *See* Psychoeducation

Effexor. *See* Venlafaxine

Eldepryl. *See* selegiline.

EMDR. *See* Eye movement desensitization and reprocessing

Emotion
  See also Anxiety; Fear
  lack of therapist attention to, 257, 261
  role of cognitive appraisal in, 240–241

Emotion theory, and panic disorder, 28–29

Enclosed place phobias. *See* Claustrophobia; situational phobias; Specific phobias

Encourage Connection, 311

Epidemiological Catchment Area (ECA) study, 16–17, 25, 53–54, 84, 86

Epidemiology
  panic disorder, 21–26
  social phobia, 53–59
  specific phobia, 84–88

Ethnicity, and social phobia, 55–56

Nonclinical panic, 20–21, 29
Nongeneralized social phobia, 50
Non–fearful panic (non–fearful PD),
    18–19
Nonverbal communication, 233–234
No Panic (United Kingdom), 314
Norepinephrine (NE), 35–36
Norfluoxetine. *See* Fluoxetine

Obsessive–compulsive disorder (OCD)
    differential diagnosis and, 115, 119
    pharmacotherapy for phobic disor-
        ders and, 268
Open–ended questions, 236, 243–244
Open vs. closed communication styles,
    233–234, 234, 236
Overt avoidance patterns, 124–125, 166

PACQ. *See* Panic Attack Cognitions
    Questionnaire
PAI. *See* Panic Appraisal Inventory
Panic
    Barlow's integrated model of, 28–29
    Clark's cognitive model of, 27–28,
        29
    cognitive appraisal and, 241
    discussion of nature of, 160–162
    nonclinical, 20–21, 29
    non-fearful, 18–19
    physical, cognitive, and behavioral
        components of, 163, 165–167
Panic and Agoraphobia Scale (PAS),
    136, 291
Panic and Anxiety Disorders Foundation
    of Western Australia (PADWA),
    313
Panic Appraisal Inventory (PAI), 136,
    291
Panic Attack Cognitions Questionnaire
    (PACQ), 136, 291
Panic Attack Diary (form), 132, 134
Panic Attack Questionnaire – Revised
    (PAQ–R), 136, 292
Panic Attack Questionnaire (PAQ), 20
Panic attacks
    See also Panic disorder; Panic disor-
        der with agoraphobia
    associated psychological disorders, 12
    biological factors in, 27–28
    diagnostic criteria, 12

differential diagnosis of PDA and,
    112, 115–117
misconceptions about panic and,
    163, 164
psychological models of, 26–28
relationship between panic and ago-
    raphobia, 15–17
situational vs. uncued types of, 12,
    27
special types of, 17–21
use of cognitive strategies during,
    263
Panic Attack Symptoms Questionnaire
    (PASQ), 136, 292
Panic disorder (PD), 11
    See also Agoraphobia without history
        of panic disorder; Cognitive ther-
        apy for panic disorder; Panic at-
        tacks; Panic disorder with agora-
        phobia
    attributions in, 31–32
    biological models of, 32–35
    biological research on, 32–38
    brain imaging studies on, 38
    breathing retraining and, 39, 40,
        154, 155, 156, 282–286
    cognitive biases and, 30–31, 247,
        248
    combined treatments and, 45–47,
        103, 152, 282–283
    comorbidity, 25–26
    compared treatments and, 45–47,
        152, 154–156, 157–160
    course of, 21–22
    descriptive psychopathology, 12–26
    development of, 21–22
    diagnostic criteria, 12–13
    economic impact of, 24–25
    epidemiology, 21–26
    exposure-based treatment of, 39, 40,
        46, 154–156, 217
    family studies and, 37
    functional impairment and, 24
    genetics research on, 37–38
    group vs. individual approaches to,
        157–160
    misconceptions about panic and,
        163, 164
    neurotransmitter findings on, 35–37
    pharmacological treatment of, 42–
        47, 152

Panic disorder, *continued*

pharmacological vs. psychological vs. combined treatments for, 152

presentation of treatment rationale and, 161, 162

prevalence of, 22–24

psychological aspects of, 26–32

psychological models of, 26–29

psychological treatments for, 39–42, 152, 154–156

recommended readings on, 299–300, 305

relapse and, 152

relationship between panic and agoraphobia and, 15–17

relationship between situational specific phobias and, 81, 103

sample treatment protocol for, 172–178

sex differences, 24

standard measures for, 135–141, 289–292

Three Components of Anxiety and Panic Monitoring Form (sample), *169*

treatment manuals for clinicians, 300

treatment plan development for, 152, 154–156

treatment strategies for, 38–47, 152, 154–156

Panic Disorder Self-Report (PDSR), 136, 292

Panic Disorder Severity Scale (PDSS), 136, 292

Panic disorder with agoraphobia (PDA)

See also Agoraphobia without history of panic disorder; Applied tension; Cognitive therapy for panic disorder; Panic disorder

biological models of, 32–38

case vignette, 14–15

combined treatments and, 152, *217*, 282–283

common phobic beliefs in, *244*

comorbidity, 25–26

course of, 21–22

descriptive psychopathology, 12–26

development of, 21–22

diagnostic criteria, 13

differential diagnosis and, 112, 115–117

economic impact of, 24–25

examination of evidence and, *251*

focus of apprehension in, 124

functional impairment and, 24

goals in cognitive therapy for, *242*

group vs. individual approaches, 157–160

misconceptions about panic and, 163, *164*

open-ended questions for assessment of, *123*

pharmacological treatment of, 42–47, 152

pharmacological vs. psychological vs. combined treatments for, 152, 154–156

prevalence of, 22–24

psychological aspects of, 26–32

psychological models of, 26–28

psychological treatment choices for, 39–42, 152, 154–156, 157–160

rational self-statements for, *254*

recommended readings on, 299–300, 305

relationship between panic and agoraphobia, 15–17

sample treatment protocol for, 178–182

sex differences and, 24

situations avoided with, *125*

standard measures for, 135–141, 289–292

subtle avoidance strategies and, *126*

treatment manuals for clinicians, 300

treatment strategies for, 38–47, 152, 154–156

Panic Frequency Questionnaire (PFQ), 135, 141, *142–143*

PAQ. *See* Panic Attack Questionnaire

PAQ-R. *See* Panic Attack Questionnaire – Revised

Paroxetine (Paxil)

See also Selective serotonin reuptake inhibitors

dose changes and, 276, 277

panic disorder and, 43, 272

social phobia and, 74, 271

PAS. *See* Panic and Agoraphobia Scale

PASQ. *See* Panic Attack Symptoms Questionnaire

information-processing biases and,
123–124
medical conditions and, 129
medical examination and, 133–134
open-ended questions in, *123*
overt avoidance patterns and,
124–125
parameters of fears and, 126–127
physical limitations and, 129
physical symptoms and, 122
skills deficits and, 129
social supports and, 127–128
subtle avoidance strategies and, 126
thoughts and, 123–124
treatment history and, 128–129
variables assessed during, *121*
USAir Fearful Flyer Program, 320

Valerian root, 279
Valium. *See* Diazepam
Varied–stimulus exposure, 202
Venlafaxine (Effexor)

drug interactions with, *274*
panic disorder and, 43, 272
side-effects of, *274*
social phobia and, 74, 272
Vicarious acquisition, 89–90, 91
Vicarious exposure, 205–206
Video resources, 193, 300, 301, 321
Virtual reality, 193, 207–208
Vomit phobia, exposure resources for,
321

Water phobias, 84, 205
drowning statistics and, 318
Web pages, 315
See also entries for specific organizations
Weight gain, and pharmacotherapy, 273
Wings–Fredom to Fly (Northwest–KLM
program), 320

Xanax. *See* alprazolam

Zoloft. *See* Sertraline

ABOUT THE AUTHORS

Martin M. Antony, PhD, is an associate professor in the Department of Psychiatry and Behavioural Neurosciences at McMaster University, Hamilton, Ontario, Canada. He is also chief psychologist and director of the Anxiety Treatment and Research Centre at St. Joseph's Hospital in Hamilton. He received his PhD in clinical psychology from the State University of New York at Albany and completed his predoctoral internship training at the University of Mississippi Medical Center in Jackson. Dr. Antony has published several books, including *The Shyness and Social Anxiety Workbook: Proven Step-by-Step Techniques for Overcoming Your Fear* and *When Perfect Isn't Good Enough* with Dr. R. P. Swinson; *Obsessive–Compulsive Disorder: Theory, Research and Treatment* with Drs. R. P. Swinson, S. Rachman, and M. A. Richter; and *Mastery of Your Specific Phobia* (patient and therapist manuals) with Drs. M. G. Craske and D. H. Barlow. He has also published numerous research papers and book chapters in the areas of cognitive–behavioral therapy, panic disorder, social phobia, specific phobia, and obsessive–compulsive disorder. Dr. Antony has received new researcher and young investigator awards from the Canadian Psychological Association (in 1999) and the Anxiety Disorders Association of America (in 2000). He is currently president of the Anxiety Disorders Special Interest Group of the Association for Advancement of Behavior Therapy (AABT) and is program chair for the 2001 AABT meeting. Dr. Antony is actively involved in clinical research in the area of anxiety disorders, teaching, and education, and he maintains a clinical practice.

Richard P. Swinson, MD, is professor and Morgan Firestone Chair of the Department of Psychiatry and Behavioural Neurosciences, faculty of Health Sciences, McMaster University, Hamilton, Ontario. He is also a professor in the Department of Psychiatry at the University of Toronto and psychiatrist-in-chief at St. Joseph's Hospital in Hamilton. Previously, he held several appointments at the Clarke Institute of Psychiatry, including vice president, Medical Affairs; chief of medical staff; and head of the Anxiety Disorders Clinic. Dr. Swinson was recently chair of the Examination Board in Psychiatry for the Royal College of Physicians and Surgeons of Canada. He has published approximately 200 scientific papers, book chapters, and reports, mostly on behavior therapy, anxiety disorders, and related topics. He has also published several books, including *When Perfect Isn't Good Enough* and *The Shyness and Social Anxiety Workbook: Proven, Step-by-Step Techniques for Overcoming Your Fear*, with Dr. M. M. Antony, and *Obsessive–Compulsive Disorder: Theory, Research and Treatment*, with Drs. M. M. Antony, S. Rachman, and M. A. Richter. In addition, Dr. Swinson was a member of the *Diagnostic and Statistical Manual of Mental Disorders* (4th ed.) subcommittees for obsessive–compulsive disorder and for panic disorder and agoraphobia.